"A thorough and comprehensive guide to managing your Mac network and an integral part of any network manager's toolkit."

— David Burk, Marketing Manager, The AG Group, Inc.

Best wishes to Ray,

Dave Kosin

MACWORLD

NETWORKING
HANDBOOK

By
Dave Kosiur and Nancy E. H. Jones

Foreword by Reese Jones
Chairman, Farallon Computing, Inc.

IDG Books Worldwide, Inc.
An International Data Group Company
San Mateo, California 94402

Macworld Networking Handbook

Published by
IDG Books Worldwide, Inc.
An International Data Group Company
155 Bovet Road, Suite 610
San Mateo, CA 94402
(415) 312-0650

Library of Congress Catalog Card No.: 91-78115

ISBN 1-878058-31-2

Printed in the United States of America

10 9 8 7 6 5 4 3 2 1

Distributed in the United States by IDG Books Worldwide, Inc.
Distributed in Canada by Macmillan of Canada, a Division of Canada Publishing Corporation; by Woodslane Pty. Ltd. in Australia; and by Computer Bookshops in the U.K.

For information on translations and availability in other countries, contact Marc Jeffrey Mikulich, Foreign Rights Manager, at IDG Books Worldwide. Fax: (415) 358-1260.

For sales inquiries and special prices for bulk quantities, write to the address above or call IDG Books Worldwide at (415) 312-0650.

Trademarks/Acknowledgments

IDG Books Worldwide has attempted to supply trademark information about the products, services, and companies named in this book. The product names are used throughout the book in an editorial manner only. No uses of product names, or the use of any trade name, convey endorsement or other affiliation with IDG Books Worldwide or the authors of this book.

The following brand names and product names are trademarks, registered trademarks, and registered trade names. They were derived from various sources, and IDG Books Worldwide makes no claim as to the accuracy of the information. The trademarks of other products mentioned in the book but not listed here are held by the companies that produced them.

3Com Corp: 3+/3+Open, 3Com; **Acius:** 4th Dimension; **Adobe Systems:** PostScript; **Alladin Systems:** StuffIt; **Aldus:** PageMaker; **Alisa Systems:** AlisaTalk, AlisaPrint, AlisaShare; **American National Standards Institute:** ANSI; **Andrew/KMW:** Emerald Technology, TwinAxcess ApLINK; **Andyne:** GQL; **Apple Computer, Inc.:** Apple, the Apple logo, AppleShare, AppleTalk, Apple IIe, Apple IIGS, EtherTalk, ImageWriter, LaserWriter, Macintosh, ProDOS, TokenTalk, CL/1, Apple Desktop Bus, AU/X, AppleLink, AppleTalk Remote Access, Chooser, Finder, LocalTalk, Inter•Poll, MacTerminal, MacX, MultiFinder, PowerBooks, Print Monitor, SNA•ps, Quadra, Mac II, Mac SE, Mac SE/30, AppleTalk Internet Router, Apple Terminal Services (ATS), Communications ToolBox, XTND; **Aperture Technologies, Inc.:** Aperture; **Argosy Software:** Software Bridge; **Asante:** MacToken; **ASD Inc.:** Planisoft; **AT&T:** AT&T Bell Labs, StarGroup Server, Unix; **Avatar:** MacMainFrame, MacMainFrame Graphics module, MacMainFrame DX, MacMainframe gateway series, Netway gateways; **Banyan:** VINES, VINES SAA gateway; **Beagle Bros.:** Flash; **Blyth:** Omnis; **Borland International:** dBASE; **Casady & Greene:** Access Managed Environment; **Cayman Systems:** GatorBox, XGator, GatorPrint CS, GatorShare; **CE Software:** QuickMail; **Claris:** FileMaker Pro, MacWrite; **Columbia University:** Columbia AppleTalk Package; **Compatible Systems:** Enhanced Network Security protocol; **Compumation, Inc.:** Print Central; **CompuServe, Inc.:** CompuServe Information Services; **Connectivite:** BOTH; **CSG Technologies:** Network SuperVisor; **Datability:** MacRAF; **Datapoint:** ARCNET; **DataViz:** MacLink Plus; **Digital Communications Associates:** IRMA, MacIRMA; **Digital Equipment Corp:** All-In-1 Mail, DEC, DEC LPS40, DECnet, DECwindows, Desktop ACMS, NAS, PATHWORKS, Ultrix, VAX, VMS; **Distributed Tecnologies Corp.:** TalkManage; **Dove Computer Inc.:** FastNet SCSI; **Fairfield Software:** ClearAccess; **Farallon Computing Inc.:** Liaison, NodeHint, PhoneNET, PhoneNET Manager's Pack, StarController, StarCommand, Timbuktu, TrafficWatch II; **Fifth Generation:** SuperLaserSpool; **Fox Software:** FoxBase+/Mac; **General Electric Corporation:** GEnie; **Gizmo Technologies:** ShadowWriter, Send Express; **Group Technologies:** Aspects; **GTE Telenet Communications Corporation:** Telenet; **Hayes Microcomputer Products, Inc.:** Hayes, HayesConnect, Smartcom, Smartmodem; **Helios USA:** EtherShare; **ICATT:** Administrator's Aid; **International Business Machines Corporation:** IBM, PC Link (PCLK), SAA, SNA; **IDEAssociates, Inc.:** IDEAcomm Mac; **Info. Present. Techn.:** Sun-Partner, uShare; **Informix:** Wingz; **Insignia Solutions:** SoftNode, Soft PC; **Intel Corporation:** Intel; **Intercon Systems:** TCP/Connect II, Planet X, NFS/Share; **International Business Software, Inc.:** DataClub; **Kinetics, Inc.:** Kinetics; **Lotus Development Corporation:** cc:Mail, Lotus 1-2-3, Vendor Independent Messaging; **MacVONK:** NetOctopus, inForum; **Mainstay:** Markup, Marco Polo; **MCI Communications Corporation:** MCI and MCI Mail; **MDG Computer Services:** NetUpdater; **Microcom:** Virex; **MicroDynamics, Ltd.:** MARS; **Microsoft Corporation:** Excel, Microsoft Mail, Microsoft Word, LAN Manager, MS-DOS, Schedule+, Xenix; **Miramar Systems:** MACLAN Connect; **Mitem:** MitemView; **Network Resources Corp.:** LT2000E; **Novell:** NetWare, NetWare SAA Service; **Nuvotech:** TurboStar; **Odesta Corp.:** Double Helix, Odesta Document Management System; **ON Technology:** Status*Mac, Instant Update, Meeting Maker; **Oracle Corporation:** Oracle; **Pacer Software:** PacerForum, PacerTerm, PacerShare, PacerLink; **Peripheral Land Inc.:** TurboSpool; **Proteus Technology:** Quota; **Sassafras Software:** KeyServer; **Shiva Corp.:** EtherGate, FastPath, NetModem, NetSerial, StarController, Hublet; **Simware:** SimMac; **Sitka Corp.:** InBox, TOPS; **Software Ventures:** MicroPhone II; **SoftWriters:** VersionTerritory; **Solana Corp.:** C-Server, R-Server; **Sonic Systems:** Radar; **Spider Island Software:** TeleFinder; **Sun Microsystems:** NFS; **Symantec Corporation:** MORE II, SAM; **Synergy Software:** VersaTerm; **Technology Works:** GraceLAN, GraceLAN Asset Manager, GraceLAN Updater; **T.I.C.:** hiBBS; **Tribe Computer Works:** LocalSwitch; **Tri-Data Systems, Inc.:** Netway; **TriK Inc.:** NetDistributor, Nok-Nok; **United Data Corp.:** ALAC; **Virginia Systems, Inc.:** Sonar Professional; **White Pine Software Inc.:** eXodus, Mac220/241, Mac320; **Wollongong Group:** PathWay Client NFS; **WordPerfect:** WordPerfect, WordPerfect Office; **Xerox Corporation:** Ethernet; **XINET:** K-AShare, K-Spool.

Dedication

To my wife, Susan, and my parents
— Dave Kosiur

To David Edwards,
who tirelessly champions the rights of AppleTalk network managers
— Nancy E.H. Jones

Acknowledgments

A book like this, which covers so many details of Macintosh networking, includes the experiences and knowledge of more than just its authors. A lot of information that we gained about networking prior to and during the writing of this book came from colleagues and friends who, like us, have been a part of networking for the last five to six years. We know we won't remember them all, and we hope that those we forget don't feel slighted. Our "grey cells" aren't quite as active as they were five years ago when we started working with Mac networks.

Special thanks go to those who have helped us shape our technical and writing skills and brought us to the point we are at today:

Brita Meng, who has taught Dave some of the better points of writing ever since he became a contributing editor for *Macworld* magazine.

Don McClure, who always challenged Nancy with questions like "Well, why *can't* I just add a zone to the zone list while the network is running?"

Kee Nethery (Kagi Engineering) and Bob Denny (Alisa Systems), who originally "roped" Dave into writing about Mac networks in the first place over five years ago.

Keith Tebo, Nancy's original office partner at Ford Aerospace, who introduced her to the OSI Reference Model and convinced her of how important it was to take formal classes on LAN technology.

Mike McCarthy, formerly of IDG Books, who played a major role in convincing Dave that this book should be written.

Others who have had a hand in influencing the course of Mac networking and this book include Diana Foster (Bechtel Corp.), Elizabeth McGee (Shiva Corp.), Steve Nelson (Novell Corp.), Brad Parker (Cayman Systems), Mike Rogers (Sitka Corp.), Dick Skeie (CE Software), Frank Slaughter (Shiva Corp.), and Greg Satz (Cisco Systems).

When it came to staying informed, there were others who helped us get information when we needed it: David Burk (The AG Group), Kim Criswell (Criswell Communications), Trudy Edelson (Farallon Computing), Carol McGarry (Criswell Communications, formerly of Cayman Systems), Sue Nail

(CE Software), Meg Owens (DCA), Ed Hopkins (Cayman Systems), and Jim Persky (Starnine Technologies). Special thanks goes to Patrick Jones (Cisco Systems), Nancy's husband, who provided us with mountains of technical information as well as an impromptu technical review of drafts of this book.

A special thanks goes to Trudy Edelson, who graciously helped us find some of the artwork that we used in this book — thank you, Farallon, for letting us use that artwork. We also thank Arne Hurty of *Macworld* for creating other artwork that we used in this book, originally for use in *Macworld* features; thanks go to Macworld Communications for letting us use that art.

An undertaking like this depends on good relations with the publishers. Mary Bednarek, Senior Project Editor, and Jeannine McDonel, Copy Editor, took us to task in our writing. It's a much better book because of their efforts, and we believe that we are now much better writers. (See, Mary, no more ambiguous "that's" and "this's"). Greg Merrell of Digital Equipment Corp. also played a crucial role as our technical reviewer.

Also, we would like to thank Nancy's doctors, Dr. Mary Imig and Dr. Kathryn Babich, who have kept Nancy calm (most of the time) and healthy through the writing of this book as Nancy's body worked on creating Sarah Elizabeth Jones during the gestation of this book.

(The publisher would like to give special thanks to Bill Murphy, without whom this book would not have been possible.)

About IDG Books Worldwide

Welcome to the world of IDG Books Worldwide.

IDG Books Worldwide, Inc., is a division of International Data Group (IDG), the world's leading publisher of computer-related information and the leading global provider of information services on information technology. IDG publishes over 178 computer publications in more than 55 countries. Thirty million people read one or more IDG publications each month.

If you use personal computers, IDG Books is committed to publishing quality books that meet your needs. We rely on our extensive network of publications — including such leading periodicals as *Macworld, PC World, Computerworld, InfoWorld, Lotus, Publish, Network World, Computer Buying World,* and *SunWorld* — to help us make informed and timely decisions in creating useful computer books that meet your needs.

Every IDG book strives to bring extra value and skill-building instruction to the reader. Our books are written by experts, with the backing of IDG periodicals, and with careful thought devoted to issues such as audience, interior design, use of icons, and illustrations. Our editorial staff is a careful mix of high-tech journalists and experienced book people. Our close contact with the makers of computer products helps ensure accuracy and thorough coverage. Our heavy use of personal computers at every step in production means we can deliver books in the most timely manner.

We are delivering books of high quality at competitive prices on topics customers want. At IDG, we believe in quality and we have been delivering quality for 25 years. You'll find no better book on a subject than an IDG book.

John Kilcullen
President and Publisher
IDG Books Worldwide, Inc.

International Data Group's publications include: ARGENTINA'S Computerworld Argentina; ASIA'S Computerworld Hong Kong, Computerworld Southeast Asia, Computerworld Malaysia; AUSTRALIA'S Computerworld Australia, Australian PC World, Australian Macworld, Profit, Information Decisions, Reseller; AUSTRIA'S Computerwelt Oesterreich; BRAZIL'S DataNews, PC Mundo, Mundo IBM, Mundo Unix, Automacao & Industria, Publish; BULGARIA'S Computerworld Bulgaria; CANADA'S ComputerData, Direct Access, Graduate Computerworld; CHILE'S Informatica; COLUMBIA'S Computerworld Columbia; CZECHOSLOVAKIA'S Computerworld Czechoslovakia, PC World Czechoslovakia, Network World, Nueral; DENMARK'S CAD/CAM WORLD, Computerworld Danmark, PC World Danmark, Macworld Danmark, Computerworld Focus, Lotus World, Macintosh Produktkatalog, Unix World, PC/LAN World; FINLAND'S Mikro PC, Tietoviikko, Tietotekniikka, Tietoverkko; FRANCE'S Le Mond Informatique, Distributique, Compu Search, Golden, Computer Direct, InfoPC, Telecoms International, Le Guide du Monde Informatique; GERMANY'S Computerwoche, Computerwoche Focus, Computerwoche Extra, Computerwoche Karriere, Information Management, Macwelt, Netzwelt, OS/2 Welt, PC Woche, PC Welt, Unix Welt, Unit, Lotus Welt; GREECE'S PC World; HUNGARY'S Computerworld SZT, Mikrovilag Magazin, PC Vilag; INDIA'S Computers & Communications; ISRAEL'S People & Computers; ITALY'S Computerworld Italia, PC World Italia Macworld Italia, Network World Italia; JAPAN'S Computerworld Japan, Macworld Japan; KOREA'S Computerworld Korea, PC World Korea; MEXICO'S Computerworld Mexico, PC Journal; THE NETHERLAND'S Computerworld Netherlands, LAN Magazine Mac Magazine, Computer! Totaal; NEW ZEALAND'S Computerworld, PC World, C World, PC World Norge, PC World Ekspress, IDG Direct Response, Multimedia and Desktop, Lotus World, PC World's Product Guide, Student's DP-Guide, Publish! World, Macworld Norge; NIGERIA'S PC World Africa; NORWAY'S Conputerworld Norge, PC World Norge CAD/CAM, Macworld Norge; PERU'S PC World; PEOPLE'S REPUBLIC OF CHINA'S China Computerworld, PC World China; IDG HIGH TECH Newproductworld; PHILLIPPINE'S Computerworld, PC World; POLAND'S Computerworld Poland; ROMANIA'S InfoClub; RUSSIA'S CADWorld, Computerworld, Networks, PC World; SPAIN'S CIM World, Communicaciones World, Computerworld Espana, PC World Espana, Macworld, PC World Autoedicion, Amiga World, Publish; SWEDEN'S ComputerSweden, Mikrodatorn, Macworld, CAD/CAM World, Lotus Windows, Svenska PC World, Lokala Natverk/LAN, Affarsekonomi Management, Attack, CAP, DataIngenjoren, Data & Telekommunikation, Maxi Data, Digital/Varlden, Unix; SWITZERLAND'S Computerworld Schweiz, Macworld Schweiz; TAIWAN'S Computerworld Taiwan, PC World Taiwan; THAILAND'S Thai Computerworld; TURKEY'S Computerworld, PC World; UNITED KINGDOM'S Lotus, Macworld; UNITED STATES' AmigaWorld, CIO, Computerworld, Computer Buyers World, Digital News, Electronic News, Federal Computer Week, GamePro, inCider/A+, IDG Books, InfoWorld, Lotus, Macworld, MPC World, Network World, NeXTWORLD, PC Games, PC World, Portable Office, PC Letter, Publish, Run, SunWorld; VENEZUELA'S Computerworld Venezuela, Micro-Computerworld Venezuela; YUGOSLAVIA'S Moj Mikro.

 The text in this book is printed on recycled paper.

About the Authors

Dave Kosiur has been involved with computers in one form or another since he was a freshman in college. Kosiur, a contributing editor for *Macworld* magazine for the past three years, has been writing for the magazine since 1987. Kosiur, who also contributes to *InfoWorld*, founded *Connections, the Newsletter for Macintosh Networking* in 1987, and served as Publisher until the end of 1991.

Before working with *Connections*, Dave, who received his Ph.D. in Geochemistry from UCLA, worked as a research geochemist for Chevron Oil Field Research Co. (COFRC). During his tenure with Chevron, he was one of the few hardy souls who brought their own personal Macs to work to replace what he'd been doing on mainframes and minicomputers. Dave also worked with an employee computer club and wrote an "unofficial" company newsletter about Macs for three years.

Even before he got hooked on computers, Dave has been an avid reader, particularly of science fiction, mysteries, and historical fiction. If he's not in front of his Mac these days, you'll likely find him in a bookstore or record store, unless he's out driving around L.A. with the top down.

Dave and his wife Sue live with a cat named Riley in the Los Angeles area, where they enjoy walking, hiking, and bicycling — smog conditions permitting.

Nancy E.H. Jones received her B.A. in Liberal Arts from the State University of New York at Albany, where she majored in history and minored in linguistics — after dabbling in forestry, geology, and journalism. At Ford Aerospace, where she began her career coordinating proposals, Nancy began spending time with "those new little computers, the Macintoshes," and soon helped set up backup procedures and handled system and file configurations. She helped set up and managed one of Ford Aerospace's TOPs networks, and then worked in virus clean-up.

In July of 1990, Nancy, who continued to support Ford Aerospace's growing AppleTalk network, began to specialize in the management and design of two divisions' AppleTalk networks. The internet she managed consisted of 45 LocalTalk networks and an Ethernet backbone with 7 transparent Ethernet bridges. She moved the internet to AppleTalk Phase 2, with a multiple zone list and network range.

In 1991, Nancy cofounded the Apple Network Managers Association. The Association brought AppleTalk and Macintosh network managers together for sharing ideas and for presenting mutual needs and requirements to network vendors. Nancy has also spoken at several Macintosh conventions on the subject of AppleTalk network management and troubleshooting.

Nancy ended her association with Ford Aerospace in 1991 so that she could devote full time to creating this book — and her new daughter, Sarah Elizabeth. Sarah Elizabeth Jones was born just as the finishing touches were being placed on the *MacWorld Networking Handbook*. Nancy will continue her work in Macintosh networking as a consultant to several corporations. Nancy, her husband Patrick, and Sarah Elizabeth live on 3½ wooded acres in the wilds of Minnesota.

Credits

President and Publisher
John J. Kilcullen

Publishing Director
David Solomon

Senior Project Editor
Mary Bednarek

Production Director
Lana J. Olson

Acquisitions Editor
Terrie Lynn Solomon

Technical Reviewer
Greg Merrell (Digital Equipment Corp.)

Copy Editor
Jeannine McDonel

Text Preparation
Shirley E. Coe

Proofreading
Charles A. Hutchinson

Indexer
Kevin Foust

Book Design and Production
Peppy White
(University Graphics, Palo Alto, California)

Contents at a Glance

Part Four: Using an AppleTalk Network 349

Part Five: Working with Other Computer Platforms 423

Appendixes 475

Table of Contents

4 **AppleTalk Protocols in Action** **83**

Part Two: Installing an AppleTalk Network **97**

5 **Network Design 101** **99**

6 **Designing a LocalTalk LAN** **113**

12 Making the Phase 2 Move 231

13 Designing an AppleTalk WAN 255

Foreword

The success of the Macintosh computer in business and education emphasizes the importance of understanding Macintosh networking in your workplace. Today, over four million Macintoshes are attached to networks, and this number is growing at over a million users a year.

Macintosh networking has become mainstream because of the Macintosh's success and because of AppleTalk's acceptance as a de facto multivendor, multiplatform standard. AppleTalk is supported today by every major server, router, and printer vendor.

Macintosh computers are often acquired by organizations that already have other types of computer and networking products. Thus it is important to understand how Macintosh networking can be combined with other systems to create heterogeneous networks that perform well.

Dave Kosiur's breadth of experience uniquely qualifies him to write this book. With personal experience as a network manager at a large corporation, he gained hands-on experience in constructing and managing a large Macintosh internetwork and its connections to other systems within the organization. In addition, he founded the highly regarded *Connections* newsletter, covering every aspect of Macintosh networking from the technology to the products to the problems. As a contributing editor for *Macworld* magazine, Dave covers current products and issues in Macintosh networking and provides insight into the future of this rapidly maturing area.

Nancy Jones managed a large network at an aerospace corporation and is the founder of the nationwide AppleTalk Network Managers Association. She brings her extensive personal experience as well as insights drawn from other corporate network managers to solve the problems of Macintosh networking.

In the *Macworld Networking Handbook,* Dave and Nancy draw on their extensive experience to explain how to build, manage, and use your Macintosh network, including solutions for cross-platform connectivity and attaching your Macintosh network to your corporate internetwork. The *Macworld Networking Handbook* will prove to be a valuable tool for beginning users looking for networking basics as well as the advanced users interested in getting more out of their network.

Reese Jones
Chairman, Farallon Computing, Inc.
April, 1992

Introduction

We believe that a Macintosh network, with its ease of use, friendly interface, and powerful capabilities, is more exciting to see in action than any other network system. Network users easily become proficient at collecting and distributing information. To provide this easy interface, however, the network administrator must deal with many complex concepts that are unseen to the end user. This book is intended to help the administrator understand networking concepts in order to design and manage Macintosh networks that run at their highest performance potential.

Why You Need This Book

There are very few sources of detailed information on the construction and management of AppleTalk networks. This book aims to fill that gap. It doesn't make any difference whether you're a user of a network, a designer of a new network, or a manager of a large established network — this book explains both the background concepts and the working details of Mac networks so that you can put the information to good use. If you're interested in making a network work better — or even just making one work! — this book will help.

Whom This Book Is For

This book is aimed at two groups of network administrators: beginning Macintosh network administrators, who may need help in understanding how to design a simple AppleTalk network for sharing printers and files, and administrators of large, challenging networks, who need information on the various aspects of managing multiple routers, servers, modems, and other network equipment.

We have written this book for a wide audience because we believe that many times, the network administrator of a small network often finds himself or herself becoming the network administrator of a large network. So this is a book you can grow with.

To get the most from this book, you should already be familiar with the basic pieces of the Macintosh interface, such as volume icons and opening the Chooser. You should also have an understanding of the basic use of the Macintosh — manipulating the mouse, and so on. If you do need to learn more Macintosh fundamentals, please study the manual *Getting Started With Your Macintosh* or the disk *Your Tour of the Macintosh*. Both come with every Macintosh computer. You can also consult other IDG books on the Macintosh for additional information. Suggested titles include *Macworld Complete Mac Handbook* by Jim Heid; *Macworld Guide to System 7*, by Lon Poole; and *Macworld Read Me First Book*, by Jerry Borrell et al.

The first section of this book will cover network fundamentals to provide background if you have never worked with a network before.

How This Book Is Organized

Material in this book has been organized as much as possible to lead you from simple and fundamental concepts to the more advanced complexities of networking. We encourage you to read this book in sequential chapter order because many of the earlier chapters provide underpinnings to discussions that appear later in the book. Also, as much as possible, we have tried to use a cross-reference icon in the margins to show you where the more detailed explanation can be found. See the section in this Introduction called "Conventions Used in This Book," for more information on the icons used in this book.

Part One: Introducing Networking

In Part One, we discuss why we think networking is so important and introduce the many exciting things that you can do with a network. We describe how information is transmitted across a network and how network protocol suites are used. You'll find that these fundamentals are very important for understanding the material presented in later sections.

Chapter 1, "Understanding Connectivity," explains what a network can do for you and your company and why we recommend the AppleTalk protocol system for Macintosh networking.

Chapter 2, "Understanding Networks," describes how signals work over your network's cable to transmit information and the basics of how the various pieces of your network — such as transceivers, repeaters, bridges, and routers — function. This chapter also introduces some basic network vocabulary that you can refer to as you continue in the book.

Chapter 3, "Understanding AppleTalk Protocols," explains network protocols, the OSI Reference Model, and the AppleTalk protocol suite.

Chapter 4, "AppleTalk Protocols in Action," gives you examples of several of the AppleTalk protocols in action. You learn, for example, which network protocols are used when a Macintosh sends a print job to a LaserWriter.

Part Two: Installing an AppleTalk Network

Part Two takes a close look at putting together AppleTalk networks, starting out with the basics of network design and layout. In this part, we cover LocalTalk and EtherTalk network design as well as the design of large (20 or more zones) networks. You'll find tips on what types of cable and connectors to purchase and what topology pitfalls to avoid.

Chapter 5, "Network Design 101," describes the various topologies you can use for designing your network and the advantages and disadvantages of each. We also introduce you to the concept of fault-tolerant network design.

Chapter 6, "Designing a LocalTalk LAN," builds on the concepts introduced in Chapter 5 and describes in detail the relations between LocalTalk and other topologies. After covering the physical limits of LocalTalk network topologies, the chapter then goes on to show you what devices, such as repeaters and bridges, you can use to extend the limits of those networks.

Chapter 7, "Installing a LocalTalk LAN," explains how to select connectors and cables for your LocalTalk network and then tells you how to install a LocalTalk LAN in either the daisy-chain, bus, passive star, or active star topology. You learn the importance of testing your network.

Chapter 8, "Designing an Ethernet LAN," describes Ethernet standards and the types of cables and topologies that can be used for Ethernet networks. The chapter then moves on to describe the hardware that's available for connecting Macs and LaserWriters to Ethernet, and what kind of performance you can expect from Macs on Ethernet networks.

Chapter 9, "Installing an Ethernet LAN," is the Ethernet parallel to Chapter 7, as it explains how to select Ethernet cables and connectors and how to wire them together to create a LAN using either coaxial cable or unshielded twisted-pair wire. The chapter also walks you through the procedures for setting up an Ethernet connection for your Mac.

Chapter 10, "Using Modems with Networks," introduces you to the terminology of modems and telephone systems and then shows you how you can share modems on a network or link a remote Mac to the network with a modem.

Chapter 11, "Designing an AppleTalk LAN," explains Apple's concept of internetworking and how you can use routers to join networks together to form larger internetworks.

Chapter 12, "Making the Phase 2 Move," describes the strategies you can use to upgrade an AppleTalk network from Phase 1 to Phase 2 protocols and goes on to outline many of the problems administrators may encounter during the upgrade.

Chapter 13, "Designing an AppleTalk WAN," is an overview of the methods you can use to connect geographically separated networks, WANs (Wide Area Networks), particularly using telecommunications services.

Part Three: Managing an AppleTalk Network

Part Three covers many of the aspects of managing an AppleTalk network, from troubleshooting physical cable problems to maintaining security for your data files. In this part, we cover procedures for troubleshooting network problems, the monitoring of network traffic, and configuring routers, as well as ways to maintain security and keep track of software usage on your network.

Chapter 14, "Fault Management," presents methods you can use to gracefully recover your network from an unexpected failure as quickly as possible.

Chapter 15, "Performance Management," describes ways to spot bottlenecks in your network's performance and how to improve the throughput of a network.

Chapter 16, "Configuration Management," explains how to configure network devices such as routers, bridges, and servers. You learn about the proprietary configuration tools currently available and the status on the development of an open software toolkit called SNMP.

Chapter 17, "Accounting and Security Management," explains how you can audit usage of networked printers and file servers and then shows how you can maintain secure access to your network resources.

Chapter 18, "Resource Management," describes some of the ways you can use resource management tools to find out what software and hardware is installed on each Mac and how this information can help you deal with some common problems.

Part Four: Using an AppleTalk Network

Part Four covers the various types of applications that you might run on your network. We discuss the setup and usage of printers, file servers, and databases, as well as the types of electronic mail and groupware currently available for Macintosh LANs.

Chapter 19, "Using Printers on the Network," describes the differences between print spoolers and print servers and how they should be installed on a network.

Chapter 20, "Moving and Sharing Files on the Network," explains how you can use file-transfer utilities and file servers on a LAN, and how distributed and centralized file servers differ from each other. The chapter also includes hints for setting up a centralized file server.

Chapter 21, "Using Networked Databases," presents an overview of the various types of databases and how they can be installed on your network for efficient use. This chapter also introduces you to the concepts of client-server computing.

Chapter 22, "Using Electronic Mail," explains how e-mail programs work and the important features that you should look for in an e-mail program. The chapter also introduces you to the types of gateways you can use to link different e-mail systems together.

Chapter 23, "Using Groupware," shows you what software is available for users so that they can work together as a group over a network. Groupware includes such items as group schedulers, document-editing programs, and document tracking and retrieval programs.

Part Five: Working with Other Computer Platforms

In this part, we turn our attention to networks that are not using AppleTalk protocols and how you can connect a Macintosh to such systems. Part Five covers non-AppleTalk networks as well as connectivity solutions to Unix, VMS, and IBM computers.

Chapter 24, "Using Non-AppleTalk Protocols," describes the various networking protocol systems currently in use and how Macs can be set up to use some of these protocols, either directly or through gateways.

Chapter 25, "Sharing Printers and Files with Other Platforms," explains how you can use printers attached to other, non-Mac systems; a major focus is on non-Mac print servers. This chapter also contains an overview of the many systems that now offer AFP-compatible file servers and explains how Macs can use the NFS filing system on TCP/IP networks, as well as some of the problems facing users attempting file exchanges between different platforms.

Chapter 26, "Running Applications on other Platforms," explains how you can use terminal emulators to attach your Mac to other computers and how the Mac can utilize X Windows, foreign databases, and distributed processing involving other types of computers.

Appendixes

Several useful appendixes supplement the information found in this book's chapters.

Appendix A, "AppleTalk Packet Formats," graphically displays the data contained in packets generated by the various AppleTalk protocols.

Appendix B, "List of Vendors," provides product and contact information for vendors that we've mentioned in the book.

Appendix C, "Glossary of Networking Terms," contains definitions of the major networking terms that we've used throughout this book.

Appendix D, "Networking Acronyms," contains a list of acronyms.

Conventions Used in This book

Certain conventions are used in this book to help you better understand the discussions.

Icons

This book features a variety of icons, which are located in the margins. The icons are intended to alert you to information you can keep in mind as you learn Macintosh networking concepts. Here is what to look for:

The paragraph denoted by the background icon provides some background information on the point under discussion.

The tip icon points to a useful hint that can save you time and trouble.

The caution icon alerts you to potential problems.

The cross-reference icon tells you where in this book you can find more detail about the subject under discussion.

The System 7 icon points you to issues specific to Apple's System 7 operating system.

Sidebars

Certain discussions in this book are expanded with sidebars — shaded boxes that often contain background information and other peripheral details. The information in the sidebars can often give you an edge of understanding and insight.

Special notations

The dollar sign ($) represents the start of a string of hexadecimal numbers. For example, an Ethernet address would be written like this: $0800899a724b.

Note that hexadecimal numbers and on-screen information and code appears in a special typeface.

Feedback, Please!

We appreciate your feedback. Please feel free to contact us in care of IDG Books Worldwide with questions or comments. You can also reach the authors electronically via CompuServe. Dave Kosiur can be reached at address 74206,3270; Nancy Jones' CompuServe address is 70400,3676.

Part One

Introducing Networking

Part One: Introducing Networking

Part One of *Macworld Networking Handbook* contains basic material about using networks and how networks work. We start out by showing you how networks can be used in different business situations and explain what actually happens on a network cable and within your computer. Then we describe the details of the AppleTalk protocol suite and give you some examples of how the protocols work.

Chapter 1 explains what we think connectivity and networking is all about and presents some typical business situations in which you might use networks. We also explain some of the unique features of AppleTalk.

Chapter 2 gets down to the details of what happens on a network cable and how your computer's data gets transmitted over the network. In this chapter, we introduce some basic network vocabulary as well.

Chapter 3 is a detailed explanation of network protocols, including the OSI Reference Model and the AppleTalk protocols. We start out with a simple explanation of AppleTalk and then discuss each protocol in detail.

Chapter 4 shows you which AppleTalk protocols are involved in some typical uses of the network.

Chapter 1
Understanding Connectivity

Whether you realize it or not, we live in an age of networks. Almost all the information we get every day arrives at our homes and our desks via some sort of network. In this context, we can define a *network* as a collection of things that share a common purpose and are interconnected in some way. Such a broad definition can include television networks, telephone networks, bank ATM networks, and computer networks, as well as non-electric networks like the postal service. In this book, however, we're going to deal only with computer networks.

But the title of this chapter is "Understanding Connectivity." How does that title relate to networks? It's simple. *Connectivity* is a term that encompasses all of the networks you come into contact with. Networks by themselves are the computers and their physical links; connectivity is what results when we humans use networks. Connectivity is the guiding principle behind networking, for connectivity is the capability to acquire and share information.

What Is a Computer Network?

A network is a collection of devices that share a common purpose and are interconnected in some way. We'll get more specific so that we can talk about computer networks, which are the subject of this book. A *computer network* is a collection of computing devices, such as personal computers, large mainframe computers, printers, and modems; this collection of devices is interconnected so that all devices can share information. Such information might include stock quotes, a printed report, or even a typed message about the next intramural baseball game. If we had to pick three words of importance from that definition, they'd be the following: *collection, interconnected,* and *sharing.*

A single personal computer connected to a printer is not a network. Neither is a computer attached to a modem. But if you connect more than one computer to a cable to use the printer and share information with each other, you have a network.

What can be connected to a network? We mentioned the basic devices — personal computers, printers, and modems. You might also connect larger computers, such as minicomputers, mainframes, and supercomputers, to your network. Or you might use a cellular modem to link a portable computer to a network. The possibilities are nearly endless. In this book, we'll introduce you to many of the common networked devices, along with the common applications of Macintosh networks.

Before we show you some examples of Macintosh networks, we'll take a brief look at how computer networks evolved from the first electronic computers to the present day.

A Short History of Networking

When electronic computers were first created, they were huge beasts of vacuum tubes and relays that required large air-conditioned rooms and teams of workers just to keep running. Not just anyone could go into the computer room and start programming the computer to solve a problem. In fact, very few people even knew how to program these computers. The usual situation was for a group of workers to coddle the big computers (called *mainframes*) as they solved their assigned problems. The computers and their support teams usually were in a large room all by themselves, isolated from the rest of the workers or users. But, as the computers represented a large corporate investment, these rooms often had large glass windows so that executives and other visitors could see the results of their investment. That situation hasn't changed much in the present, either — the glass rooms and large computers are still around and are likely to stay around for some time to come.

As these large computers became more sophisticated, they could actually process more than one job at a time; this capability became known as *time-sharing*. Time-sharing led to the first attempts at networking, more properly known as *terminal networking*. Each user could sit at a computer terminal located somewhere in the building and submit jobs to the computer for processing. The computer queued jobs according to available resources and requirements and ran a few of them at the same time, spitting back results to the users at their terminals (or on a printer). But the idea of handling the contention between all these users' terminals and the submitted jobs is similar to what we face today with local area networks (LANs) consisting of micro-computers.

Eventually came the PC revolution. Now we have more computing power on our desktops than existed in the early mainframe computers. But until LAN systems came along, each PC was fairly isolated from the other PCs. In fact, *sneakernet* was the main transport for exchanging data. One thing changed with the introduction of PC LANs with respect to control of communications. With mainframes, most, if not all, of the intelligence was located at the mainframe and not the terminals; communications control was located at the mainframe. With PC LANs, however, the computing intelligence was distributed among the computers, and the control had to be distributed. So communications control was built into the network itself.

Sneakernet is a common term denoting a non-network method for transferring files between computers. With sneakernet, you transfer the files by walking — in your sneakers, of course — from computer to computer with a floppy disk containing the files. The term is variously called *Nikenet, Adidasnet,* or *Reeboknet* — pick your favorite shoe manufacturer.

There's a tendency to associate the term networking with the smaller Mac or DOS-based computers and workstations. This reflects a frequent pairing of the term network with LAN, or *local area network*. But there's more to connectivity than just networking as we've defined it here. Connectivity means connecting to and exchanging data with any kind of computer, small or large, wherever it may be. So, although most of this book focuses on LANs, we will devote an entire section to using a Mac to connect to larger computers, with or without a LAN.

Sharing Information and Resources

The common work environment these days necessitates working with other people, either in your own company or with your customers. That means that if you're not networked now, you probably soon will be.

Networks are built for two main purposes: sharing resources and sharing information. Resources can include such tangible items as expensive computer peripherals — laser printers, imagesetters, slide makers, and so on. Information, on the other hand, is likely to be the lifeblood of your enterprise. All those sales reports, parts inventories and orders, sales contacts, and personnel histories are integral requirements of the business.

You might say that you can share all this information without a network; after all, you've already got sneakernet, so you can copy your files to a floppy disk and take them down the hall to someone else's Mac. That may work in some situations. But what about the times when the person you're sharing data with is in another building, another city, or across the country, and the person needs the data "right now"? In these cases, sneakernet just won't cut it. You need a real live network to make data exchange easier, regardless of the scale.

One of the most important advantages of sharing information on a network is the capability to continually update information. As an example, imagine what the New York Stock Exchange would be like if every stock transaction had to be hand-carried to a computer operator, who entered the transaction and then printed out a report for every interested party. Even worse, imagine that this manual exchange had to be accomplished with the interested parties residing all over the country, and that each party required delivery of the information at the same time. That's what would happen without a network. By the time some of the reports were printed, they'd most likely be out of date.

With a network, the transaction can be entered once and that data shared immediately with anyone who's interested. You can get the same type of interaction by sharing data in special files (usually in a database installed on a file server) with the other members of your workgroup. The data might include only your company's current inventory, but with a network, everyone gets the same data at the same time. This sharing of information from one central source also ensures that duplicate, perhaps incorrect, data isn't being circulated.

In our opinion, sharing information is a more important justification for networks than sharing resources. It's true that not everyone has a personal LaserWriter, and networks are, in fact, good for sharing printers. But printing reports and memos is only a small portion of what networks can help you accomplish by sharing information. Even more importantly, future networks are likely to offer even more opportunities to share and use information than you thought possible. But we're not going to get starry-eyed here about future prospects. We're concerned here with what networks can do now.

One of the appeals of networking is its versatility — you can do so many different things with a computer network. If you surveyed a group of network users, you'd probably get a different response from each of them, where each pointed out a different way that they used a computer network to their benefit. We'll go through a few examples to give you a flavor of how networks help you work.

Using electronic mail and groupware

Electronic mail, commonly called *e-mail*, is just what its name implies: an electronic form of paper mail that follows the same type of conventions used by intercompany mail or the U.S. Postal Service. You type a note on your Mac, select the names of the people it's supposed to go to, and send it over the network. (We'll give more details of e-mail in Chapter 22.)

A new class of computer software, called *groupware*, is similar to e-mail. Groupware is designed to make the exchange of information among a group of workers easier by having the networked computers take care of some of the details. For example, the computers can keep track of a group's schedules. They might also track different versions of a report and propagate the changes to that report among the workgroup. We'll discuss groupware in Chapter 23.

Relieving telephone tag

When Steve Jobs introduced the Macintosh computer at Apple Computer, he claimed that he wanted to make the Mac an information appliance as simple to use as the telephone. But, as we all know, the downside of telephones is that the person you're trying to reach sometimes isn't there to take your call. Often, we're left talking to an answering machine or voice mail. Conversely, even if a human being is answering phones for you, your desk may get covered with slips of paper from past phone calls that you weren't able to take.

Fortunately, computer networks don't suffer from the same problems as telephone networks. With products like electronic mail, your computer can take care of relaying information to others whether or not they're available at the time. So instead of passing telephone messages back and forth as you try to talk to each other (rather than each other's voice mail), you can compose a lengthy discussion of a subject and mail it to your co-worker. The co-worker can sit down, read your message, think about it, and compose a suitable reply. Each of you gets to do this at your leisure, and you'll have accomplished something when the process is finished. If nothing else, the hassle level is reduced when compared to playing telephone tag.

Of course, you can't always avoid telephone tag, even if everyone in your company uses e-mail. But what about all of your clients and contacts in the outside world? Even here, electronic mail may be of some help. A receptionist answering your phone can use e-mail to send you all the telephone messages, rather than writing them down and adding to the pile of papers on your desk.

Scheduling meetings

Meetings are one of the most common activities of businesses. Keeping track of all the meetings you have to attend as well as their agendas can often seem like an overwhelming task. But there are ways to use a computer network to keep track of, and schedule, meetings more easily than with paper-based systems.

You can use e-mail to send notices to your co-workers about a proposed meeting. You might include the agenda for the meeting or even attach a spreadsheet or graphics to be discussed at the meeting. When the other workers receive their e-mail, they can read your proposal and send back a reply; they may confirm that they'll be there, give you an excuse why they can't make it, or even offer comments on your agenda. All this can be done via e-mail, without using a single piece of paper.

As mentioned previously, groupware software can accomplish the same thing. One type of groupware handles meeting schedules, including searches of workers' schedules for open time slots to identify a feasible date and time. A product called Meeting Maker (ON Technology) does this for networked Macs.

Using a shared database

Databases have become a common way to store and share information over a network. That's because everyone who accesses the data stored in a database sees the same data, and any changes are propagated to everyone else using the database. Databases also offer security options which you can use to control access to the data. For instance, some users might be able to change, or update, the data, while others could only use the data to generate reports. We'll mention more about networked databases in Chapter 21.

Passing around sales contacts

If you work in a sales organization, you may have a method for sharing new sales contacts. You may receive some leads meant for someone else's territory, for example, or it may be that the sales team distributes the workload of new leads. This is another area where networked computers can help.

One way of maintaining a collection of sales information to be shared is to set up a shared database on a file server. This database can compile essential information about each sales lead and may even include assignments. Because this shared database is centrally located on the network, sharing data is easier than if each salesperson were to store sales information in a separate database on his or her own Mac.

Tracking inventory

Tracking your company's inventory is another use for a shared database. The inventory database might be more complicated than our previous example, as it probably contains information on parts availability, suppliers, pending orders, and similar items. Because some of this data can be compartmentalized, it's probably best suited for what's known as a relational database (see Chapter 21).

This centralized database can be accessed in various ways by groups within the company. The receiving department can update new parts shipments, and the accounting department can generate billings directly from the same database. Sales can check the status of previous orders, and managers can track the product flow into and out of the company. The basic data that everyone sees is the same; it's just that each user employs an interface to the data that's specific to the user's needs. Because data is stored in a central location, it's easier to verify that everyone's talking about the same numbers, and that everything's up to date.

Sharing files

Assume that it's time to prepare a special sales report that requires input from a group of your co-workers. Here again, using the network can make your job easier.

First, you should realize that what we mean by "the network" isn't geographically restricted. Your co-workers may be all in the same building as you or may be scattered around the city, the state, or even the world. With a properly designed network, this geographic scatter makes no difference.

The basic function of the network is to exchange ideas and files among the workers. You may choose a simple file-transfer program to send word processing and graphics files to the other worker, or you may decide to keep all the files necessary for the report on a file server that everyone can access. Tracking files, however, is a bit easier if everyone works on the files from a central location, as on a file server.

There are also some groupware products designed to make some of the steps of report generation easier. With some of these products, you can work with the rest of your co-workers on a report document at the same time, seeing each other's changes as they occur. Such a process might be difficult to coordinate if the work team were located all over the world, though. Another way is to use groupware that coordinates different versions of the document, showing the changes suggested by each team member to the document's owner.

We hope that this gives you a feel for what you can do with a computer network, with a minimum of hype — we work with networks every day, so we know that the hype doesn't do anything to improve connectivity.

Macs and Connectivity

We live in a multinational world. In similar fashion, our businesses run in a multi-computer world. It's more common for companies to have a network using more than one vendor's computers than it is to see only one type of computer throughout the company. In this multi-computer world, no vendor's computer can afford to be an island unto itself. Connectivity, or the ability to share information with other types of computers, is de rigueur. Like many other computers, Apple's Macintosh computers offer many ways to connect to other computing systems and different types of networks to exchange data. Throughout this book, we're going to show you how Macs can be connected using their built-in networking support, called AppleTalk, as well as how Macs can connect to other systems.

AppleTalk and networking

This book is primarily about AppleTalk. Why? The answer's fairly simple: AppleTalk is the network of choice for connecting Macs. This preference stems from two reasons. First, AppleTalk support has been built into every Mac since the first one rolled off Apple's assembly lines; and, second, the user interface to networks provided by AppleTalk is probably the easiest to use of any currently available.

Don't underestimate the advantage the Mac has provided by including a built-in interface to networking since the first Macs were manufactured. Building AppleTalk support into the Mac has made it easy for users to experiment, as they discover what works in a network, what doesn't, and whether a network will solve their problems or create new ones.

By incorporating AppleTalk within the Mac, Apple also gave developers a single standard to use when creating network applications. No longer did developers have to worry about the type of network interface being used or whether any network drivers (the interface to the network card) were installed. Network support came with each Mac, and activating it was as easy as clicking on a button in the Chooser. That made some parts of network development easier than before.

But back to the user. One of the distinguishing features of the Macintosh has been Apple's attention to detail regarding the user interface, making it as easy and intuitive as possible to do things without reading many manuals. Right from the beginning, Apple paid a great deal of attention to the user interface for networking. It was a natural outgrowth of creating the Macintosh and its distinctive user interface. Apple made sure that the ease of use that the Mac is known for extends to networking as well.

One of the principal mechanisms for making the network interface more tractable for the user is AppleTalk's use of *named entities*. This means that with AppleTalk, you choose the networked devices, such as laser printers and file servers, by their names, not by some cryptic number, as is common in other networking systems. Your Mac also has a name on the network, which makes it easier for others to identify the Mac, either to send information or to deal with a problem.

AppleTalk also allows you to create logical subdivisions of your network, called *zones*, making it easier for users to find services on the network. These subdivisions can be named appropriately for your company, as with zones for Accounting, Marketing, Sales, and Engineering; or zones might be Bldg. 1-First Floor, Bldg. 2-First Floor, and Bldg 2.-Second Floor. (For details, see Chapters 2 and 11.)

Connecting to other computers

We said that no computer can afford to act as an island. The Mac is no exception. Fortunately, both Apple and third-party vendors have seen to it that the hardware and software you may need to connect to other computers are available for the Macintosh. This is true whether the computer is a personal computer running DOS, or a larger computer running Digital's VMS operating system, one of IBM's mainframe-based operating systems, or Unix. The Mac can connect to, and communicate with, them all.

As Apple has attempted to guide other vendors to providing support for connectivity to other computers, the company has also attempted to guide the vendors in the use of the Mac interface and its approach to networking. Thus, when using the Mac, you'll see that although you may use a variety of network services on other types of computers, the interface to those services will look like the same one you use on an AppleTalk network with your Mac. This perhaps gives the Mac the most transparent interface to multivendor networking available at this time, making the Mac a "universal client" to all kinds of network services. Later in this book, we will demonstrate how this "universal" connectivity can be achieved.

Summary

In this chapter, we've presented the basic concept of connectivity and shown you some examples of how you can use networks. This chapter presented the following points:

✔ A network is a group of devices that are interconnected for a common purpose.

✔ Computer networks are only one of many different kinds of networks that we come into contact with on a daily basis.

✔ The main reasons for networking are sharing resources and sharing information.

✔ Every Mac has built-in support for Apple's AppleTalk networking system.

✔ Tools are available for connecting the Mac to almost every kind of major computer.

In Chapter 2, we'll discuss some of the basics of networks before we get into the details of AppleTalk and Macintosh networking.

Chapter 2
Understanding Networks

So far we've introduced you to some examples of how you can use networks in your business. But a network isn't just something you install and forget about. The networks themselves are far from transparent — aside from doing such tasks as transferring files or sending faxes differently, you're usually aware of the wires and connectors that have been added to your computer to connect to the network. In this chapter we'll focus on the various aspects of any physical network: the cables, the electrical signals transmitted on those cables, how your computer is attached to the network's cables, and how your computer communicates with other computers. We'll also introduce you to the basics of other network devices that are used to build networks larger than those found on a single floor of a building or contained in a single building. Then we'll point out some of the concepts of AppleTalk networking.

The Components of the Network

A network needs both hardware and software to work. On the hardware side, there are the cables used to carry the network's signals, the connectors between a computer and the network cable, and any electronics required to interface the computer to the network. As you'll see when we discuss networking protocols in Chapter 3, "Understanding AppleTalk Protocols," these items form what's known as the *physical layer*.

In order for these electronic items to do something useful, you need some software on your computer to communicate with the network hardware — this is the job of one or more software drivers that work with your computer's operating system. The most basic functions of the drivers form a network's *data link layer*, but drivers can also perform network functions that are defined by other protocol layers.

Network media

Networks can be constructed out of almost anything that can transmit a signal (excepting smoke signals). Whereas copper cabling is the most common means of carrying network signals, there's an increasing use of fiber-optic cables that use photons, or light signals, rather than electrons to carry the signals. Some networks also use wireless setups, such as infrared light or radio frequencies, to transmit signals over short distances (for example, within a large room). Large networks are often created using microwave or satellite links to connect smaller geographically distant networks, such as when a large multinational corporation needs to link together all of its branch offices.

Throughout this book, we'll focus on the various types of cables that use electrical signals for a network because those cables make up the majority of networks today. We won't cover fiber-optic or wireless networks, except in passing.

The two most common cable types for networks are *coaxial* cables and *twisted-pair* cables (see Figure 2-1). Coaxial cable looks like the cable for your cable-TV hookup. These cables use a center conductor for transmitting a signal and are surrounded with insulation and a wire braid or similar conductive sheet to shield the conductor from outside interference. This shielding makes these types of cables ideal for use in noisy environments, such as factories. Shielding also reduces the strength of the signal that is broadcast out of the wire, reducing the chance of interception and snooping. Any wire carrying an oscillating electrical signal acts as an antenna, broadcasting the signal to the space (air or vacuum) outside the wire.

Twisted-pair cables are constructed just as their name indicates: These are pairs of insulated copper wire wound around each other, much like strands of DNA. These pairs are placed with other twisted pairs inside a larger insulated casing. The twists within a pair (measured by the *pitch*, or number of twists per foot) help reduce the electrical interference between signals transmitted on the wires (this interference is called *crosstalk*). Simple twisted-pair cable may contain only 2 or 3 pairs, but the heftier twisted-pair cable, such as that used for corporate phone installations and networks, may contain 50 or more pairs.

Networks use two types of twisted-pair cable — *unshielded* and *shielded* (refer again to the diagram in Figure 2-1). The shielding performs the same function as the shielding in coaxial cable — it reduces the interference from electrical sources outside of the cable. In general, however, the electrical interaction between the

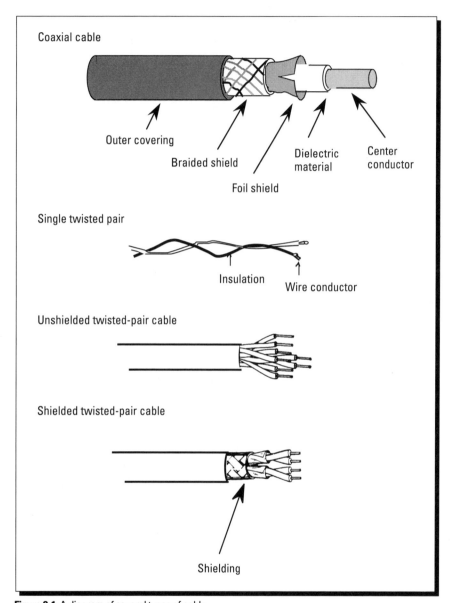

Coaxial cable

Outer covering

Braided shield

Foil shield

Dielectric material

Center conductor

Single twisted pair

Insulation

Wire conductor

Unshielded twisted-pair cable

Shielded twisted-pair cable

Shielding

Figure 2-1: A diagram of several types of cable.

shielding and the cable it protects means that a signal cannot be transmitted as far in a shielded cable as in a similar cable without the shielding. When deciding between unshielded and shielded cable, therefore, your choice should be guided by the amount of noise in your network environment, as well as by the length of your network cabling. (See Part Two, "Installing an AppleTalk Network," for more details.)

The wire used in twisted-pair cable is solid, not stranded, copper wire. The thickness of the wire is most often expressed as American Wire Gauge (AWG). The diameter of a wire is inversely related to the AWG number; thus, 24 AWG wire is thinner than 22 AWG. This is because the AWG number is the number of wires of that size that can fit in a standard area.

Cable connections

The purpose of the network cable is to transmit electrical signals, which are received and processed by each computer's electrical interface to the network. We'll go into detail on the nature of these signals in the following section. What we want to emphasize here is that each computer, or other networked device (such as a printer), requires an electrical interface between itself and the cable. This interface is known as a *transceiver,* because it both transmits and receives the network signals.

Part of the transceiver's job is to distinguish between true network signals and noise. The transceiver also converts the analog electrical signals traveling on the network cable to the binary 0s and 1s (digital bits) that computers can understand and process.

> A *transceiver,* which transmits *and* receives the network's signals, distinguishes between true network signals and noise and also converts analog signals to binary signals.

In many cases, the transceiver is a small box connected by a cable to the *network interface card* (NIC), also called the *network interface unit* (NIU), that's installed in your computer. This is the setup for one type of Ethernet cable, called *thick-wire* Ethernet (see Chapter 8, "Designing an Ethernet LAN," for more information). Network interface boards for the remaining two major types of Ethernet, *thin-wire* Ethernet and *10BaseT,* or *twisted-pair* Ethernet, use a transceiver that's part of the NIC. With Apple's LocalTalk wiring scheme, the transceiver is built into each Mac and LaserWriter; an external connection box is connected to the network cable, and a cable connects this box to the transceiver's port on the Mac or LaserWriter (see Figure 2-2).

The external connection device that connects to the network cable is also often called a *medium attachment unit,* or MAU. This term is usually restricted to external connection devices that include a transceiver, such as the one just described for thick-wire Ethernet. A MAU connects to the NIC or NIU via an *attachment unit interface* (AUI) cable, or *drop cable,* which plugs into the AUI socket on the NIC.

What's in the computer?

Whether or not the network transceiver is located outside of your computer, the remainder of the electronics for processing a network signal is found

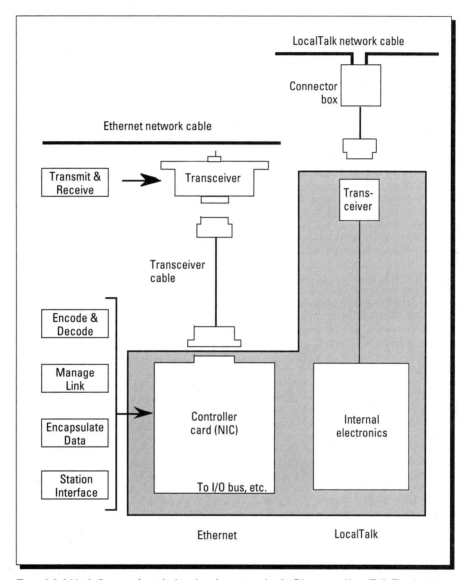

Figure 2-2: A block diagram of a typical workstation connection for Ethernet and LocalTalk. The shaded area represents the computer's hardware.

within your computer. A Mac has a chip on the motherboard that can interpret LocalTalk signals and communicate with the microprocessor and its operating system. For Ethernet, most Macs require an interface card (or an external box using the SCSI or a serial port), which includes buffers for storing incoming and outgoing packets and the rest of the processing electronics. The newer Mac Quadras have Ethernet built into the motherboard. In either case, the operating system must include software that can communicate with, and control, the network interface. This type of software is called a *driver*.

An Introduction to Network Signals

The electrical signals that are transmitted over network cables are much more complex than the alternating current that's flowing in your home's electrical wiring. We'll discuss in this section the basics of how network signals are created and how to combat the problems of noise and other interference.

> A driver contains the computer instructions to process incoming bits and to recognize their patterns according to certain rules known as *protocols.* When the computer is sending data to the network, the driver also ensures that the outgoing bits are properly arranged so that your computer can communicate with other computers.

Creating signals

We've said that signals are transmitted throughout a network by cables. These signals resemble the alternating current in your home's electrical supply. The signals change, or *oscillate,* continuously from one voltage to another in a regular manner.

Electrical signals are usually specified with two numbers. The first number is the signal's *amplitude*, or the difference between the maximum and minimum voltage. The second number is the signal's *frequency*, or how many times per second it cycles from maximum to minimum voltage and back again. A signal that has a smooth oscillation between the voltages is called a *sine wave,* which resembles a smooth-topped hill next to a broad, smooth valley.

But computers deal with binary digits — the 0s and 1s that have no values between them. If the maximum voltage of a sine wave means "1" and the minimum voltage means "0," what do all the rest of the voltages in the sine wave mean?

In order to make electrical signals represent 0s and 1s on a cable, engineers have combined sine waves together to form a *square wave.* The trick is to use a number of varied sine waves, each with a different amplitude and a different frequency (see Figure 2-3). The resultant square wave now remains most of the time at either the maximum or minimum voltage, and the transition from one to the other is very rapid compared to the period the wave spends at the maximum or minimum.

To take this concept further, we can use the maximum of the square wave to represent a binary 0 or a 1 from the computer and the minimum of the square wave to represent the other value of the binary 0 or 1. Figures 2-4 and 2-5 are diagrams of this concept. The maximum and minimum threshold values

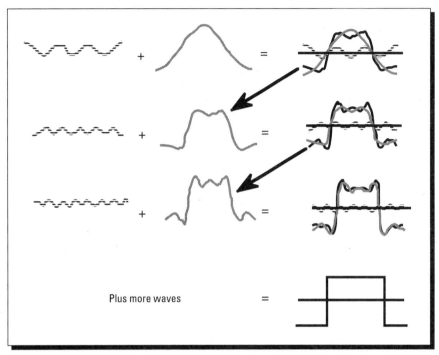

Figure 2-3: These sine waves of various amplitudes and frequencies are added together to make a square wave. The horizontal black line represents the result of addimg waves together.

indicated by the jagged lines in Figure 2-4 represent the maximum and minimum voltages that the transceiver's electronics can detect as a signal. Any wave that falls between the maximum and minimum threshold values (as shown in Figure 2-5) is not detected by the transceiver because the wave is smaller than either the maximum or minimum threshold value.

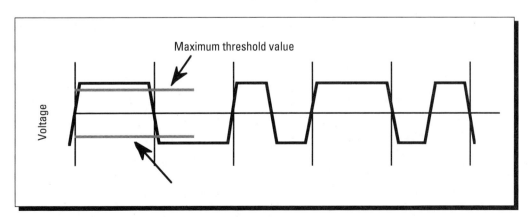

Figure 2-4: A typical square wave used for a network signal.

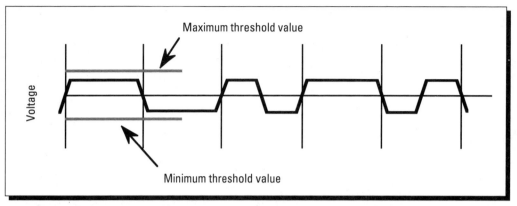

Figure 2-5: An example of a weakened square wave signal that is lower than the transceiver's threshold.

Erroneous signals

Nothing in life is perfect, and neither are electrical wires and cables. The laws of physics are such that wires resist the flow of electrons from one end of a wire to the other. This is called *resistance*, which is measured in *ohms* and varies from one kind of wire to another. Wires also resist changes from one voltage to another, such as when a sine wave passes through. This phenomenon, called *impedance*, is also measured in ohms, partly because impedance is electrically related to the resistance.

Resistance and impedance are two of the reasons why your computer's signal may never make it to another computer on the network. Both of these cable properties act to absorb a signal, weakening it and dissipating the absorbed energy as heat. If the cable's length between the two computers is too great, your signal may be reduced to a low enough voltage that the receiving computer never "hears" it (refer to Figure 2-5). That's why all networking schemes have limits to the maximum distance between the first and last computer on the network. There are also devices called *repeaters*, which can boost, or *amplify*, the network signals. We'll explain these devices later in this chapter.

Electrical signals don't always retain their original shape as they pass through a wire because the impedance of a wire changes with the frequency of the signal. Let's go back to our square wave, which is composed of multiple sine waves, each having a different frequency. A wire's impedance acts with different strength on the waves making up the square wave in a process called *attenuation*. With enough attenuation, the signal may no longer resemble a square wave, and the transceiver may not recognize it as a network signal (see Figure 2-6).

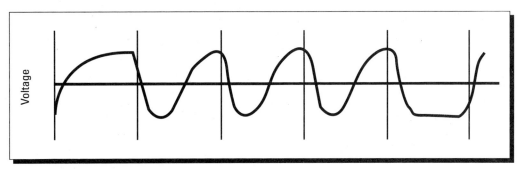

Figure 2-6: An example of an attenuated square wave.

Encoding signals

A transceiver can have problems even with a good strong signal. That's because a transceiver receiving a signal has to be synchronized with the transceiver that sent the signal, meaning that the receiving computer must know where the signal starts and where the signal ends. If the receiving transceiver doesn't detect the beginning of a signal at the right time, chances are good that it will eventually miss one of the bits in the frame — this is most likely to happen when there's a long string of binary 0s or 1s.

A transceiver with an extremely accurate clock might carefully measure the width of the square wave representing a 0 or a 1 and thereby keep track of the signal, counting binary digits as it goes along. But any drift or inaccuracy in the clock eventually causes the transceiver to lose track of a digit. It's not only difficult to create a clock this accurate, it's also expensive. Fortunately, there are *encoding* methods that keep one transceiver synchronized with another transceiver.

Rather than depending on the width of a square wave signal to represent a bit, most network systems rely on different representations, or *encodings*, of 0s and 1s. A basic encoding method is called NRZ, or *non-return to zero* (see Figure 2-7). In NRZ, two separate voltage levels, one positive and one negative, are used to represent the two binary digits, 0 and 1. One form of NRZ encoding, NRZ-level or NRZ-L, uses a negative voltage to represent a binary 1 and a positive voltage to represent a binary 0.

However, all the NRZ encoding methods make it difficult to detect where one bit ends and another begins. A more popular and reliable encoding method is *Manchester encoding* (see Figure 2-7), which is used, for example, by Ethernet networks. Manchester encoding always has a transition from high to low

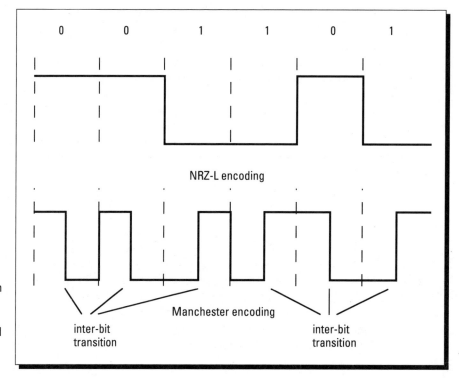

Figure 2-7: An example of NRZ-L encoding and Manchester encoding.

voltage (or vice versa) within the signal that represents one bit. By detecting this additional transition, a transceiver can always tell that it has detected one bit. The presence of this predictable transition within each bit's representation makes it possible for transceivers to remain synchronized. Such encodings are called *self-clocking codes*.

Getting the Message Through

Imagine that you're in a crowded room, perhaps at a cocktail party, with a group of people, all of whom are talking at the same time. In this chaotic scene, your chances of holding a decent conversation for any length of time are pretty slim. But now imagine something even worse: Each person in the room is talking non-stop, without taking a breath. Now, you probably can't understand anything at all.

Networks have to deal with the same sort of problems. Two conditions are necessary on a network to ensure that two computers can communicate with each other reliably. First, no computer can transmit data on the network endlessly. Second, each computer must have a system for giving way to another computer so that it can transmit data on the network.

Networks deal with the first problem by dividing your computer's data into groups of bits called *frames,* or *packets.* In addition to the data that you send from your computer, a frame contains information about the source and destination of the data — the network address of the computers on the network.

The packet further contains information about which rules, or *protocols,* were used by the computer to create the frame. If you send more data than will fit into one frame, your computer divides the data into smaller groups and sends as many frames as necessary to transmit all the data. So now you've got your computer saying something, but still taking a breath every so often.

We still haven't dealt with the problem of having more than one computer transmit on the network at the same time. If a group of computers were to start transmitting their signals simultaneously on the network, the signals would mix together unintelligibly, much like the commotion at the cocktail party. None of the computers could distinguish the original signals.

Network designers have developed a number of ways to deal with this problem, which is commonly called *contention.* We'll briefly describe the two most common ways of overcoming network contention. These methods are known as *carrier sensing* and *token passing.*

Each computer on the network has a specific network address. This address identifies the computer as the sender or receiver of a frame. You may wonder why contention is a problem if every computer has an address — can't a signal be sent from one computer to the right destination much as you'd drive a car from your house to a friend's?

Unfortunately, electrical signals don't work that way. Electrical signals are transmitted in both directions along a cable from their source. Thus, every computer's transceiver on the network must listen to the network cable to see whether the frame that's passing by is meant for it — if it is, the transceiver copies the frame and passes it on to the computer (see Figure 2-8). This process is similar to having a party line for your telephone; everyone's phone rings for an incoming call — you know whether the call is for you only when you answer the phone.

We'll take a closer look at the different methods that networks commonly use for dealing with contention problems.

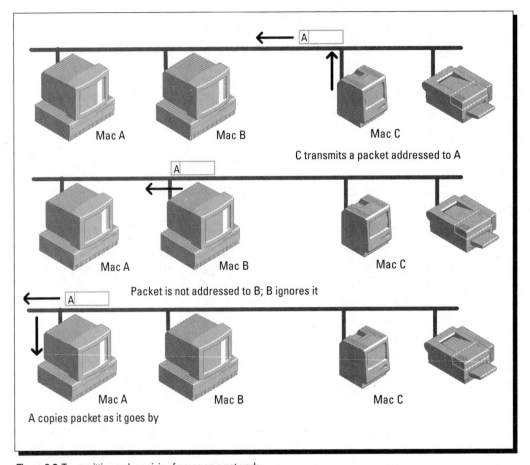

Figure 2-8: Transmitting and receiving frames on a network.

Carrier sensing

The idea behind carrier sensing is that a computer can listen to the network to see that no signal is being transmitted before it transmits its own signal. When the network is idle, the computer transmits its own packet, while continuing to monitor, or *listen* to the network.

In some cases, two or more devices may decide to transmit at about the same time. Their packets will interfere with each other, a situation known as a *collision*. What a computer does to prevent or detect a collision is the distinguishing factor for the two major types of carrier-sensing networks. These types are called *carrier sensing multiple access with collision detection*

(CSMA/CD) and *carrier sensing multiple access with collision avoidance (CSMA/CA)*. The words *multiple access* in this terminology simply mean that more than one computer is operating on the network.

In CSMA/CD, a transmitting computer stops transmitting its data on the network when it notices that a collision has taken place (see Figure 2-9). If you think back to our cocktail party analogy, this is like a person who waits silently for a period before saying anything; if anyone else starts talking when he does, he stops talking.

CSMA with collision avoidance (CSMA/CA) parallels our cocktail party with a new twist. Here, rather than simply waiting for a silence, our speaker says "excuse me" or coughs to alert the others and then starts talking. The key here is that the speaker does something to grab everyone's attention before speaking. Drawing a comparison to a network, the computers each listen for such an attention-getting signal in the form of a particular packet, called a *carrier burst*, to see whether the cable is going to be used by another computer. If a computer detects this packet, it knows that another computer is going to use the cable and that data will follow; if there is no carrier burst, the first computer can send one of its own to start a conversation.

Token passing

Token passing is different from both of the carrier-sensing methods we just described. As the name suggests, token passing involves sending an electronic *token* packet on the network from one computer to the next; this token gives the receiving computer permission to transmit data. When that computer is finished sending its data, it then passes the token on to the next computer (see Figure 2-10). This is much like going around a table at a meeting and asking each person at the table if that person has anything to say.

Of the networks that we'll be discussing in this book, Apple's LocalTalk network uses CSMA/CA to deal with contention on the network, whereas Ethernet uses CSMA/CD. And, although we won't be saying much about token ring networks, many IBM computers and their clones are wired together using token passing rings. Macs can also be attached to token ring networks and use the TokenTalk driver to communicate with each other.

Devices for Larger Networks

So now you know that such conditions as noise and resistance place both distance and node limitations on your network cables. But suppose you need for Mary to talk to Paul, and they're at opposite sides of a long building, or even across the street. How do you overcome the distance and node limitations? How do you create a larger network?

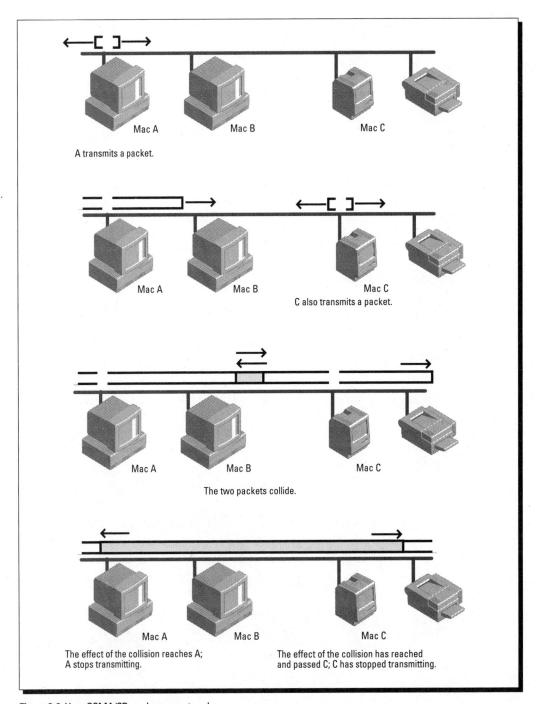

Figure 2-9: How CSMA/CD works on a network.

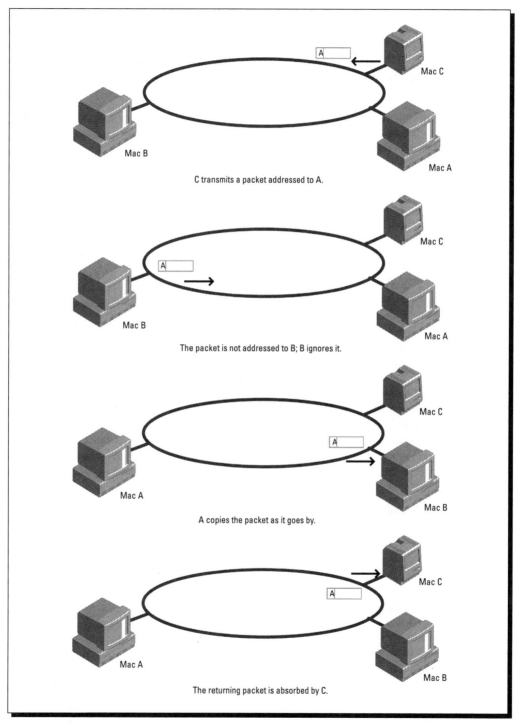

C transmits a packet addressed to A.

The packet is not addressed to B; B ignores it.

A copies the packet as it goes by.

The returning packet is absorbed by C.

Figure 2-10: Transmitting tokens and frames on a token ring network.

You can go beyond these limitations by using any of the devices known as *repeaters, bridges,* and *routers.* These devices enable you to connect cables together to form larger and larger networks. Each device type in its turn is a step up in performance and flexibility, but also a step up in complexity for the network administrator. We'll explain each of these devices in order of their increasing complexity. We'll show you how and when each device can be used and point out the limitations of each device as well.

Repeaters

You can use a repeater to link two network cables of the same type. AppleTalk networks use two primary cable types: LocalTalk and Ethernet. A repeater can link two LocalTalk cables to make a longer LocalTalk cable, or two Ethernet cables to make a longer Ethernet cable.

The primary purpose of a repeater is to amplify and reclock the electrical signal (see Figure 2-11). A signal traveling along a cable is gradually weakened by the resistance of the path, making the voltage of the wave too low to be heard by the receiver. A repeater solves this problem by reissuing the signal at full strength across to the second cable. Obviously, the placement of the repeater is important. The repeater must be located at some place along the cable where it can still detect the incoming, somewhat weak, signal.

A repeater has two primary limitations. The first is that a repeater strengthens a signal, but does so only for two passes. Once a signal has gone through the second repeater in a row, the signal is no longer strong enough to be repeated a third time. Secondly, a repeater does not solve the problem of too many collisions. The number of collisions goes up with the number of nodes in use on a segment. When the number of collisions causes the network to fail or to slow to a crawl, you need to move up a step and install a bridge.

Bridges

A bridge also combines two like cable segments and performs all the functions that a repeater does. Beyond this, the bridge adds some traffic-handling capability. A bridge maintains a table that informs it about which nodes are located on either side of it. As a packet travels on the network, the bridge retrieves it and checks its header. If the packet and its destination are on the same side of the bridge, the bridge does nothing. But when the destination is on the other side of the bridge, the bridge passes the packet across (see Figure 2-12). In this way, only the traffic that is destined for the other side gets across. Local traffic stays local. Most bridges today are called *learning bridges,* which means they collect information that they need for the address table. Previously, the administrator had to enter the address table and maintain it manually.

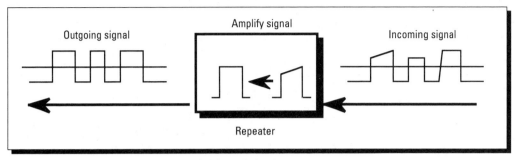

Figure 2-11: An example of a repeater processing network signals.

Again, there are two primary limitations to a bridge. First, a bridge only looks at the address to determine whether the packet should be passed across. A certain type of packet, called a *broadcast packet*, has a destination of everyone on the network. As your network grows, such broadcast packets can overwhelm the network, and the bridge can do nothing to limit the broadcasts. As your network traffic increases, you will need to put routers in place.

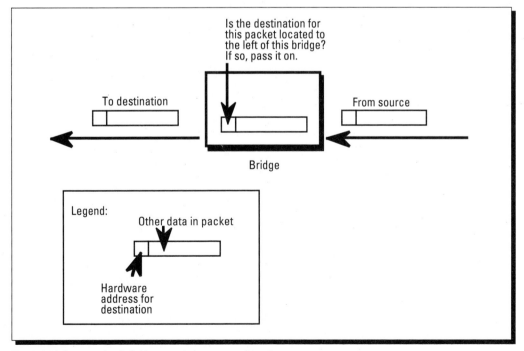

Figure 2-12: An example of a bridge processing a network packet.

A second limitation with a bridge is that it can join only like segments. If you want to connect a LocalTalk cable to an Ethernet cable, you will need to use a router.

Routers

A router does more than just link two cable segments together and filter traffic. A router actually links two networks together. When you put a router in place, it creates a separate designation for each cable and calls each a network. Each network then has its own designator, a network number, so that the router can keep track of it (see Figure 2-13).

With bridges and repeaters, you make a single larger network. But with a router, you are joining multiple networks. So what does this mean to you? With a router in place, the administrator can define areas physically. In addition to source and destination node addresses, each packet now contains network addresses for both source and destination. If you place another router as a link between network cables on a second floor and third floor, for example, you can look at any packet and identify the floor of source or destination. With no router — if you used a bridge, for example — there would be no network address. You would have only the node address, so the packet wouldn't tell you whether the node was from the second or third floor.

A router is capable of performing many advanced traffic-flow procedures. As we mentioned previously, a router does not pass broadcast traffic. If information in a broadcast packet is needed on the other side, the router itself creates a packet, using its own address as the source and then sending the information. In some cases, multiple devices may be sending out information in a broadcast format. With a router, this information goes across only once. Information regarding node addresses also is not passed on by the router. The router looks at the network-address destination portion of a packet and passes it across when the destination-network number matches.

Because a router joins two separate networks, it can also join two different types of cable segments. The router changes the packet as necessary and sends it across in the new format.

Although routers can link networks that are countries apart by using telephone serial links, routers do have traffic limitations. A router is usually slower than a bridge because the router does more processing of packets, maintaining network numbers, and filtering packets. Also, routers add to the data traffic on the network. On networks with more than one router, the exchange of route information creates additional overhead.

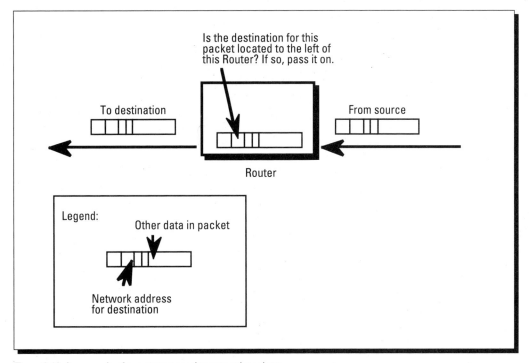

Figure 2-13: An example of a router processing network packets.

A Basic Networking Vocabulary

In this chapter, we've focused on the physical aspects of a network. Occasionally, we've used some terminology that deals more with the logical or organizational aspects of networking, such as network addresses. We'll be dealing extensively with the logical organization of networks, so we'll take some time now to introduce some of the vocabulary that you'll need to know. Remember also to check Appendix C, "Glossary of Terms," for further reference.

Should you use a repeater, a bridge, or a router?

Use a repeater when the network is very small. For LocalTalk, you should have no more than 48 active nodes (see Chapter 15, "Performance Management"). Use a bridge in busy but small physical areas. Use a router when the network's physical area is large or spans more than one floor of a building, or when you need to join two dissimilar cable segments.

Previously, we referred to *network devices*. It should be fairly obvious by now that a network device is just about any type of computing device that you can attach to a network. This includes Macs, DOS computers, file servers, printers, and even modems. When any device is attached to a network, it is commonly referred to as a *network node* and is assigned a *network address*. This network address is unique for each node. Many network systems require an administrator to assign the network address to the node; some, like AppleTalk, allow the node to select one for itself. We'll say more about AppleTalk's method later in this chapter.

Network nodes can also be subdivided into *sockets,* which have their own identifying number for tracking purposes. Each socket on a network node is associated with a single process or application on that node. Thus, if you're printing a document on a networked printer and using electronic mail, the network sees two sockets defined on your computer: one for the print job, the other for your electronic mail.

Networkers also have a specific name for most of the networking tasks that your computer performs; each task is called a *session.* It's convenient to think of a session as a conversation between your computer and another node on the network. Following the example in the preceding paragraph, your computer is running one session between itself and the printer and another session between itself and the mail server.

Note that we said that most, but not all, of your computer's network tasks are sessions. Occasionally your computer searches the network for a particular device — it may be looking for *any* file server, for example. To do this, the computer sends a *broadcast* over the network. This broadcast is just what its name implies; it is not addressed to any node in particular. Every node on the network receives the broadcast and decides how to respond, if it responds at all, based on the contents of the broadcast. Because the broadcast isn't directed to one node in particular and there may be no response, a conversation doesn't take place between two nodes. Broadcasts, therefore, aren't considered sessions.

In a previous section in this chapter titled "Devices for Larger Networks," we introduced you to networking devices that can be used to create larger networks. In our discussion of routers, we mentioned that routers connect two or more networks to form a larger network. How does the router know which network is which? When you install a router, you assign a unique network number to each network. When you have a router on your network, packets are directed to their destination by the router, based on both the network number and the network address of the destination. (For convenience, many network systems, such as AppleTalk, combine the node's network address and network number into a single internet address.)

An Overview of AppleTalk Networks

The primary focus of this book is AppleTalk networking, even though we'll talk about other ways of networking Macs in Part Five, "Working with Other Computer Platforms." Before going into detail on the AppleTalk networking protocols, wiring and applications, we'll cover some of the basic concepts of AppleTalk networks.

Dynamic node addressing

As we explained in the section about networking vocabulary, AppleTalk uses both a node address and socket number to identify a network task. Devices using AppleTalk are designed to select their node addresses *dynamically*. This means that the first time a device is attached to an AppleTalk network, it randomly selects a tentative node address from a range of numbers, as defined within the AppleTalk specifications.

The device broadcasts that address to the network. If no other node is already using that address, the new device uses the selected address and stores it for future use. If another node already has the desired address, the new device selects another address at random and tries the process all over again until it selects an unused address.

Because an AppleTalk device stores its selected node address, it tries to use the same address the next time it is turned on (or when it is reattached to the network, if the device is a Mac Portable or PowerBook). This usually means that, after the device is attached to the network and the selection process is completed, the same address is used over and over again. On occasion, however, an AppleTalk device may need to go through the process of selecting a new address. When a new device is attached to the network and turned on, the new device may select an address formerly used by an older device. Also, if you reconfigure your network, possibly by adding a router, your AppleTalk devices will go through the process of selecting new addresses.

Note that because each Mac stores its node address in PRAM (Parameter Random Access Memory), the address will be cleared if you replace the Mac's battery, so the Mac will need a new address when it's reattached to the network.

AppleTalk names

Even though AppleTalk networks transmit and route network traffic based on numeric addresses, we human users are more comfortable working with named objects. AppleTalk relies on converting, or *mapping,* node addresses to names to make network access easier for users. AppleTalk also lets network administrators logically group nodes into *zones* to make navigation through a network easier.

We'll take a brief look at AppleTalk's named services first. When a device is attached to the network and provides a network service for other users, or *clients,* to use, the type of service usually has a name associated with it. These names, which represent types of services, usually show up in your Mac's Chooser with an associated icon. Some examples are AppleShare, which is a file server; LaserWriter, which is a networked laser printer; and MS Mail, which is an electronic mail server.

When installing any of these services on the AppleTalk network, an administrator has the option of giving the device a name. Thus, you may have on your network AppleShare servers named Finance, Legal, and Marketing. Or, your LaserWriters may have names like "Word Processing," or "Bldg. 3, 1st Floor," or "London." In any case, these names show up in the Chooser when you're looking for a particular server or printer, so you don't need to know the device's numeric address in order to use it.

We also said that AppleTalk lets a network administrator combine nodes into a logical group (provided your network has a router installed). These named groups are called *zones.* The main idea behind zones is to make it easier for a user to navigate through the network. For example, you might have a network that runs through three stories of a building (see Figure 2-14). If your network includes a router or two, you could decide that all devices on the first floor would be in a zone called "1st Floor," all devices on the second and third floors are in the "Upper Floors." (Note that the "Upper Floors" zone includes two routers.) When a user on the second floor starts looking for a laser printer on the upper floors, he can use the Chooser to see a list of zone names, select the "Upper Floors" zone, and select the LaserWriter icon to find all the laser printers on in that zone (see Figure 2-15). If no zones were created (even if a router is part of the network), the user would see all of the laser printers in one list (see Figure 2-16).

The AppleTalk internet

Recall that the router calls each cable segment that is attached to it a *network.* If each of these segments is called a network, what do you call the entire network? A network of networks? Or a Network with a big N? That's a bit awkward. Besides, you'd have problems discussing the "big-N" Network, as opposed to one of the router's "little-n" networks. Apple chooses to call the entire aggregate of networks connected via routers an *internet.*

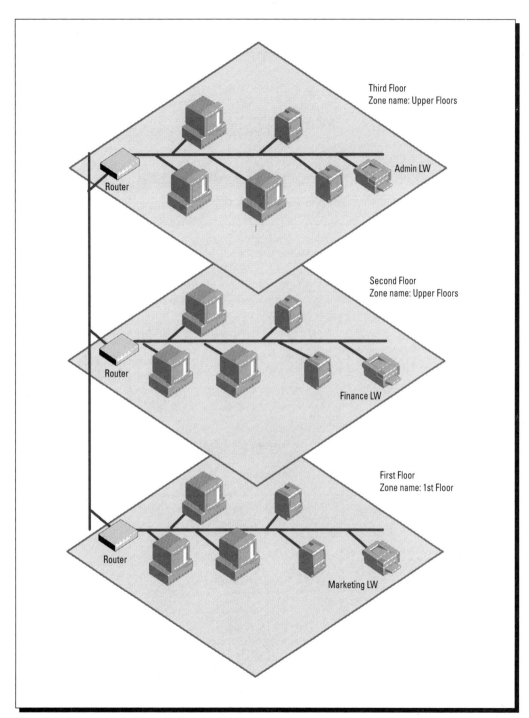

Figure 2-14: A three-story building with three AppleTalk zones.

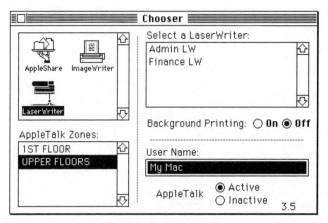

Figure 2-15: The user sees only the Admin LaserWriter and Finance LaserWriter when selecting the Upper Floors zone in the Chooser.

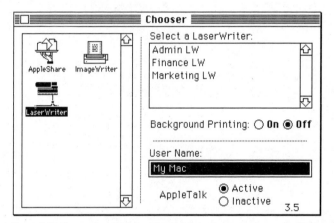

Figure 2-16: The user sees all three laser printers because the network has no zones.

Apple's use of the term *internet* is not the same as *The Internet,* which is a large international telecommunications network used by many universities to connect their computers.

Within an AppleTalk internet, each cable segment has one or more network numbers associated with it. The original AppleTalk specifications allowed only a single network number per cable. When AppleTalk specifications were upgraded to Phase 2 in June, 1989, Apple allowed Ethernet and token ring cables to have more than one network number. In either case, the AppleTalk router is responsible for maintaining the list of network numbers and their associated cables (see Chapter 3, "Understanding AppleTalk Protocols," and Chapter 11, "Designing an AppleTalk LAN").

Summary

This chapter introduced you to the vocabulary of networking and presented some concepts basic to an understanding of how a network operates. We've covered the following points:

✔ The most common networks use coaxial cable or twisted-pair cable. Some also use fiber-optic cabling or wireless connections, such as infrared or radio frequency.

✔ A computer requires both hardware and software to connect to a network. The hardware includes both a cable connector and a transceiver to understand network signals. The software is called a driver.

✔ The binary 0s and 1s understood by a computer are transmitted as a square wave over the network cabling.

✔ These network signals can be weakened by the cabling, or interfered with by external noise sources.

✔ Digital encoding schemes make it easier for transceivers to stay synchronized with each other in order to correctly receive data.

✔ Networks use either a carrier-sensing technique or token passing to control communications between computers.

✔ A repeater can be used to amplify the network signal. A bridge can link networks using the same type of cabling to create larger networks. A router can link networks using dissimilar cables to create larger networks and control traffic on the network.

✔ AppleTalk uses names to identify networked services to the user. It also uses names to show the user logical divisions of the network.

Now that we've covered the basic concepts of networks and how they work, in the next chapter we'll look at AppleTalk specifications in details.

Chapter 3
Understanding AppleTalk Protocols

Love may make the world go 'round, but network operations are set in motion by *protocols* — the rules that determine everything about the way a network operates. Protocols govern how applications access the network, the way data from an application is divided into packets for transmission through a cable, and which electrical signals represent data on a network cable.

You can accomplish a good deal on a network without being aware of protocols. But knowing about protocols can help if you're ever called upon to troubleshoot a network or if you want to understand what's happening with a router, a laser printer, or a mail server. Each protocol is assigned a different network function, so you can use the protocol definitions to see how the parts of a network relate or to understand the steps that an application must go through in order to perform on a network.

When the guts of a networking system are designed, a suite of protocols is defined so that the proper hardware can be manufactured and programmers can adopt a standardized method of communicating with that hardware. Protocols may be defined by a single vendor as with AppleTalk, or by a group of vendors, as with Ethernet. In other cases, an international committee defines the protocols for a network, as with the OSI protocols.

More than one kind of networking system is currently available for computers — names such as Ethernet, TCP/IP, SNA, DECnet, AppleTalk, FDDI, and so on come to mind. Each system has its own rules for how the network should work. And, as you might expect, the rules aren't interchangeable from one network to another.

In this chapter, we'll discuss the internationally accepted OSI Reference Model for open systems, which helps vendors design networks that can communicate with one another. Using this model as a framework, we'll cover in detail the AppleTalk protocols, what they do, and how they interact with one another.

Introducing the OSI Reference Model

In an effort to standardize a way of looking at network protocols, the International Standards Organization (ISO) created a seven-layer model that defines the basic network functions (see Figure 3-1). This model is called the *OSI Reference Model*. The letters OSI stand for *Open Systems Interconnection*. In many network operating systems, you can pigeonhole each protocol into one layer of this reference model. In other cases, it's not so easy. Occasionally, a protocol spans more than one layer of the model. In still other cases, some layers may be missing entirely. But once you categorize the protocols according to the OSI Reference Model, you'll find it easier to compare the component functions of the various networks.

> The seven layers of the OSI Reference Model group network functions into general categories; comparing various protocols to this standard model will help you understand various networking systems.

Two important principles are at the heart of the OSI Reference Model. First, there's the concept of open systems. Each layer of the model is assigned specific network functions, which means that two different networking systems that support the functions of a selected OSI layer can exchange data at that level. For the moment, though, this is more often true on paper than in practice.

Second, the OSI Reference Model depends on the concept of *peer-to-peer communications*. What this means is that data created by one layer in the OSI Reference Model (such as the network layer) and transmitted to another device on the network pertains only to the same layer on that device. In other words, intervening layers do not alter the data; the other layers simply add to the data found in a packet to perform their assigned functions on the network.

Protocol suites are designed in distinct layers to make it easier to substitute one protocol for another. You can say that protocol suites govern how data is exchanged above and below each protocol layer. (In fact, the graphical representation of these protocols in vertical layers is why protocol suites are sometimes called *protocol stacks*.) When protocols are designed, specifications set forth how a protocol exchanges data with a protocol layered above or below it. As long as you follow those specifications, you can substitute a new, supposedly better, protocol for one currently in the suite without affecting the general behavior of the network.

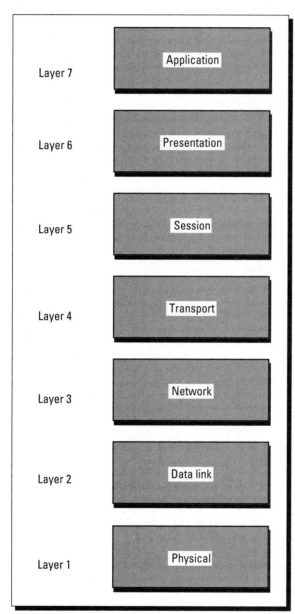

Layer 7	Application
Layer 6	Presentation
Layer 5	Session
Layer 4	Transport
Layer 3	Network
Layer 2	Data link
Layer 1	Physical

Figure 3-1: The OSI Reference Model sets a standard for network protocols.

We'll offer some examples and explain the purposes of each layer, which we'll list here in descending order. For now, you can think of the layers as dealing with the following questions:

Layer 7 — The application layer: What data do I want to send to my partner?

Layer 6 — The presentation layer: What does the data look like?

Layer 5 — The session layer: Who is the partner?

Layer 4 — The transport layer: Where is the partner?

Layer 3 — The network layer: Which route do I follow to get there?

Layer 2 — The data link layer: How do I make each step in that route?

Layer 1 — The physical layer: How do I use the medium for that step?

To further explain the OSI Reference Model, we'll use a non-computer example — the process of a fax communication — to illustrate what happens in different layers of the model, starting from the top and working down the layers.

Suppose that you want to fax a report to a correspondent in another, non-English-speaking country. Deciding to send the report is your job as the user, but the actual job of setting up the report for transmittal is the job of your staff, which compares here to layer 7, the *application layer*. The report itself and any translations necessary are part of layer 6, the *presentation layer* (see Figure 3-2).

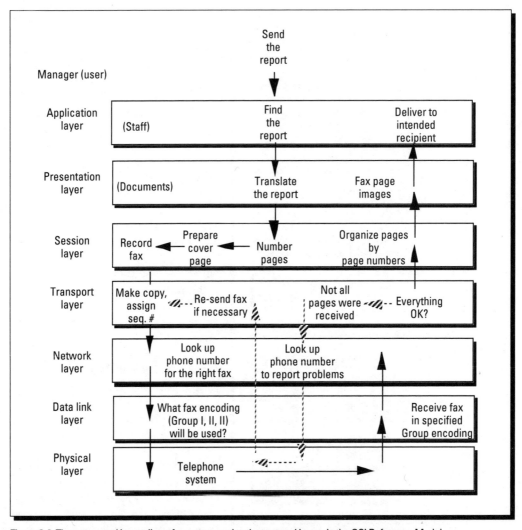

Figure 3-2: The steps used in sending a fax correspond to the protocol layers in the OSI Reference Model.

The preparation of this report for fax transmission is a good example of how the top two layers, the application and presentation layers, work together, because the various tasks to accomplish the presentation layer — finding the report, translating the report, and then preparing the fax page images — may be handled by different members of your staff as discrete functions within the application and presentation layers. Storing the original report and its final translated copy is the job of the presentation layer, for example, but it's the job of the application layer to find and track the report. In short, there's a continual conversation going on between the staff at the application layer and the documents at the presentation layer.

Once the document is ready to be transmitted, someone has to prepare the cover page, which usually states how many pages are in the transmission. This is the job of layer 5, the *session layer*. The session layer also has the responsibility of recording and checking pertinent details of the fax, such as the address of the recipient, the recipient's correct title, and the size of the fax document. This is an important task because lower protocol layers will request information from the session layer in order to maintain a two-way conversation between the sender and the recipient.

The next lowest layer in the model, layer 4, the *transport layer*, takes care of numbering the pages of the fax document in sequence, copying the fax for storage, and assigning a sequence number for easier tracking. All these tasks are necessary to ensure reliable transmission of the fax. If something goes wrong with the transmission, the transport layer can recover a copy for re-sending. Also, numbering the pages ensures that the pages are sent and received in the proper order. Numbered pages also make it easier to determine whether a page was not received and identifies an unreadable page that needs to be sent again.

Now you have a fax document, and you know what to do if all of it or parts of it don't make it to the intended recipient. Which fax do you call to get the document to intended recipient? The transmittal sheet may simply say that the report is from Bill in the Accounting Department and that it is to be sent to Pierre in Corporate Finance. Layer 3, the *network layer,* keeps track of people's locations according to department and location in the company. But someone needs to look up the phone number for Pierre's fax number. This *mapping* of logical to physical addresses, as it's called, is the role of layer 2, the *data link layer*.

Actually getting the report pages sent from one fax to the other requires that both faxes use the same data format (Group I, II, or III, in the case of faxes — the two faxes negotiate this once they're connected). We're not talking about the format of the fax document with such considerations as pagination and paragraph setup, but the way that the bits representing the image of the fax page are sent. This *encoding* (and *decoding* on the receiving fax) of the bit patterns is also a part of the data link layer.

Layer 1, the *physical layer* is pretty much what its name implies. Following our fax example, the physical layer becomes the physical wiring scheme or the telephone service between the two offices.

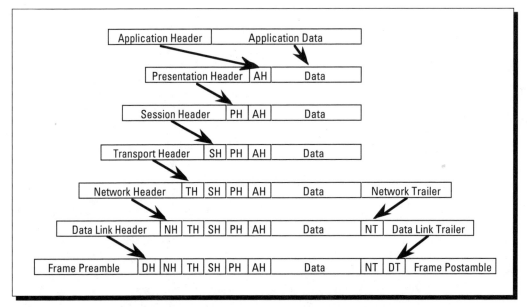

Figure 3-3: Your data is prepared for a network with headers and footers that supply protocol information.

In a later section, you'll see that real data exchange on a network isn't very different from this fax example. One important thing is different, however, and that is the form that data takes as it is passed from layer to layer, or protocol to protocol. Each protocol adds some information to the original data on the sending computer so that the receiving computer knows the rules to follow as it decodes the data packets and reconstructs the original data (see Figure 3-3). This added protocol information is either prepended or appended to the data in the form of *headers* and *footers*. Under no circumstances is your raw data transmitted on a network.

In the next section, we'll discuss the protocols themselves. We'll first give you an overview of AppleTalk protocols, and then we'll examine each of the protocols in sequence, according to the layer their functions belong to.

Introducing AppleTalk Protocols

AppleTalk, the name for Apple's proprietary network architecture, is a layered suite of protocols that easily fits the OSI Reference Model. As you see in Figure 3-4, quite a few protocols make up the AppleTalk suite. Although they fall into distinct layers according to the OSI model, it's useful to further classify the

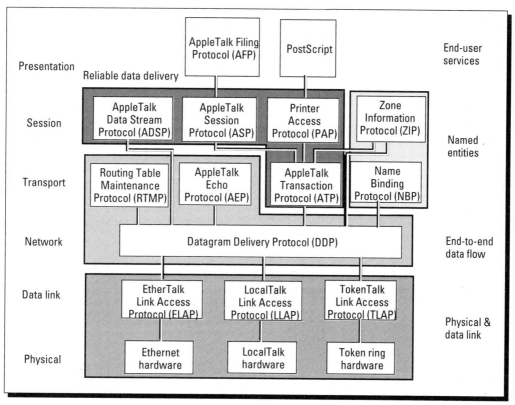

Figure 3-4: The AppleTalk protocol stack is arranged here by function.

protocols according to their functions. These functions can be described as follows, in order from bottom to top:

1. The physical and data link functions

2. The end-to-end data flow functions

3. The named entities functions

4. The reliable data delivery functions

5. The end-user services

Looking at Figure 3-4, you'll see the physical and data link functions grouped together at the bottom of the diagram. This physical and data link category contains the Link Access Protocols, or LAPs. Think of this category as the network hardware interface — the network's cable and the hardware needed to communicate with that cable (see Chapter 2, "Understanding Networks"). The AppleTalk Address Resolution Protocol (AARP) also belongs in this category because it's intimately linked to the Ethernet and token ring LAPs (AARP is not shown in the protocol layer diagram, as this protocol is usually included within the definition of each LAP).

Moving upward on the diagram, notice the end-to-end data flow category. End-to-end data flow (the flow of data from one network socket to the other) is controlled by the following three protocols:

❖ Datagram Delivery Protocol (DDP)

❖ Routing Table Maintenance Protocol (RTMP)

❖ AppleTalk Echo Protocol (AEP)

These protocols see to it that data is properly transmitted from the source to the correct destination on the network. Only the DDP packets actually transmit your application's data; the other two protocols control and test the route your computer's data packets take to their destination.

> End-to-end data flow means getting the data from one network socket to another; AppleTalk protocols in this category make certain that data is transmitted to the right destination.

However, the end-to-end data flow protocols are not concerned with reliability in transmitting the data on the network. That's the function of another group of four protocols:

❖ AppleTalk Transaction Protocol (ATP)

❖ Printer Access Protocol (PAP)

❖ AppleTalk Session Protocol (ASP)

❖ AppleTalk Data Stream Protocol (ADSP)

Take another look at Figure 3-4. You will see that in general the preceding four protocols are layered above the end-to-end data flow protocols, which means that they ensure reliable data delivery without knowing the source and destination of the data. These protocols pass on their data to the lower protocols, which take the responsibility for finding the right destination.

So far, we've classified the protocols according to functions that are needed to get data from one place to another. We could stop here and have a functioning network system. But such a system would be difficult to use because users must select other destination nodes by a numeric network address that wouldn't be easy to remember. Apple's solution is to assign names to every network device or service, which we'll explain further in the section on the Name Binding Protocol.

The two protocols responsible for handling these named devices and services so that they are easy to use and so that the network understands what the users want are the Name Binding Protocol (NBP) and the Zone Information Protocol (ZIP).

The final category, end-user services, represents what the user will probably want to do with the network. AppleTalk defines two fundamental user services: file sharing and printing. File sharing is defined by the AppleTalk Filing Protocol (AFP); printing is covered by PostScript. Although PostScript isn't owned by Apple (it's patented by Adobe Systems), it is included in the protocol stack because it's a common interface for networked printer output on Macs. (Apple's first laser printers mainly supported PostScript as the page description language.)

If you're new to AppleTalk or don't need to figure out what each protocol is doing on the network, you may want to stop here. Up to this point, the chapter has presented a broad overview of the various protocols and their functions. You can skim the rest of the chapter if you're interested. But if you're curious about how the protocols accomplish their functions, or if you need to understand their operations for troubleshooting purposes, continue with the next section, which covers the AppleTalk protocols in more explicit detail. (Details on the AppleTalk packet formats are found in Appendix A.)

A Detailed Look at the AppleTalk Protocols

The next sections provide an in-depth look at AppleTalk protocols. Users, who are mainly concerned with end-user services, generally deal with protocols from the top of the stack downward; from layer 7, the application layer, down to layer 1, the physical layer. We'll start our discussion of the protocol suite, however, with the lower layers (see Figure 3-5) and work our way upward. It's more convenient to proceed in this direction; as you get to the higher layers in the protocol stack, you'll find that many protocols often use the same protocol in a layer below them. Working our way up from the bottom, therefore, makes tracking these relations easier and reduces repetition.

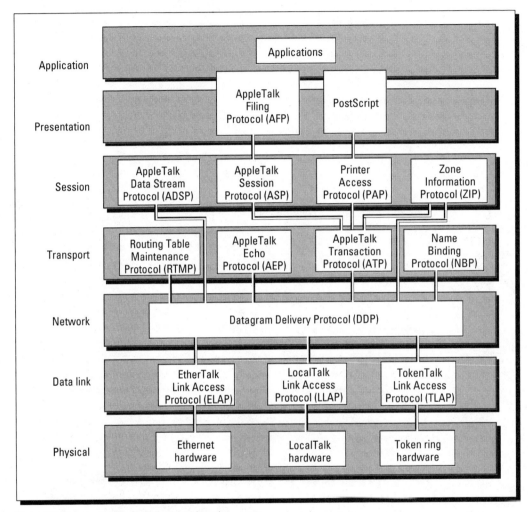

Figure 3-5: The complete AppleTalk protocol stack.

Layer 1 — the physical layer

Referring again to Figure 3-5, notice layer 1, the physical layer of the protocol stack, which is responsible for handling the network hardware. Standard network hardware, such as that defined for Ethernet and token ring networks can be used with AppleTalk. Apple has also defined its own network hardware, called *LocalTalk*, which uses a synchronous RS-422A bus for communications. Bits are encoded on the cable using FM (frequency modulation) 0 encoding (see Figure 3-6). FM 0 is a biphase encoding technique that provides self-clocking (see Chapter 2, "Understanding Networks" for more information).

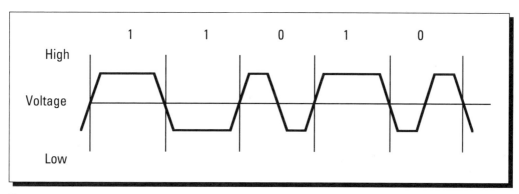

Figure 3-6: LocalTalk uses FM 0 encoding.

With this method, a transition occurs at the beginning and end of each bit; 0s also have a transition in the middle — the 1s do not. LocalTalk's transmission speed is 230,400 bps (bits per second).

To prevent unwanted reflections of the LocalTalk signals, Apple's network connectors contain an internal 100-ohm resistor for unused ports. Farallon's PhoneNET connectors do not include internal resistors, but require insertion of a 120-ohm resistor into unused ports to counter reflections. In each case, the transformers used within the connectors provide ground isolation as well as protection from static discharge.

Layer 2 — the data link layer

The next layer upward in the AppleTalk protocol stack is layer 2 — the data link layer. The data link layer, which is responsible for interfacing to the network hardware, includes three protocols called LAPs (for Link Access Protocols). The original LAP defined by Apple was the ALAP (AppleTalk Link Access Protocol). With the passage of time, ALAP was renamed LLAP (LocalTalk Link Access Protocol) to distinguish it from other LAPs that were defined for Ethernet (ELAP) and token ring (TLAP) hardware. A few other LAPs have been defined by third-party vendors; the most notable one is the ARCNet LAP.

Each LAP is designed to handle what is known as *dynamic node ID assignment.* Simply put, this means that a node picks its node number whenever it starts up. This also means that a node does not necessarily have the same ID each time it starts up.

The procedure for dynamic node ID assignment is relatively simple. When a node starts up, it randomly assigns itself an ID. The node then tests this ID by transmitting a control packet on the network to discover whether another node has that ID. If the ID is not being used, the node keeps that ID. If the ID is in use, the node must select a new ID and try again. As you might guess, this can lead to heavy traffic on a large network. Nodes joining the network late in the game have more existing node IDs to conflict with and may retry a number of times to get an unused ID.

> With *dynamic node assignment,* a node picks an ID by random choice and then sends a control packet out to see whether this number is taken; many tries to get an unused number can be necessary on a busy network.

Things are a bit simpler if a node has been on the network previously, as when the node was originally connected to the network. In such cases, the Mac stores its previous address to use as its first try for dynamic node assignment. Thus a previously configured, unchanged network should experience only one round of node requests as each Mac is restarted, with each Mac using its assigned ID from its previous time on the network.

The LocalTalk Link Access Protocol is a CSMA/CA protocol, which means that it uses collision avoidance to handle contention on the network (see Chapter 2, "Understanding Networks"). LLAP expects the network cable to be clear for an interdialog gap (IDG) of 400 microseconds plus a random wait period before a transmission is initiated by a node. Each packet in the transmission is separated by no more than 200 microseconds (the interframe gap, or IFG).

LLAP can choose to send packets either to a single node in a *directed transmission* or to all nodes in a *broadcast transmission*. In both cases, LLAP sends a Request-to-Send packet (lapRTS) to the destination node. For a directed transmission, the destination is the node ID; for the broadcast transmission, the node ID has the address of **$FF** in hexadecimal (or 255 in decimal). When the transmission is directed, LLAP waits for a Clear-to-Send packet (lapCTS) from the destination node and then transmits a data packet to the destination. In the case of a broadcast, however, the source node simply waits for one IFG and then broadcasts the packet.

The LocalTalk LAP defines two types of packets, which are specified in the LLAP type field (see Appendix A). If the type field contains a value in the range 128-255 (**$80-$FF**), the LLAP packet is a control packet and does not contain a data field. On the other hand, if the value is between 1 and 127 (**$01-$7F**), the LLAP is a data packet. Data packets can contain up to 600 bytes of data.

Two other LAPs are worth noting at this point. These are the EtherTalk LAP (ELAP) and the TokenTalk LAP (TLAP). *EtherTalk* is Apple's name for AppleTalk protocols running on Ethernet, whereas *TokenTalk* is Apple's name

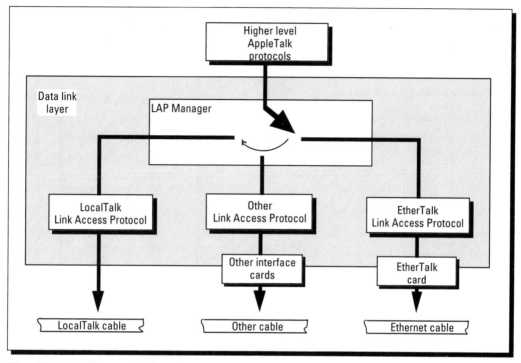

Figure 3-7: The LAP Manager handles switching among the different media.

for AppleTalk running on token ring networks. In each case, because of the modularity of the AppleTalk protocol stack, all the protocols above the data link layer function independently of these LAP definitions. In other words, once you get to the protocols starting at the network layer and above, it doesn't matter what network medium you're working with.

One advantage of working with layered protocols is that switching among the different media is handled within the data link layer by the LAP Manager (see Figure 3-7). The most common interface to this at the user level is the Control Panel Network cdev in System 6.0.x (and earlier) or the Control Panel Extension in System 7.

When Apple first introduced EtherTalk as an extension of the AppleTalk Phase 1 protocols, the Ethernet version 2 definition was used, as defined and promulgated by DEC, Intel, and Xerox (see Chapter 8, "Designing an Ethernet LAN"). When Apple upgraded its protocols to Phase 2, it adopted the IEEE standards for Ethernet and token ring, so that the EtherTalk packets now followed the IEEE 802.3 definition. The two packet types are defined differently (nothing's

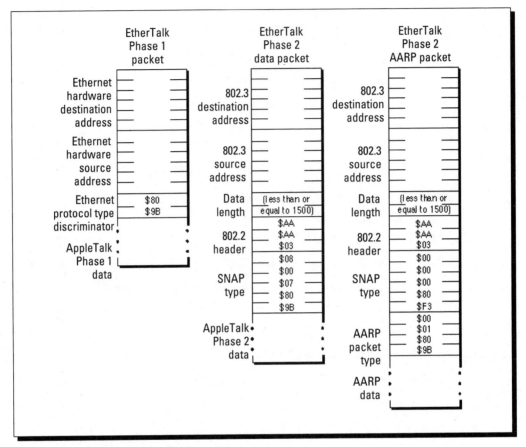

Figure 3-8: A diagram of the types of EtherTalk packets.

simple), and a computer set to recognize one packet type does not recognize the other type (see Figure 3-8). This is one reason you can have EtherTalk Phase 1 and EtherTalk Phase 2 Macs on the same network, but they cannot communicate with each other unless a transition router is present (see Chapter 12, "Making the Phase 2 Move").

In both EtherTalk types, Apple has registered the EtherTalk packet as Ethernet type **$809B** with Xerox, the company responsible for maintaining the international registry of Ethernet packet types. In the Phase 1 data packet, the Ethernet type field follows the hardware source address, as shown in Figure 3-8. However, since EtherTalk Phase 2 packets use the IEEE 802.2 Logical Link Control (LLC) to promote connectivity over different data links, the Ethernet type is contained in the SNAP type field. (SNAP is the acronym for Sub-Network Access Protocol.) The SNAP field requires added information, namely an organization code, which is **$080007** in Apple's case. (The full protocol type, which combines the organization code with the Ethernet type, is **$080007809B**.)

The TokenTalk LAP did not exist before the introduction of AppleTalk Phase 2, and there's only one definition of token ring packets. Consequently, TokenTalk doesn't suffer from the packet-typing problems just discussed for EtherTalk. AppleTalk follows the IEEE 802.5 standard for token ring packets. By supporting the 802.5 and the 802.2 LLC standards (in addition to 802.3 for Ethernet), AppleTalk can transmit data over an internetwork composed of LocalTalk, Ethernet, and token ring networks.

When Apple introduced EtherTalk, it also had to create a protocol that could map a hardware address to an AppleTalk protocol address. This protocol is known as the AppleTalk Address Resolution Protocol, or AARP. One reason for the existence of this protocol is AppleTalk's use of dynamically assigned 8-bit addresses, whereas Ethernet and token ring use a statically assigned 48-bit address. Under AppleTalk Phase 2, which also added AARP support for token ring, the SNAP protocol type defined for AARP is **$00000080F3**.

AARP uses an Address Mapping Table (AMT) to simplify mapping between hardware addresses and protocol addresses. By keeping the most recently used addresses in the AMT, AARP can efficiently map addresses as needed. If an address is not contained in the AMT, AARP sends a request to the protocol address desired and adds the appropriate information to the AMT when the desired device replies.

AARP is also used to register a node's dynamically assigned address on the network (for non-LocalTalk networks). To accomplish this, AARP first assigns a tentative random address (one that's not already in the AMT); then AARP broadcasts AARP probe packets on the network to determine whether another node is using the tentative address. If no other node is using the selected address, the address is made permanent. If, however, another node is already using that address, AARP randomly picks another address and repeats this procedure until a usable address is found.

Layer 3 — the network layer

The third layer in the AppleTalk stack, the network layer, is responsible for accepting data from the layers above it and dividing the data into packets that can be sent over the network. Because the network layer creates the packets, it's also used to define the way packets should be treated if they've been damaged in transit.

Only one protocol, the Datagram Delivery Protocol (DDP), is present in the AppleTalk Network Layer. DDP is an important protocol because it communicates between two sockets on the network. The datagram defined by DDP is limited to 586 bytes of data and includes a checksum so that the destination node can verify the integrity of the data.

Prior to the introduction of AppleTalk Phase 2, only one type of DDP header existed, as what is now known as the *short DDP header*. The short DDP header uses both the source and destination sockets for addressing and is still used when both sockets are on the same network. (Remember that the internet address is the 8-bit socket number and the 8-bit node ID, as defined in the LAP.)

> **AppleTalk Phase 1 used *short DDP headers,* which addressed source and destination sockets by their 8-bit socket numbers and 8-bit node numbers.**

Phase 2 introduced the *long DDP header,* designed to accommodate Apple's extended network addressing scheme. The extended network internet address is defined as the 8-bit socket number, plus the 8-bit LAP-assigned node ID, plus the 16-bit network number assigned by DDP. In this way, AppleTalk Phase 2 overcame the restriction of 256 nodes per network, raising the limit to a nearly astronomical 16 million. Note, however, that the socket number assignment hadn't changed, still allowing only 256 sockets per node. Of the 256 sockets, only 128 are available for actual use because the first 64 are reserved by Apple, and the next 64 are set aside for unrestricted experimental use.

> **AppleTalk Phase 2 uses the *long DDP header,* an extended address of the 8-bit socket number, 8-bit node ID, and 16-bit network number.**

Each DDP packet contains the *hop count,* which is AppleTalk's way of tracking the number of routers the packet travels through from source to destination. In AppleTalk, a packet can traverse no more than 15 routers, which is to say that 15 is the maximum hop count. Every time a DDP packet passes through a router, the router increments the hop count by 1 hop as the router regenerates the packet.

Layer 4 — the transport layer

The next layer up from the network layer is layer 4, the transport layer, which includes four protocols. Referring again to Figure 3-4, notice that two of these protocols are for end-to-end data flow, one is for reliable data delivery, and the last is for using AppleTalk's named entities. The four protocols are as follows:

❖ Routing Table Maintenance Protocol (RTMP)

❖ AppleTalk Echo Protocol (AEP)

❖ AppleTalk Transaction Protocol (ATP)

❖ Name Binding Protocol (NBP)

In the following sections, we'll explain each of these protocols in detail.

The Routing Table Maintenance Protocol (RTMP)

The Routing Table Maintenance Protocol (RTMP) maintains information about internetwork addresses and connections between the various networks. Most of this protocol's work is performed on what is known as an *internet router*. RTMP defines the rules for information exchange between routers so that they can maintain their routing tables, as well as the rules for the information contained within each routing table.

> RTMP, the Routing Table Maintenance Protocol, is a master address controller, keeping up with addresses and exchanging information with routers.

Take a brief look at the AppleTalk routing table shown in Figure 3-9. Each entry within a routing table consists of five items:

1. The network range

2. The distance in hops to the destination network

3. The port number of the destination network

4. The node ID of the next router (also called the *entry state*)

5. The status of each port

The routing table contains an entry for each network that a datagram can reach, within 15 hops of the router. The table is aged at set intervals as follows:

❖ First, the status of all entries is changed from good to suspect.

❖ Then the router sends an RTMP packet to all routers within its tables.

❖ If a response is not received within a set period of time, the entry for the nonresponding router is set to bad and removed from the routing table.

The data contained in the routing table is cross-referenced to the Zone Information Table (ZIT), which is needed to map networks into zones (see Figure 3-10). We'll go further into the relationship between the routing table and the Zone Information Table when we discuss the Zone Information Protocol later in this chapter.

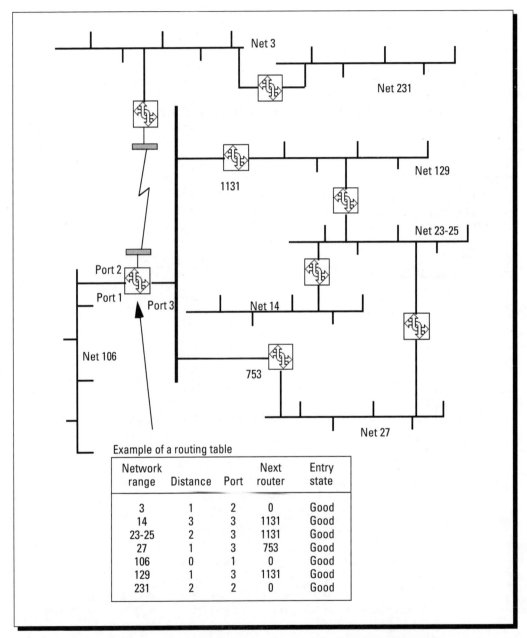

Figure 3-9: This sample AppleTalk internet shows the construction of a routing table for one of the routers.

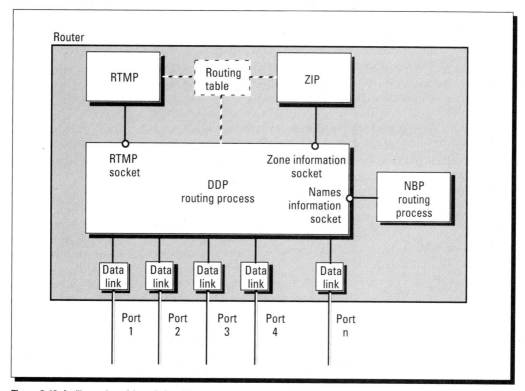

Figure 3-10: An illustration of the relationships between RTMP, ZIP, and NBP within a router.

The Routing Table Maintenance Protocol (RTMP) was originally assigned three packet types: the RTMP Request packet, the RTMP Data packet, and the RTMP Response packet. A fourth packet type was added in AppleTalk Phase 2 — the RTMP Route Data Request packet (RDR). The Route Data Request can be used by a nonrouter node (such as a network management program) to acquire the routing table of a specific router, or this request can be used by a router to load a routing table without waiting for the other routers to update their tables at the usual interval of 20 seconds.

The AppleTalk Echo Protocol (AEP)

The AppleTalk Echo Protocol (AEP) is used to send a datagram from one node to another and cause the destination node to return, or *echo*, the datagram to the sender. To implement this process, each AppleTalk node has an echoer socket.

Because the function of the AEP is comparatively uncomplicated, this protocol has only two packet types: the Echo Request and the Echo Reply.

Yet despite its simplicity, the AEP can prove to be useful on a network. First, this protocol can determine whether a node is accessible before any sessions are started. Second, a programmer can use the AEP to estimate the round-trip delay time for a data transmission between two nodes. (Apple now includes other mechanisms for timing round-trip delay times with AppleTalk version 56, released with System 7.0. Later versions of AppleTalk also include these new features.)

The AppleTalk Transaction Protocol (ATP)

The AppleTalk Transaction Protocol (ATP) uses three types of transactions: the ATP Transaction Request (TReq), the ATP Transaction Response (TResp), and the ATP Transaction Release (TRel). The ATP is one of the methods that AppleTalk uses to ensure that DDP packets are delivered to a destination without any losses (the other is the AppleTalk Data Stream Protocol). ATP accomplishes this by requiring a reply to every ATP transaction. In other words, every time that ATP is requested to send a packet, the receiver socket must report the outcome of the transfer. The first action is referred to as a *transaction request*, and the report of the action is a *transaction response*.

Because ATP maintains a conversation between two sockets by pairing transaction requests with transaction responses, ATP can deal with three possible network errors:

1. A transaction request is lost on the network.

2. A transaction response is lost or delayed on the network.

3. A responder becomes unreachable.

ATP determines whether these conditions occur by using a timer; if the timer expires before a response is received, ATP retransmits its original request. ATP will stop trying to retransmit when it gets a response or when the maximum retry count is reached.

Because ATP can retry packet transmissions that are required because of a lost packet, data may not arrive in its original sequence. This condition can lead to problems. One way of handling the problems of lost or delayed transactions is to enable an automatic retry mechanism. If a response is not received within a set period of time, the requester will retransmit a Transition Request (TReq), and the process is repeated until the response is received or the maximum retry count is reached. (If the maximum retry count is reached, the requester is notified that the responder is unreachable.) This approach is called the ALO (*At-Least-Once*) transaction. If ALO transactions are used, it is up to the responder to handle retransmission of responses to duplicate requests.

To counter the difficulty of handling duplicate requests, ATP can be programmed to operate in XO (*Exactly-Once*) transactions. By maintaining a transactions list, ATP can filter out duplicate transaction requests (caused by a lost transaction response, for example) and re-send transactions as needed. On small networks, such as a single AppleTalk network, ATP XO transactions can be quite effective. In an internet, however, packets may arrive at their destination in an order different from the order in which they were sent (by traveling through different routers, for example). This situation requires additional program control to ensure proper sequencing. Alternatively, a different protocol, such as ADSP, can be used.

The third ATP transaction, the ATP Release, is used to close a transaction session once all data has been transferred and acknowledged. Each of the transaction types — request, response, and release — is represented by a TID (Transaction Identifier), which appears in the ATP request packet and has a maximum size of 16 bits. The limited size of the transaction identifier ($2^{16} = 65,536$) can lead to *roll-over*, or repeated use of the same TIDs for transactions involving large numbers of packets. ATP can send more than one ATP response packet in sequence as a reply — the maximum number of ATP response packets for a single request packet is 8.

The Name-Binding Protocol (NBP)

The Name Binding Protocol (NBP) is important in the AppleTalk scheme of things. As you recall, to maintain communications, the network itself operates with *numeric internet addresses*, but the AppleTalk user works with *named entities*. AppleTalk internally represents any named entity, which is a network service such as a file server or a network device such as your Mac, according to the following conventions:

    object:type@zone

In this line, *object* is the name of the user or service name, *type* is the entity classification, and *zone* is the logical zone of the AppleTalk internet.

Given these conventions, then, consider the following line:

    Bldg. 3 Printer:LaserWriter@California

In this line, Bldg. 3 Printer represents the *object*; LaserWriter represents the *type*; and California represents the *zone*. These conventions are only used internally by AppleTalk protocols; the Chooser serves as the user's interface to

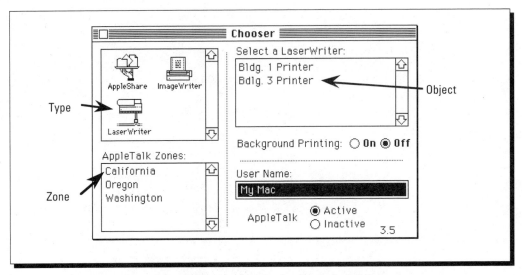

Figure 3-11: The Chooser is the user's interface to selecting named entities on AppleTalk.

named entities (see Figure 3-11). When you select one of the icons shown in the Chooser, you're selecting the device *type*; the *zone* list is shown below the list of icons, and the list of *objects* matching the selected type is displayed in the right half of the Chooser.

The Name Binding Protocol handles the translations between the numeric internet addresses and alphanumeric entity names. The NBP Protocol maintains a table of *mappings* (a names table) between internet addresses (a node) and name socket clients (named entities) that reside in that node. Because each node maintains its own list of named entities, the names directory within an AppleTalk network is not centralized, but is a distributed database of all nodes on the internet.

This approach to storing entity names requires that a socket that needs to communicate with a named service must first find out where the service is by requesting its location. This request is made via the NBP Broadcast Request (BrRq) packet, which names the desired entity and requests the network address for that named entity. On a single network, each node responds to the NBP Broadcast Request (BrRq) and searches its internal names table for a match. When a match is found, NBP sends a LookUp-Reply to the requesting socket, including the address of the named entity (see Figure 3-12). If the request is made on an internet, the router forwards the BrRq to each network in the specified target zone, causing the affected nodes to perform the search of their names tables.

In the example in Figure 3-12, the workstation sends an NBP LkUp for AFP

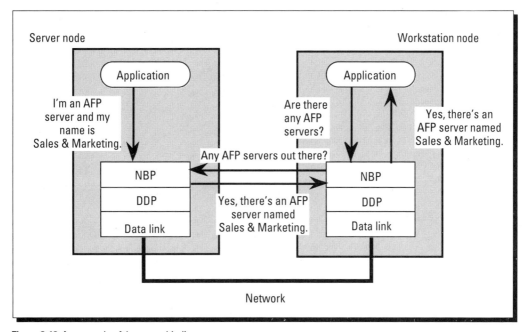

Figure 3-12: An example of the name-binding process.

servers. The server node named Sales & Marketing then replies that it is an AFP server and supplies its network address.

Including the name lookup feature just described, NBP provides a total of four services to accomplish this search:

1. Name registration

2. Name deletion

3. Name lookup

4. Name confirmation

Name *registration*, which takes place on each node, is used to build the names table. Name *deletion*, the opposite of registration, occurs when an entity has its name and socket number removed from the names table. The final is name *confirmation*, which can be used to validate a name-address binding, to see whether it has changed since the last lookup.

Layer 5 — the session layer

Situated atop the transport layer is layer 5, the session layer. The main purpose of this layer is to manage the conversations among end users (hence the word *session*) and to synchronize communications between applications located throughout the network.

As with the transport layer, the session layer contains four protocols. In this case, three of the protocols (AppleTalk Data Stream Protocol, AppleTalk Session Protocol, and Printer Access Protocol) are related to reliable data delivery. The remaining protocol, the Zone Information Protocol, is used for handling named entities on the network.

The AppleTalk Data Stream Protocol (ADSP)

Like the AppleTalk Transaction Protocol, the AppleTalk Data Stream Protocol (ADSP) is responsible for reliable transmission of data between two sockets. Unlike ATP, however, ADSP provides full-duplex byte-stream delivery, which means that a conversation between two computers can take place in both directions at the same time. ADSP also includes flow control, so that a fast sender does not overwhelm a slow receiver.

ADSP uses the concept of a *connection-to-connection* data exchange between two nodes. Only when both nodes have established a connection end by using ADSP can data be exchanged between them. If only one node is able to establish a connection end, the connection is called *half-open* and can be automatically closed by that node if a second connection end at the other node fails to be established within a preset time interval.

After a connection is established, ADSP uses a 32-bit sequence number to ensure the sequential flow of data between connection ends (compare this to ATP's 16-bit transaction ID). ADSP also uses packet sequencing to make certain that packets are received in the correct order. Every ADSP data packet contains a number identifying the packet's sequence in the data stream — the receiving node compares this number with its own counter to track the next expected packet. If the two numbers coincide, the packet is accepted; otherwise, the packet is discarded.

ADSP is also capable of controlling the rate at which data is sent from one node to another, a process known as *flow control*. Flow control keeps a data transmitter from overwhelming the buffer space of a slower receiver. To accomplish this controlled rate, the receiving node periodically updates the transmitting node by reporting the amount of available buffer space. As a side benefit of this mechanism, two nodes participating in a connection can negotiate a suitably sized window to take advantage of larger bandwidth networks (which is something ATP cannot do).

The AppleTalk Session Protocol (ASP)

Many AppleTalk communications between a workstation and a server occur during a session between the two. Once a connection is made between a workstation and server, it's up to the AppleTalk Session Protocol (ASP) to pass the commands that make up a session. ASP ensures that the commands are delivered in the same order as they were sent and returns the results of these commands to the workstation.

The AppleTalk Session Protocol uses two protocols in the transport layer to do its job. ASP employs NBP to obtain the address of the server's session listening socket so that it knows to which address it should direct commands. ASP also uses ATP to provide the transport service for its packets. ASP does *not* perform two important tasks: first, it does not ensure that consecutive commands are completed in the order they were sent to the server; second, ASP does not allow the server to send commands to the workstation, as it can only use the attention mechanism to alert the workstation.

Within ASP, four basic processes occur. The first two are rather obvious: These are the processes of opening and closing a session. The third, called *session request handling*, conveys the commands from workstation to server and returns the replies of the server. Fourth, there's *session management*, which, in this case, uses a tickler packet to make sure that both ends of the connections are still operational. The following discussion of PAP will give more information on tickler packets.

The Printer Access Protocol (PAP)

As its name implies, the Printer Access Protocol, or PAP, takes the responsibility for maintaining communications between a workstation and a printer (or print service). PAP functions, therefore, include setting up and maintaining a connection, as well as transferring the data and tearing down the connection on completion of a job.

Understanding ADSP packets

ADSP uses two types of packets to set up and maintain connections: *control packets* and *data packets*. Control packets can be used to probe or acknowledge a connection, open or close a connection, or negotiate a retransmission of a series of data packets. The second type of packets, data packets, are just what the name suggests: These are packets designed to exchange data using DDP. Up to 572 bytes of data can be stuffed into a packet. (The DDP type field equals 7 for ADSP packets.)

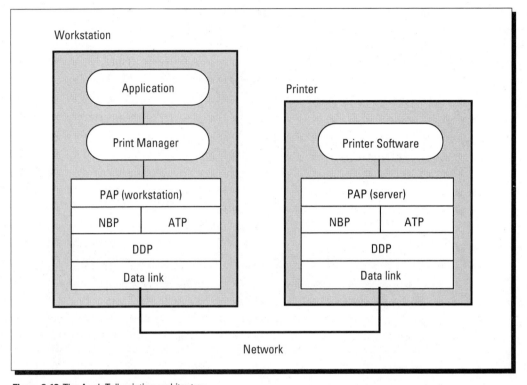

Figure 3-13: The AppleTalk printing architecture.

When a connection is established, either socket client can send or receive data. This two-way communication is necessary because printers often must control the amount of data sent (by asking for the next page) or reply with the printer's status.

As with other protocols in the session layer, PAP relies on NBP to find the addresses of named entities. PAP also depends on ATP for sending data (see Figure 3-13). On a workstation, the application uses the Print Manager software to communicate with the PAP. The client, or workstation, side of PAP then maintains a session with the networked printer (a PAP server) to print the required pages.

The Printer Access Protocol covers five basic processes: opening a connection, transferring data, closing a connection, determining a print service's status, and filtering duplicate requests. (Because PAP uses ATP, duplicate packets can be received from a node; see the previous description of ATP for an explanation of the problems involved.)

One of PAP's capabilities is to handle half-open connections, which occur when one side of the connection goes down or terminates without informing its partner.

To cope with half-open connections, PAP maintains a connection timer at both ends. If the connection timer expires before any packets are received, the connection is terminated.

When a device such as a Laser-Writer is busy processing a job, it's doing very little on the network. Under such circumstances, the client of the LaserWriter periodically sends out *tickler packets* to the LaserWriter to make sure that it's still working.

To assist in maintaining a connection, PAP also sends tickler packets periodically. As you might expect, ticklers are used to keep the other end informed that the device is actually still on-line, even if it otherwise appears that nothing's happening. Many printers spend most of their time processing the data, while ignoring nearly everything else; sending a tickler tells the user that something is happening and that the printer hasn't gone down.

The Zone Information Protocol (ZIP)

One of the unique features of AppleTalk is its use of logical groupings of networks. These logical groupings are presented to the user as names. The groupings are called zones — each AppleTalk zone consists of a collection of AppleTalk networks. Working in concert with the Routing Table Maintenance Protocol (RTMP), the Zone Information Protocol, or ZIP, helps routers maintain a mapping of network numbers to zones for the entire internet.

ZIP creates and maintains a Zone Information Table (ZIT) in each router. Each entry in the ZIT is a *tuple* (pair), matching network numbers and zone names. (The zone names are initially supplied by a network administrator.) In AppleTalk Phase 1, a tuple matches a single network number with a zone name. In routers using AppleTalk Phase 2, the tuple matches a range of network numbers and a list of zone names.

A fairly simple relationship exists between the Zone Information Table (ZIT) and a routing table within a router: An incoming NBP packet includes the zone name, which the router compares with entries in the ZIT. The router then matches the network number obtained from the matching ZIT tuple to that in the RTMP table to find the port that the packet should be routed to. (With AppleTalk Phase 2, a zone name may point to a range of network numbers; this range of numbers still directs the router to a single port.)

ZIP packets are defined with a DDP packet type of 6. Three types of ZIP packets are used: the Query, the Response, and the Extended ZIP Reply. The first two are nearly self-explanatory; a ZIP Query contains a request for a zone list, and the Response packet returns the zone list. The third packet type, the Extended ZIP Reply, is used if the zone list cannot fit into a single packet.

Two new packet types were added with AppleTalk Phase 2. The new packet types, which are used when a node starts up, are the ZIP GetNetInfo (GNI) and the ZIP GetNetInfoReply (GNIR). The new packet types make it simpler for nonrouter nodes (such as your workstation) to obtain the name of any zone on the internet. ZIP GetNetInfo tells the node which zone it has chosen to be in (from the node's original setup); otherwise, the zone name is set to local (*zone* = *), and a GetNetInfoReply (GNIR) from the router tells the node which zone to use (if it's not specified). ZIP GetNetInfoReply also provides a multicast address for the zone.

Layer 6 — the presentation layer

The next-to-last layer is the presentation layer, which handles issues related to data files and formats. In addition to file formats and translations between formats, tools such as data encryption and data compression are part of the presentation layer.

Only two protocols, the AppleTalk Filing Protocol and PostScript, are part of the presentation layer. The first protocol is used to provide remote access to files on a network. The second, PostScript, is the well-known page description language used by many printers. We won't be covering PostScript in any detail in this book.

The AppleTalk Filing Protocol (AFP) provides both Mac and non-Mac work-stations with a means of accessing files on a file server's shared disk while still using a workstation's native file system commands. To accomplish this, AFP employs an AFP translator to convert native file system commands into AFP calls that will be understood by the server (see Figure 3-14).

A program can either directly issue AFP calls, or the AFP Translator can translate calls from the native file system to AFP calls. Only AFP calls are transmitted on the network to the AFP server.

It's up to the application developer to design a translator for the native file system in use. Apple currently includes translators for the Macintosh, Apple II (ProDOS), and MS-DOS file systems.

AFP uses the AppleTalk Session Protocol to open and maintain a session between the workstation and the server. Before this occurs, the workstation uses the Name Binding Protocol to look up the file server's name and obtain its address. Once a connection is established, the workstation uses AFP to log onto the server, after which the server and workstation exchange information regarding the level of access to the server's files that has been granted to the workstation.

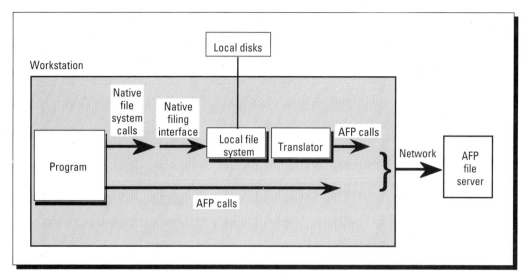

Figure 3-14: The AFP file access model.

Many details of AFP, especially as they pertain to servers, will be discussed later in this book in the chapter on file sharing (see Chapter 20, "Moving and Sharing Files on the Network").

Layer 7 — the application layer

The top layer of the OSI model is the application layer, which is the layer of most interest to you as a user. This is the layer at which all of your programs are going to work. And at this level you'll decide if an application is going to use the network to access other files or to send and receive electronic mail. AppleTalk has no specific protocols for the application layer — very few network systems do.

Protocol Locations in the Macintosh Operating System

As mentioned at the beginning of the chapter, protocols are rules for how networks should behave. By themselves, protocols are not software. It's up to the operating system or application to implement the protocols in software. In the case of AppleTalk, Apple includes most of the network software as a series of driver resources that are part of the Macintosh operating system. The programming interfaces to these drivers are included in what Apple calls the AppleTalk Manager.

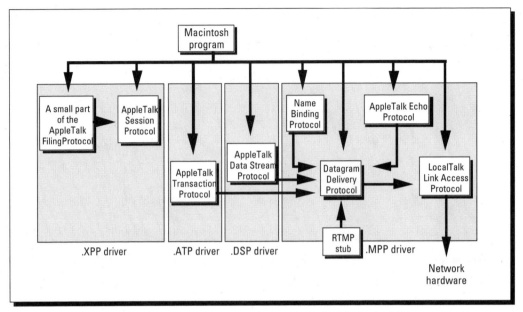

Figure 3-15: This schematic shows which Mac drivers contain the code for the different AppleTalk protocols.

Macs include four AppleTalk drivers: .MPP, .ATP, .XPP, and .DSP. These drivers are resources available to any application on the Mac. Most Macs already have these drivers within their ROM; if the drivers are not in ROM (or have been patched by a later version of the system), the AppleTalk Manager software is read from disk and loaded into the system heap.

As you can see from Figure 3-15, the .MPP driver implements the LocalTalk Link Access Protocol for connecting to the network hardware, as well as the DDP, AEP, and NBP protocols. The .ATP driver has only one protocol associated with it (as the name implies), the AppleTalk Transaction protocol, handling both transaction requests and transaction responses.

The .XPP driver is the eXtended Protocol Package. Within the .XPP driver are the workstation (or client) side of ASP and a portion of the AppleTalk Filing Protocol, the part responsible for sending AFP commands to the file server. Other software has the responsibility for translating native file system calls to AFP calls. With the introduction of AppleTalk Phase 2, the .XPP driver also includes part of the Zone Information Protocol functions.

Because ADSP was introduced as a protocol after the initial rollout of AppleTalk, ADSP was usually added as a separate system file when needed. (Often the programs that used it included ADSP as part of the installation process on the Mac.) If you have a Mac running System 7, Apple has added a .DSP driver to the system; the .DSP driver implements ADSP and removes any need for the separate ADSP file found in other systems.

A Macintosh can also include additional AppleTalk connection files, such as those used for EtherTalk and TokenTalk. An AppleTalk connection file has the file type adev and contains the code for a specific type of LAP for that data link (ELAP for EtherTalk or TLAP for token ring, for instance). When you're using the Network panel in the Control Panel to select a different network interface, you're asking the LAP Manager to select and load a new adev file.

The Evolution of AppleTalk Protocols

Networks are dynamic systems, and the protocols used to define them can change. These changes are often introduced to take advantage of new technology or to address limitations in the original specifications. First, we'll look at how Apple altered its protocol suite with the introduction of AppleTalk Phase 2; then we'll move on to an overview of some of the mechanisms that Apple is currently using to introduce new protocols.

AppleTalk Phase 2

When Apple first created AppleTalk, its designers defined the network protocols for small networks that would be easy to install and maintain. But AppleTalk quickly grew popular, and its easy installation encouraged networks that outgrew the expectations of AppleTalk's architects. A variety of problems began to crop up on the larger networks that used multiple routers and corporate backbones, notably on those using Ethernet. To resolve the inadequacies of the original AppleTalk release, AppleTalk Phase 2 was released in 1989 with a redesigned suite of protocols.

Prior to the development of Phase 2, AppleTalk networks were restricted to 254 nodes per physical cable. For users with a large Ethernet backbone and Macs scattered throughout the plant, this arrangement quickly became unsatisfactory. Now, with Phase 2, AppleTalk uses the concept of *extended addressing*. Rather than relying on the limited 8-bit node identification number, Phase 2 networks using extended addressing employ a network address that consists of the 8-bit node number plus a 16-bit network number. This expands the network node limits to 2^{24} addresses, or over 16 million nodes on a single network. Note that each workstation can be assigned to a different network number, even though all workstations are on the same cable (see Figure 3-16).

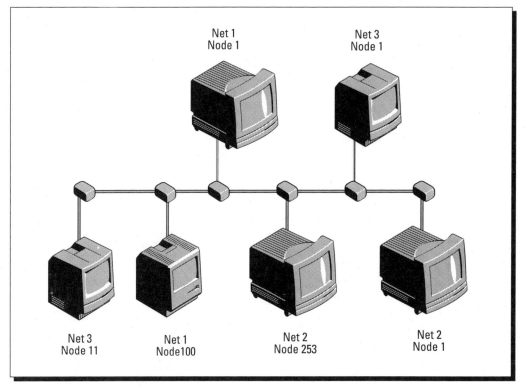

Net 1
Node 1

Net 3
Node 1

Net 3
Node 11

Net 1
Node100

Net 2
Node 253

Net 2
Node 1

Figure 3-16: An example of an extended network.

> AppleTalk Phase 2 accommodates larger networks with its system of extended addressing. Networks using extended addressing are referred to as *extended* networks. LocalTalk is a *nonextended* network.

But not all networks running Phase 2 are extended networks. LocalTalk does not implement extended addressing, for example. EtherTalk and TokenTalk networks, however, do implement extended addressing. This means that LocalTalk networks are still limited to 254 nodes per cable.

Along with the extended addressing scheme just described, extended networks enable you to assign a range of network numbers to each network. In the past, all nodes on a single physical cable were assigned one network number. Under Phase 2, that's no longer the case.

The coexistence of extended and nonextended networks also prompted a change in the way AppleTalk DDP packets are defined. For nonextended networks, especially LocalTalk networks, the DDP packet format remained as it was and became known for containing the short DDP header. Short DDP headers are also used when the source and destination sockets have the same network number. The newer long DDP packets, containing the long DDP header, are meant for extended networks and include the full internet addresses of the source and destination sockets.

The dynamic aspect of addressing AppleTalk nodes has also changed somewhat from Phase 1 to Phase 2. In the past, a node selected a provisional address when it started up on the network. Now under Phase 2, this provisional address includes both the node's ID number and network number. If a node must start with a provisional address, it communicates with the nearest router to determine whether the network number found in its provisional address falls within the network range of the router. If not, it selects one of the network numbers supported by the router. If there is no router on the network, the node uses the provisional address as its final address. This makes it easier for large networks, such as those entirely on Ethernet or token ring, to function without using a router to assign network numbers.

AppleTalk Phase 2 introduced several new mechanisms for reducing traffic. One of these is the way the AppleTalk routers periodically exchange data packets, called RTMP Data packets. RTMP Data packets contain routing tables to create an up-to-date map of the internet; this map tells the router what the best path is to forward a data packet on to its destination.

Phase 2 uses a routing technique called *split horizon*. Split-horizon routing is much more efficient than the routing method used in Phase 1, which was to send out routing information regarding what all routers know about all ports. With split-horizon routing, the router recognizes that a different set of information is needed for each port (the "horizon"). The router therefore "splits" the routing information that it knows about, the router sends routing data only out a port that the networks listening to the port really need.

An example of split-horizon routing is shown in Figure 3-17. In the figure, router X has two ports: port B and port A. Three routers are attached to the Ethernet cable that is attached to port A. The three routers each have one LocalTalk network attached. Off port A, router X therefore has a total of four reachable networks: three LocalTalk networks (net 1, net 2, and net 3) and one EtherTalk network (net 4). Off port B, router X has two reachable networks: one LocalTalk network (net 5) and one EtherTalk network (net 6). Router X will advertise the two routes that are reachable via its port B only out of port A. In other words, the RTMP Data packet that router X sends out of port B will *not* contain routing information regarding the networks that are reachable via port B (nets 5 and 6). Likewise, router X will not send an RTMP Data packet with routing information regarding the four networks (nets 1, 2, 3, 4) reachable via port A out of port A.

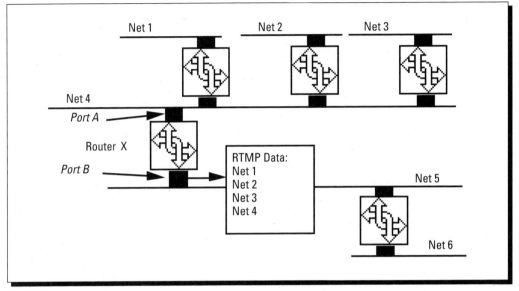

Figure 3-17: An example of split-horizon routing.

Another method that reduces traffic and provides convenience for users is the Phase 2 support for *multiple zones per network cable.* Multiple zones on one network enable the administrator to set up logical areas to group services. For example, putting all of the Engineering department's Ethernet file servers in a zone called Engineering will enable users to quickly find their file servers in the Chooser. The reduced traffic benefit comes because the name lookup requests (NBP LkUp) are sent only to nodes in a particular zone rather than to all the nodes on the Ethernet. For more information about AppleTalk routers, see Chapter 2, "Understanding Networks," and Chapter 11, "Designing an AppleTalk LAN."

AppleTalk Phase 2 uses another mechanism for reducing network traffic, that of *directed broadcasting.* In the past, AppleTalk devices would broadcast packets to all nodes on a given network. On an Ethernet network, for example, broadcast packets would be received by AppleTalk nodes as well as non-AppleTalk nodes (VAXes, Unix boxes, and so on). These non-AppleTalk nodes had to receive the broadcast packets and then process and discard them, thereby reducing the node's efficiency.

With directed broadcasting, AppleTalk nodes register to receive packets from a multicast address (defined by DDP). Non-AppleTalk nodes do not register on that address, so they cannot receive or be interrupted by AppleTalk broadcasts. Routers on Phase 2 internets can also assign various zone multicast addresses to the network nodes. Using these zone multicast addresses, a router can then broadcast packets to nodes within selected zones on the network.

Finally, AppleTalk Phase 2 includes support for certain networking standards. This support includes IEEE 802.3 for Ethernet and 802.5 for token ring. Also, for internets requiring more than one network media (such as networks containing both Ethernet and token ring), AppleTalk Phase 2 uses the IEEE 802.2 Logical Link Control specification, enabling AppleTalk packets to be sent over the entire network.

Introducing the new AppleTalk protocols

When Apple introduced the Phase 2 protocol suite, no protocols were added other than those in the physical and data link layers. Most of what Apple changed in Phase 2 was accomplished by changing definitions and variables within the existing protocols.

The new protocols that Apple has been developing for networking in 1991 and 1992 are, in some cases, additions to the current protocol stack. And, in a change from past practices, the development of some of these protocols has been undertaken with advice from network vendors and designers outside of Apple.

The AppleTalk Update-Based Routing Protocol (AURP) has been designed to make it easier for users to connect LANs into wide-area networks (WANs) and reduce routing table updates over the WAN link. Much of the work here was done in conjunction with an Internet Engineering Task Force (IETF); for more details, see Chapter 13, "Designing an AppleTalk WAN."

At the physical and data link layers, Apple developed a new protocol for using telecommunications links between a single user and a network. Introduced at the same time as the Mac PowerBooks in late 1991, Apple Remote Access Protocol (ARAP) lets a Mac user dial into a network and use any of the network services as if the Mac were physically attached to the network. Apple plans to expand ARAP to use other telecommunications protocols, such as the Point-to-Point Protocol (PPP) familiar to the Unix and Internet communities.

Finally, Apple has also decided to implement another foreign, or non-AppleTalk, protocol to assist in network management. Apple has been working on MIBs (Management Information Base) for both Macs and AppleTalk routers for use with the Simple Network Management Protocol (SNMP), which was originally defined for use with TCP/IP networks. (For more details, see Chapter 16, "Configuration Management.")

Summary

After reading this chapter, you should have an overall understanding of how protocols govern the functions of a network. AppleTalk protocols were explained and illustrated within the standard framework of the OSI Reference Model. The following topics were covered:

▶ The OSI Reference Model is a seven-layer model that defines basic network functions.

▶ Protocol specifications set forth how a protocol exchanges data with a protocol in the layer above or below it.

▶ The AppleTalk protocols fall into distinct layers according to the OSI Reference Model, but they can be further classified according to their functions.

▶ The physical layer of the protocol stack handles the network's hardware.

▶ The data link layer contains the AppleTalk Link Access Protocols (LAPs), which are responsible for interfacing to the network hardware.

▶ The network layer, containing the AppleTalk Datagram Delivery Protocol (DDP), is an important layer that is responsible for accepting data from the layers above it and dividing the data into packets that can be sent across the network.

▶ The transport layer includes four protocols that are responsible for end-to-end data flow, reliable data delivery, and the use of AppleTalk named entities.

▶ The session layer, which contains four protocols, manages network conversations among end users.

▶ The presentation layer handles issues related to data files and formats, and includes two protocols.

▶ The application layer is the layer at which most of the network's programs work. AppleTalk has no specific protocols for the application layer.

▶ AppleTalk Phase 2 was released in 1989 with a redesigned suite of protocols, including new protocols in the physical and data link layers. Most of the changes were accomplished by changing definitions and variables among the existing protocols.

▶ Apple has been developing new protocols that will be additions to the current protocol stack.

In the next chapter, you'll see the AppleTalk protocols in action, as we examine the sequences of AppleTalk protocols in network functioning.

Chapter 4
AppleTalk Protocols in Action

In this chapter...

We discuss the sequence of AppleTalk protocols for a variety of actions, including the following:

✔ Registering your Mac on the network

✔ Selecting a printer

✔ Printing on the network

✔ Using an AppleShare server

With so many protocols in the AppleTalk stack, a number of activities may result from each simple action that you perform on a network. Some of the protocols discussed in Chapter 3, such as RTMP and ZIP, are invisible to you as a user because they are meant primarily for such network devices as routers. But you do use the information that these protocols maintain on the network, even if you use it indirectly. We selected a few common network actions that you or your Mac ordinarily perform to show you which protocols are used for these actions and to illustrate how the protocols are used.

This chapter will discuss the following network tasks:

❖ *Registering your Mac on the network:* What procedures does the Mac follow for dynamic node addressing when you first turn on your Mac?

❖ *Selecting a printer:* What happens when you open the Chooser and select a LaserWriter on the network?

❖ *Printing on the network:* What is the sequence of protocols used in printing to a LaserWriter?

❖ *Using an AppleShare server:* What protocols are used when you select an AppleShare server, log onto it, and mount a volume?

To help explore which protocols are used and in what sequence, we've included two charts that help explain each session. The first, Figure 4-1, is a

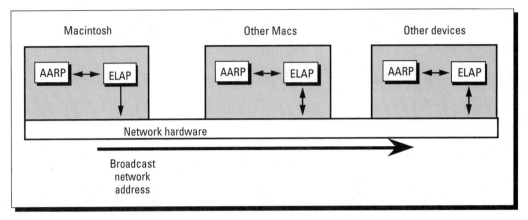

Figure 4-1: This diagram shows the protocol flow for dynamic node number assignment.

simple flow chart showing the flow of control and data through the AppleTalk protocol stack. The second, Figure 4-2, is a network activity chart, which shows you what protocol data is exchanged between the devices involved in that task.

Registering Your Mac on the Network

For the first action, we'll look at the protocols used when your Mac attempts to assign itself a node number dynamically, using the AppleTalk Address Resolution Protocol (AARP) over EtherTalk.

Remember that a Mac randomly picks an address the first time it's used on the network; if the Mac has already succeeded in obtaining a legitimate network address from a previous connection to the network, it attempts to use that address first. Either way, your Mac must broadcast its selected address on the network to ensure that there are no conflicts.

The part of AARP used for network addressing is the AARP Probe. As an example, we'll discuss how the AARP Probe is used on Ethernet (see Figure 4-1). If the node is on a LocalTalk network, LLAP Enquiry packets are used to determine if the node address is unique.

When you turn on your Mac, the operating system instructs the AppleTalk Address Resolution Protocol (AARP) in your Mac's network interface (in this case, Ethernet, as signified by ELAP in Figure 4-1) to broadcast an AARP probe packet with the selected address. Any other AppleTalk node on the network receives the AARP Probe and compares your Mac's suggested address with its

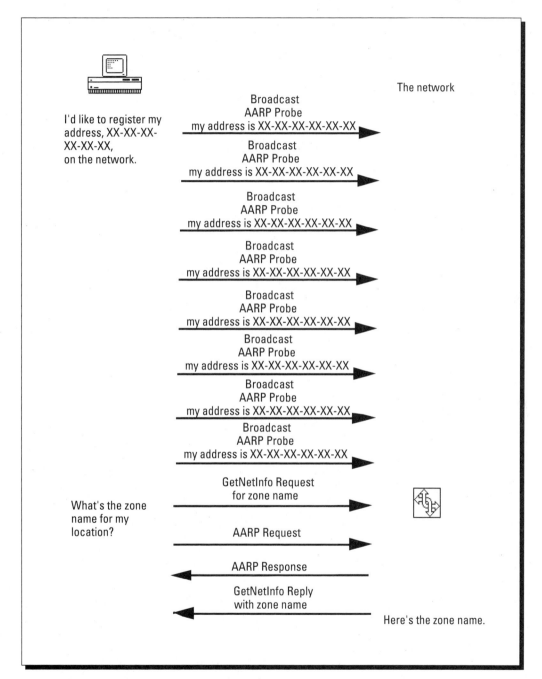

Figure 4-2: Network activity for dynamic node assignment.

own. If the two addresses do not coincide, the node does nothing further. If the two addresses are identical, the node sends an AARP reply to the originator node of the AARP probe, informing it that the desired address is already being used.

As you work your way through the network activity diagram (see Figure 4-2) for the AARP procedure, note that the Mac first looks for its selected address ten times. If, after those ten broadcasts, the Mac does not receive notification from another device on the network that the address is already in use, the Mac uses that address for further communications.

Selecting a Printer

The most common interface to an AppleTalk network that you see is the Chooser DA on the Mac (see Chapter 2, "Understanding Networks"). If you're on a network, the Chooser displays icons for each available networked resource, such as the LaserWriter, AppleTalk ImageWriter, AppleShare, NetModem, and so on. When you select the LaserWriter II icon, you're presented with a list of available printers.

How does all this happen? For this activity, most of the action revolves around the Name Binding Protocol (NBP), as you see in Figure 4-3. When you select the icon of a LaserWriter in the Chooser, the type of device is set (in this case, to LaserWriter). A character string for controlling the search is defined, as follows:

"=:LaserWriter@*"

In this string, the equal sign means that any name is allowed, and the @* refers to the local zone. The name inserted between the colon and the @ (at sign) is the type of device that you want to find. The name lookup request now goes to all nodes in the zone for lookup. Any node (in this case, any LaserWriter) that has a match will respond.

Once the list of LaserWriters is displayed by the Chooser and you select one, that device's name is stored for future use. That's why you don't always have to select the same LaserWriter every time you want to print.

Note in Figure 4-3 that the top diagram indicates the flow of information as the Mac makes a name request; the lower diagram indicates the flow during the LaserWriter's reply. In both events, the Name Binding Protocol (NBP) sends the name request to the Datagram Delivery Protocol (DDP), which inserts the name lookup request into the DDP data field and then prepends the socket number of your Mac.

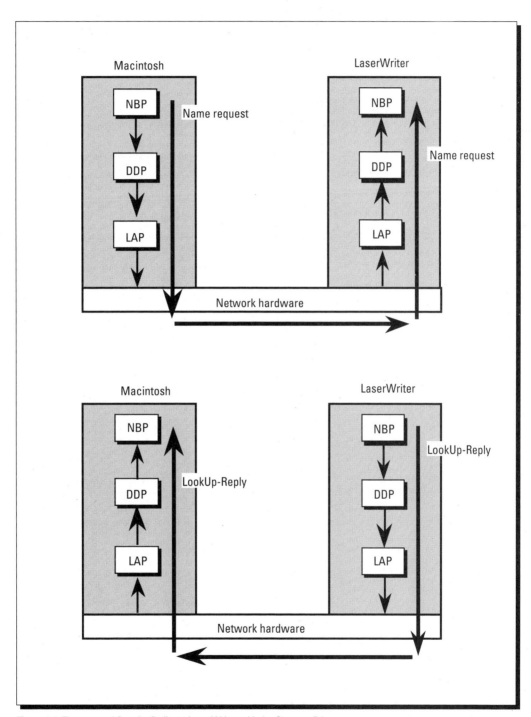

Figure 4-3: The protocol flow for finding a LaserWriter with the Chooser DA.

This data is then sent on to the Link Access Protocol (LAP), which adds the node ID of your Mac to the data and constructs a packet according to the network protocols being used (LocalTalk, Ethernet, or token ring, for example; see Appendix A for the differences in packet formats).

The Chooser DA instructs the NBP to search the selected zone for all devices of the type "LaserWriter." When the search is completed, NBP presents a list of the names to the Chooser for display. If you're working within an internet that has zones, you also select the zone to be searched; the name of the zone replaces the asterisk.

Printing on the Network

Printing a file on a LaserWriter involves other protocols, particularly the AppleTalk Transaction Protocol (ATP), as you see in Figure 4-4. When you issue a command to print a document, your application uses the Print Manager to establish a connection with the printer.

First, the Print Manager uses the Name Binding Protocol (NBP) to find the AppleTalk address of the currently selected printer by issuing an NBP broadcast with the name, device type (that is, LaserWriter), and zone name of the desired LaserWriter. When the LaserWriter replies with an NBP packet containing its node address and socket number, the Printer Access Protocol (PAP) then opens a connection with the printer and proceeds to send the data to the printer. PAP uses the AppleTalk Transaction Protocol (ATP) to send the print file to the printer.

Once the data is divided into a size that ATP can deal with (a maximum of 578 bytes of data per packet), ATP keeps track of the necessary number of packets and sends the data on to the Datagram Delivery Protocol. Next, DDP adds the socket number for this session, followed by the Link Access Protocol (LAP), which adds the node ID and forms the final packets that are transmitted on the network cable.

Figure 4-5 summarizes the process of selecting a LaserWriter and starting to print to that LaserWriter. If a router is present on the network, the router intercepts the NBP BrRq (Broadcast Request) and propagates NBP LkUp packets to create a list of LaserWriters, which it then forwards back to the Mac. If there is no router, the Mac will send an NBP LkUp packet on its own.

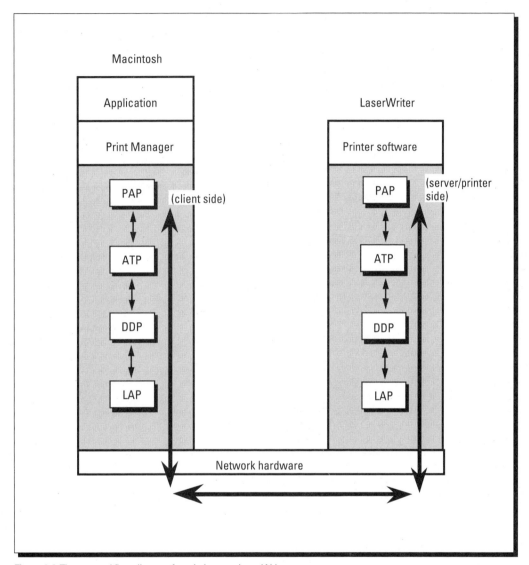

Figure 4-4: The protocol flow diagram for printing on a LaserWriter.

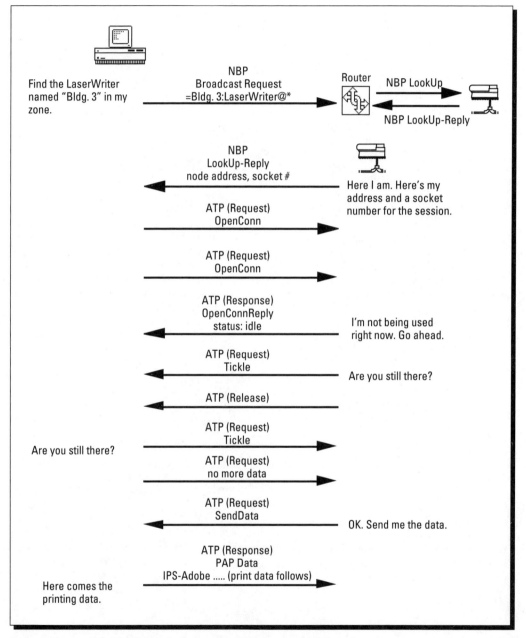

Figure 4-5: A network activity diagram for finding a LaserWriter and then printing to it.

In the upper two-thirds of the diagram, you see the flow of packets as the user's Mac selects the LaserWriter named Bldg. 3 in that Mac's zone, and then initiates a session for transferring the printing data. Once the LaserWriter indicates that it's ready to print (the next-to-last packet in the diagram, an ATP Response containing the SendData Response), the Mac uses ATP packets to send the data created by the Printer Access Protocol (PAP).

Using an AppleShare Server

When you use an AppleShare server, the initial procedure is much the same as for selecting a printer. First, you use the Chooser DA to find the list of available file servers in the selected zone, and then you select the appropriate server from the list. This mainly involves the Name Binding Protocol (NBP), as with the printer selection (see Figure 4-6). The only difference is that the NBP data contains a string that directs a search for AFP servers in the zone named MyZone:

"=:AFPServer@MyZone"

Note in Figure 4-6 that the top diagram shows the protocols involved in sending out a name request for an AFP server on the network (along with its interception by an AFP server); the lower diagram shows the flow back to the requesting Mac from the AFP server, telling the Mac the server's name.

Once the AppleShare file server is selected, you then proceed through a log-in session, in which the AppleTalk Session Protocol (ASP) handles the transmission of your name and a password from your workstation to the server (see Figure 4-7). Then ASP delivers a list of the available server volumes to your Mac. Once you select the volume that you want to mount and use with your Mac, the AppleTalk Filing Protocol (AFP) takes over and shows you which folders can be accessed and what files are in any folder that you open.

Figure 4-8 summarizes the major parts of the session to first select an AppleShare server and then to log in and mount a server volume on your Mac's desktop. Note that the session as illustrated does not include actually selecting and opening a file on the server. Note that, as in Figure 4-5, when a router is present, the router is used to acquire a list of available servers in response to the Mac's NBP Broadcast Request (BrRq).

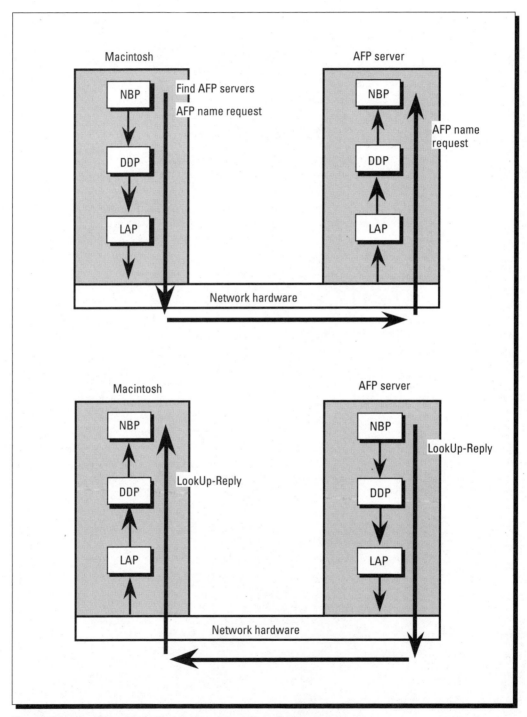

Figure 4-6: A protocol flow diagram for selecting an AppleShare file server.

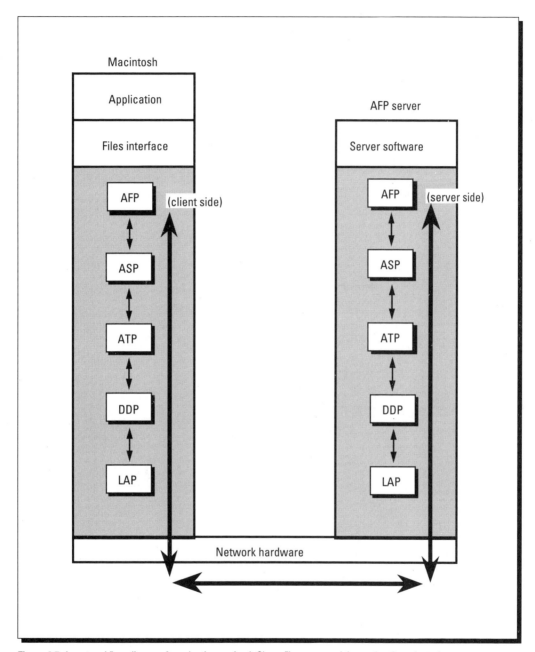

Figure 4-7: A protocol flow diagram for selecting an AppleShare file server and then using the selected server.

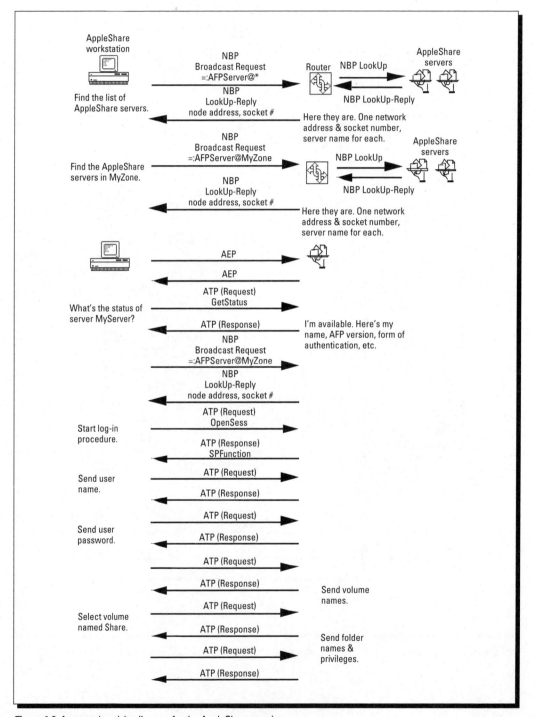

Figure 4-8: A network activity diagram for the AppleShare session.

Summary

In this chapter, we illustrated the sequence of AppleTalk protocols as they complete some of the tasks you commonly require on a network. The diagrams of common network sessions presented here gave you a sampling of what goes on with your AppleTalk network behind the scenes of the user interface. Network managers may also find these descriptions useful in determining what protocols and packets to analyze with a network packet analyzer when problems strike.

The following subjects were covered:

✔ The AppleTalk protocols are used in a certain sequence when your Mac starts up.

✔ When the Mac registers itself on the network, the AARP (AppleTalk Resolution Protocol) process is used.

✔ During printer selection, the NBP (Name Binding Protocol) starts the process by sending a name request to look for LaserWriters on the network.

✔ The protocols involved in the execution of commands include the NBP (Name Binding Protocol), the PAP (Printer Access Protocol), and the ATP (AppleTalk Transaction Protocol).

✔ Selecting a server is similar to selecting a printer: The NBP (Name Binding Protocol) looks for servers in the zone you specify.

The next chapter outlines the fundamentals of network design, where we discuss the process of matching your needs to the various options available.

Part Two

Installing an AppleTalk Network

Part Two: Installing an AppleTalk Network

Part Two contains the "meat" of designing and installing AppleTalk networks for Macintosh computers. This is where you'll learn about network topologies, how to design an AppleTalk network, what kind of cables you can use for LocalTalk and Ethernet networks, and how to install network software on a Mac. Once we show you the details of designing and installing Macintosh Local Area Networks, we'll then take you to the more complex world of multirouter internetworks and wide-area networks.

Chapter 5 is intended to be an introduction to the two main aspects of network design: the user's needs and the physical topology of networks.

Chapter 6 extends the discussion of network topologies to LocalTalk and PhoneNET networks. We explain the limits of the topologies and the cables you use for the networks.

Chapter 7 gets down to the nitty-gritty of actually wiring a LocalTalk network, as we show you how to install wall jacks, bus networks, and star networks. We also provide some hints on testing your installation.

Chapter 8 moves on to Ethernet networks for Macs. Like Chapter 6, this chapter concentrates on the topologies you can use with Ethernet cables, and details some of the restrictions you can run into when setting up an Ethernet network. We also provide some information on what kind of performance you can expect from Macs running on Ethernet.

Chapter 9 is the Ethernet equivalent of Chapter 7. It includes information on how to select and install Ethernet cables, connectors, and transceivers. You learn about the types of interfaces you can use to connect Macs to Ethernet.

Chapter 10 introduces you to some of the terminology surrounding modems and telecommunications and then shows you the ways that you can share modems on an AppleTalk network, as well as how you can dial into an AppleTalk network with a modem.

The next chapter, Chapter 11, covers the details of installing and maintaining AppleTalk networks that have at least one router. It explains how AppleTalk routing works and also shows you how you can use a non-AppleTalk network as a back-bone network for combining AppleTalk networks.

Chapter 12 discusses the approaches you can take to converting an older Phase 1 network to one using the newer Phase 2 protocols of AppleTalk. The chapter concludes by examining some of the problems you can run into when converting to a Phase 2 network.

The final chapter in this part, Chapter 13, introduces you to the terminology of wide-area networks and how they can be used in conjunction with AppleTalk networks.

Chapter 5
Network Design 101

In this chapter . . .

✔ Checklists you can use to determine users' network needs

✔ Different network topologies for wiring your network

✔ Advantages and disadvantages of each topology

✔ Fault-tolerant network design

Designing a network requires care and attention to detail. As you plan your network, you are combining physical and human factors: You must deal with the cables and devices that make up the physical network, and you must consider the people who use the network as well. This chapter presents the fundamentals of network design, which are applicable to almost any type of network, even those not using AppleTalk. The material covered in this chapter forms the basis of knowledge you can apply to network design and installation, as detailed in the rest of this Part of the book.

Using a Top-Down Approach to Network Design

Although we can talk of network functions in terms of the layered protocols found in AppleTalk and the OSI Reference Model, the fundamentals of network design don't involve all the OSI protocols. Rather, network design involves the two extreme ends of the protocol stack: layer 1, the physical layer, and layer 7, the application layer. In fact, it would be more correct to say that the uppermost layer of network design is not even part of the OSI model. In fact, this is the *eighth* layer — the user.

The best network design philosophy takes a top-down approach, beginning with the people who will use the network. Despite the fact that installation starts at the bottom, with cables and the physical apparatus of the network, you'll get the best results from your network if you start with top-down design concepts.

As you investigate what your network users need, or what you *think* they need, you'll need to ask questions about individual Mac use and what your users will expect from the network. To assist you in making a thorough evaluation, we've drawn up several lists of questions that you'll need to ask, beginning at the individual level.

Determining the needs of the network users

Only rarely will users be active on a network for the entire day or even most of their working day. Network traffic is usually sporadic, so many small as well as large networks do well even at the relatively low speeds of LocalTalk (230,400 baud). Installation of larger bandwidth networks, such as Ethernet, is usually driven by the need for large file transfers, access to large databases, and support for many users. Access to other computers using Ethernet, such as a Unix or a VAX/VMS computer, may be another justification for installing Ethernet. Consider the following questions as you judge the adequacy of network types for your work environment:

> A top-down approach to network design means that you'll begin your network plan by assessing the users' needs.

✔ **Will LocalTalk speeds suffice for the user?**

The occasional use of e-mail and networked printing doesn't necessarily require faster networks.

✔ **Are transfers of large amounts of information routinely involved?**

If so, consider an Ethernet segment on your network for those users who will be transferring large amounts of information.

Setting up the network for print services

Often, the reason for installing a network is to share expensive printers among members of a workgroup. Depending on your workgroup, you may have to select printers with multiple paper trays, color output, or envelope feeders. When selecting your printers and how they'll be connected to the network, consider these questions:

✔ **What kind of printing will these users need?**

Will their finished output be mainly business correspondence and reports? Lots of graphics?

✔ **Will the users require any color output?**

Most color printers are expensive — restricted access to these printers may be required.

✔ **Will your workgroup need special paper, such as company letterhead or transparencies?**

If so, you should consider printers that include multiple paper trays or can be used with special paper-feeder attachments.

✔ **Will your users be addressing envelopes?**

Again, a special tray or feeder attachment may be required.

✔ **Does your network need central or individual control over printer queues?**

If you need centralized control, consider installing a print spooler.

✔ **Will users on Ethernet require access to a printer?**

Some PostScript printers, including one made by Apple, now include Ethernet connections. Others can be connected with special adapter boxes, or you can use a print spooler that connects to both Ethernet (for the users) and LocalTalk (for the printers).

Providing for modem sharing and remote access

Your users may need to access by modem such outside telecommunications services as an e-mail system, a stock quotation service, or an information bank. Or the users may need a modem to dial into another computer. Your company employees may travel with notebooks or other portable computers and need access to network services, possibly a database or printer. Consider the following modem issues:

✔ **Will the users require a modem?**

If many of your users have a need to access outside telecommunications services, computers at other sites, or network services such as a printer or company databases, you will want to consider modem services.

✔ **Will employees use the modem frequently or can one be shared on the network?**

Modem-sharing devices and modem servers are a good solution for sharing one or more modems on a network. Heavy users of a modem probably should have their own.

✔ **Do you want users on the road or in other building sites to access your network?**

Some of the devices for sharing modems allow dial-in access to the network. The Shiva NetModem and Farallon Liaison are two examples of modem-sharing devices.

Evaluating file-sharing needs

Next to printing, the most common use of a network is to share files. Your file sharing may require either point-to-point file transfers or group sharing of files on a file server. Dedicated servers use a computer solely to provide the services, whereas *distributed*, also called *peer-to-peer* servers, allow your Mac to be both server and client at the same time.

These questions will help you evaluate your file-sharing needs:

✔ What kind of file server will be appropriate?

Servers come in various flavors: dedicated (centralized), distributed (peer-to-peer), or background.

✔ Will the file sharing in System 7's or TOPS' peer-to-peer file services suffice (see Chapter 20, "Moving and Sharing Files on the Network"), or will a dedicated file server be required?

System 7's file sharing and TOPS are good for small workgroups of fewer than ten users. A dedicated file server is appropriate for larger workgroups and large databases.

✔ Will the users be accessing a database? And will the database file be shared among the users?

The more complicated a database becomes, the more essential it is to install the database file on a dedicated server.

✔ Are point-to-point file transfers enough?

You don't need a dedicated file server for users to send files occasionally to one another. File-transfer programs or e-mail will do this job.

After you resolve these questions to the satisfaction of yourself, your management, and your users, you can move on to questions regarding the physical plant, or the physical layout of the network. In the next sections, you'll find a few questions worth asking to help you make decisions about physical layout.

Planning for the distribution of users and services

Designing the physical layout of your network depends on such matters as the distance between users, the location of wiring closets, and the availability of existing wiring. Try to answer these questions when planning:

✔ **How close are each of the users to one another? How closely do they work together?**

You may have to install routers and repeaters to get everyone on the same network. Assigning zone names to different areas of the network can make it easier for members of a workgroup to work together and use the network's resources.

✔ **Are the users grouped together?**

Again, physical groupings make it easier to connect networks to a backbone to form a larger network.

✔ **Is the distance between groups large or small?**

Even backbone networks may not be enough. You may need to use repeaters, or you may have to plan a wide-area internet.

Evaluating the physical plant

The actual installation of the network depends on a number of factors, many of which you may not be able to control. Here are some of the installation factors:

✔ **Will you use existing wiring or install new wiring?**

Someone has to check the integrity of the wiring. Special connectors may be needed if you use existing wiring systems.

✔ **Is there space in the existing utility closets for your planned network equipment, such as StarControllers and routers?**

Everyone jostles for space in utility closets; hopefully there's some room left for your new network. Make sure other users of this space know what belongs to the network.

✔ **Who will install the wiring?**

The installer should be certified to handle network (or data) wiring. A regular phone installer usually is not aware of the problems associated with data transmissions at high speeds — that is, networks. Have all the network wiring checked after installation to make sure everything works, and have these checks done in your presence and *before* you approve payment for the job.

✔ **Who will be responsible for maintenance of the wiring?**

Your original wiring contractor might get called in if you need to rewire an entire floor of a building. But someone within the company should be responsible for reassigning wall jacks or changing wires at a hub without calling a contractor.

✔ **Where can you set up print stations?**

Because so many people use printers, ready access to printers is a must. Give some thought to procedures for maintaining the printers, including paper and toner refills. Make sure that your users know the rules.

✔ **Where can you install file servers, mail servers, or networked modems?**

All these services require some degree of security and should probably be in a locked room, or at least one with limited access.

✔ **Are there any noise sources (fluorescent lights, faxes, copy machines, motors, and so on) near the wiring?**

Watch out for these noise sources, especially if you're using unshielded twisted-pair wiring for your network.

✔ **Is there sufficient air flow or air-conditioning in the utility closet?**

Routers, modems, and StarControllers generate a lot of heat and should be cooled to run well. If these devices overheat, the network may go down.

After you work your way through these lists of questions, you should have a good idea of what the users expect to do with the network, as well as some of the equipment or services that you'll have to install on the network.

Introducing Network Topologies

Network design is a compromise between what your users want and what you can provide. When it comes to connecting all the users into a network, the main constraint in designing a network is not the users' needs, as we outlined in the top-down approach, but how you can wire the network. The various layouts that you can follow to wire a network are called *network topologies*, which is the focus of this section of the chapter.

When you design a network, you will choose from four basic network topologies: the daisy-chain, bus, star, and ring. We'll begin with the daisy-chain.

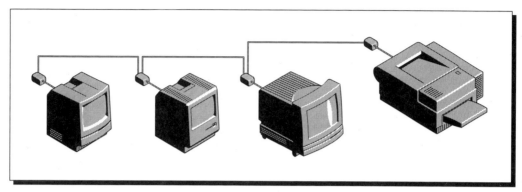

Figure 5-1: An example of a daisy-chain network.

The daisy-chain network

The *daisy-chain* network is a simple one that's easy to set up, but one that should be restricted to small workgroups. This topology consists of separate links between each device on the network, with a terminating resistor at each end of the chain (see Figure 5-1).

One problem with a daisy-chain is its fragility. If someone disconnects one of the network cables from a connector, for instance, the original network is broken in two. Also, because the network connector is the link between two neighboring cables, the connector must stay in place even when you move a device on the network. Daisy-chains are good only for shorter length networks because the introduction of so many interfaces (two for each connector) weakens the signal on the cable.

Daisy-chain networks do have a few advantages. They're easy to set up and therefore don't cost much, as you're only buying network cables and the connectors. That makes daisy-chains particularly useful for a small network, such as when you have two or three Macs and a LaserWriter that you need to link together in your office. A better network topology, even for small networks, is the bus network, which we describe next.

The bus network

A straightforward network configuration is the *bus*, or *backbone*, topology. Simply think of the bus as a linear cable with each device attached directly to this central cable. The connection is often called a *tap*. Just as with any straight line, there are two ends to the bus — these ends must be terminated electrically with a resistor to complete the bus (see Figure 5-2).

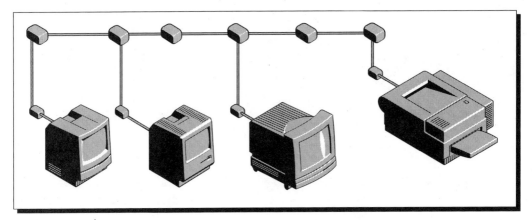

Figure 5-2: An example of a bus network.

The major difference between daisy-chain and bus networks is the continuity of the main cable of the bus. Because the bus can be a single length of cable, there are fewer interfaces on the cable to weaken a network's signal. Also, you can attach taps anywhere along the length of the bus and leave them unused (in wall jacks, for example) without affecting the signal of the bus. Thus you can lay out a bus cable and place taps anywhere that you'd expect to install a network device. Use the taps you need now and leave others for later expansion.

Bus-based networks are good for small- to medium-sized networks and are very useful when you're planning to install the wires within a wall, but need to allow for expansion of the network. A good way to extend a bus network is with a repeater — not by soldering two lengths of cable together. And, if you make connections available (in wall jacks, for example) in currently unused offices as you install the bus, you'll be able to add users to the network without added wiring.

Bus networks suffer from some of the same disadvantages as daisy-chains. First, a break in the network cable disrupts the entire network. Note, however, that these breaks can be less likely to occur than with a daisy-chain. The daisy-chain network cable leads right to the network connector for your Mac, so someone may accidentally break the network by unplugging a cable from the connector. On the other hand, the bus cable will most likely be hidden in the wall, and the network connector is part of the wall jack, reducing the chance of disconnecting the connector from the network cable.

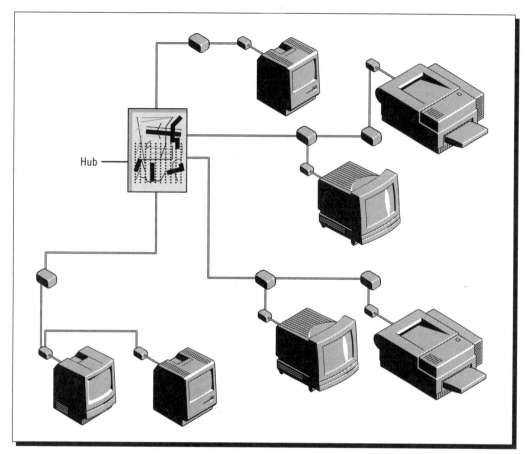

Hub

Figure 5-3: An example of a passive star network.

The star network

Many people are already using a type of *star* network topology, although they probably don't realize it. Most phone systems are wired in a star topology. Your phone is wired to a central location in a utility closet, as are all the other phones on your floor. The main thing to remember is that each device has its own set of wires to attach it to the central location, commonly called a *hub* in networking.

This hub may be no more than a wiring panel or punchdown block for gathering all the wires in one place — such an arrangement is called a *passive star* (see Figure 5-3).

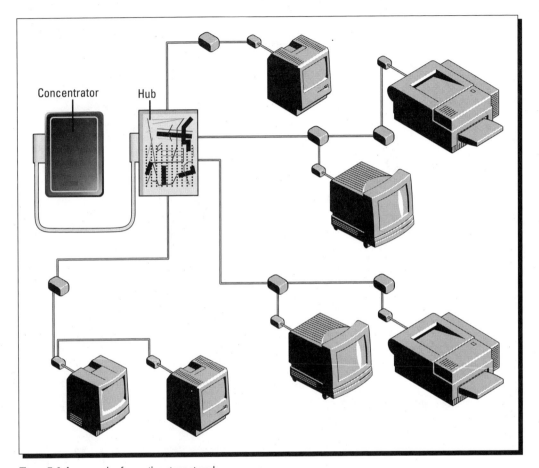

Figure 5-4: An example of an active star network.

In an *active star*, the hub is an active device on the network that amplifies any signal it receives before passing the signal on to other wires connected to it (see Figure 5-4). The amplifying device is usually called either a *concentrator* or a *multiport repeater*. We'll see in later chapters that active stars are popular both for LocalTalk and Ethernet networks.

One advantage of a star network is that it's easier to troubleshoot than other networks. It's a fairly easy matter to determine which device is having or causing problems by testing the different wires making up the star. These wires are commonly called *branches* or *legs*. Usually, there is one device per branch, so finding the problem wire isolates the problem device. The hubs used for active stars generally include electronics for testing each branch and for disconnecting a branch if necessary, as when there is too much noise on the branch.

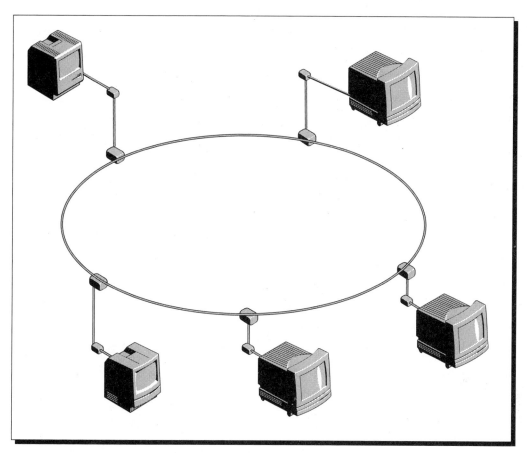

Figure 5-5: An example of a ring network.

The one disadvantage of a star network is that the network won't work when the hub fails. This isn't too likely with a passive star because only wiring connections and no additional electronics are involved in the hub. On the other hand, the multiport repeater that's used as the hub for an active star contains electronics that will, at some point in time, fail.

The ring network

With LocalTalk, PhoneNET, and Ethernet networks, you're told time and again not to create a closed loop in the network cable. But other networks, such as the token ring, require a closed loop in order to work. As you might expect, these are called *ring topologies*. Mac users are likely to encounter this topology if they're using TokenTalk, which sends AppleTalk protocols over token ring networks (see Figure 5-5).

Because the ring network depends on a closed topology, any break in the network cable will stop the network from working.

Selecting a Network Topology

Deciding which topology, or set of topologies, to use for your network isn't a cut-and-dried decision. But we'll offer here a few suggestions and points to consider when you're designing your network.

First, daisy-chain and bus networks are good for small networks. If you're going to install the wiring in the wall, use the bus topology and install wall jacks for the network connection. Bus networks also work well for medium-sized networks of 10 to 40 Macs, provided you don't have to run the bus cable every which way to connect all the cubicles or offices.

If the users are going to be fairly dispersed, however, such as over an entire floor of a building or even on multiple floors, plan to use a star topology. Whereas passive stars may be okay for small dispersed workgroups, you'll find it easier to troubleshoot and reconfigure a network if you have an active star topology. And if you're running token ring, you don't have much choice but to use a ring topology.

Second, remember that only the smallest networks are configured as a single topology. As networks grow, they eventually incorporate more than one topology. With growth prospects in mind, bus and active star networks are best-suited for expandability and work well together.

When designing your network, you should keep the following issues in mind. Each has a bearing on what topology or topologies you select:

✔ **Determine the average distance between nodes.**

This distance will quickly tell you if you're exceeding recommended wiring limits or if installation will be more costly for a given topology. For example, wiring a dispersed workgroup for a bus topology will probably cost more than wiring the same workgroup for a star topology.

✔ **Decide whether certain network services, such as a file server or printer, will be centrally located with users located at peripheral sites.**

If so, a star topology is probably your best bet.

✔ **Determine how many sites (or workgroups) will be connected via the network.**

A series of stars connected to a backbone, or a series of stars connected to a centrally located star, will be best when you have more than two or three sites.

✔ **Determine whether you're going to use existing wiring or install new wiring.**

If you use some existing phone cables (which PhoneNET allows, for example), a star topology will be best, because the topology matches that used by the phone companies.

✔ **Keep in mind how difficult it may be to install new wiring in some locations.**

Also remember that, someday, you or someone else will probably have to access the network wiring to repair it.

Designing Fault-Tolerant Networks

Fault tolerance is the capability of a system to continue functioning when some component of the system fails. This concept is most often applied to file servers on networks, but it also applies to network design in general. (See Chapter 14, "Fault Management," and Chapter 20, "Moving and Sharing Files on the Network," for more information on these issues.)

> Designing for network fault tolerance means planning for alternate routes in the event of breakdown.

The basic precept of fault-tolerant network design is this — the network manager should plan to provide users with alternate paths to crucial services. If a fault-tolerant design is in place, and one path between a user and a file server — such as through a router — goes down, the user is left with an alternate way of reaching the server. That alternate path might be another, slower network (LocalTalk instead of Ethernet, for instance) or even a modem link. But as long as such a path is available, the path allows users to continue with their work even if part of the network goes down.

Here are some examples of fault-tolerant network design:

❖ If your network spans more than one building, plan more than one link between each building; don't install all the links in the same conduit.

❖ Try to run an extra pair of wires to each workstation (this is especially easy in twisted-pair cables) for use in case the original connection is broken.

❖ When wiring to a hub, wire as many devices as possible with their own wiring runs; in other words, avoid daisy-chains and, if possible, buses.

❖ If you're wiring together more than one hub in a larger network, provide a second connection between the hubs as a standby connection; if possible, also provide a standby hub to take over the network if one of the hubs goes down.

Summary

In this chapter, we've covered the fundamental topologies of network design. We discussed the advantages and drawbacks to each type of network so that you can plan a design suited to your needs.

We discussed the following topics:

✔ Plan your network with a top-down approach that keeps the users' needs in mind.

✔ When designing your network, keep in mind the types of services that need to be installed. Such services can include print services, modem sharing and remote access, and file-sharing needs.

✔ Keep the physical layout in mind when designing a network.

✔ Network topologies are the various layouts used to wire a network. Four basic network topologies are the daisy-chain, the bus, the passive star, and the active star topologies.

✔ Fault-tolerant network design involves planning for alternate paths to crucial network services.

In the following chapter, we'll guide you through the design of a LocalTalk network.

Chapter 6
Designing a LocalTalk LAN

In this chapter...

✔ Using different topologies with LocalTalk

✔ Selecting hardware for your network

✔ Calculating wiring limits for LocalTalk and PhoneNET wiring

✔ Choosing devices to extend your network

We've introduced you to how networks operate, particularly AppleTalk networks, but haven't yet covered much about how to install a network to use AppleTalk and the services it provides. In this chapter, we'll cover rules and tips for designing networks using LocalTalk and related media, such as PhoneNET. The next chapter will go into the details of installing the network you've designed.

Remember that AppleTalk is the suite of networking protocols developed by Apple and is *not* a network cable or connector. The original transmission medium developed by Apple to run AppleTalk protocols is called LocalTalk, which uses shielded twisted-pair cable. A popular alternative to LocalTalk cabling is PhoneNET, originally developed by Farallon Computing, which uses unshielded twisted-pair cabling similar to that used by your telephone system. In this chapter, we'll talk about designing networks with these two transmission media.

Getting Acquainted with LocalTalk and PhoneNET

Apple's LocalTalk networking system is designed to run at a speed of 230,400 baud (or bits per second) over shielded twisted-pair cable. The specifications for LocalTalk are a part of the physical and data link layers of the AppleTalk protocol suite (see Chapter 3, "Understanding AppleTalk Protocols"). Farallon Computing pioneered a similar wiring scheme, using unshielded twisted-pair cabling to transmit at LocalTalk speeds — the original idea and the connectors actually began with a group of students at BMUG (Berkeley Mac Users Group).

Since the first Mac rolled off the assembly lines in 1984, each Mac has had built-in networking support for AppleTalk. In LocalTalk, this was accomplished by the Serial Communications Controller (SCC) chip that controls the two serial ports found on each Mac. Later Macs, starting with the IIfx, used a custom chip for controlling the serial ports, but the resulting LocalTalk support stayed the same.

Selecting a Network Topology

As discussed in Chapter 5, "Network Design 101," four main types of topologies are used for wiring networks: daisy-chain, bus, star, and ring. Because we're concentrating on LocalTalk here, we'll cover only the daisy-chain, bus, and star networks in this chapter.

To help guide you as we discuss the ins and outs of the various network topologies, we've set up an example of a building with 15 offices and one copier room. All but two of the offices have Macs, but you'll also need to support Macs in the two empty offices at some later date. The laser printer and a Mac for print spooling and file services are installed in the copier room. Now let's look at the different ways in which you can wire these offices for LocalTalk.

The daisy-chain topology

The daisy-chain network is the simplest to construct, especially if you're using LocalTalk or PhoneNET connectors. Just plug the network connector box into each Mac, connect a network cable from one box to the next, then from that box to the next, and so on (see Figure 6-1). But remember that if one of the cables breaks or is disconnected from the connector box, your network's down.

Daisy-chains are good for small networks, but when they get beyond 10 or 12 devices, this type of network gets hard to troubleshoot and maintain. Also, note that the daisy-chain is the only network topology that you can create with LocalTalk, unless you use adapter cables, which we'll cover in Chapter 7, "Installing a LocalTalk LAN."

The bus topology

If you don't like the idea of wires hanging around your cubicles, you're better off using a bus, or backbone, topology for your network. In the bus topology, you use one cable for the entire network and tap into the main cable with another wire that leads to your network connector. Often, these backbone cables are run through the walls of your building, and the taps are made at wall jacks, much like the phone system. As this means stringing a new cable in the wall, the bus topology is also recommended for small workgroups. You can also install the wire along the baseboard and attach new jacks to the wall if you want — it's all a question of neatness and available resources.

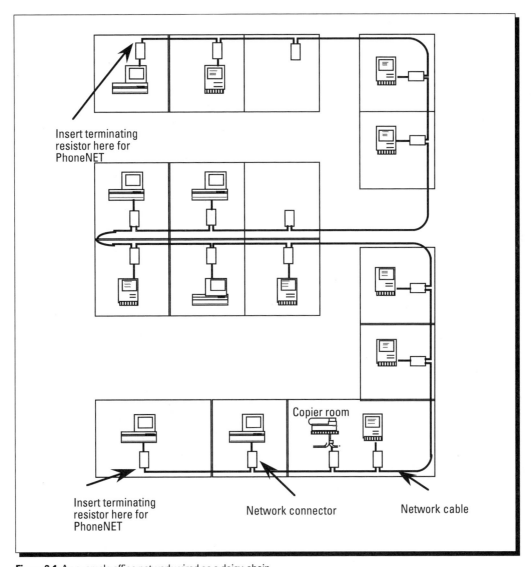

Figure 6-1: An example office network wired as a daisy-chain.

If you plan to install a bus network, plan also on using PhoneNET connectors or their clones. Apple's LocalTalk connectors are not meant for any topology other than a daisy-chain.

Figure 6-2 shows the example network as a bus network. Note that the two empty offices also have been wired to the bus, as indicated by the circles

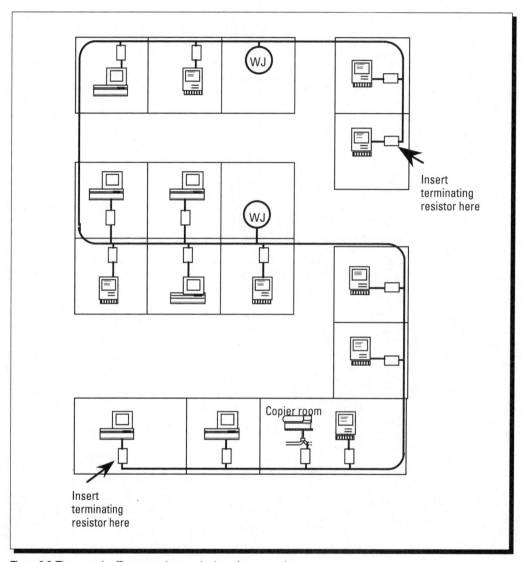

Figure 6-2: The example office network now wired as a bus network.

marked WJ (for wall jack). You can connect a new computer to the network in those offices simply by plugging a PhoneNET connector into the wall jack.

The passive star topology

Phone wiring in most buildings meets the specifications for PhoneNET wiring, so you can use the existing phone wiring to create a PhoneNET network. To do this, all you need to do is to attach each Mac to a phone jack and reconnect the phone

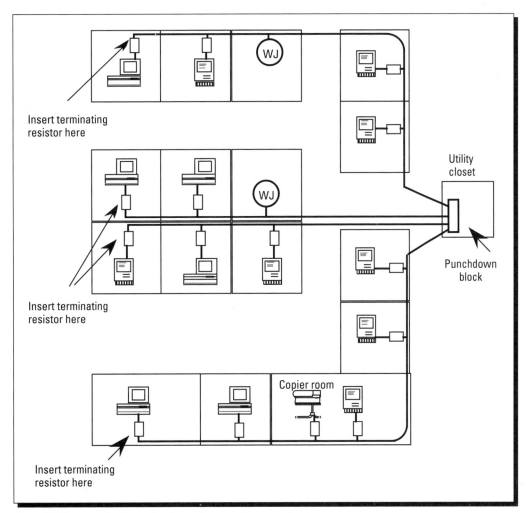

Figure 6-3: The example office network wired as a passive star network.

jack to the utility closet, just as if you were installing a phone. Of course, you don't use the same two wires that the phone uses; there's usually an extra pair in the cable that will do the trick. Then you wire all the leads from each phone jack together in the phone closet, at a device called the *punchdown block,* and you've got a passive star (see Figure 6-3). We'll cover the details of that part of the installation in Chapter 7, "Installing a LocalTalk LAN."

Note in Figure 6-3 that each branch of the passive star has more than one device attached to it. In this example, we wired each branch as a bus, but that's not required. Note that the two empty offices also have been wired to the bus, as indicated by the circles marked WJ. You can connect a new computer to the network in those offices simply by plugging a PhoneNET connector into the wall jack.

Passive stars can be very limiting when designing a PhoneNET network. This is mainly because the ends of the network wires are joined in a passive star. When a signal from a Mac on one branch reaches this common connection point, the signal's power is divided among all the branches of the passive star. Because the passive star doesn't provide any means for amplifying the signal, the network signal is weakened each time it reaches the common connection point.

When you're designing a passive star network, try to use no more than four branches, and don't attach other passive stars to any of the branches. To determine how long each of your passive star's branches can be, divide 3,000 feet (for 24 AWG wire) by the number of branches in your star, and use the remainder as your branch's maximum length, as in the following formula:

maximum branch length = (wiring limit/number of branches)

If you're going to attach other cables to a branch, you should also subtract four times the length of those cables from the remaining length to determine the maximum branch length:

maximum branch length = (wiring limit/number of branches – 4 x length of added cables)

In both formulas, if you're using 24 AWG wire, the wiring limit is 3,000 feet, whereas the wiring limit is 4,500 feet for 22 AWG wire and 2,000 feet for 26 AWG wire. If you use more than four branches, you still use the same formulas, but for installation, you should use no more than a total of four terminating resistors on the network.

From our discussion, you can see that passive stars are limited; they can often be more trouble than they're worth. Because each branch of the passive star is not electrically isolated from the others, the branches are limited in length.

The passive star limits you even further by the number of devices you can install on it; the connection of each branch to the others reduces the network signal. For example, Farallon recommends no more than 16 devices on a 3-branch passive star of 1,800 feet, whereas a backbone network of the same length can support 48 devices. If you have small network in which the users are not located centrally, a passive star can be a simple start to creating a network. But as you expand your network, either by adding more devices or incorporating more-distant users, you should be prepared to convert your passive star to another topology, usually an active star.

The active star topology

Because of the wiring-length limits for a passive star, you're usually better off using an active star topology, which creates a more reliable network, even though it is more expensive to set up. Buy a StarController or TurboStar LocalTalk hub and install it in your phone closet. You can wire your star just as we described for the passive star, connecting the wires from each device into a punchdown block in the utility closet. The difference is that you then plug a feed cable from the punchdown block to the active hub. Now, instead of each wire contributing to the length of your network (as it did in the passive star), each Mac's cable is electrically isolated from the other, and the network signal is amplified when it passes through the active hub. This means that you're not stuck with calculating branch limits (as you were with the passive star) and that each branch of an active star can be set up following the rules for a daisy-chain or bus network, depending on how you want to connect devices to the active hub (also called a *multiport repeater*).

Note that in Figure 6-4, the example network wired as an active star, the branches drawn in the center of the diagram, as well as the two at the top and bottom of the drawing, have multiple devices attached to them. Four computers at the right of the drawing are attached individually to the star. Also note that the two empty offices also have been wired to the bus, as indicated by the circles marked WJ. You can connect a new computer to the network in those offices simply by plugging a PhoneNET connector into the wall jack.

Because each active star's branch is electrically isolated from the rest of the network, you're free to make any of the branches a daisy-chain, a bus, or even a passive star or another active star. The active hubs available for LocalTalk are designed for a maximum of four wire runs for each port. Thus, if you're planning to wire more than one device per port (the StarControllers have 12 or 24 ports; the TurboStar has 16), you have a great deal of flexibility in choosing your wiring runs.

The best approach when planning for network troubleshooting is to keep as few devices as possible on each wiring run. Therefore, it's better to use a separate wiring run for each device and connect it to the desired port at the punchdown block or patch panel than to use one wiring run for the same four devices. This way, when something goes wrong, you can physically disconnect and isolate a problem wire or device without adversely affecting the rest of the network. Of

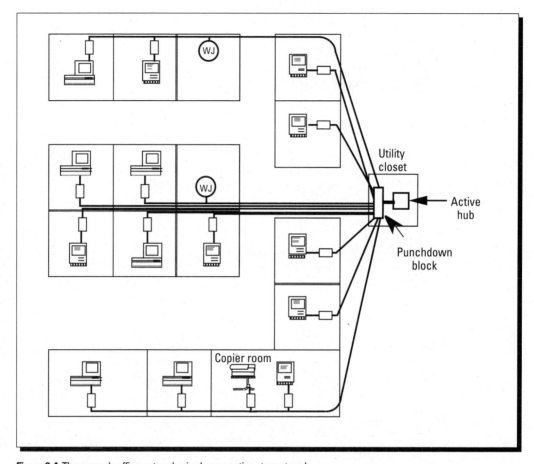

Figure 6-4: The example office network wired as an active star network.

course, if you're planning to connect more than four devices per port, you have no choice but to use some wiring runs for more than one device. And, in some cases, you may not be able to run enough wires to use one run per device.

We mentioned that each branch of an active star can have its own topology. This is particularly useful in larger networks, since you can create a hierarchy of active stars for your network. As each branch of an active star can be individually disconnected or tested without affecting the rest of the network, this hierarchy makes it easy to find a problem network and then to isolate it from the others.

Understanding the Limits for Network Topologies

Each topology has limits on the length of wire that can be used, either for the entire length, as in a bus topology, or for each branch, as with star topologies. You're also limited as to how many devices you can attach to a given topology. These limits vary with wire gauge. Table 6-1 presents the wiring and device limits for LocalTalk and PhoneNET for the different network topologies and typical gauge wire.

Table 6-1: Limits for Network Topologies*

	Daisy Chain	Daisy Chain	Backbone	Passive Star (3 branch)	Passive Star (4 branch)	Active Star**
Max length (ft)	LocalTalk	PhoneNET				
22-gauge wire	1000	—	4500	4500	4500	3000
24-gauge wire	—	—	3000	3000	3000	2000
26-gauge wire	—	1800	1800	1800	1800	1500
Max nodes	32	24	48	16	12	varies***

Notes:

  * All limits are cited for PhoneNET cabling, except for the daisy-chain topology, where both LocalTalk and PhoneNET wiring are considered. All lengths are given in feet.

 ** The maximum lengths specified for the active star are the length for each branch. Total length of the network should be the maximum length of each branch times the number of ports in the active hub.

*** The maximum number of nodes depends on the networks attached to each port of the active hub and on the number of ports in the active hub.

Extending Network Limits

If the network length limits we mentioned in Table 6-1 aren't long enough for your needs, you may want to consider using a repeater to extend the reach of your network. If you want only to extend the length of one network cable, a single-port repeater will do the trick. On the other hand, if you want to wire a star topology and use long network cables, you can use either a multiport repeater, such as the Farallon StarController or Nuvotech Turbostar, or a packet-switching hub, such as the Tribe LocalSwitch.

Multiport repeaters (we've also referred to them as *active star hubs*) amplify and reclock any network signal as it passes through the hub, retransmitting the signal to all other ports of the hub. A multiport repeater handles network traffic much like a conference call — everyone hears every conversation on the network. A packet-switching hub, on the other hand, works more like the phone system and is able to isolate network traffic on one port from traffic on other ports, exchanging packets between ports only as necessary. The packet-switching hub is able to do this because it inspects each network packet to determine the destination of the packet; it then forwards the packet to the appropriate port and only the devices attached to that port will see (or "hear") the packet.

When should you use which device? Multiport repeaters deal only with electrical signals and retransmit the amplified signal to all of the network branches attached to the repeater, so a multiport repeater cannot be used to isolate traffic on one wiring branch from traffic on another wiring branch. But multiport repeaters are good for extending the scope (or length) of your network because they amplify signals.

Packet-switching hubs can be used in the same way as multiport repeaters, because they, too, amplify the signal. But you should plan to use these devices for more than just repeater replacements, as they're more expensive. Packet-switching hubs are good for isolating network traffic on one wiring branch from that on another branch.

But this traffic isolation is good for improving the performance of your network only if users aren't continually accessing centralized services, but are more likely to exchange information in reasonably well-defined workgroups. Thus, if you have a single laser printer or file server and everyone on the network must use those devices, a packet-switching hub won't help increase network performance. On the other hand, if you have a number of users running the File Sharing feature under System 7, or if each workgroup has its own printer and/or file server, a packet-switching hub will most likely increase the network's performance. This happens because each branch of the network is isolated from the other and only those packets that need to get from one branch to the other are passed on by the hub. Multiport repeaters won't make any difference in such cases.

To further illustrate this point, we've constructed a network with multiple workgroups wired in a star topology. Notice in Figure 6-5 that the network has a multiport repeater installed at the hub. The figure illustrates where various network packets go. If the Mac labeled "A" is printing to LaserWriter "B," the packets it generates travel throughout the network and are seen by Macs C, D, E, F, and H, and LaserWriter G as well. None of those devices can start using the network until Mac A has finished with LaserWriter B.

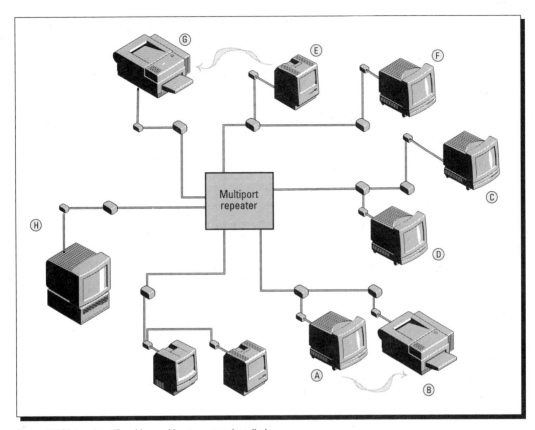

Figure 6-5: Network traffic with a multiport repeater installed.

A similar network is shown in Figure 6-6, but this one has a packet-switching hub in the middle of the star. In this case, the packets generated by Mac A printing to LaserWriter B are not transmitted beyond the hub, so the other devices don't see these other packets.

Thus, as you can see in the figure, Mac C can exchange a file with Mac D on one cable that's attached to the hub, since that cable is isolated by the hub from the cable connecting Mac A and LaserWriter B. The other network task, Mac E printing to LaserWriter G, is also unaffected by the other two uses because the packet-switching hub can relay the packets between the two cables involved without transmitting those packets to the other cables. If Mac H wants to send a file to Mac F, which is on the same cable as Mac E, it must wait until Mac E is finished printing because packets transmitted from Mac H through the hub to Mac F will collide with those generated by Mac E.

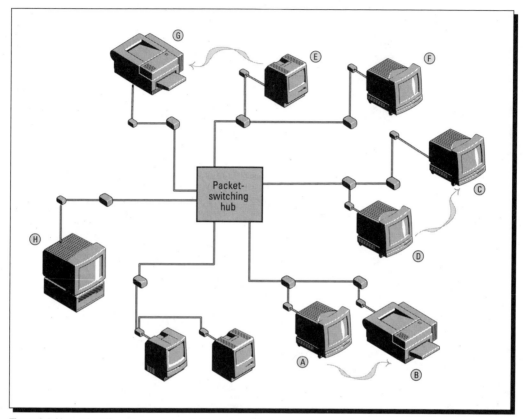

Figure 6-6: Network traffic with a packet-switching hub installed.

Although we'll cover the subject of routers in more detail in Chapter 11, "Designing an AppleTalk LAN," it's worth noting here that you can also use routers to isolate traffic between networks. This can be a more cost-effective solution than the packet-switching hub if you only have a few workgroups or networks. But be aware that packet-switching hubs can process network traffic faster than routers and that a router may become a bottleneck in your network.

Bear in mind that your network's performance can be greatly affected by where you locate your network services, such as print spoolers, file servers, and e-mail servers. We touched on that point when discussing packet-switching hubs, and we'll be concentrating on that aspect of network design and optimization in Chapter 15, "Performance Management."

Summary

This chapter introduced you to the layout of LocalTalk and PhoneNET networks for different network topologies. We also presented the wiring and device limits for each of the topologies. The chapter included information on when to use multiport repeaters (active star hubs) or packet-switching hubs to extend your network and isolate network traffic.

In this chapter, we covered the following topics:

✔ LocalTalk is Apple's hardware for installing your network.

✔ An alternative to Apple's LocalTalk cabling is PhoneNET, originally developed by Farallon Computing.

✔ You can lay out LocalTalk networks in the daisy-chain, bus, and star topologies.

✔ Each network topology has limits on the length of wire used; you can, however, calculate these wiring limits for both LocalTalk and PhoneNET.

✔ You can use repeaters and packet-switching hubs to extend your network.

In the following chapter, you'll learn more about LocalTalk networks, as we cover the details of installation.

Chapter 7
Installing a LocalTalk LAN

In this chapter . . .

✔ How to select the proper connectors and cables for your network

✔ How to make your own cables

✔ How to install a daisy-chain network

✔ How to install a bus network

✔ How to install a star network

✔ How to set up your Mac's network software

In Chapters 5 and 6, we covered some of the details of planning and designing a network. Now we'll show you how to install and test both simple networks as well as the larger, more complicated LocalTalk networks. Before you read this chapter, you should read Chapter 6, "Designing a LocalTalk LAN," which deals with the basic types of LocalTalk networks.

Selecting Cables and Connectors

The first thing you should know about your Macs is that all of them have built-in support for networking. Apple calls its networking system *AppleTalk*. You don't need to buy any special software to make a network of Macs work together. But you will need some hardware. You can choose either Apple's own cabling system, called *LocalTalk*, or a popular alternative called *PhoneNET*.

Using standard cabling and wiring kits

Apple offers LocalTalk connectors and wiring kits for use with Macs and LaserWriters (see Figure 7-1). The LocalTalk kit uses shielded twisted-pair cable, which is less affected by outside interference, or *noise,* but is limited to maximum lengths of 300 feet. The standard LocalTalk cable that comes with each Apple LocalTalk connector is 6½ feet (2 meters) long. If you need longer cables, you can buy a LocalTalk wiring kit and make your own cables. The LocalTalk connectors for your Mac are self-terminating, which makes it easier to set up or change a network without added pieces. (We'll describe the process of terminating your network cables shortly.)

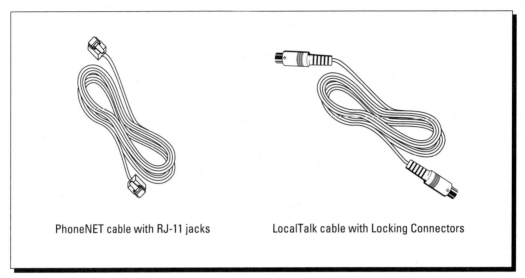

PhoneNET cable with RJ-11 jacks   LocalTalk cable with Locking Connectors

Figure 7-1: Both PhoneNET and LocalTalk cabling types can be used for an AppleTalk network.

The most popular wiring scheme for Mac networks is PhoneNET, mainly because it can use existing phone wires. This is particularly helpful if you have a spare pair of wires in your phone cable that can be set up for the network, especially in prewired buildings with wiring closets and such. In a small office, though, you can get by just as well with the modular cords that come with the PhoneNET connectors. The modular cords are thinner and a bit easier to bend than Apple's LocalTalk cables. Other custom-made cables for PhoneNET can extend over distances as great as 1,000 feet. Because they are not shielded as LocalTalk cables are, PhoneNET cables are not recommended for high-noise environments, such as in factories near electrical motors or elevators.

Because most modular cable is not twisted pair, you shouldn't use it for long network wiring runs; we suggest lengths of not more than 50 feet. If you need longer wiring runs, use a cable that is known to contain twisted pair, such as *station cable,* which is the 22-gauge twisted pair often used by phone companies. (See the next section for details on making your own cables.)

If you must combine two or more existing networks, and if some use Local-Talk cabling and others use PhoneNET, you can use a LocalTalk-PhoneNET adapter cable to link the two types of cables together. This adapter cable is also handy when you're installing an active star network because you can use it to connect existing LocalTalk daisy-chains to the phone jacks for the star. Remember, though, whenever you mix cables in this manner, your total length is limited by the LocalTalk cable specifications.

We offer a word of warning here about the insulation used for these cables. Buildings use one of two methods for circulating room air. Circulation is either through airspaces within the building's ceiling, often called *plenum air returns*, or through air ducts. Cables can be purchased with either of two types of insulation: PVC (polyvinyl chloride) or Teflon. If you're planning to install network cables within a plenum air return, you should avoid using PVC-insulated cable. PVC releases poisonous gases when burned, and the plenum return can carry flames and the poisonous gases rapidly through the building. If you have any questions about the type of network cable that you should install in air spaces, check with your local fire codes.

The Apple LocalTalk 2-meter and 10-meter cables are PVC-coated and should be run through metal conduit when they are installed through walls or ceilings. The LocalTalk Custom Wiring Kit uses Teflon-coated cable.

Making your own cables

Stock cable lengths usually fall in the range of the 6½-foot length provided with connectors, up to the 50-foot modular cables. These lengths still may be too short for your network. For a bus or star network, you may not be able to purchase the proper twisted-pair cables in the lengths you need, complete with connectors or terminators. Your best bet then is to make your own cables.

There is more than one type of telephone wiring, and not all of it is twisted-pair. Quad, the wiring found in homes, has four parallel wires in one cable. Wiring plants in many older buildings were installed using thick multiconductor cables, whereas some modern buildings have been wired with a flat cable known as *silver satin cable*. These cables are not suitable for high-speed (10 Mbit/sec) LANs, but they can be used at LocalTalk speeds. If you use existing wiring, find out as much as possible about its electrical characteristics before using it.

If you make your own modular extension cables, such as for a PhoneNET daisy-chain, you can use modular cable from a supplier like Radio Shack, which offers the cabling in 50-foot lengths, as well as on reels for longer cabling. Farallon also offers a modular cable construction kit for creating custom cable lengths. Once you cut the cable to the lengths you want, you'll need to trim away the outer jacket of the cable from the four wires in the modular cable. Place the wire ends within the four slots of an RJ-11 connector and then use a crimping tool to drive the connector's pins into the wire. Above all, be consistent: always match the same color wire to the pin number of the connector. (Each wire in the cable can be distinguished from the others by the color of its insulation.) If you have to buy all the equipment you need to make the cables, don't scrimp when buying the crimping tool; we've found that the cheaper crimping tools don't always push the RJ-11 connector pins into the wires evenly, and you can end up with an intermittent connection.

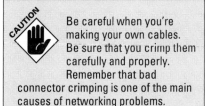

Be careful when you're making your own cables. Be sure that you crimp them carefully and properly. Remember that bad connector crimping is one of the main causes of networking problems.

As we said previously, if you're planning to make your own cables for a bus or a star network, use 22-gauge or 24-gauge twisted-pair cable that contains solid wire. The 22-gauge version (which has an outer tan-colored jacket) is often called *station cable* by phone installers. You can use the typical four-conductor (two-pair) cable to create a bus or to run a branch for a star, leaving the extra pair as a replacement in case the first pair malfunctions.

Remember that the maximum distance for reliable use of PhoneNET cables is a function of the wire thickness used within the cables. A common wiring, especially for telephone installations in businesses, is 24-gauge. The tan-colored, 22-gauge phone cable just mentioned is most often found in homes. Network buses and branches for stars should be installed with 22-gauge quad cable, which has a solid copper core for each wire.

You can also make your own LocalTalk cables, using wiring kits from either Apple or third-party vendors. For LocalTalk, you'll need a soldering iron instead of a crimping tool because you have to solder each wire of the cable to the pins found in the LocalTalk connector. It's a bit more work than crimping RJ-11 jacks for PhoneNET, but a soldered connection is more reliable.

Setting up connectors

Each type of cable, whether LocalTalk or PhoneNET, requires its own special connector box. The LocalTalk connector boxes have two ports for connecting network cables. Each port is *self-terminating*, which means that you don't have to add a terminating resistor at the end of each network cable segment (see Figure 7-2). The most common PhoneNET connectors and their clones also have two ports for the network cables, but require a terminating resistor at both ends of the network segment — we'll get into the details of placing terminating resistors later in this chapter when we discuss specific network topologies. There's a third type of connector, Farallon's StarConnector, which is internally terminated and has only one port for connecting a network cable — this connector is designed only for star topologies with one device per wiring run. Each connector, whether LocalTalk or PhoneNET, connects to a Mac's printer port with a short cable.

No matter which wiring system you choose, you may need to buy more than one type of network connector. All the newer Macs and LaserWriter IIs use the smaller

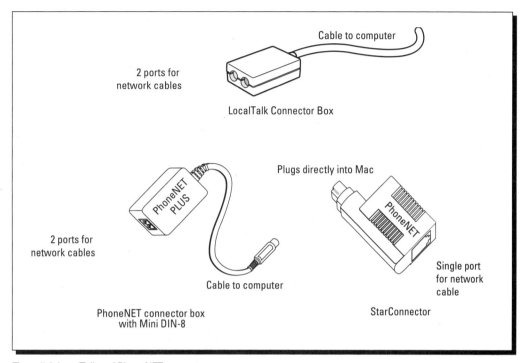

2 ports for
network cables

Cable to computer

LocalTalk Connector Box

PhoneNET
PLUS

Plugs directly into Mac

PhoneNET

2 ports for
network cables

Cable to computer

Single port
for network
cable

PhoneNET connector box
with Mini DIN-8

StarConnector

Figure 7-2: LocalTalk and PhoneNET connectors.

mini-DIN-8 connector for their printer ports, which is where the network connects
to the Mac. The older LaserWriters from Apple and some other PostScript printers,
as well as the venerable Mac 512, use a larger DB-9 connector (see Figure 7-3).
The DB-9 connector is also used for LocalTalk cards for DOS computers. Check
the printer port of each of your Macs and LaserWriters before you purchase your
connectors. In Figure 7-4, you see the location of the printer port on the Mac
Classic series (including the Mac SE and SE/30) and the Mac II series.

Other types of connectors are available for use with the PhoneNET system.
Nuvotech offers a PhoneNET-compatible connector that includes an internal
terminating resistor. In this case, the resistor is not the normal 120-ohm
resistor, but a smaller resistor that attempts to weaken, or *dampen,* the reflected signals sufficiently so as not to interfere with the original network
signal. The problem here is to decide what is sufficient dampening. The 120-
ohm resistor used with PhoneNET connectors absorbs enough of the signal to
prevent a reflection and thereby prevent interference with the original signal.
Resistance values of less than 120 ohms, such as those used with the Nuvotech

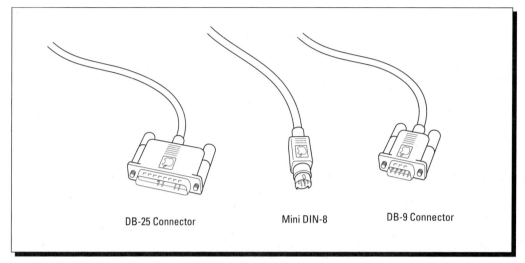

DB-25 Connector   Mini DIN-8   DB-9 Connector

Figure 7-3: Connector types for connecting to a Mac.

connectors, don't completely absorb the signal's energy. Although this may not be a problem on a short cable with a strong signal, reflections from lower-value terminating resistors can lead to interference with a weak signal, as you may have on networks with long cable lengths.

Choosing wiring accessories

If you're going to install either a passive or an active star network, you'll choose from various wiring devices that organize your wiring and make installation easier. Devices that you'll need to know about are the *harmonica block*, the *punchdown block* (also called the *type 66 block*), and the *patch panel*.

Harmonica blocks are good for small networks, as they come in 12-port models and have sockets for RJ-11 jacks (see Figure 7-5), which means that you can use them with modular cables. Changing a cable is as easy as plugging a new one into the proper RJ-11 socket. One end of the harmonica block has a socket for a 50-pin Amphenol connector — you'd use a cable with Amphenol connectors on both ends to connect the harmonica block to a concentrator (a StarController, for example).

Instead of a harmonica block, you can use a punchdown block (see Figure 7-6) for connecting your wiring runs to the active hub. A common type of punchdown block is the *type 66 block,* as named by AT&T and used in many

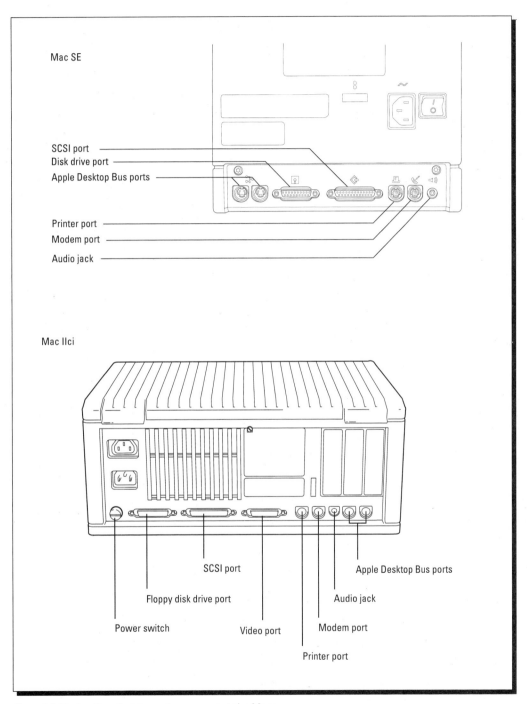

Figure 7-4: The location of printer ports on representative Macs.

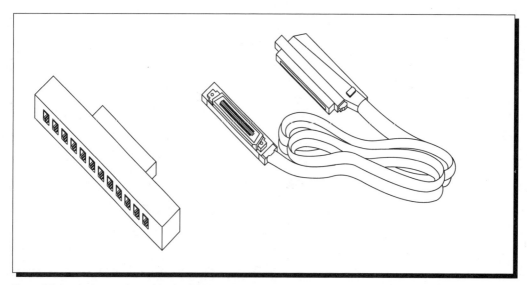

Figure 7-5: A typical 12-port harmonica block with mating Amphenol cable.

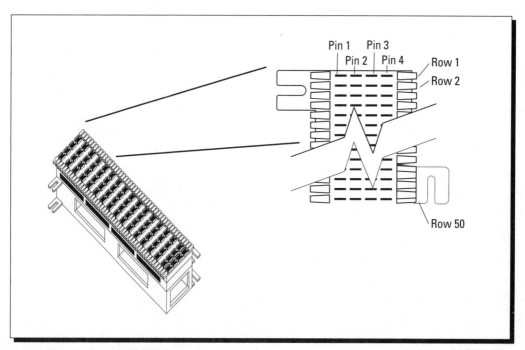

Figure 7-6: A type 66 punchdown block.

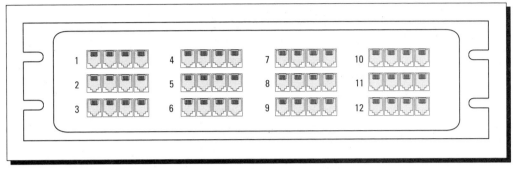

Figure 7-7: A typical patch panel with four RJ-11 jacks per port. This extended view shows contacts, or pins.

phone installations (some companies also call them *telco splice* blocks). The punchdown block has fifty rows of four insulated contacts; in each row, contacts 1 and 2 are electrically connected, as are contacts 3 and 4. To connect a wire to a contact, you place the wire between the jaws of a retaining clip that's attached to the contact, and then use a special punchdown tool to force the wire into the retaining clip — hence the name punchdown block. You *punch* the wire *down* into the retaining clip. As you force the wire into the clip, the clip slices through the wire's insulation to make electrical contact with the wire's conductor.

Punchdown blocks are especially useful if you're working with network cables that are collected in a wiring closet. Wiring closets are usually short on space, so using a compact, wall-mounted wiring device like a punchdown block helps to keep your cables organized and makes it easy to add or exchange wires in a star network.

Like the harmonica block, a punchdown block has a 50-pin Amphenol connector so that you can run a cable from the punchdown block to your star's multiport repeater or a packet-switching hub.

The third device we'll discuss here, the patch panel, is a cross between the harmonica block and the punchdown block. Like the harmonica block, the patch panel is designed to accept RJ-11 jacks. But like the punchdown block, the patch panel has places for connecting more than one wire per port. Patch panels usually offer four RJ-11 jacks per hub port (see Figure 7-7). Because a patch panel has more jacks per port, you can use one for easy connection of multiple wiring runs to each port of an active hub. Again, like the harmonica block and punchdown block, the patch panel has an Amphenol 50-pin socket for connection to an active hub.

If you're running only one device per port, you don't really need a patch panel, but you may want to use one for future expansion capabilities. If you have multiple wiring runs to a single port, with or without a patch panel, just remember that the total length of the runs attached to one port is subject to the usual wiring limits and number of nodes of a passive star network (with four branches if you use all four jacks on the patch panel). Patch panels have a distinct advantage if you have to rewire your network because they don't require special tools to connect the wires to the panel. (Of course, you will need wiring runs ending in RJ-11 jacks in order to make the connections.)

There are some differences in installing any of these devices for passive stars and for active stars, but we'll cover those differences later in this chapter when we discuss installing each type of network topology. Next, we'll start putting together some networks using the cables and wiring devices we've just described.

Installing a Daisy-Chain Network

The simplest network to create is a daisy-chain. All you need to do is connect the network connectors with network cables; then plug the connectors into the computers, and you're done. But we'll go through this procedure step by step.

Following is a shopping list of the items you'll need:

❖ One Apple LocalTalk or Farallon PhoneNET Plus connector for each Mac

❖ One similar connector for each LaserWriter

❖ Either LocalTalk or PhoneNET cables

We'll assume that all of your Macs and the LaserWriter are installed relatively close to one another. That proximity will make installation a bit simpler, although it's certainly not a requirement.

If you decide to use LocalTalk wiring, all you need to do is plug the network connectors into each Mac and LaserWriter and then plug the LocalTalk cables into the connectors. The connectors should be plugged into the printer port of each Mac. In Figure 7-4, you saw the positions of the different ports on the back of some of the more common Macs.

Start with one Mac. First plug a cable into its network connector, and then plug the other end of that cable into the next Mac's network connector. Repeat the process until all of the Macs and the LaserWriter are connected. You've just created a *daisy-chain* network (see Figure 7-8).

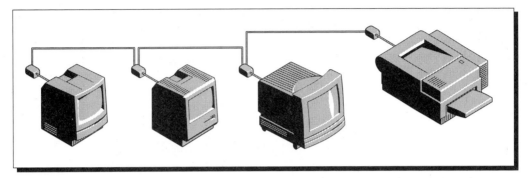

Figure 7-8: A daisy-chain network.

 If you are installing a PhoneNET system, you'll need to take an extra step. As described previously, you plug the connectors into your Macs and run cables from each network connector to the others. You also have to *terminate* the network. To terminate the network, you use special resistors that come with the PhoneNET connectors (see Figure 7-9). You will need two RJ-11 jacks with terminating resistors for a PhoneNET installation.

If you connected all the cables correctly, you should have a PhoneNET connector with an open socket at each end of the daisy-chain. These two connectors define the ends of your network. To make the network run smoothly, you should install terminating resistors on these connectors. Take the resistors that are soldered to the clear plastic RJ-11 jacks and place one jack into each PhoneNET network connector that has an empty socket. Your network is now terminated.

We'll move on to a network that is more complicated, but one that offers more expandability options — the bus network.

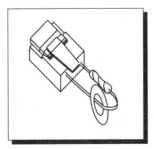

Figure 7-9: An RJ-11 jack with terminating resistor.

Installing a Bus Network

We presented a sample layout for a bus network in Chapter 6, "Designing a LocalTalk LAN." In that example, we explained how to use wall jacks and place taps in the bus cable to form the network. Now, we'll show you a way to wire those wall jacks to the bus to form the network.

The bus network is a fairly custom installation, inasmuch as the length of the bus is determined by your building's layout. You'll probably start with a reel of cable that you'll cut to your specifications. First, check the cable while it's still on the reel. Use an ohmmeter, a cable tester, or a time domain reflectometer (TDR) to verify the continuity of the cable (see Chapter 9 for use of these instruments). Ohmmeters are the simplest tools for this task, but they won't indicate the position of a break if one has occurred in the cable. On the other hand, cable testers can locate the break to within a few feet, and TDRs can pinpoint the break, with an error factor of within an inch or two.

Once you pull the cables to their locations, be sure to test the cables again for shorts or breaks that may have occurred during the installation. Mark the cable every five meters with white tape and a cable number. (Do this beforehand if the cable is being pulled through conduit or inaccessible areas.) Then add colored labels bearing the cable number in a neighboring location, such as a baseboard, and mark the location of the cables on a building plan. This way, when you have a break in the cable, a TDR or other cable tester can pinpoint the break, and your systematic labeling of cables will lead you right to the problem.

You can use wall-mounted phone jacks for tapping into a PhoneNET bus network. Once you've pulled your cable through the wall, leaving some slack in the cable, remove the phone jacks where you intend to tap into the bus cable. Strip the outer insulation from about two inches of the cable, and then strip about one inch of insulation from the two wires in the cable that will be used to carry network signals.

Be careful not to cut any of the wires. If you accidentally cut a wire, solder the two ends together; do not simply twist them back together. Take the two stripped lengths of wire and wrap them around the screw terminals in the phone jack.

Be consistent in following the color schemes of the wires and the labels of the phone jack. For example, as the red and green wires are usually used for the phone system, use the yellow and black wires (the remaining colors in a quad cable) for your network. Attach the stripped black wire to the terminal marked "B," and the stripped yellow wire to the terminal marked "Y" (see

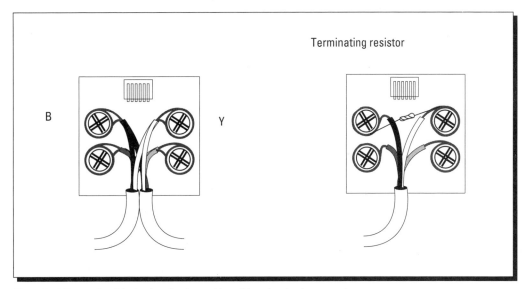

Figure 7-10: Exposed wall jacks showing the position of the wires for the network.

Figure 7-10). Mount the phone jack back into the wall and continue with the rest of your phone jacks. Be sure to install a 120-ohm terminating resistor between the black and yellow terminals of the wall jacks at each end of the bus cable, as shown in Figure 7-10. The wall jack on the right-hand side of the drawing shows where to install a terminating resistor.

To use the bus that you installed in the wall, all you need to do is plug a PhoneNET connector into your Mac (or other network device) and run a modular extension cable from the connector to the wall jack. You're now ready to use the network.

Note that because you've installed a terminating resistor at each end of the bus, you don't need any further terminating resistors. Thus, if you use regular PhoneNET connectors to connect a Mac to the wall jack, the unused RJ-11 socket in the connector should remain empty. Also, remember that you shouldn't use StarConnectors to connect devices to a bus.

In some cases, you may want a dual wall jack for your network connection so that you can use one plug for a phone and the other for the network. The process of connecting the wires is the same as described above, except that only the network wires are connected to one jack, whereas the phone wires are connected to the other jack (see Figure 7-11).

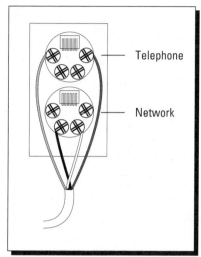

Figure 7-11: An exposed dual wall jack showing wire positions for the network and for the phone.

As we've said before, star networks are easily the most versatile topology and make troubleshooting simpler. We'll explain next what it takes to install both passive and active star networks.

Installing a Star Network

If you're installing either a passive or an active star network, you'll most likely be using the wiring, or utility, closets of your building. The utility closet is where the phone installers connect your office phones to the phone system. As we pointed out in the preceding chapter, the phone system also uses a star network to link together the phones in a building.

Initially, we'll assume that you are installing only one device per branch. Later, we'll explain the star's wiring options when you use more than one device per branch, but for this time around you won't add party lines. To set up a star, you need some type of wiring distribution block for connecting the network branches — we'll say that you're using a punchdown block rather than a patch panel.

Install the punchdown block on a wall in the utility closet; then pull a separate length of cable from the block to each wall jack that you intend to use. Wire each wall jack. For the moment, because you are installing one device per wall jack, you can simply cut the wire, strip the ends, and attach the wire ends to the terminals. If you're using regular PhoneNET Plus connectors, attach a terminating resistor to the wall jack terminals (refer again to Figure 7-10). If you use the newer StarConnectors, which are already terminated, you don't need to use a resistor in the wall jack.

If you want to connect a few wall jacks together to support more than one device per branch, you should wire the intermediate wall jacks using the same method as we described for the bus, stripping the wires without cutting them. The last wall jack in the branch can be connected to the cut ends of that wire run. Only the last wall jack in the run — the one farthest from the utility closet — should be terminated.

Most of what we've just described applies to both passive and active stars. But recall that in Chapter 6 we explained that there should be no more than four terminating resistors on a passive star, regardless of the number of branches. So take care if you're installing a passive star.

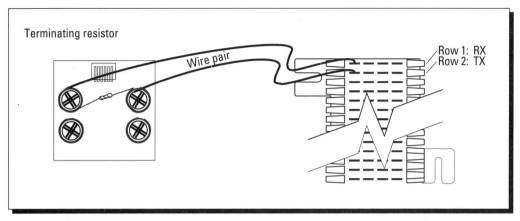

Figure 7-12: Wiring run from the phone jack to the punchdown block.

Back at the punchdown block, connect the wires coming from each wall jack to the block (see Figure 7-12). Yellow wires should be connected to one row of pins; black wires should be connected to the next row of pins. Now use a jumper wire to connect all the yellow wires together, and use a second jumper to connect all the black wires together. You now have a passive star. Farallon also offers a passive wiring kit, which includes a special jumper plug that mates with the punchdown block's Amphenol socket and eliminates the need for the jumper wires.

You may not be able to pull each wire pair separately, as you may have a number of wires that are simply connected to unmarked pins on a punchdown block in the utility closet. If so, you'll need to determine which wire pair goes to which wall jack or room. The best way to do this is to emulate telephone install-ers. Obtain a tone generator, which costs about $30 from wiring suppliers, and a listening unit, which costs around $50-$60. Attach the tone generator to the wire pair in one room, and then return to the utility closet with the listening unit. If you wave the listening unit like a wand over the pins of the punchdown block, you'll hear a tone. The tone gets louder as the listening unit gets closer to the pair that's connected to the tone generator. When you touch the wires with the listening unit, the tone is ear-splitting. You've just located the wire pair that leads to the desired room. Now, you need to move the tone generator to another wall jack and repeat the process until you've identified and labeled all pairs on the punchdown block.

If you've just completed a wiring layout for an active star network rather than a passive star, you don't run any jumper wires on the punchdown block. All you do is mount your active hub (a StarController, TurboStar, or LocalSwitch) nearby. Then, run a cable with Amphenol 50-pin plugs from the socket on the punchdown block to a similar socket on the active hub. Plug in the active hub, turn on the power, and your active star is ready for action.

Whether you use punchdown blocks or patch panels to create your star network, you can create a hierarchy of networks by combining active stars. This combination is especially effective when it comes to troubleshooting the physical layers of your network. For example, you may use one or more active stars to wire the networks on each floor of a building, and then connect each of those stars to a master hub for the entire building. A problem that occurs with one branch on a particular floor can be isolated from the rest of the network by shutting down that branch at its active hub. If the problem involves an entire workgroup wired to one active hub, you can isolate the workgroup by shutting down the branch that leads from the workgroup's hub to the master hub.

Testing the Network

Some of the simplest, but most useful, cabling tests that you can perform involve only an ohmmeter. Under the right conditions, you can use this instrument to determine if a cable is damaged or cut. We'll go through two exercises next, using an ohmmeter to test your network cables.

If you're testing wires that are connected to wall jacks, the first thing you should do is to create a test cable from a small piece of modular extension cable, of one to three feet in length. Install an RJ-11 plug on one end; strip one inch of insulation from the yellow and black wires at the other end. Then, after attaching the yellow and black leads to your ohmmeter, you can insert the RJ-11 end into the wall jack that you want to test.

Because you cannot have any PhoneNET connectors attached to the network when you're performing an ohmmeter test, it's a good idea to perform this test right after installing the cables. If you must use this test at a later time, you'll have to disconnect all your users from the network, a situation which can be bothersome to everyone. You can use diagnostic software to perform other tests that check a cable's continuity and do not involve physical changes to the network. Such tests are particularly useful for a fully installed network. For more information on such tests, see Chapter 14, "Fault Management."

To test a bus network, simply plug your test cable into a wall plug and measure the resistance (see Figure 7-13). The resistance should measure 60 ohms, plus about 30-50 ohms for every 1,000 feet of cable. If the resistance is infinite, your cable is cut or has suffered other damage. It may also simply be lacking a terminating resistor, so check this out before jumping to conclusions about the condition of your cable. On the other hand, if the measured resis-

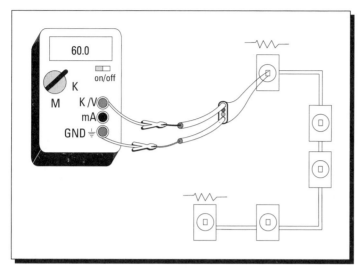

Figure 7-13: An ohmmeter used to test a bus cable.

tance is near zero or just 30-50 ohms per 1,000 feet of cable, you either have a shorted cable or you've left a PhoneNET connector plugged in somewhere along the cable. Obviously, the ohmmeter is not an infallible, definitive test, but it can point you in the right direction if you're checking cables.

With a star network, you can perform similar tests, except that you'll test at the punchdown block instead of at the wall jacks. Measure the resistance across the two pins that correspond to one wiring run; the resistance should measure 120 ohms, plus the usual 30-50 ohms for every 1,000 feet of cable. Again, if the resistance is infinite, the cable is either cut or lacks a terminating resistor. If your cable has been shorted, as with a bad crimp, the resistance will be near zero or approximately 30-50 ohms for every 1,000 feet of cable on the run. Don't forget that you may have left a PhoneNET connector plugged into the wiring run.

If you go back and plug a PhoneNET connector into the wall jack at the end of the wiring run, you should be able to measure a resistance between 0 and 100 ohms. If the resistance is more than 100 ohms, either you have a bad connection or the cable may be too long.

When you work with punchdown blocks, there's always a chance that the wiring installer has confused a network run with a phone line. If you can measure the DC voltage of a wiring run (using a voltmeter), you should measure no voltage on a network wire pair. On the other hand, if you're testing a live phone line, there will be some measurable voltage (not enough to harm you), and you know that someone has connected the wrong line to the network.

Setting Up Your Computers

Now that your network wiring is in place, you can start connecting your Macs and other network devices to the network. Remember that when you're using wall jacks that already have a terminating resistor installed in them, you should not install another terminating resistor in the PhoneNET connector. Also, recall that you should not use a StarConnector in such a case.

As we pointed out in previous chapters, AppleTalk devices such as the Mac and a LaserWriter dynamically poll the network to assign node numbers to themselves. This makes network startup easier for the user, but it can make matters trickier when you're troubleshooting the network later — and you *will* find yourself doing some troubleshooting later. A network doesn't see the node numbers change after the first time the devices are used and node numbers are assigned, because each device tries to use the same node number it had the last time it was turned on and attached to the network (see Chapter 2, "Understanding Networks").

You may be interested in assigning your own node numbers right from the start; perhaps you want to follow a particular scheme based on location. Farallon's NodeHint INIT is a handy utility that lets you pick a node number that the Mac will try to assign to itself whenever it starts up. Keeping a log of all node numbers and assigning them every time you attach a Mac to the network can work particularly well with LocalTalk and PhoneNET networks. This technique doesn't work with LaserWriters, of course, because you cannot install the INIT on a LaserWriter.

You may also want to assign specific names to each Mac and LaserWriter that is part of the network. In fact, if you have more than one LaserWriter, you *must* assign names to them.

Assigning a name to a Mac is easy. For Macs running System 6.0.x, simply select the Chooser DA and enter an appropriate name in the space provided (see Figure 7-14). Keep in mind, however, that anyone using that Mac can open the Chooser and change that name. If you want to prevent the name from being changed, get the public domain utility called ChooserUser. This utility lets the network administrator control who can change the name in the Chooser by setting a password to protect against any changes.

If you're running System 7 on your Mac, you need to choose **Control Panels** from the Apple menu and then open the **Sharing Setup** control panel. The part labeled **Network Identity** in the **Sharing Setup** window (see Figure 7-15) contains a field where you enter the name for your Mac.

Now turn on all your Macs and the LaserWriter. When your Mac is ready, select the Chooser DA (or extension if you're using System 7) from the Apple menu. At the lower right-hand side of the Chooser window, you'll see the word **AppleTalk** with two buttons, one marked **Inactive,** the other marked **Active** (see Figure 7-16). If the **Active** button isn't checked, check this now.

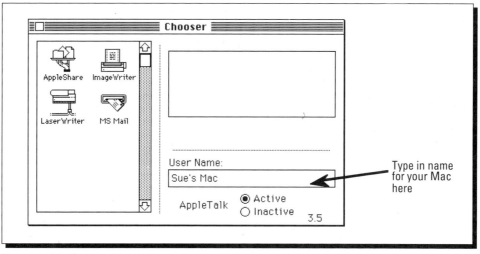

Figure 7-14: The Chooser shows where you name your Mac under System 6.0.x.

This step activates your Mac's built-in support for AppleTalk networking so that your Mac now becomes part of the network that you built.

To assign names to LaserWriters under System 6.0.x, use the Namer application that comes with the LaserWriter. Install this application on one Mac that is attached to the network. Turn on one LaserWriter at a time and run Namer to

Figure 7-15: The Sharing Setup extension shows where you name your Mac under System 7.

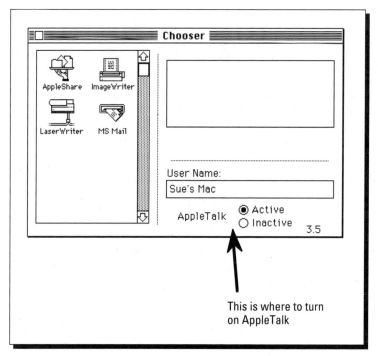

Figure 7-16: Choose the Active button to turn on AppleTalk.

assign a new name to that LaserWriter; simply cycle through each of the LaserWriters on your network. System 7 has a new application for naming LaserWriters — this application is called the LaserWriter Utility 7.0, but it does the same job as the Namer.

So far, we've talked only about attaching Macs and LaserWriters to your network. You may want to connect some DOS-based computers to your network as well. If you do, you'll need to install a LocalTalk card in each PC. These cards are available from Dayna Communications, Daystar Digital, and Farallon. The cards include software that allows a PC user to print to a LaserWriter and log into AppleShare file servers. Some readers may be familiar with the AppleShare PC card and software from Apple. That product was turned over to Farallon in 1990 for further development and is now being sold by Farallon as part of its PhoneNET Talk line.

Summary

This chapter introduced you to the types of cables, connectors, and added wiring devices that you can use for installing LocalTalk and PhoneNET networks. We also discussed wiring for daisy-chain, bus, and star networks.

In this chapter, you learned the following points:

✔ When selecting the cables and connectors for your network, you can choose from Apple's own LocalTalk kit or a popular alternative, PhoneNET.

✔ Making your own network cables may be your best bet especially if your network doesn't fit the standard length parameters offered in the ready-made kits.

✔ Wall jacks can be wired for bus and star networks.

✔ Various wiring devices, including the *harmonica block*, the *punchdown block*, and the *patch panel* can organize your wiring and make installation easier.

✔ Certain types of networks require terminating resistors to make the network run smoothly.

✔ You can assign a network name to individual Macs either through the built-in Chooser or by using the public-domain utility, ChooserUser.

In the next chapter, we'll address the design of Ethernet local area networks.

Chapter 8

Designing an Ethernet LAN

Running a network at the LocalTalk speed of 230 kbits/sec may not be fast enough for your needs, even on a well-designed network. The slow speed of LocalTalk just won't handle the large file transfers that you may need for CAD files, page-layout files, and 24-bit-deep color images. Nor will this speed accommodate multiple-user access to large databases.

Ethernet, which has been a network standard for some time, is a good upgrade path for providing faster networks for Mac users. Ethernet speeds up many network tasks for Mac users by a factor of three to five times, and the prices of interface cards have now dropped to a point where the added cost of $200-$300 per card is worth it. Ethernet cabling can be more expensive than LocalTalk wiring, but even that is changing, as Ethernet on twisted-pair cable has been standardized and is becoming more popular.

An Introduction to Ethernet

Ethernet is a set of protocols for only the two lowermost layers of the OSI Reference Model: the physical and the data link layers. The protocols of a network operating system, such as AppleTalk or TCP/IP, are then layered atop Ethernet to form a complete network.

But AppleTalk doesn't have to be the only protocol running on the Ethernet cable. Ethernet is called a *multiple protocol medium*. This means that Ethernet can support protocols from different network operating systems at the same time, a feature that adds to its versatility.

Ethernet packets include data about protocol types in order to distinguish among the various network operating systems. Thus you can have an Ethernet network with AppleTalk, DECnet, IPX, XNS, and TCP/IP protocols all being transmitted on the same cable without any extra effort on your part, although network management may be an issue. The AppleTalk machines know which protocols are for them, the DEC computers know that they should be handling DECnet (or TCP/IP), and so on down the line.

Three companies, Digital Equipment Corp. (DEC), Intel, and Xerox (known in networking circles collectively as "DIX"), were responsible for formulating the first working Ethernet networks and the specifications, published in the 1970s. These specifications have been upgraded since their original publications and are now known as the *Ethernet version 2 specifications*, which were published in 1982.

The IEEE (Institute of Electrical and Electronics Engineers) is a standards-making body that depends on the participation of many company representatives. Companies such as DEC, Intel, Xerox, and Apple, among others, cooperate in the formulation of electrical, communications, and networking standards. The IEEE is a neutral body and thus can obtain broader support for a standard from a variety of companies than if a similar standard were suggested by a single corporation, or even a set of corporations such as DIX. Many standards defined by the IEEE often find their way into similar standards from the ISO (International Standards Organization; see Chapter 3, "Understanding AppleTalk Protocols").

Although the DIX Ethernet specifications predate those from the IEEE, we'll take a look at the IEEE specifications first, because we discuss these most frequently in this book. The IEEE Ethernet standards fall within a category called the Project 802 standards, which include both Ethernet and token ring networking standards; these standards are structured in a typical layered scheme, as in the OSI Reference Model, as you can see in Figure 8-1. The Ethernet standards are labeled *802.3* in the diagram. Note the layer labeled *802.2: Logical Link Control*. This is the specification that allows network running different media to *interoperate,* or to exchange data. AppleTalk's support of LLC came in Phase 2 and was discussed in Chapter 3, "Understanding AppleTalk Protocols.")

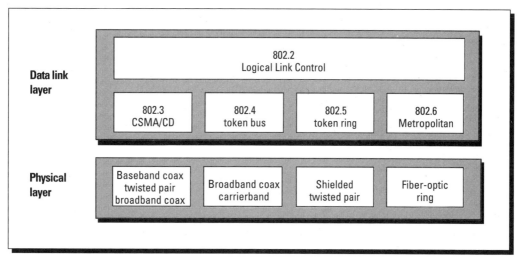

Figure 8-1: The IEEE 802.x networking standards.

The IEEE 802.3 Ethernet standards currently include five 802.3 specifications:

1. 10Base5, also called *thicknet*

2. 10Base2, also called *thinnet*

3. 10Broad36, also called *broadband Ethernet*

4. 1Base5, also called *Starlan*

5. 10BaseT, also called *UTP Ethernet*

A standard for Ethernet over fiber-optic cable is currently being formulated; this standard will be called 10BaseF. See Table 8-1 for a summary of the main features of these standards.

Table 8-1: IEEE Ethernet Specifications

Specification	Medium	# Devices	Max. Segment Length (meters)
10Base5 (thicknet)	coaxial cable	100	500
10Base2 (thinnet)	RG58 coaxial cable	30	189
10BaseT (UTP)	unshielded twisted-pair	1 per branch	100
10Broad36	RG9 CATV coaxial cable	1,023	3,800

The labels used by the IEEE to distinguish the different types of Ethernet (10Base2, 10BaseT, and so on) form a shorthand notation for the salient features of each specification. Each label covers the type of signal transmission, the speed of the network, and the maximum distance of a network segment. In the last case, though, the IEEE has deviated from its older conventions, using the *T* in 10BaseT to signify the type of cable. We'll review next the features used to define these networks.

Ethernet networks can propagate signals in one of two ways — baseband or broadband transmissions. *Baseband* means that the signal is transmitted at its original frequency without modulation. Baseband uses digital signaling, as opposed to the analog signaling used by broadband systems. *Broadband* networks use the same type of cables and transmission devices as cable TV and implement a range of frequencies for transmission. In the IEEE labels, *Base* tells you that the network uses baseband transmission, whereas *Broad* tells you that this is broadband.

The number prefix represents the transmission speed in Megabits per second (Mbits/sec). Most Ethernet networks run at a speed of 10 Mbits/sec. An older version that currently is little used is the Starlan network, which has a transmission speed of 1 Mbit/sec.

The suffix after Base or Broad tells you the approximate maximum length of a network segment in 100s of meters (some rounding of numbers is used in assigning the labels, as you can see for 10Base2 in Table 8-1). In the 10BaseT specification, the *T* stands for *twisted*, as in twisted-pair wire, so this is a qualitative term, rather than a distance limit. 10BaseT is commonly referred to as *UTP Ethernet*, where *UTP* stands for *u*nshielded *t*wisted-*p*air.

Although the IEEE labels do not include information about the number of devices that you can install on an Ethernet network, certain limits exist that vary with the medium you use. These limits are shown in Table 8-1. 10Base5 and 10Broad36 can accommodate the largest number of devices per network segment. As you'll see, 10BaseT networks are multibranch star networks, where the only limit on the number of devices is the capacity of the active hub used for the star.

We mentioned previously that, in fact, two different standards exist for Ethernet — the IEEE 802.3 standard and the DIX, or Ethernet version 2, standard. An important difference between the IEEE 802.3 and Ethernet version 2 standards is the packet format. If you compare the two packet types, as shown in Figure 8-2, you'll see that the Type field used in Ethernet version 2 to specify protocol types (XNS, AppleTalk, DECnet, and so on) is located

IEEE 802.3 packet format

Destination	Source	Length	Data	CRC
6 bytes	6 bytes	2 bytes	46-1500 bytes	4 bytes

Ethernet 2 packet format

Destination	Source	Type	Data	CRC
6 bytes	6 bytes	2 bytes	46-1500 bytes	4 bytes

Figure 8-2: A comparison of the Ethernet 2 and IEEE 802.3 Ethernet packet formats.

where the Length field is in the IEEE 802.3 packets. This means that a network device obtains incorrect information if it expects one type of Ethernet packet (Ethernet version 2, for example), but in fact receives the other type of packet (IEEE 802.3). To alleviate this problem, some implementations of Ethernet drivers are smart enough to handle both types of Ethernet packets at the same time.

This difference in packet format can cause problems in AppleTalk networks. Apple's original specifications for EtherTalk used the Ethernet version 2 packet format; then Apple switched to IEEE 802.3 for AppleTalk Phase 2 (see Figure 8-3). This becomes a problem when you use an Ethernet bridge, as is common in large corporate networks, to filter out AppleTalk packets and then switch some, or all, of your AppleTalk networks to Phase 2. If you want to continue filtering AppleTalk, you'll have to reconfigure the filtering bridge for the IEEE 802.3 packets carrying AppleTalk data. (See Chapters 12, "Making the Phase 2 Move," and Chapter 16, "Configuration Management," for more details.)

Now that we've reviewed the different Ethernet standards and the differences in packet formats, we'll explain what cables can be used for Ethernet and what network topologies you can build with these cables.

Cabling and Network Topologies

Ethernet packets are routinely transmitted over both electrical media, such as coaxial cable and twisted-pair wires, and optical media, such as fiber-optic cable. You can create larger networks by connecting Ethernet networks with microwave

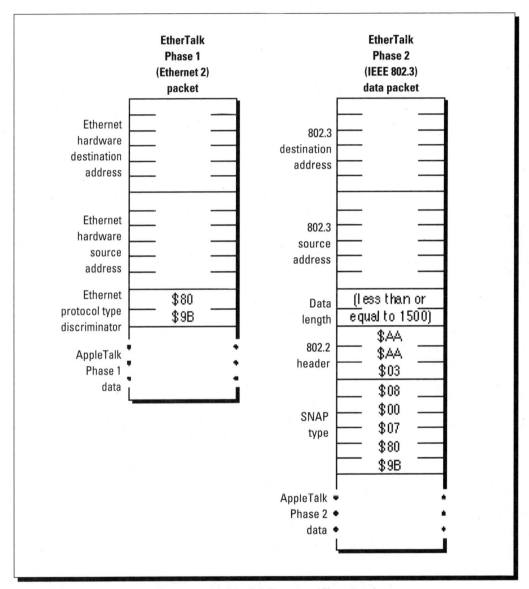

Figure 8-3: The format differences between Apple's EtherTalk Phase 1 and Phase 2 packets.

or laser links. And, within the past year, vendors such as Motorola, with its Altair system, have made it possible to use wireless (radio-frequency) links within offices to tie together workstations using Ethernet technology.

Four transmission media for Ethernet are currently popular: thick coaxial cable (10Base5), thin coaxial cable (10Base2), twisted-pair cable (10BaseT), and

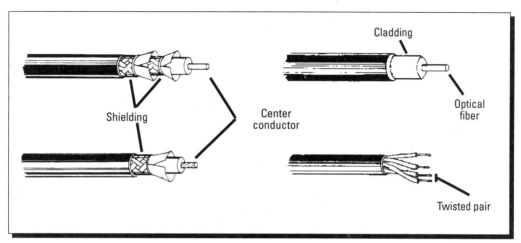

Figure 8-4: Types of cables for Ethernet.

fiber-optic cable (see Figure 8-4). Each of these media poses restrictions on the network topologies you can use for your Ethernet network.

When 10Base5 thick coax cable was first standardized for Ethernet, there were few, if any, workstations and PCs around. Network installers routinely ran thick coax as a bus for connecting a series of mainframe computers or minicomputers. Thick coax is still used primarily as a bus or backbone network to connect either subnetworks or buildings. In many cases, newer installations are using fiber-optic cable for Ethernet (among other protocols, such as FDDI, or Fiber Distributed Interface) as a backbone cable.

Thin coax, or 10Base2, is also primarily used to create bus networks, although it is restricted to shorter lengths than with 10Base5. In addition, thinnet multiport repeaters can also be used to create stars out of thin coax cabling.

An appealing Ethernet medium for an office workgroup environment is unshielded twisted-pair cable, the wire used in many phone installations. However, unlike thicknet or thinnet Ethernet, UTP Ethernet requires additional hardware to create a complete network. UTP Ethernet requires an active controller, or *hub*. This hub contains control circuitry for monitoring the condition of each UTP branch, as well as the repeater circuitry for amplifying the Ethernet signal for each port. Only one device can be connected to each port of the hub, so no daisy-chaining of devices is allowed with 10BaseT. Recently, vendors have started to offer multiport repeaters for 10BaseT, enabling you to connect more than one device to a 10BaseT branch.

The hubs currently offered for 10BaseT Ethernet offer further advantages to the network designer. Because the hubs can be connected to each other, several star networks can be arranged in a hierarchy, so network management and troubleshooting can progress from the top downward to the subordinate networks. Many hubs are built on a chassis that contains extra slots for modules that connect to other media. This makes it a simple task to connect your UTP Ethernet star network to fiber-optic or thicknet Ethernet backbones.

The wiring normally called for in 10BaseT is 26 to 22 AWG, which corresponds to the wire gauge of telephone twisted-pair cables. Remember that you need two pairs of wiring for each node. Before you think seriously about using your existing phone wiring for an Ethernet network, however, look before you leap. Older cabling may not be of sufficient quality to support the full 100 meters between a device and the hub. Or your wiring contractor may have used substandard wiring that's not capable of transmitting the 10-Mbps Ethernet signal without heavy noise and other interference.

Once again, good planning can help prevent problems in the future. If you're working with an existing wiring plant, be sure that each run you plan to use for the network is capable of handling Ethernet signals. Making the proper measurements (such as with a time domain reflectometer or other measurement devices) can tell how much you should expect from your existing wiring. Make sure that you know where the wires go — do they pass sources of intermittent noise, such as heavy machinery or elevators? Checking each length at different times of the day helps to discover problems now, so that you won't have to deal with them later. Some substandard wiring may still be used if its length is less than the maximum recommended by the 10BaseT standard. But if you have any doubts about the wire, don't use it — you'll save yourself much grief later.

The advantages of UTP Ethernet

Because UTP Ethernet connects nodes at an active hub or *concentrator*, this type of Ethernet network is advantageous for network management. The star topology joins the legs to a common hub, so diagnosis of network problems is simple. Each leg of the star can be individually isolated and tested at the hub to determine which one is causing the problem, and then the defective leg can be disconnected for repairs without affecting the rest of the network. The bus topology, used for thickwire and thinwire Ethernet, is more complex to troubleshoot because it requires continuity of the entire network; disconnecting any segment breaks all network operations.

For any of the cabling schemes we've described, you can install a repeater to amplify the signal whenever excessive length of the network becomes a problem. Recall that the repeater is a physical layer device (see Chapter 2) and, as such, it does not filter network addresses or any of the network signals. Be aware that Ethernet limits you to two repeaters per network. When you must subdivide the network to control network traffic, you can use routers, which we discuss in more detail in Chapter 11, "Designing an AppleTalk LAN."

Selecting Macintosh Ethernet Hardware

When we described the options for connecting Macs to a LocalTalk network in Chapters 6 and 7, you saw that options for making a connection depended only on the wiring you selected — you had only to select the proper connection box. One reason for this is Apple's inclusion of the LocalTalk transceiver within every Mac that's shipped. With Ethernet, the story is a bit more complicated because the type of Ethernet cable you use determines what type of network interface you'll need. Ethernet transceivers are designed differently for each type of cable.

You can use one of three approaches for connecting a Mac to Ethernet. You can use a router to connect a LocalTalk network to Ethernet; you can use an external device that connects to a single Mac via either the SCSI port or a serial port; or you can use an internal card for a single Mac. We'll briefly explain each in turn.

Using a router to connect LocalTalk to Ethernet

If you're interested in connecting two or more LocalTalk networks via an Ethernet backbone, you should use a router. Among other routers available for this are the Shiva FastPath, Cayman Systems' GatorBox, Compatible Systems' Ether•Route, NRC LT2000E, Apple's AppleTalk Internet Router, and Farallon PhoneNET Liaison. The first four are hardware routers, and the latter two are software for installation on a Mac. Each product is capable of sending and receiving AppleTalk packets inside Ethernet packets.

Using an external device

The second alternative is designed with a single Mac in mind, which is to use an external box that connects to either the Mac's SCSI port or its printer port. Most of these devices are designed for use with the Mac's SCSI ports, but one from Dayna is available for connecting to your Mac's printer port. For the SCSI-based devices, you either plug the box into your Mac's SCSI port or make the box a part of your daisy-chain of SCSI devices; then install the Ethernet driver software and plug the box into your Ethernet network. Installing a serial-based box is much the same, except that you plug the box into the Mac's printer port and then install the software.

When should you use one of these external interfaces? First, think of all those Mac Pluses and Classics with no expansion slots in them. Second, you may have a Mac SE or SE/30 with its single slot already allocated to another board, possibly an accelerator or a second monitor. The external boxes are excellent choices for Ethernet connectivity in either of these cases. Also, you may want to select an external box for a Mac Portable or PowerBook, as no vendors currently offer an internal Ethernet board for the portable Macs.

Using an internal card for a single Mac

Last, but most important, are the internal Ethernet cards for any of the Mac LC, Mac SE, Mac SE/30, or the Mac II series. As you'll see in a later section on Ethernet performance, your Mac can achieve its best Ethernet performance by using an internal card.

The common Ethernet adapter cards support both 10Base5 and 10Base2, so it's easy to use these cards to connect a Mac to an existing Ethernet network. Thinnet Ethernet is probably the most popular form of Ethernet at the moment, but 10BaseT systems are likely to become the favored wiring scheme for new offices and workgroups. Many of the newer cards are available with either 10Base5 and 10BaseT connectors or 10Base2 and 10BaseT connectors; some cards now offer all three connectors on a single card.

If you're short of internal slots, as with the Mac IIsi, you can now purchase multi-function cards from some of the video monitor manufacturers, such as E-Machines and Mobius Technologies; these cards combine the video interface for an external monitor with Ethernet support. Asante has also developed an Ethernet card that piggybacks onto a Radius video interface card for use in the IIsi.

Selecting media adapters

We noted that many vendors now either support 10BaseT as an option or have added it as a standard part on their Ethernet cards. If you're already using an Ethernet network and switching to 10BaseT because of office expansion or relocation, you can use your older Ethernet interfaces for 10BaseT by buying a media adapter.

These 10BaseT media adapters are designed to plug into a 10Base5 socket and accept an RJ-45 plug with 10BaseT wiring. With these converters, you can use your existing Ethernet units (cards, external boxes, or routers) without any need to upgrade further.

With its new Ethernet Cabling System, Apple also anticipated that you may on occasion want to change your network media. The new Apple EtherTalk cards do not include an on-board transceiver or socket for a particular Ethernet cable; instead the cards have a special interface port called the AAUI (Apple Attachment Unit Interface) into which you plug a special media adapter/transceiver box. This approach lets you change network media just by changing the external adapter/transceiver box, but it offers no particular advantage over some of the current Ethernet cards that other vendors offer with all three (10Base5, 10Base2, 10BaseT) connectors on a single card.

Note that Apple's AAUI is the standard method for connecting the new Mac Quadras and the LaserWriter IIg to Ethernet. These devices have built-in support for Ethernet, but do not include transceivers.

Connecting Laser Printers to Ethernet

One of the most popular devices on any network is the laser printer. But most laser printers, including Apple's LaserWriters, include only a LocalTalk port for connection to a network. If you're working with a mixed network of LocalTalk and Ethernet, that's all right, because you can always place your laser printers on a LocalTalk segment of the network.

But what do you do if you're using only Ethernet cabling? A few laser printer models are now available with built-in Ethernet support; these models are Apple's LaserWriter IIg, Hewlett-Packard's LaserJet IIIsi, and Talaris' PrintStation. However, most laser printers on the market require another method for connecting to Ethernet. For those laser printers without built-in Ethernet connections, you can use either software installed on your Mac or self-contained hardware to connect a laser printer to an Ethernet network.

The software for connecting laser printers to Ethernet are software routers for AppleTalk: These are Apple's AppleTalk Internet Router and Farallon's Liaison. Both can be installed to run in the background on a Mac that has both LocalTalk and Ethernet connections. The Ethernet connection is the connection normally used by the Mac, whereas the LocalTalk connection is used for the laser printer. This is a reasonable, low-cost solution, but bear in mind that the availability of the link depends on the reliability of the Mac running the router software; if the Mac becomes unavailable, as during a system crash, users will be unable to access the laser printer.

A more reliable solution is to use hardware that is solely dedicated to the task of linking LocalTalk-based laser printers to an Ethernet network. The EtherPrint/EtherPrint Plus series from Dayna Communications and Ether•Write from Compatible Systems are just such devices. They contain anywhere from one to six LocalTalk ports for laser printers and one Ethernet port for attaching to the network. These are not full-functioned AppleTalk routers (see Chapter 11, "Designing an AppleTalk LAN"), so they shouldn't be used for other devices (such as Macs), but they do the job of connecting laser printers to Ethernet quite well. Of course, you can also buy AppleTalk routers to perform the same function as these printer interfaces do, but the routers generally are two to four times more expensive and aren't worth considering for this task unless you have devices other than laser printers to attach to the LocalTalk ports.

Another solution, which we'll discuss in detail in Chapter 19, "Using Printers on the Network," and Chapter 25, "Sharing Printers and Files with Other Platforms," is to use a computer as print server, attaching the computer to the Ethernet network and the laser printer to the print server/computer.

Understanding Ethernet Performance

When you're transferring large graphics images or CAD files, using a large multiuser database, or simply adding more users to your network, the 10-Megabit/sec speed of Ethernet can be mighty appealing. But be careful — just because Ethernet transmits data 44 times faster than LocalTalk's 230-kilobit/sec speed, file transfers between two Macs won't be accomplished 40 times faster, because most of today's computers cannot send or receive data that quickly.

Differences in Ethernet hardware

If you read articles about Ethernet board performance for MS-DOS computers, you'll note that the authors spend much time discussing buffer sizes, bus architectures, and the width of the data bus. Partly because of the uniformity of the Mac's bus architecture, there's less variation in Ethernet board performance among Macs than for IBMs and compatibles.

While working with Macworld Labs, we noted little difference in performance among the various Ethernet boards for a given type of Mac. Despite differences in data bus width (16 bits vs. 32 bits) and RAM buffers for caching packets (8K to 32K), all the boards performed about the same under such typical conditions as when transferring data from a hard disk. In general, you can use Ethernet to increase your data throughput by a factor of five over the throughput rate for LocalTalk.

The cause appears to be the Mac operating system's control of the SCSI bus and the hard disk. As long as data is transferred through the Mac's SCSI Manager, the rate of data transfer from a hard disk through the CPU and onto the Ethernet is fairly constant. Even when we tried using an SCSI accelerator card — one employing DMA (Direct Memory Access) to the CPU — we noted little improvement in the transfer rates. This means that with the current system (either 6.0.x or 7.0) there's very little reason to pick one Ethernet interface card over another because of its features.

In certain situations, the more advanced cards, such as those using a 32-bit data path, can be used to good advantage. When we tested the boards by transferring data directly from the RAM of one Mac to the RAM of another, there was a noticeable difference between boards. Thus, if you're using a database or other distributed application that loads much of its code and data into memory, your best bets for an Ethernet card are those from Asante, Cayman, and Interlan. These cards all have a data bus width of 32 bits. This advantage can also extend to Macs running A/UX, which doesn't use the SCSI Manager to control disk access. Some programs that do depend more on Ethernet card speed and CPU speed rather than file-access rates are windowing software, such as MacX (Apple Computer Inc.) and eXodus (White Pine Software Inc.). These X Windows server programs receive a large number of commands and data over the network from the X Windows client in order to create a display.

Another thing to keep in mind when considering board performance is the type of network you'll be on. For a large network with heavy traffic performing large file transfers (24-bit color images, for example), you may get slightly better performance from boards with larger buffer sizes. Some vendors offer boards with at least two sizes. Regular applications don't need the extra buffer, but large file transfers, A/UX, and X Windows can benefit from the increased buffer size.

Differences among interfaces

The results of our Ethernet tests at Macworld labs are summarized in Figure 8-5. In the figure, we compare the performance you can expect from Macs running on Ethernet to the same Mac on LocalTalk. We chose to divide the results according to the type of device that you'd use to connect a Mac to Ethernet: LocalTalk-to-EtherTalk routers, SCSI-based external boxes, and internal cards. The rectangles with square corners represent SCSI-based external interfaces, whereas the rounded rectangles represent Macs with internal Ethernet adapter boards.

If you glance at the figure, you'll see that routers behave about the same as a LocalTalk network. That's because the bottleneck for LocalTalk-to-Ethernet routers is the LocalTalk network that they're attached to. A router's best advantage is that you can use it to connect a network of Macs to Ethernet without buying an interface card or a box for each Mac. This is particularly useful if you anticipate only occasional use of the Ethernet network by each Mac user.

The figure also indicates that the SCSI-based Ethernet interfaces are slower than internal cards. We believe that this is due to the Mac's use of the SCSI bus, which transmits data at a slower rate than either the Nubus interface found in Mac IIs or the PDS (Processor-Direct Slot) found in the Mac SE and SE/30 models.

Differences among Macs

By looking only at the results obtained using internal cards, we can compare the performance of different Mac models. As expected, the Mac SE/30 performs about the same as the Mac IIcx when both are using internal cards because they use the same microprocessor. Once again, this shows that the data bus (Nubus vs. PDS) is not the controlling factor in disk transfers to and from Ethernet because the SE/30 and the Mac IIcx use different buses. Although we haven't run a full suite of tests with the newer Macs, such as the Mac IIsi, we expect the IIsi to perform similarly to the SE/30, as its processor is only 25 percent faster than that of the SE/30s. Thus, the Mac SE/30 and the newer Mac IIsi can be good server machines for a network.

The IIci and IIfx Macs are strange beasts. Because the Mac IIci has built-in video, some of the microprocessor's compute cycles must be devoted to handling video-related events that would ordinarily be performed by intelligence on a video card. When we tested Ethernet performance, a Mac IIci using the built-in video performed the same as a Mac IIcx. Installing a video card in the IIci improved its Ethernet performance by about 15 to 20 percent, which is about the same improvement others have noted for non-network-related IIci benchmarks.

If you thought that the Mac IIfx would make a super server for your Ethernet network, think again. Certainly, its 40-MHz clock speed is an impressive sounding improvement over the rest of the Mac line, running at 16, 20, or 25 MHz. But, thanks to the SCSI Manager software currently used in Systems 6.0.x and 7, the IIfx isn't much faster than the IIci for file transfers over the network. Other tests that we've seen with AppleShare 3.0 indicate that the Mac IIci and IIfx are roughly equivalent in performance, and that the new Quadra 900 is about 50 percent faster than either the IIci or IIfx.

As an Ethernet workstation, a Mac SE with an internal card offers about 75 percent of the performance of either a Mac SE/30 or a IIcx. For RAM-to-RAM data transfers, the discrepancy can become even wider, running as low as 34 percent, when comparing the worst SE card to the best IIcx card.

On the whole, if you're concerned primarily with file transfers or other activities involving your Mac's hard disk, you'll get a performance increase for the Mac II series of up to five times of that offered by LocalTalk by going to Ethernet. For a Mac Plus or Classic with an external SCSI interface, the perfor-

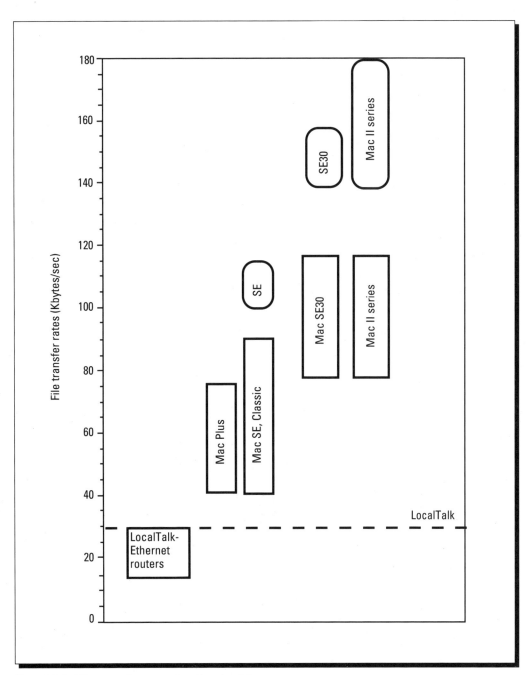

Figure 8-5: An Ethernet performance chart for various Macs.

mance increase is about double; for the Mac SE, it's threefold with an external interface, and with an internal card the increase is 3.7. For those whose work involves large memory-based transfers over the network, such as with X Windows, you can expect speed gains as high as 11 times that of LocalTalk.

When you're comparing our results to your own network experiences, bear in mind that these numbers represent upper limits for each process (disk-based transfers and RAM-based transfers). Much like the EPA's mpg ratings, the numbers represent unique, though standardized, conditions that most likely are not the same for your circumstances. Use these figures as a comparative guide, realizing that your mileage may vary.

Summary

In this chapter, we've presented a historical overview of the development of Ethernet networking standards. Then, we explained how various cabling types can be used in different network topologies. The following points were covered:

✓ IEEE 802.3 and Ethernet version 2 use different packet formats.

✓ For Ethernet, you can use two types of coaxial cable or unshielded twisted-pair (UTP) or fiber-optic cable.

✓ Thicknet and thinnet Ethernet are usually wired in bus topologies, whereas UTP Ethernet uses an active hub and is wired as a star.

✓ Macs can be connected to an Ethernet network with a router, an external box using the SCSI or serial port, or an internal card.

✓ Macs on Ethernet perform network tasks about five times faster than on a LocalTalk network.

In the following chapter, we'll cover the details of installing cables, connectors, and other hardware for a working Ethernet LAN.

Chapter 9

Installing an Ethernet LAN

Installation of an Ethernet LAN for a few Macs isn't much different from a LocalTalk LAN installation, although the number of products and vendors for Ethernet is far greater in the marketplace than for LocalTalk.

Chapter 8, "Designing an Ethernet LAN," introduced you to the types of cables that can be used to create Ethernet networks. In this chapter, we'll get into the details of installing the cables and the connectors that you'll need to connect your Macs to Ethernet. Then, we'll discuss the types of Ethernet transceivers, how to connect these transceivers to the cables, and then how to connect your Macs to Ethernet.

Installing Ethernet Media

When you install an Ethernet network, you need to consider three aspects of the network hardware: the type of cabling that you want to use, the methods that you'll use for tapping into the network cable, and the type of transceiver you'll use for your Mac. First, we'll show you how to select and install Ethernet cables and connectors, and then we'll explain how to attach various types of cables, taps, and transceivers to the Ethernet cable.

Installing cables and connectors

As we pointed out in Chapter 8, there is more than one cabling standard for Ethernet networks — thick coax, or *thicknet;* thin coax, or *thinnet;* and unshielded

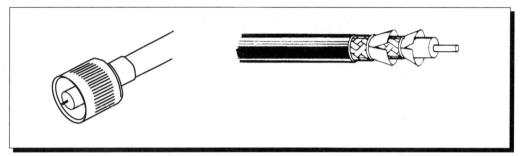

Figure 9-1: 10Base5 Cable and N-type connector.

twisted-pair. Fiber-optic cable is also used with Ethernet networks.
In this section, we're going to concentrate on three popular media for Ethernet: thick coaxial cable for 10Base5, thin coaxial cable for 10Base2, and twisted-pair cable for 10BaseT. We won't include fiber-optic cable in this discussion. Fiber-optic cable requires special installation procedures that are best left to professionals.

10Base5 coaxial cable

Thick coaxial cable for 10Base5, the original Ethernet medium, uses a 50-ohm coaxial cable as the backbone for the network. The cable has an outer diameter of 0.37 to 0.41 inches, depending on the type of insulation; also note that the 10Base5 cable has two layers of shielding (see Figure 9-1). Many vendors offer 10Base5 cable according to the DEC cable number as a cross-reference. In this case, the cable is called BNE2A (plenum cable) or BNE2B (PVC insulation).

Each thicknet cable segment is limited to 500 meters and can support no more than 100 transceivers per segment. You can link cable segments with repeaters to create even larger networks, provided that the greatest distance between the two most-distant nodes of the network is no more than 2.5 kilometers and also that you don't use more than two repeaters between bridges or routers.

Thick coax is available in either pre-made standard lengths or on a reel for making your own cables. Standard pre-made lengths are 23.4, 70.2, 117, and 500 meters (76.8, 230.3, 383.9, and 1,640.5 feet).

Thick coaxial cable has a few limitations. First, it's harder to install, especially around corners, than other cable types, because it is more difficult to bend without damaging the internal wires. Second, the cable requires a transceiver and a carefully placed tap to link a device to the network. If you're using thicknet cable, you must also run a transceiver cable, or *drop cable,* from your

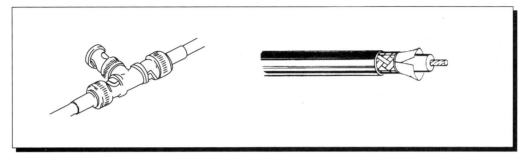

Figure 9-2: 10Base2 Cable and BNC-type tee connector.

Mac's Ethernet interface board to the transceiver that's attached to the coaxial cable. The drop cable can be no longer than 50 meters in length.

Thick coaxial cable uses N-type connectors. Adding the N-type connectors to the ends of cables is a somewhat complicated process. To connect an N-type connector to thick coax, you'll need cable cutters, wire strippers, and a soldering iron; you may also need a crimping tool, as you'll see in a moment.

The dielectric separates the shielding (foil or braid) from the central conductor. The amount of shield and dielectric you cut away to reveal the central conductor depends on the manufacturer of the connector, so check the specifications that come with the connectors. After stripping the outer insulation, you'll need to roll back the braid to expose the dielectric and central conductor; the braided shield makes contact with the outer sleeve of the connector through a series of washers that are squeezed together when you screw the outer sleeve over the end of the connector assembly. The central conductor is either soldered or crimped to a central pin, depending on the connector's manufacturer.

10Base2 coaxial cable

Coaxial cable for 10Base2, or thinnet, is quite popular because it is more flexible and less expensive than thickwire and because it can be used without large transceivers and taps (see Figure 9-2). Thinnet coax cable is also a 50-ohm coaxial cable, but it has a smaller diameter than thicknet coax — thinnet coax is 0.20 inches in outer diameter. DEC's thin coax H8243 is PVC insulated cable, and its H8244 is plenum-rated cable.

Thin Ethernet cable has a maximum limit of 189 meters, with fewer stations on the cable than for a thicknet segment; thin Ethernet cable allows 30 devices, as compared to 100 devices for thicknet. Note that a tee connector (for a transceiver) and a barrel connector both count as a device. Like thicknet, thinnet cannot have more than two repeaters between bridges or routers. There must be a distance of at least 0.5 meters (19 inches) between transceivers.

You can purchase thin coax either in pre-made standard lengths or on a reel for making your own cables. Standard pre-made lengths are 1.8, 4.5, and 9 meters (6, 15, and 30 feet).

Adding the BNC connectors to the ends of cables is also a fairly involved process. After stripping the outer insulation, you have to roll back the braid to expose the dielectric and inner conductor and then solder the conductor to the BNC connector. Then you screw down the outer sleeve of the connector over the braid. As with the N-type connector, the central pin can be either soldered or crimped to the central conductor of the cable. The process takes some time until you become accustomed to doing it and certainly isn't as easy as crimping RJ-11 or RJ-45 jacks onto twisted-pair cable.

If you're somewhat concerned about the bultk of thinnet cable lying throughout your office, you can extend a thinnet cable with twisted-pair wire by using a *balun*. Baluns derive their name from their purpose, as they *bal*ance the *un*balanced impedances of the two types of cable, minimizing signal reflections and other losses. Many cabling vendors offer Ethernet baluns to link thinnet and twisted-pair cable.

Using a thinnet-to-twisted-pair balun is not the same as wiring your office for unshielded twisted-pair Ethernet (10BaseT). When you use baluns, you're merely substituting one type of cable for another. You'll need two baluns for each length of twisted-pair cable, one for the end that adjoins the rest of the thinnet network, and the other for the connection at your Mac. Also, baluns restrict you to shorter lengths of twisted-pair cable than does 10BaseT. The limit is usually around 150 feet instead of 330 feet and varies with the type of twisted-pair wire and the balun manufacturer. Note that with baluns, unlike 10BaseT, only a single pair is required.

10BaseT unshielded twisted-pair

10BaseT networks are designed only to be installed as an active star. Each branch of the star from the network device to the 10BaseT hub, or *concentrator,* is limited to 100 meters. The wiring normally specified in 10BaseT is 26 to 22 AWG with solid copper conductors, a wiring setup which corresponds to many telephone twisted-pair cables. Remember that you'll need two pairs of wiring for each node (see Figure 9-3).

Be sure to check any preexisting cable that you intend to use for 10BaseT. Older cabling may not be of adequate quality to support the full 100 meters

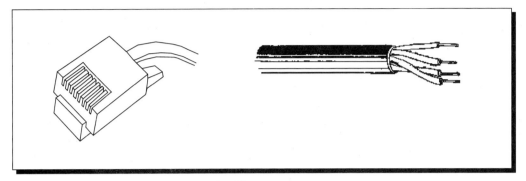

Figure 9-3: An RJ-45 jack and two-pair twisted-pair cable.

between a device and the hub. Or you may have substandard wiring that cannot transmit the 10-Mbps Ethernet signal without interference.

When you're wiring your network, you should take care not to run any other data traffic (especially from another network, such as token ring) on the same cable; the unshielded twisted pairs are not protected from interference from other, non-Ethernet, signals that may be generated within the same cable bundle.

If you use standard phone wire to install your 10BaseT Ethernet network, the insulation color codes for each wire in the bundle make it easy to keep pairs together. All telephone pairs are color coded. For instance, standard four-pair station cable contains orange, blue, green, and brown pairs, which are identified as follows (a stripe is a thin band of color):

Orange pair
   White wire with orange stripe
   Orange wire with white stripe

Blue pair
   White wire with blue stripe
   Blue wire with white stripe

Green pair
   White wire with green stripe
   Green wire with white stripe

Brown pair
   White wire with brown stripe
   Brown wire with white stripe

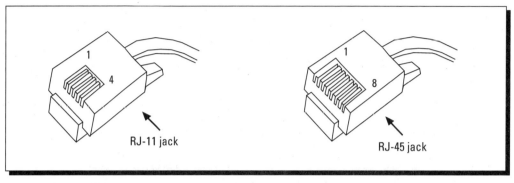

Figure 9-4: RJ-11 and RJ-45 jacks.

Usually, phone installers use the blue and the orange pairs to connect a phone system to a wall jack, leaving the green and brown pairs unused. Check with your phone installer to make certain that you know which wire pairs are unused before you install your network using existing wire. Double-check the wires used in your installation by investigating the wall jacks in a few scattered locations throughout the building on your own.

When wiring your connections, take precautions against splitting pairs. In other words, be sure that you maintain the same color mates for each pair used within the cable. If you don't follow a common color pairing, you'll most likely mix up the wires and the Ethernet signal won't be transmitted. This is particularly important with 10BaseT Ethernet, which uses one pair of wires as the transmitting pair and the other as the receiving pair.

Connections are made with RJ-45 plugs, those eight-conductor cousins of the familiar RJ-11 plugs (see Figure 9-4). Your home phone system probably uses at least one RJ-11 jack. Be careful when selecting the plugs, because without careful examination, the two plugs look confusingly similar; their main distinguishing feature is the number of conductor blades at the end of the jack. The RJ-11 jack has only four conductors, but the RJ-45 jack has eight. 10BaseT specifications expect the transmitting pair to be connected to pins 1 and 2, and the receiving pair connected to pins 3 and 6 (see Figure 9-5).

Installation tips

When you're installing coaxial cables of over 50 meters, it's a good idea to divide the cable into shorter segments with barrel connectors (see Figure 9-6). Then, if something goes wrong, you need only to replace a short segment of cable. Dividing the network into short sections also makes it easier to diagnose network problems. For a diagnostic test, replace the barrel connector with two

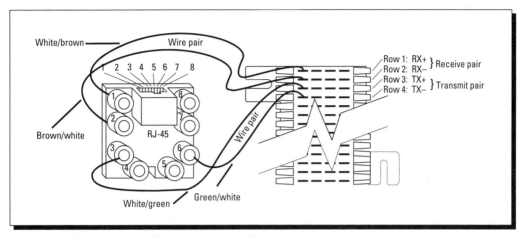

Figure 9-5: A wiring run from a wall jack to a punchdown block.

terminators (one for each cable, of course), and then check to see how the two new networks perform. We call this the *divide-and-conquer* method of network diagnosis (see Chapter 14, "Fault Management").

But don't just randomly pick any length for subdividing segments. The IEEE recommends that Ethernet coaxial cable be subdivided at lengths of 23.4 meters (76.8 feet), or multiples of that length, in order to minimize internal signal reflections. These reflections will reduce the signal strength for large networks. On small networks, such as those covering a single floor of a building, these reflections probably won't cause problems.

When you're wiring your network, remember that coaxial-cable Ethernet segments must be terminated at both ends with 50-ohm resistors, and that one end of the network should be grounded to earth or building ground. Don't

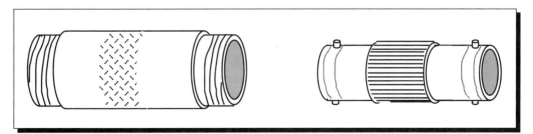

Figure 9-6: Barrel connectors for 10Base5 (left) and 10Base2 (right).

bother making your own terminators — many vendors offer ready-made terminators that mate with the connectors for either thick or thin coax. Some of these premounted terminators also include a wire on the end that can be used to make your grounding connection.

Another point about grounding is that you should not ground a cable segment in more than one place. If you do, you're likely to create interfering currents in the cable because of differences in the ground voltage. Even in the same building, all electrical grounds may not be at the same voltage level.

Two types of cable insulation — PVC and Teflon — are offered for most cable types. Generally, you should use Teflon cable (also called plenum cable) in any plenum air return in the building; if you wish to install PVC-insulated cable in these areas, the cable must be installed within a conduit. When PVC burns, it releases poisonous cyanide gas and is therefore a health hazard. Fire codes regulate insulation types, so check with the appropriate regulatory agencies before installing either Teflon or PVC cable (see Chapter 7).

When you install Ethernet cabling, place the cables perpendicular to any power wiring and at least six inches away from power cables. Also, keep cables at least six inches away from lighting fixtures.

Using transceivers

Very few Macs have built-in support for Ethernet (only the Quadras do), and none of them include built-in transceivers for Ethernet. To make the physical link between your Mac and the Ethernet cable, you need to tap the cable and attach an Ethernet transceiver to the tap.

There are two types of taps: *intrusive* and *nonintrusive*. A nonintrusive tap does not disrupt cable operations, so you can install this tap while the network is running. Many transceiver/tap devices for 10Base5 Ethernet are nonintrusive because they require drilling only through the cable's outer insulation and dielectric, and because they use a needle-like spine to connect to the center conductor of the coaxial cable (see Figure 9-7). During installation of an intrusive tap, you must disrupt, or break, the cable connection. An example of an intrusive tap is the BNC tee for thinnet cabling, which connects two cable segments together at two ends of the tee and provides the connection to the transceiver at the remaining end of the tee (see Figure 9-9).

10Base5

For 10Base5 Ethernet, the transceiver itself includes the *tap*, which is a needle-like protrusion (also called a *spine*) that connects the transceiver to the cable. Because the spine must make contact with the center conductor of the cable and no other

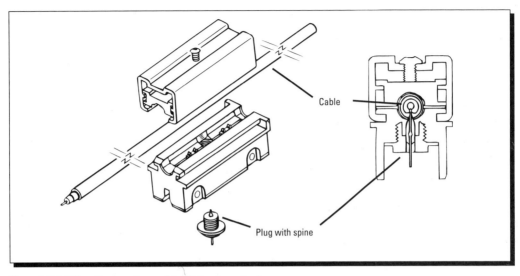

Figure 9-7: A 10Base5 transceiver and detail showing spine tap.

Figure 9-8: A 10Base5 transceiver cable and AUI on an interface card.

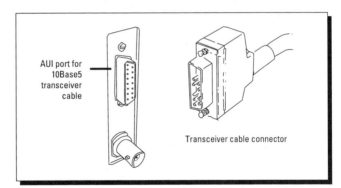

Figure 9-9: Two types of 10Base2 taps: a regular BNC tee and a wall plate with a special connector cable.

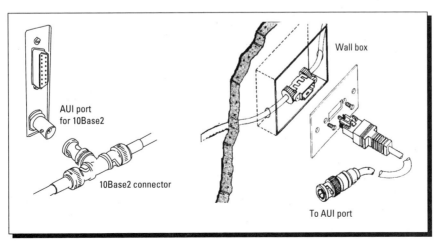

conductor (such as the shielding, or braid), transceivers are designed for specific cable diameters. Make sure that you order transceivers and cables that match.

To connect the 10Base5 tap to your Ethernet board, you'll have to run a special transceiver cable (also called a *drop cable*) between the two. This transceiver cable offers a great deal of design flexibility. For example, you can install the transceivers in the ceiling and run transceiver cables in two segments: one from the transceiver to a special wall socket, and the second from the computer to the wall socket.

Installing a tap usually requires that you use a tapping tool for clamping and aligning the cable, along with a screw-in device for piercing the shielding and dielectric of the cable to get to the conductor (see Figure 9-7). As mentioned previously, the dielectric separates the shielding (foil or braid) from the central conductor.

In some cases, you can use a drill bit to pierce the cable. Never, however, use an AC-powered drill, as the power drill can cause a ground loop throughout the cable, shorting out and ruining every transceiver connected to the cable.

The spine, as shown in Figure 9-7, is then screwed into the cable from the side opposite the clamp (top assembly in Figure 9-7), and then the drop cable is screwed into the plug containing the spine.

The final connection needed for a thicknet installation is the transceiver cable that runs from the transceiver to the Ethernet controller in the computer (see Figure 9-8). Most transceiver cables are relatively thick, stiff 15-pin cables with a D-style connector that attaches to the transceiver. Some transceiver cables use screws to lock the connector, but most now have a sliding-lock system.

Carefully check the locking mechanism: occasionally, the controller cable with a sliding-lock system does not stay attached to the wall box used for a transceiver cable connection, even when the units have compatible sliding locks.

A few companies have recently introduced other types of transceiver cables resembling twisted-pair cable. Standard transceiver cable is limited to lengths of about 50 meters, with shorter lengths for thinner cables. Some of the newest connectors using shielded twisted-pair wire to link a transceiver and the controller are good for 250-meter distances; such systems can make it easier for office microcomputers to link to a thicknet backbone. Wiring vendors also offer a more flexible transceiver cable called *office transceiver cabling;* the distance limit for this more flexible cable is 12.5 meters (41.25 feet).

10Base2

For thinnet connections, a BNC tee most frequently serves as the tap (see Figure 9-9) and plugs directly into the on-board BNC socket for the transceiver that is part of the Ethernet controller.

Because the BNC tee is intrusive, you should be careful when connecting and disconnecting workstations. Because each workstation is directly connected to the network cabling, it's a good idea to physically anchor the cable to the workstation so that an energetic user moving the workstation won't rip apart the connector or controller board. In order to maintain the continuity of the network, you should disconnect your workstation from the network by unplugging the tee from the BNC connector on the controller board, not by unplugging one end of the tee from the thinnet cable.

Although the most common way of setting up a simple thinnet network is to use coaxial cables with tee and barrel connectors, many wiring vendors offer systems for installing special in-wall taps (see Figure 9-9). The end of the tap is connected to a faceplate mounted on the wall; a special 50-ohm coaxial cable has the usual BNC connector for plugging into your interface card on one end and a locking connector that mates with the faceplate on the other end.

There are a few other ways to install 10Base2 cabling. In 10Base2, the transceiver is most often located on the interface card. (Some cards, like the newest ones from Apple, use an external transceiver for all Ethernet connections.) If you don't like the idea of stringing thinnet cables to each computer, you can use an external thinnet transceiver, which allows you to keep the thinnet coax closer to the wall. Then you just run a small transceiver cable from the thinnet transceiver to the interface board in the computer, much as you would with thicknet transceivers. With the growing popularity of the in-wall wiring systems we just described (see Figure 9-9), the added cost of external transceivers usually isn't worth it.

You can also use multiport transceivers for 10Base2 coax to connect a cluster of workstations to a single tap. But this approach is also expensive, so a better approach is to use unshielded twisted-pair cable and a 10BaseT hub.

10BaseT

10BaseT is a star-based network that allows only one device per branch, so there is no tap for connecting an interface card to the network. All you need to make the network connection is an RJ-45 plug on the end of the wiring run; insert this plug into the RJ-45 socket on the interface card.

Many sophisticated wiring systems for buildings allow you to run a 10BaseT cable to a wall jack. Then, when you need to attach a computer to the network, you simply use a length of twisted-pair cable with RJ-45 plugs on both ends to connect the computer to the wall jack and, thus, to the network. Just remember that the total length of the wiring run, including the cable from the concentrator to the wall jack, plus the cable from the wall jack to the computer, must be less than the 100-meter limit of 10BaseT.

Because 10BaseT is the latest Ethernet standard, vendors have developed a way to support 10BaseT on older interface cards, as well as offer new cards with built-in transceivers. If you're already using an Ethernet network and switching to 10BaseT, you can use your older Ethernet interface cards for 10BaseT by buying a media adapter. These 10BaseT media adapters are designed to plug into a 10Base5 socket on the interface card and to accept an RJ-45 plug with 10BaseT wiring.

10BaseT hubs

As mentioned previously, 10BaseT networks require an active hub, or concentrator, to work properly. However, as you'd expect, all hubs are not alike.

First, consider their construction. A hub may be a closed box with a fixed set of ports, or it may be a rack-like box with slots for different modules. Also, hubs may feature an added built-in port for thicknet or thinnet Ethernet or even fiber optics; others may require you to purchase a special card or module in order to connect to different Ethernet media.

Another consideration is the method of connecting the hub to the network cables. Depending on your situation, you may get by with RJ-45 jacks on the hub, which is good enough for small networks. Or you may want a hub that can connect directly to a punchdown block with an RJ-21 50-wire connector (much like Farallon's StarController; see Chapter 6). RJ-45 jacks are the eight-conductor cousins of the familiar RJ-11 plugs so often found in telephone systems and PhoneNET installations.

Another difference in hubs is in the way they implement the 10BaseT specifications. Some specifications designate only minimum requirements, giving vendors much latitude in design. An example of this latitude is the way a hub is designed to handle a line that has too many collisions on it (too many collisions may indicate a problem on the line). That line, by specification, is to be disabled after 30 or more consecutive collisions, but different vendors have chosen to disconnect the line anywhere from 30 to 90 collisions. Some hubs try to reenable the line after a set period of time; others do nothing but turn on an LED to indicate that a problem has occurred.

A final consideration is that you can buy hubs that perform only the most basic network management functions: disconnecting noisy lines, flashing LEDs, and so on. Other hubs support extensive software packages for managing a network. Farallon's StarController EN falls somewhere in between the high and low ends, offering the StarCommand software, which can be used with both PhoneNET and Ethernet StarControllers. On the other hand, the Synoptics and Cabletron hubs support extensive network management via SNMP (Simple Network Management Protocol, originally developed for TCP/IP networks; see Chapter 16), which is important for heterogeneous networks.

Installing an Ethernet LAN

To set up your own Ethernet network for a group of Macs, your best choices for cabling are either thinnet or unshielded twisted-pair. At the moment, thinnet is cheaper than unshielded twisted-pair. It's not that the cable is cheaper, but the added cost of a hub for 10BaseT to run Ethernet on unshielded twisted-pair wire adds significantly to the network cost. A small workgroup can do without that added cost, especially since the network management options of many 10BaseT hubs are usually not required for small workgroups. This situation may change quickly, though. At the time of this writing, low-end 10BaseT hubs are being introduced at prices under $500.

Installing 10Base2

If you decide to go with thinnet, remember that the network will be laid out in the bus topology (see Chapter 8, "Designing an Ethernet LAN"). That means that you'll be stringing a thinnet cable from workstation to workstation, tying cables together with tees, and plugging those tees into the network interface. This method worked fine in our own office — we simply ran the thinnet cable along the baseboard and used small cable clamps nailed to the wall to hold the cable in place.

But what if your workstations aren't close to the wall? Running two coaxial cables, thin as they may be, to your Mac may be hazardous.

Why two cables? Remember that there's a cable coming from the Mac to the left of you that connects to the tee on the back of your Mac; then the cable continues the network connection from your tee to the Mac to the right of you. If you're concerned about these two cables, you can buy an external thinnet Ethernet transceiver that connects to the DB-15 port of your interface card, which lets you put the thinnet connection farther away from your Mac. This port is usually meant for the thicknet transceiver cable, but it works for any external transceiver. Because most Ethernet cards already have an on-board thinnet transceiver, the extra transceiver is an added cost. An extra transceiver, however, is one of the few ways you can put a greater distance between your Mac and the network connection. Or you may find the new in-wall systems more to your liking.

Don't forget those terminating resistors — one at each end of the thinnet bus. For Ethernet, the terminating resistor is 50 ohms. Don't make them; buy them to be sure that you have the proper resistance. If you use Apple's new Ethernet Cabling System, the terminators are built into the thinnet connectors.

When it's time to add other Macs to your Ethernet network, first make sure that no one's using the network. Then disconnect the cable from one of the tees and add the lengths of cables and the tees for the new workstations. When we first installed our office network, we purchased pre-made 15-foot and 20-foot thinnet cables from a network vendor and connected the cables with tees instead of barrel connectors. Any time we had to add a new device to the network, all we needed to do was to plug the device into one of the unused tees — we didn't even have to bring down the network to do this.

This method, however, may not work in high-noise environments, such as factories, because the unused tee can act as an antenna and introduce inter-ference on the network. In these environments, it's better to use barrel connectors to connect the lengths of cable and substitute tees for the barrel connectors whenever you want to add a device to the network.

We have one last bit of advice about thinnet Ethernet. If you make your own cables, don't be tempted to make them too short, such as when you are planning to connect two Macs that are close to each other. Because of the wavelength of the Ethernet signal, the minimum length of cable between two nodes must be at least 2.5 meters (about 8.2 feet).

Another handy device to use with thinnet Ethernet installations is the multiport transceiver. Even though the Ethernet adapter for your Mac will probably have a built-in thinnet transceiver, you may find it more convenient to install a multiport thinnet transceiver in locations where three or four Macs are close to one another. To set this up, plug the multiport transceiver into your thinnet network and then run transceiver cables (such as those used for thicknet transceivers) from the multiport transceiver to each of your Macs. Some vendors also refer to multiport transceivers as *fan-out* transceivers.

Installing 10BaseT

If the idea of thinnet cables lying all around doesn't appeal to you, or if your Macs are scattered throughout the site, making it next to impossible to stay with a simple bus topology, you'll probably want to set up a network using unshielded twisted-pair.

Remember that if you plan to use existing twisted-pair wire (such as the extra pairs in your phone cable), you'll need to have two pairs of wire available for

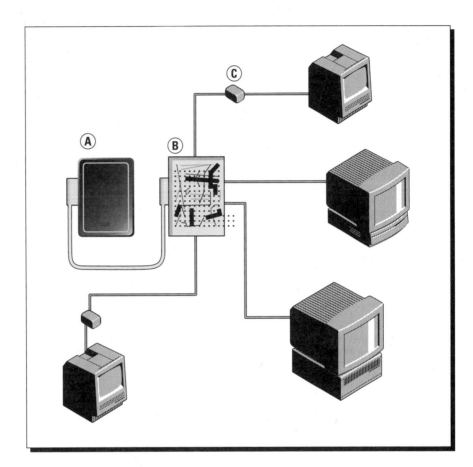

Figure 9-10:
A typical
workgroup
10BaseT
installation.

the connection, not the single pair that PhoneNET requires. Lay out your
network with a star topology and place the hub in your wiring closet or a
similar location.

As we cautioned previously (see Chapter 8), you are limited to one network
device per hub port. You can buy many types of hubs, choosing from 6-port
hubs, 8-port hubs, 12-port hubs, and so on. Some hubs are self-contained
boxes with no expansion options; others give you an empty rack enclosure
with a built-in power supply and slots for the boards that you want. Some
hubs have no network management software whatsoever; others offer all the
bells and whistles you'll ever need. The market for 10BaseT hubs has become
highly competitive, so shop around for your exact needs. Almost all hubs have
a second network connection of some type so that you can connect them to a
backbone network, which may be thinnet, thicknet, or fiber-optic cable (see
Figure 9-10).

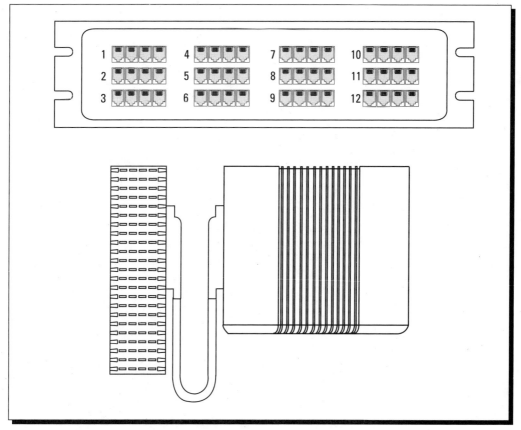

Figure 9-11: A 10BaseT hub connected to a punchdown block.

If you're using 4-wire telco cable running from your workstations (or wall plugs) to the wiring closet, your cables will most likely terminate at a punchdown block. This will be similar to a typical PhoneNET installation (see Chapter 7), except that you're using four wires for each connection instead of two; also note that each wire is connected to a row of its own (refer again to Figure 9-5). You'll then use a 25-pair cable to attach the punchdown block to your hub (see Figure 9-11), just as the PhoneNET StarController, TurboStar, or LocalSwitch is connected to a punchdown block for LocalTalk networks. If you're not working within the existing telephone company wiring system, you may find it just as convenient to run 4-wire cable from your workstations directly to a patch panel feeding the hub or to the hub itself; some hubs have RJ-45 receptacles built in for this particular purpose.

Now that we've covered some ways that you can construct your Ethernet network, we'll move on to a crucial aspect of the installation — testing the network.

Testing the Network

When you're installing a new network, it's wise to test the cabling before it's installed. For large installations, check the cable while it's still on the reel. You can perform a simple test with an ohmmeter, but a better method is to use a *time domain reflectometer* (TDR). The TDR sends electrical pulses down the cable and checks for returned signals; electrically flawless cables take an infinite time to return a signal. If return signals are received, the TDR can tell you the exact distance to the fault in the cable.

You can run a similar test with a simple box called a *cable scanner*, but the scanner will not be as accurate in pinpointing a problem as the TDR. The downside of the TDR is that it uses an oscilloscope monitor to display signals. Although the signals give you a great deal of information, the monitor usually requires training to interpret properly.

Once the cable is pulled, it's advisable to test again to verify that the cable is solid. A short or a break may have occurred with handling because repeated bending of coaxial cable can cause shorts. As you install the cable, it's a good idea to mark the cable every five meters on a piece of white tape indicating the distance from the end and the cable number. Then place colored labels with the cable number written on them in a neighboring location, possibly the baseboard or ceiling. Next, mark the location of the cables on a building layout. Should you have a break in the cable, a TDR can indicate the exact distance of the break from your test location, and the systemized labeling of your cables will lead you to the problem area.

Should you have reason to doubt the integrity of your transceivers (either a thicknet box or the thinnet ones mounted directly on your controller board), you'll need to construct a loop-back connector (see Figure 9-12). These connectors are fairly simple to make and can prove quite useful for eliminating some components from the checklist as you work your way toward isolating a network problem. To use the loop-back connector, all you have to do is disconnect the suspected computer from the network, plug the loop-back connector into the interface card, and run the interface card's diagnostic software. If the card passes all the diagnostic tests, you can be sure that the problem is not with the card, and then you can reattach the computer to the network.

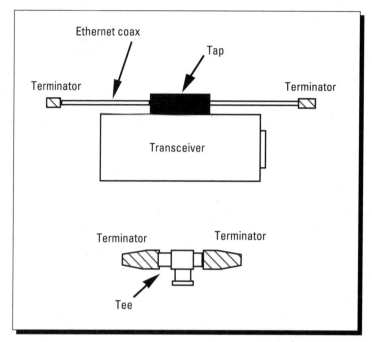

Figure 9-12: Loop-back connectors for thicknet and thinnet Ethernet.

Other test instruments are simpler, such as the hand-held TDR with a digital display and fewer functions, sometimes called a *hand-held scanner*. These simpler devices can usually tell you whether a twisted-pair cable is acceptable for use with token ring or 10BaseT Ethernet, although they don't report actual measurements for the appropriate parameters. Instead, hand-held scanners flash messages like "Good" or "No Good" on the digital display when you're testing a cable. Table 9-1 shows when to use these devices for testing network wiring problems.

Table 9-1: Capabilities of Testing Instruments

	Ohmmeter	Hand-held scanner	TDR
Resistance	•	•	•
Split pairs		•	
Open cables	•	•	•
Shorts	•	•	•
Cable length	•	•	•

Connecting Macs to Ethernet

You'll follow two basic steps to install Ethernet on a Mac. First, you install the hardware interface, either an external box or an interface card (see Chapter 8); then you install the Ethernet software drivers in the Mac operating system.

The hardware

Ethernet cards for the Mac come in two varieties. First, there's the standard adapter card, which usually has two connector ports: one for a thicknet transceiver cable and one for thinnet Ethernet. The thinnet Ethernet transceiver is built onto the card. Some new cards have all three connectors on-board — thicknet transceiver cable, thinnet, and 10BaseT. Newer cards are built to comply with Apple's new Ethernet Cabling System. These cards do not feature any built-in Ethernet transceivers. Instead, you purchase an external transceiver for the type of cable that you plan to use. Most network installers are accustomed to the older style of Ethernet adapters; with these adapters, all you do is bring the Ethernet cable to the computer — or use a transceiver cable when you're using thicknet.

The adapters for the Apple Ethernet Cabling System have two relatively minor advantages. First, if you're changing your network medium, all you need to do is change the external media adapter rather than the card. Second, Apple's media adapters for thinnet Ethernet are self-terminating, just as with its LocalTalk Cabling System. This means that you won't worry about installing the proper terminating resistor at each end of the thinnet bus, although this is no great advantage, because we've never found that to be much of a problem. Apple's Ethernet Cabling System does make it more convenient to attach the newer LaserWriter IIg and high-end computers (the Quadra series) to Ethernet.

The Mac has always been designed for easy use. Installing Ethernet on a Mac is no exception. An Ethernet adapter board is simple to install in the Mac II family because of the Nubus bus architecture, which frees you from setting board switches to register the board's slot address on the system. Compact Macs (SE, SE/30) require that installation of internal boards be done by trained personnel, because disassembly of the Mac is necessary.

A caution about the Apple Ethernet cable system

Both the 10Base2 and 10BaseT transceivers (Apple Ethernet Thin Coax Transceiver and Apple Ethernet Twisted-Pair Transceiver) draw power from the Mac. However, the external 10Base5 transceiver (Apple's Ethernet AUI Adapter) has its own six-foot power cord and requires an electrical outlet nearby.

Most older Ethernet boards require you to select the Ethernet medium you're going to use. Some boards have an internal switch that you must set; others have a socket with a multipin jumper that you must change. The better ones place the switch near the connectors, at the outside of the boards, so that you can make a change after the board has been installed. (After working with many vendors' cards, we've found that each installation step is clearly explained in the vendors' instruction manuals and shouldn't pose any problems.) Still better is a *smart board,* which automatically senses the port being used. Smart boards are available from Farallon and Asante.

The software

Some board vendors include a simple diagnostic program so that you can check the status of the board after it's installed. Usually, the diagnostic program tells you whether the board is electrically sound and whether it can see the Ethernet network. Some diagnostics let you send a sample packet to another computer on the Ethernet, which should return a reply to verify that your computer can use the network. If you cannot find a diagnostic program for your Ethernet board, try Neon Software. Neon includes a program as part of its Netminder Ethernet package that tests all Ethernet boards that Netminder Ethernet works with.

All board manufacturers have settled on using Apple's Installer program for installing their Ethernet driver software. This compatibility makes it a simple matter to complete installation of your Ethernet board and its software. In keeping with the trend toward AppleTalk Phase 2, most Installer scripts install only the Phase 2 drivers. If you need Phase 1 support over Ethernet, you must execute a special Installer script for the Phase 1 driver, or you can simply copy another file to your system folder. In Apple's case, for example, you can copy the EtherTalk Phase 1 file to your system folder once you've used the Installer to install the Phase 2 driver. Apple's latest drivers for Ethernet boards under System 7 can also support Phase 1 if you think it's absolutely necessary — the driver can be found only on the System 7 Group Update CD-ROM disk.

If both drivers are installed, you can select either one or the other by using the Network cdev in the Control Panel (or Control Panel Extension in System 7). The icons in the Network cdev distinguish between the Phase 1 and Phase 2 EtherTalk drivers — the Phase 1 driver has single-headed arrows, and the Phase 2 driver has two-headed arrows within the icon (see Figure 9-13).

In most circumstances, you'll probably have only one Ethernet card installed in your Mac. But, on some occasions, you'll want more than one card. The Mac may, for example, be configured to be a router (using Liaison or the AppleTalk Internet Router). Or perhaps you're setting up the Mac as an Ethernet packet analyzer and want to use one card for the analyzer and another for your

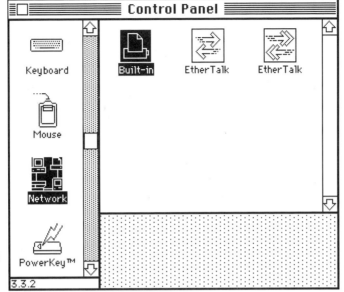

Figure 9-13:
The Network cdev, showing the LocalTalk driver (labeled Built-in) and two EtherTalk drivers.

regular network functions. Prior to System 7, you were restricted to using boards from the same manufacturer if you installed more than one Ethernet board in a Mac. The .ENET driver in System 7 (EtherTalk 2.2.1) has been rewritten to allow mixing of boards from different vendors in the same Mac.

Summary

In this chapter, we explained in detail how to install an Ethernet network. The following points were covered:

✔ 10Base5 coaxial cable (thicknet) is best used for bus networks. This type of cable requires that you use a transceiver with a tap to connect a workstation.

✔ 10Base2 coaxial cable (thinnet) is easier to install and uses a BNC tee connector to connect to your network interface card; thinnet is also best suited for bus networks.

✔ 10BaseT twisted-pair cable requires a star network with a concentrator at the center of the star; 10BaseT requires two pairs for each connection and an RJ-45 jack to plug into your network interface card.

✔ A TDR (time domain reflectometer) can give you the most information about wiring problems, but it requires some skill and training to use; simpler hand-held cable scanners are often sufficient for diagnosing network wiring problems.

In the next chapter, we'll switch direction somewhat to show how you can use modems with AppleTalk networks.

Chapter 10
Using Modems with Networks

Telecommunications, as a technology that uses such devices as modems and PBXs, is a science deserving a book or two on its own. In fact, just mention the word *network* to some people, and they start thinking about statewide or nationwide networks involving telephone company services. We'll investigate the ties between some of these services and internetworks in Chapter 13, "Designing an AppleTalk WAN." For the moment, this chapter will focus on using modems on your LAN.

An Introduction to Modems

Modems exist because of the current fundamental difference between the way computers and telephone systems work. Computers work with the 0s and 1s of digital signals (see Chapter 2), whereas analog signals are transmitted over phone lines (see Figure 10-1). These analog signals look like the sine waves illustrated in the figures in Chapter 2. To enable one computer to communicate with another over a phone line, we need a device that can convert digital to analog signals and then back again. This is the function of the modem.

The word *modem* derives from the two words *mo*dulate and *dem*odulate, which describe the device's primary functions. First, a modem modulates a digital signal, or data from the computer, into analog form so that it can be transmitted over a phone line. The analog wave is called a *carrier wave.* Second, the modem demodulates that transmitted analog signal back into digital form so that the receiving computer can understand it. The specific techniques that a modem uses to transform digital signals into analog signals and vice versa are called *modulation protocols,* distinguishing them from network protocols, such as those covered in Chapter 3, "Understanding AppleTalk Protocols."

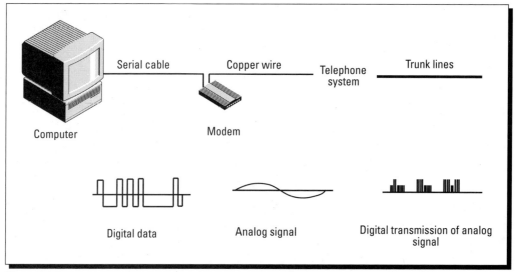

Serial cable — Copper wire — Telephone system — Trunk lines

Computer — Modem

Digital data — Analog signal — Digital transmission of analog signal

Figure 10-1: Data as it moves from a computer through a modem to the public-telephone system.

Modems are generally classified according to their raw speed of transmission; the *raw speed* is what a modem can achieve without the use of data-compression techniques (which we'll discuss later). A modem's raw speed is determined by the modulation protocols it uses. *High-speed modems* are those that feature raw speeds of 9600 bits/sec or higher; we'll refer to other modems, such as those running at 2400 bits/sec, as *low-speed modems*.

A high-speed modem has a raw speed of 9600 bps or higher; a low-speed modem runs at 2400 bps. You'll have fewer network-related transmission failures and shorter connection times with a high-speed modem.

Whether you're sending an e-mail message or transferring a large file from a remote file server, it's best to work with the fastest modems possible. When you're trying to connect to a net work, the timing of network protocols can cause transmission failures if you use a slow modem of less than 2400 bps. Also, faster modems mean that your connection time is shorter, so your cost for the call is less. In addition to the speed gained by modulation techniques, we'll see how error correction and data compression can affect a modem's speed.

Modem terminology

We'll define some terms that you're likely to run into time and again in discussions of modems. First, there are the terms *baud rate* and *bits per second* (*bps*), which are used to explain a modem's speed. *Baud rate* describes the number of signal changes per second. In a simple system where a signal change represents a single bit of information, baud rate and bits per second measure the same thing. However, if special modulation techniques are used — we'll explain these shortly — baud and bits per second are not identical, because a signal change can represent more than one bit. The baud rate is restricted by the fixed bandwidth of the telephone line, but the rate of data exchange, or bits per second, is not. This is because the modulation scheme may pack more than one bit per baud. So it's clearer to describe modems and their data-transfer rate in bits per second than by baud.

> Baud rate is the number of signal changes per second; in some cases, a signal change can represent more than one bit, so bits per second and baud rate may not always be the same.

Modems can communicate with each other in either of two modes: *half-duplex* and *full-duplex*. In half-duplex mode, data is sent over the connection in only one direction at a time; the sending modem must wait for the receiving modem to acknowledge receipt of the data before sending the next block of data. But in full-duplex mode, data can be sent in both directions at once. Full-duplex communications are usually more than twice as fast as half-duplex, because the acknowledgments of received data found in half-duplex communications are not used in full-duplex mode.

> In half-duplex mode, data goes in one direction a time; in full-duplex mode, data moves in both directions at once.

It's entirely possible that two modems can exchange data at a rate faster than the attached computers can process it. To ensure that no data is lost in such cases, the modem-computer connection uses some type of *flow control*. Flow control is usually accomplished by either a *software handshake* or a *hardware handshake*. The software handshake, or *in-band flow control*, inserts the special characters Ctrl-S (also called XON) and Ctrl-Q (also called XOFF) in the data stream to control data transmission and prevent data loss. For example, a modem will transmit XOFF to the host computer if it is sending data too quickly to be transmitted or stored in the memory buffer. The modem will transmit XON when it's ready for more data.

The hardware handshake, or *out-of-band flow control*, uses an electrical signal sent from the computer to the modem over a wire in the modem cable; for computers using the standard EIA-232 interface to a modem, the hardware handshake signal is transmitted on pin 4 (RTS, or Ready-to-Send) and received by the modem on pin 5 (CTS, or Clear-to-Send). One reason for hardware handshaking is to eliminate any confusion of the software handshake control characters with actual data; some encoding methods process control characters as well as data characters, leading to errors.

> Flow control keeps the computer from receiving data faster than it can process it.

Many modem cables offered for Macintosh modems are not wired to use hardware handshaking. If you plan to configure a modem to use hardware handshaking, be sure that the cable for connecting your modem and the Mac has pins 4 and 5 wired as we've described.

Telephone terminology

Telephone systems have a vocabulary all their own, but we'll touch on a few definitions that are pertinent to our discussion of modems. These definitions are mainly concerned with the types of phone lines used for modem-based communications.

The most common phone line, such as the one in your home, is the *dial-up line*, which uses two wires to connect your phone jack to the phone network. Because only two wires are used, this type of line is also referred to as a *2-wire circuit*, or a *2-wire connection*.

It's also possible to use a 4-wire circuit, but these are usually installed for leased lines. Two or three years ago, before the development of new modem standards to transmit data at speeds of 9600 bps and above on 2-wire lines, companies needing 9600-bps speeds with full-duplex transmission required 4-wire circuits. In a 4-wire circuit, one pair of wires is used for transmitting data, and the other pair is used for receiving data.

> The most common line used for modem communications is the dial-up line, which is a 2-wire circuit; leased lines are 4-wire circuits, where one pair of wires transmits data and the other pair receives data.

Leased, or *private*, *lines* are dedicated phone lines supplied by the telephone company and permanently connect two or more locations. Leased lines can use either a 2-wire or a 4-wire connection. Leased lines offer the user reduced costs for high-volume data transmission, predictable line characteristics, and improved signal-to-noise performance; the latter two factors contribute to more reliable data transmission. Leased lines are occasionally referred to as *data lines* because of their improved properties for data transmission.

The telephone channel used for transmitting voice or data signals can transmit frequencies between 300 and 3400 hertz and thus has a bandwidth of only 3100 hertz. Originally, the rate of oscillation in repeating signals (see Chapter 2), such as those used on phone lines, was measured in cycles per second. Over 20 years, the scientific and engineering communities agreed to name the unit of oscillation as the Hertz (abbreviated Hz), after a scientist who did much of the original research on electromagnetic waves.

Modem Protocols

You've read about networking protocols frequently in this book. Modems have a series of protocols, or standards, all their own. These standards come from three sources:

❖ Bell Standards (from AT&T)

❖ CCITT (Consultative Committee for International Telegraph & Telephone) Recommendations

❖ EIA/TIA (Electronic Industry Association/Telecommunications Industry Association) Standards

Today, most new modem standards are created by CCITT, which is a United Nations agency concerned with standards for data communications. The most important standards are the V-series standards from CCITT, mainly because they are designed for international data communications.

Modems can use three types of standards: modulation standards, error-correction standards, and data-compression standards. We'll look at each type separately.

Modulation standards

As explained previously, a modem works by modulating digital data into an analog carrier wave. To represent the digital data, the modem alters the frequency, amplitude, and phase of the carrier wave. Low-speed modems generally use only two frequencies during transmission. These two frequencies

The ISDN system as an alternative to modems

ISDN (Integrated Services Digital Network) is a telephone system that replaces all analog services with digital services. With ISDN, *all* signals are digital, whether they originate from your home phone or computer or are cross-country carrier signals. Because all signals are digital, ISDN does not require a modem. An ISDN adapter, which formats the data for the ISDN phone lines, takes the place of a modem to connect a computer to the phone system. The basic ISDN service (called the Basic Rate Inter-

face, or BRI) can transmit data at speeds of up to 128 kbits/sec.

The Regional Bell Operating Companies (RBOCs) have started to offer ISDN services to homes and businesses in the last few years, but only in restricted geographic areas. We don't see the widespread use of ISDN happening until the ISDN adapters approach the cost of other devices, such as 2400-bps modems.

are called *states* of the carrier wave. Because of the phone line's restricted bandwidth of 3100 Hz, high-speed modems must employ more than two states during transmission. Ensuring that modems use the same states is the job of the modulation scheme.

The most common low-speed modem these days is the 2400-bps Hayes-compatible modem. Typically, the 2400-bps modem supports four modulation standards: Bell 103, Bell 212A, CCITT V.22, and CCITT V.22bis.

> Hayes-compatible modems use a set of commands first standardized by Hayes Microcomputer Products, Inc., for controlling their modems. Modem vendors other than Hayes usually offer compatibility with the Hayes command set and add their own proprietary commands.

The Bell standards were developed by AT&T Bell Labs and are U.S. standards. Modems following the Bell 103 standard operate at 300 bps, whereas modems using the Bell 212A standard operate at 1200 bps. In a 2400-bps modem, these standards are included so that you can connect to older modems — some computers still use 300-bps or 1200-bps modems.

The CCITT V.22 standard is a 1200-bps standard similar to the Bell 212A standard, but it's an international standard generally used outside the United States. One 2400-bps standard in use by all of these modems in the United States, as well as internationally, is the CCITT V.22bis standard. In the CCITT standard, *bis* denotes second; that is, the V.22bis standard is an enhancement to the 1200-bps standard, CCITT V.22.

In order to transmit data at 2400 bits/sec, modems using V.22bis use two carrier signals, or states — one for the originating modem and one for the answering modem. The originator transmits at a frequency of 1200 Hz; the answering modem transmits at a frequency of 2400 Hz. Each carrier is modulated at 600 baud so that the modem sends four bits of data per baud (remember that baud equals signal change).

Modulation schemes for high-speed modems have also been standardized by the CCITT. The CCITT standard for full-duplex 9600-bps communications on dial-up lines is V.32. To send data at 9600 bits per second, V.32 modems group the data into 4-bit encodings or symbols and transmit them at 2400 baud.

Full-duplex describes simultaneous signal transmission. With each modem transmitting its signals at the same time as the other, the modem must sort out its transmitted signal from the signal it receives. To accomplish this, V.32 modems use a feature known as *echo cancellation*. An echo canceler models the echoes of the transmitted signal produced by the modem's circuitry, as well as the network. The output of the echo canceler can then be subtracted from the received signal before it goes into the modem receiver for processing.

V.32 data signals are typically weaker than similar signals from slower modems, partly because more data is transmitted per second. This speed makes the individual data signals harder to detect. To counter this, V.32 incorporates an advanced coding technique known as *trellis encoding,* which allows the modem to examine several consecutive signals for known patterns before interpreting the signal.

Transmission rates even higher than V.32's 9600 bps are possible on ordinary phone lines. In 1991, the CCITT established a V.32bis standard that supports a data-transmission rate of 14,400 bps. To accomplish this, V.32bis modems use even better echo cancellation than V.32 and improved receiver technology.

If you want to send as much data as possible in the least amount of time, you can keep improving modulation schemes, but this isn't the only way to get better throughput rate on a telephone line. Two further important processes are *error correction* and *data compression.*

Error-correction standards

Modems without error-control standards cannot provide error-free data communications. Noise and other phone-line anomalies prevent any standard modem without error control from delivering error-free data.

Two major error-correction standards are currently in use. One is the CCITT V.42 standard; the other is Microcom's MNP error control (MNP levels 2-4, shown in Table 10-1), which has become an ad hoc standard because of its wide-spread implementation by Microcom and other vendors.

Table 10-1: The Microcom Networking Protocol (MNP) for Modems

Level	Purpose
1	Asynchronous, byte-oriented, half-duplex data exchange
2	Asynchronous, byte-oriented, full-duplex data exchange
3	Synchronous, bit-oriented, full-duplex data exchange
4	Adaptive packet size for synchronous, bit-oriented data exchange
5	Data compression
6	Negotiation and use of higher speeds and alternate modulation (similar to V.29)
7	Enhanced data compression

At high speeds, modems are more prone to error. To counter this hazard, the V.42 error-correction standard uses a CRC (cyclic redundancy check) concept similar to that used by the XMODEM file-transfer protocol found in most telecommunications programs for microcomputers. V.42, however, applies the CRC method to *all* exchanges of data, not just file transfers. The main drawback to V.42, as with any error-correction method, is that when numerous errors are detected, the throughput rate suffers as blocks of data are retransmitted.

As a compromise that recognizes the popularity of Microcom's MNP standards, CCITT included MNP Levels 2-4 as an option in the V.42 standard. But any future enhancements in V.42 will be built on the V.42 LAP-M protocol, not the MNP protocols. LAP-M stands for Link Access Protocol-Modem. Link access protocols have been developed by CCITT for other links, such as X.25, and the LAP-M protocol is built atop the previous work.

Besides the CCITT standards, some ad hoc standards for modems are still in use. The most notable of these are PEP (Packetized Ensemble Protocol) and MNP (Microcom Networking Protocol). PEP is a proprietary error-control and data-compression protocol developed by Telebit for use in its modems; PEP enables Telebit modems to transfer data at speeds of 14,400 bps. Various systems, especially those using Unix computers, make use of Telebit Trailblazer modems with PEP to achieve greater throughput. MNP is a series of protocols developed by Microcom, which are identified by a level number, from Level 1 to Level 9. Many modems other than those from Microcom include some of the MNP class protocols.

Data-compression standards

Technically, data compression uses mathematical algorithms to eliminate redundancies by reencoding data into shorter code. Throughput increases proportionally as the code decreases in length. This is most often quoted as the *compression ratio*; a compression ratio of 4 to 1, for example, means that the raw data can be compressed to one-fourth of its original size.

Note, however, that the amount of compression depends on the type of data being transmitted. Compression algorithms work by recognizing repeated patterns in data and substituting shorter symbols for those patterns. The more repetition a data file has, the greater the compression. Generally, compression ratios for such files as graphic images, spreadsheets, and ASCII text fall in the range of 2.7 to 3.5.

The V.42bis standard provides the first "official" method for compressing and decompressing data in modems. Several proprietary techniques, such as Microcom's MNP5 technique, have been available for some time, but because they were proprietary, it was difficult, if not impossible, for different vendors' modems to communicate. As an international standard, V.42bis addresses that very problem. V.42bis uses an algorithm similar to computer programs that produce compressed files, such as ARC and ZIP files on a DOS computer, or StuffIt files on the Mac. Again, as with V.42, V.42bis is applied to *all* data communications, not just file transfers. It is possible to achieve compression ratios of up to 4 to 1 with V.42bis.

How Modems Are Used on a Network

You can use modems with networks through two types of access. First, you can share modems for dialing out of the network, thus reducing the cost of telecommunications for your network. You can also use a modem to dial into a network, which is a convenient way to access files and network resources while you're on the road.

Sharing modems on a network

If you've used a modem with a terminal emulator program such as MicroPhone II (Software Ventures), VersaTerm (Synergy Software), or MacTerminal (Apple), to connect to another computer or bulletin board service, you can imagine what it would be like to give all your network users a modem to do the same. Even for use of only a few minutes a day, buying modems for everyone is an expensive proposition (especially with 9600-bps modems, which can cost from $500 to $1,500).

You can offer modem services to your users with another method. You can set up modem-sharing via the network by installing one of three systems:

❖ A NetModem (Shiva)

❖ A C-Server (Solana) or NetSerial (Shiva) with a modem

❖ HayesConnect software using either an internal SmartModem 2400M board or external modems

Using these systems, your networked users can access those networked modems just as if they were locally attached to the modem port of their Mac. If the one modem gets to be heavily used, you can always add another net-worked modem or two to create a modem pool for users. In a *modem pool*, a waiting user will automatically be directed to the next available modem.

Although the principle of creating a modem pool is the same for the three products we've listed, their implementation differs. In the case of the C-Server, three RS-232 ports are in one box, and each port can be assigned to a different modem.

The NetModem has only one RS-232 modem port per box; therefore, you must buy one NetModem for each modem that you plan to attach to your network. When you access the NetModems via the Chooser, you then select the NetModems by name to create the pool that you want. If the first modem selected is busy, the NetModem software tries the second, then the third, and so on, until you get a modem that's available for your use.

The HayesConnect software controls any external device connected to a Mac's serial port, but it can also control the Hayes internal modem board, the SmartModem 2400M. If you install five or six 2400M boards in a Mac, you can use HayesConnect to make that modem pool available to other users on the network.

An advantage to most of these products is their flexibility. If you use any of these devices, you can start out with low-speed 2400-bps modems and switch to higher speed 9600-baud modems as the demand requires. In the meantime, you continue to use the same device as the point of attachment to the network; you then need only to buy a new modem. If, on the other hand, you start out with a NetModem, you'll need to buy an entirely different unit when you want to upgrade to a higher speed.

If you plan to set up networked modems, you're always likely to face one problem — that of immediate access to a local (directly connected) resource, as opposed to queued access to a shared resource. Will your users always be content to wait for a networked modem to become available for their use? Or will users be impatient and want the immediate turnaround offered by a modem directly attached to their Macs?

Gaining remote access to the network

Many of us are so accustomed to working on a network that we want to take these services with us as we travel. But at the moment, we're limited to using modems, particularly high-speed modems, for remote connections to an AppleTalk network. Cellular modems are also in the offing, but they've yet to become routine telecommunications devices. Wireless mobile networks aren't here yet, either.

To start a remote connection to an AppleTalk network, you use your Mac and a modem to dial into another modem that's attached to the network. That network's modem may be controlled either by software, such as Liaison (Farallon) or AppleTalk Remote Access, or by hardware like the NetModem, NetSerial, or R-Server. Whether control is by software or hardware, the function is to make your remote Mac look like a node on the AppleTalk network, even though it's connected via a phone line.

Unfortunately, when it comes to remote access to AppleTalk, there are no standards — at least not yet. Shiva, Solana, and Farallon each offer their own versions of dial-in software for the remote user. And they're not interchangeable. For example, you cannot use Shiva's dial-in software to call up a modem that's controlled by Liaison.

Apple started the ball rolling toward a standard for remote access to an AppleTalk network. Apple recently announced an AppleTalk Remote Access Protocol (ARAP) in conjunction with their new AppleTalk Remote Access program and the PowerBooks. Apple's version of ARAP is proprietary, although the specifications are published. Apple is working with third-party vendors to extend the protocol, particularly to include PPP, or Point-to-Point Protocol, originally designed for use with TCP/IP networks.

What products are available for remote access to an AppleTalk LAN? For software-only products, there's AppleTalk Remote Access from Apple, or Liaison from Farallon. On the hardware side, there are more choices — the NetModem (V2400 and V.32 models) and NetSerial X232 from Shiva, C-Server and R-Server from Solana, InterBridge from Hayes, and ComTalk from APT Communications, all of which include their own software for remote access.

AppleTalk Remote Access is meant strictly for remote users who are dialing into a network; it is not meant for sharing modems to dial out of a network. Both the calling and receiving Mac must be running AppleTalk Remote Access and System 7 for the link to work. Features in this program include a dial-back option for security, restriction of calls to a time limit, and a log of caller activity. Although installation of AppleTalk Remote Access is controlled by the network manager, using a new concept called the *security zone,* the program is designed for setup and usage by an individual. This means, among other things, that a network manager cannot review from one location the logs of all remote access nodes on the network, but must go to each Mac that is running AppleTalk Remote Access to review the logs.

Besides handling modem access and modem sharing on a network, Liaison can act as a router between LocalTalk, EtherTalk, and TokenTalk networks. Two of Liaison's significant features for modem access are its log of incoming calls and

Accounting for modem usage

Network managers usually want logs of modem-related phone calls so that they can track illegal attempts to access the network and for calculating phone charges. But it's usually difficult to collect all the logs. This is especially true if you have more than one modem that's used for connecting to the network. You can either arrange for the "keepers" of those modems to send you the logs, or you can use a program like Timbuktu to log onto the controlling Macs and obtain a copy of the logs.

its option of call-back security. The security feature is useful for companies preferring controlled access to a network. As a remote user, this is the basic routine:

1. You dial the proper phone number.

2. You enter your name and password.

3. The system hangs up.

4. The system calls you back at a prearranged phone number.

With the exception of the Hayes InterBridge, each of the hardware devices for connecting a modem requires only that you have a modem and the proper access software on your remote Mac. Hayes requires you to have a modem and another InterBridge to connect to the other network. In effect, you are creating your own personal network on the road by connecting the Mac to the InterBridge. Then the two InterBridges are acting as half-routers (see Chapter 13, "Designing an AppleTalk WAN"). This is both an expensive and a bulky proposition for the traveler. So the other choices in this category are better than the InterBridge.

The R-Server, C-Server, InterBridge, and NetSerial comprise one class of devices. Each includes a serial port for attaching a modem, and all handle modem speeds up to 19,200 bps. The R-Server and InterBridge are designed to act also as half-routers between two AppleTalk networks, whereas you can use the C-Server and NetSerial to connect other serial devices to the network, such as plotters and printers.

Shiva's NetModems (the V2400 and V.32) are in a class unto themselves. Shiva chose to build in the modem hardware instead of providing a serial port for connecting the modem of your choice. This makes for a more compact device, as you have one box instead of two, but you're tied to the Shiva hardware

---

Calling in as you travel

The link is ready. The only disadvantage? The call-back doesn't work if you're traveling from city to city and need to connect to the central network. This is because you can store just one phone number for each user. If you're always traveling between the same offices, you can make call-back work for you by having a different account for each city and phone number that you expect to call from. For instance, you could have one account identified as Dave-NYC, another as Dave-LA, and a third as Dave-Boston.

with little chance of upgrading. Of the two, the preferred product is Shiva's 9600-bps NetModem V.32 because it provides greater throughput, cutting down on your connection charges.

The Shiva EtherGate is also more or less in a class of its own by virtue of its unique options. Each of its serial ports is programmable, so the EtherGate can act as an EtherTalk router, as well as handling half-routing and dial-in access (with an appropriate modem attached to one serial port). The newer NetModem/E from Shiva also falls in this category, offering the added feature of access to DOS computers, using the IPX protocol to access a NetWare network.

Although remote access to a network is a good way of sharing resources, you may on occasion prefer to eliminate the overhead of the network protocols by setting up a point-to-point link between two computers. These point-to-point links are especially useful when you're working with another user, sharing screens or documents, or if you want faster file transfers between the user and an e-mail server.

Some network services, such as e-mail servers, allow you to call them directly without becoming part of the network. In such cases, you may be required to enter a special password when you call, or to accept a call-back from the server, before the connection is finalized. The one advantage of a direct line to the server is that you can usually exchange mail with the server faster than by dialing into the network, as the AppleTalk protocols are not involved in your link. The one disadvantage to this approach is that the servers can monitor only one incoming phone line, which can mean many busy signals if you set up quite a few remote users.

E-mail servers can also establish their own links to other servers via a modem. This setup is an alternative to having two half-routers with modems to connect two remote LANs (see Chapter 13, "Designing an AppleTalk WAN"). The servers can be set up to queue outgoing e-mail until a certain number of messages is reached, or until a specified time is reached (or both). Then one server takes control of its attached modem, calls the other server, and exchanges any waiting mail. You can also instruct some e-mail servers to send mail whenever single messages or high-priority messages are waiting. Use this option carefully if you don't want a large phone bill.

Just as with an individual user calling the e-mail server, the server-to-server modem link is good only for that particular service, which here is e-mail. When the two servers connect, they're not connecting to the rest of their attached networks, so users on one network do not see the other users. To share other services and resources between two separated networks, you have to set up half-routers with modems and have one network call the other (see Chapter 13).

Summary

In this chapter, we first gave you a fundamental grounding on modems and the standards they use. Then we described how you can use modems with networks.

The following points were covered:

✔ Modems running at high speeds of 9600 bps or more require data-compression and error-correction schemes.

✔ Macs need special cables to use hardware handshaking.

✔ For international connectivity, the best standards to use are those from the CCITT.

✔ Network users can share a modem to dial out.

✔ Remote users can become a network node either with software, such as AppleTalk Remote Access, or with hardware, such as the NetModem.

✔ Some network services, like e-mail servers, support direct dial-in connections to the server, bypassing the network.

In the following chapter, we'll tell you how to design an AppleTalk internet.

Chapter 11
Designing an AppleTalk LAN

The Evolution of the AppleTalk Network

Originally, AppleTalk networks were designed as small multinode LocalTalk systems that enabled Macintosh users to send print jobs to a very nice 300-dpi Apple LaserWriter. But somehow the users pushed this simple concept into accommodating anything from an entire floor of an office building to acres of buildings with 10,000 users. Along the way, Apple and other vendors came up with methods, such as EtherTalk and LocalTalk-to-EtherTalk routers, for stretching the original system to do this much work.

Network Geography Terms: LAN, MAN, and WAN

LAN, MAN, and WAN are acronyms that indicate the size and scope of a network. LAN stands for *Local Area Network*, MAN for *Metropolitan Area Network*, and WAN for *Wide Area Network*. Although these terms overlap in general use, we'll define each of the network types with the following brief descriptions.

A LAN is usually considered a network that is located at one geographical site; the network is connected with privately owned cabling (your own fiber-optic or copper) and without the use of public-telephone (such as AT&T), microwave, or satellite links.

In some networking systems, such as that used with Novell Netware, users refer to a LAN as a grouping of nodes around a file server and refer to each file-server group as another LAN. Although each LocalTalk network that is attached to an AppleTalk network backbone can be thought of as a separate LAN, it is standard to consider all connected AppleTalk networks at a site as one LAN.

The term MAN is used when two or more LAN sites within a metropolitan area are connected to form a larger network, either with public or private wiring. Once the network extends past a metropolitan area, as from Los Angeles to San Francisco, for example, the network is called a WAN. With a WAN or a MAN, you may require special features not usually needed at the LAN level, such as redundant paths for the connections. These special long-distance network features are covered in Chapter 13, "Designing an AppleTalk WAN."

This chapter focuses primarily on the principles involved in construction of AppleTalk LANs. We also discuss AppleTalk LANs that have TCP/IP backbones, which can be found in sites that don't allow AppleTalk to run across their Ethernet segments.

The Basics of AppleTalk LANs

An AppleTalk LAN can consist of a single isolated network, or it can be a collection of AppleTalk networks that are joined with *routers*. This collection is called an AppleTalk *internet*.

As explained in previous chapters, AppleTalk can run on several cabling types; the two most common types are LocalTalk and Ethernet. AppleTalk can also run over token ring (TokenTalk) networks. From a user's perspective, this means that all those nifty features such as a zone list in the Chooser and AppleShare are available, no matter what type of cabling the Macintosh is plugged into. However, if you want to join networks that are running on dissimilar cabling types, such as LocalTalk and Ethernet, you must use a router.

The early AppleTalk protocol stack

The AppleTalk protocol stack includes two protocols that weren't written by Apple: the TOPS protocol and the Kinetics protocol. TOPS was an early software protocol and product for distributed file sharing. Apple soon offered the AFP (AppleTalk Filing Protocol) and its own product, the Apple File Share server. Both products and protocols still exist, although the TOPS protocol is not officially recognized. In addition, Kinetics wrote code that allowed its gateways, the original FastPaths, to communicate over an Ethernet network. The Kinetics code was a protocol system that was replaced by Apple's EtherTalk. With the FastPath Model 5, this early Ethernet protocol has been phased out. (FastPath Model 4s still use the Kinetics protocol to search for other FastPaths over Ethernet when using the configuration software.)

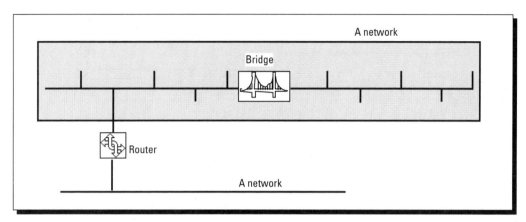

Figure 11-1: Two networks connected with a router; one of the networks has two segments connected by a bridge.

Although each AppleTalk network is limited to one cabling type, each can consist of multiple cabling topologies. You can join bus, daisy-chain, or star topologies and amplify their network signals by adding repeaters and bridges. So you can have, for example, an AppleTalk network consisting of an Ethernet network with two Ethernet thicknet segments joined with a bridge, or you can have a Local-Talk network with ten LocalTalk segments joined together at a multiport repeater.

Two cable segments connected by a bridge don't function as individual networks because the bridge does not label each of the cable segments with a separate identity (network number). Figure 11-1 shows two networks joined with a router; one of the networks has two segments joined with a bridge. Two AppleTalk segments joined by a bridge simply make one larger network — not two networks and not an AppleTalk internet. (For more information about bridges, repeaters, and segments, see Chapter 2, "Understanding Networks.")

An AppleTalk *internet,* which is a collection of AppleTalk networks, may combine several cable types, such as LocalTalk cables connected to Ethernet cables via a router. Or the internet may consist of several networks of the same type, as with a series of LocalTalk networks that are linked with LocalTalk-to-LocalTalk routers (see Figure 11-2).

If you want to join a LocalTalk cable to an Ethernet cable, you'll need a router; only a router can join dissimilar cabling types.

AppleTalk routers, such as Cayman GatorBoxes and Shiva FastPaths, have two primary functions. The first is to route packets to the appropriate physical location of the network according to a packet's destination address. The router's second function is to locate services, such as LaserWriters, within logical areas called *zones.* To understand the first function, you need to know how the

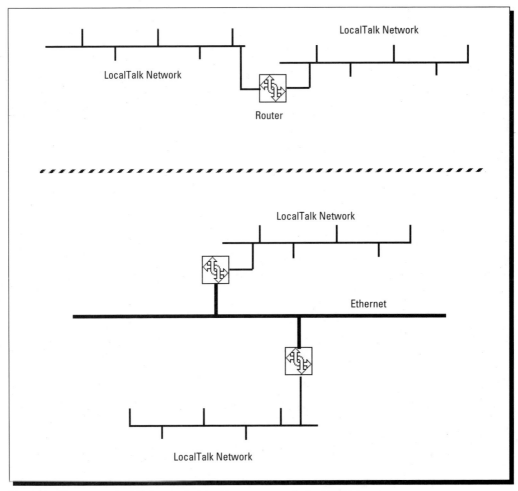

Figure 11-2: Two or more AppleTalk networks joined by routers to make AppleTalk internets.

AppleTalk network numbering system works. To understand the second, you need to learn about two further AppleTalk conventions, that of binding names to network services (with NBP) and the assignment of zone names to logical areas over an AppleTalk internet (with ZIP). We'll explain these conventions in the next sections.

The AppleTalk Network Routing System

The primary function of an AppleTalk internet router is to get data packets to their destinations. Just as the U.S. mail system uses ZIP codes with street addresses to locate mail destinations, AppleTalk internet routers use a network-plus-node numbering system to identify each network and its location (ZIP code) before zeroing in on the node location (street address).

Two AppleTalk network numbering systems are currently in use: *extended* and *nonextended*. Nonextended network numbering is the original AppleTalk numbering system and is still used for LocalTalk networks. Extended network numbering, introduced with AppleTalk Phase 2, allows each physical segment attached between two routers to be composed of multiple *logical networks*. Because extended network numbering and routing is more complex, we'll begin with the processes involved in nonextended networks. Once you fully understand the nonextended network system, you'll better understand the extended system.

Keep in mind as you read through the next sections on network numbering and routing that the user doesn't need to understand these processes to use the network. Only the network administrator, who must assign network numbers and choose the placement of routers, needs to understand these processes.

The AppleTalk Phase 1 nonextended network

The term *nonextended network* came into use to distinguish between the old and the new systems only after extended routing was introduced with AppleTalk Phase 2. A nonextended network supports a maximum of 254 nodes. Each port of a router can route only to one nonextended network. As you'll see later, this setup is less complex than extended routing, where each router port can route to an extended network composed of multiple networks within a range.

Not only are there differences between nonextended and extended networks, differences occur in the routing algorithms between AppleTalk Phase 1 and AppleTalk Phase 2. We'll explain routing operations in AppleTalk Phase 1 in the following sections.

How AppleTalk routers identify the nonextended network

Imagine a router with two physical ports. Attached to each of these ports is an Ethernet cable, and both cable connections look the same. The router must know when a data packet from one Ethernet cable needs to be passed to the other. The router differentiates between the two cables by creating a *port descriptor file*.

Before describing the port descriptor file, we'll add another piece to this picture. Suppose that a second router is attached to the other end of one of the

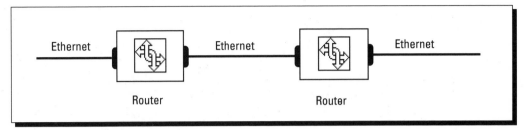

Figure 11-3: Here, two AppleTalk routers connect three Ethernet cables to create an AppleTalk internet of three EtherTalk networks.

cables and that this router also has two ports. For simplicity, we'll say that the cable attached to the second port is also an Ethernet cable. Now we have the configuration that you see in Figure 11-3, with two routers and three Ethernet cables.

Nonextended network numbering means that each cable (or collection of cables, where two or more are connected with bridges or repeaters) attached to router port is still a separate network. Each of the three cables shown in Figure 11-3 is a single and separate EtherTalk network.

The two routers need a method for telling each other about the EtherTalk networks that are attached to them. For example, they must tell each other which network is attached to which port. At this point you're probably itching to label these cables with something like a, b, c, and then the routers with tags of 1 and 2. If so, you're on the right track. Both routers must give an identifying label to each network and must also identify themselves to each of their ports with an identifying label.

It would be confusing if routers said, "that network is the cable attached to my right port." So the routers use a process similar to the way we name things to distinguish items or people. Routers are computing devices, and, as such, they use numbers to name networks attached to them and to name their ports.

Each port on a router has a *port descriptor file* that contains these items:

❖ *Port ID,* a number that identifies the port for the internal processing use of the router

❖ *Network number,* a unique number that labels the cable attached to the port as a separate network

❖ *Network address,* a number that designates the port's address on the network

The number that identifies the network is called the *network number.* The number is assigned by an administrator, who enters it into the configuration file of the router. If you study Figure 11-3, you'll see that the two routers have a single network in common. So now what happens? Both routers must agree to use the same network number. Otherwise, it would be like a conversation where two people referred to the same woman by two different names, one person calling her Mary and the other referring to her as Jeannine. The administrator must make sure that the configuration files of the two routers use the same number to identify the network that is in common.

We'll say more about node addressing in nonextended networks later in this chapter. For a thorough explanation of the dynamic node address procedure, see Chapter 3, "Understanding AppleTalk Protocols."

> A router is also a node on a network, so it has a node address just like all other nodes, such as Macintoshes or LaserWriters. The router's node address is acquired dynamically in the same manner that other AppleTalk node addresses are acquired. For the nonextended network, a node sends out an AARP probe when it boots up. This probe packet asks whether any other nodes on this network are using the address it has chosen. If a device answers the node's probe affirmatively, the node randomly selects another address and probes again. In this way, each node on the network acquires a unique address.

The port ID is assigned by the router for its own internal processing. The Cayman GatorBox, for example, assigns an ID of Port 1 to its LocalTalk interface and Port 2 to its Ethernet interface. The router uses the port ID to identify to itself the ports that are receiving or sending packets.

The port ID is used by the router to send a packet out onto the correct attached cable. If a router's table tells it that network number 15 is attached to Port 1, the router knows to send a packet out of Port 1 when it receives a packet destined for that network. Figure 11-4 diagrams logical locations: shown here are locations of the network number, the node address for the router, and the internal port ID.

Dynamic vs. static acquisition

You see the terms dynamic and static often in this chapter. Dynamic acquisition means that the computer node (Macintosh, router, and so on) acquires information on its own. The process of sending out an AARP probe, waiting for a response, and sending out a second probe is based on an algorithm contained within each node's AppleTalk software set. Most processes in AppleTalk are dynamic.

Static acquisition depends on a table of information that must be set up by a human administrator. The computer (node, router, and so on) does not change this information. In some network systems, an administrator must create a table of node addresses and then assign a unique address to each node. The node does not decide for itself what the address is.

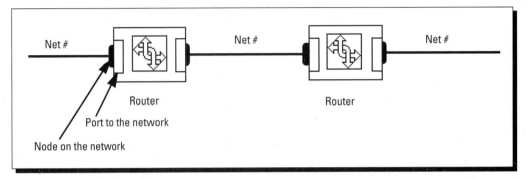

Figure 11-4: Node, port, and network numbers.

How Phase 1 routers develop routing paths

How does a router know about networks that are not adjacent to itself, but on the other side of another router? The method for acquiring this information is specified in the Routing Table Maintenance Protocol (RTMP). This protocol describes a dynamic system for networks to be added to or deleted from the internet. Instead of a single static network chart that an administrator creates and maintains, RTMP specifies that each router will learn about new routes from the other routers and will *time-out* routes after a certain period if the route is no longer broadcasted to the network by a local router.

Each router builds a routing table. This routing table is the key to the dynamic routing operations of an AppleTalk internet. The table is built through constant router-to-router communication. Every ten seconds, each router sends an RTMP Data packet to the network. Routers use the information that they receive in the RTMP broadcasts to build their routing tables. For each route (path to a network) in the routing table, the following pieces of information are included:

1. The number of the network.

2. The distance in hops to get to the network.

3. The port through which the router learned about the network (the port where it received the broadcasted RTMP Data packet).

4. The hardware node address of the router that sent the broadcast, referred to as the *source router* (when multiple routers send the same route, the one closest in hops is entered).

5. The *entry state* of the route (whether good, suspect, or bad). This state is used in the route aging process (described later in this chapter).

These five items of information are used by the router to determine the best path to forward a data packet to its destination network and node.

As explained previously, each router obtains the information for its routing table from the RTMP Data packets it receives from every router on the network every ten seconds (under healthy traffic conditions). Each RTMP Data packet contains the node address of the *source router*, or the router sending the broadcast, and one or more *routing tuples*.

A *tuple* is a combination of two related items; in the routing tuple, the two items are a network number and the distance the network is away, as measured in *hops*. Each router that a packet must go through to reach a network is counted as one hop. To visualize hops, suppose that you are on a car trip to visit your parents. You tell your anxious children in the back seat, "Four more towns to go through to get to Grandma's." If each town represents a router, Grandma's house is four hops away.

In AppleTalk Phase 1, a router sends out a broadcasted RTMP Data packet with routing tuples for every network that it knows about. So, for 60 networks, the router should send out an RTMP Data packet with 60 tuples. Sometimes, in larger Phase 1 internets, there are so many tuples to broadcast that a router splits its tuple list into two or more RTMP Data packets.

Broadcast packets, unlike data packets, are *not* forwarded across a router. Each router prepares a new RTMP Data packet, with its address as the source address, that includes tuples that it discovered from other ports (from the receipt of RTMP Data packets). Now the router sends the new packet out each of its ports, a process referred to as the "router *sourcing* the packet." In this manner, routing tuples are distributed across an internet, even though the broadcast packet is limited to each network. Keep in mind that the source address is that of the router sourcing the packet, not of the original router that is directly attached to the network referred to in the tuple.

Before sending out a set of tuples, the router increases by one hop the distance of the routes that it hears about from other routers from their RTMP Data packets. In other words, if it receives a tuple of network 20: 3 hops, the Phase 1 router adds this to its routing table and reports it in its next broadcast of tuples as network 20: 4 hops. By this, the router is saying: "Yes, I know about this route, but I am one hop farther away than the router I heard about it from." If the tuple is reporting a route that the source router is directly attached to, the distance in the routing tuple will be set to 0 hops.

The hop count is used by the receiving router to determine the best route for sending data. Suppose, for example, that a router receives two RTMP Data packets; one contains a tuple that reads network 34: 3 hops; the other packet contains a tuple that reads network 34: 1 hop. The tuple that is one hop away is entered into the routing table; the tuple that is three hops away is thrown out. A router can receive two or more tuples for a network with the same hop count. When this happens, the first entry is deleted and the last router's information for that route is entered. This step ensures that the most-up-to-date information is entered.

How Phase 1 deletes a route

When a router shuts off, as when the administrator turns it off, the router crashes, or the power fails, the routes that were directly attached to that router are no longer valid. For example, if a router told all the routers on network 3 that it had a route to network 27 that was attached to its other port, and then the router was turned off, the route to network 27 through this router would no longer be valid. The router stops advertising these routes because the router is no longer running. But when and how do the other routers on the internet delete this defunct route from their routing tables?

Routers use an algorithm called the *aging process* to delete routes that are unconfirmed and therefore considered invalid. Recall that every 10 seconds, each router sends out an RTMP Data packet with all the routes that it knows about (in routing tuples). If a router does not receive a tuple for a particular route from one of these packets within 80 seconds, the route is purged from the table. But, before the route is purged, it goes through three labels: good, suspect, and bad.

When a route is received via a routing tuple from an RTMP Data packet, the route is entered into the routing table with an *entry state* set to *good*. At this point, a *validity timer* is started. If the tuple for the route is received again within 20 seconds, the route is reentered with an entry state of *good,* and the validity timer is reset. If the tuple is not received again, at 20 seconds the entry state of the route is set to *suspect.* If the tuple is not received after 20 seconds more, the entry state is set to *bad.* Two further expirations of the validity time, or 40 additional seconds, bring the total to 80 seconds from when the validity timer was set. The route is now purged from the routing table.

In Phase 1 networks, however, every router reports in its RTMP Data packet every network's route that it knows about, even those not directly attached to the network. This causes a ping-pong effect on top of the aging process.

Keep in mind that each time a tuple is received, the validity timer for that route entry is reset to good. Routers will send tuples with an incremental hop count for each route to which they are not directly attached. Remember, each time a router sends out a tuple, it increases the hop count by one, saying, "Yes, I know about this route, but I am one hop farther away than the router I heard about it from." Only the router that is directly attached to the network begins its tuple with 0 hops.

After the directly attached router stops running and discontinues broadcasting RTMP packets, the ping-pong effect plays out this way:

1. Router A sends a tuple for network 25 one hop away (25: 1).

2. Router B receives this tuple and sends it back out as network 25 at two hops away (25: 2).

3. Router A receives this tuple and sends it back out as network 25 at three hops away (25: 3).

4. Router B receives this tuple and sends it back out again as network 25 at four hops away (25: 4).

The ping-pong increments continue until 15 hops are reached. *A route is no longer valid when it is 15 hops away.* At this point, the router purges this route from its table and no longer advertises it.

You can see from this procedure how much traffic takes place to confirm and delete routes. The more routers that you have attached to a network — an Ethernet backbone with multiple LocalTalk networks attached, for example — the more overhead traffic you will see. This overhead has been reduced somewhat with Phase 2. As an administrator, you can also decrease the amount of overhead by limiting the size of each network, restricting the number of routers attached to each network. If you have an Ethernet backbone network with multiple routers attached to it, consider installing EtherTalk-to-EtherTalk routers to divide the backbone into two or more networks.

How Phase 1 routes packets between nonextended networks

What actually happens when a packet comes into a router? Following is the step-by-step process:

1. The router looks at the AppleTalk destination address of the packet. The destination address tells it the network number and the node address where the packet needs to be sent.

2. The router looks at its routing table to find the entry for the network number that the packet specifies. This table entry tells the router from which port it discovered this route — the port where the router received the RTMP Data packet that contained the tuple with this network number.

3. The router looks to find the node address of the router that sourced the RTMP Data packet. Then, the router prepares a new header for the data packet, using the destination hardware address belonging to the router that sourced the tuple.

This procedure is referred to as *switching,* as it compares to switching tracks on a railroad to keep a train on a path to its destination.

The AppleTalk Phase 2 extended network

Many things stayed the same with the new Phase 2 routing code. But several critical changes did occur: the way that each network is identified by network numbers and the way that routers select the routes that go into their RTMP Data packets. The new network numbering is called *extended,* and the new routing is called *split horizon.*

You'll need to understand thoroughly the previous discussions about AppleTalk Phase 1 nonextended networks because we'll be building on that information. Keep in mind as we discuss the extended network format that AppleTalk Phase 2 specifies TokenTalk and EtherTalk as *extended* networks, but that LocalTalk is still considered a *nonextended* network.

How AppleTalk routers identify the extended network

Extended means that each network, defined as a physical segment between two routers, may have more than one network number. Instead of a single number, such as 15, to designate the cable's network identity, the router now uses a network *range.* The cable may be identified with a range of n-y, for example, 15-16. This new numbering system means that the physical segment between two routers can be a range of multiple networks.

In general use, the term *network* refers to a grouping of computer devices that can communicate with each other over a cable (or other medium, such as infrared or fiber). When a router is introduced, the term network takes on a more precise

---

Two addresses in each packet

Each AppleTalk packet has two address spaces. The first is the data link address space; for EtherTalk addresses, this is the *Ethernet hardware address.* The second space is for the network layer address, also called the DDP or *AppleTalk address.* Each address space has a destination address and a source address. The

AppleTalk address at the network layer specifies the final destination node address. The hardware address at the data link layer specifies the next destination in line. As the packet passes through, each router changes this address to the hardware address of the next router in the path to the final destination.

meaning: A network is now a set of addresses. Returning to our comparison with the U.S. mail, each network is like a ZIP code. You can have multiple ZIP codes within a city. A ZIP code helps to distinguish between like addresses: there may be two 151 Meridian Avenue addresses, but each will have a different ZIP code. One full address might be 151 Meridian Avenue, 23411; the other could be 151 Meridian Avenue, 42411, identifying two unique destinations. The street address is equivalent to the AppleTalk node address. In AppleTalk, each network has only 256 addresses because of the size of the address field in the packet. And, where you are limited to 256 unique street addresses, you need more ZIP codes to identify all the unique street address destinations.

The network range cannot overlap with the network range for other cables. You cannot, for example, create a network range of 15-16 and a range on the next cable of 12-15. If you do, the routers will argue over the rights to network number 15. Then, packets destined for network 15 can end up on either cable, but the destination node, which is searched for after the packet reaches the destination cable, can be on only one of those cables. A packet sent to the wrong network 15 is lost, and the user's communication to that device is unavailable or intermittent.

Also note that you can't break down a number range to apply one number of the range to half of the network cable and the other number to the other half. How would you tell the router that within network range 14-17, network 16 starts at the fire hydrant on the blue wall? Routers look only at the network number in the packet, having no knowledge of the physical points on your network. In extended network numbering, each node is randomly assigned a network number during its start-up procedures. Compare this to assigning randomly chosen ZIP codes for two houses side by side on a street. Then, each new house built is given a random ZIP code from the range of codes assigned to that street.

So what good is a network range? Each network number within a range establishes a *logical network*. Each logical network can have a maximum of 256 addresses. (Nodes 0, 254, and 255 are reserved; therefore, only 253 actual devices are possible per network.) Instead of expanding the 8-bit node address field in the packet, an extended network allows for more than 253 nodes by permitting more than one logical network to occupy a cable. So now the node address field contains both the 16 bits for the network number and 8 bits for the node address, for a total of 24 bits.

The 16-bit address space allows for 65,536 logical networks. 65,536 networks multiplied by 253 addresses per network brings the extended AppleTalk network up to an astronomical 16,580,608 nodes. But don't try this on your network, because Ethernet and other cable types cannot physically withstand anywhere close to that many nodes.

How Phase 2 routers develop routing paths

Sometimes, in larger Phase 1 internets, there are so many tuples to broadcast that a router splits its tuple list into two or more broadcasted RTMP Data packets. This overhead problem with large networks was one of the main reasons that AppleTalk Phase 2 was created.

In AppleTalk Phase 2, routers use a process called *split horizon*. This process significantly shortens the length of the RTMP broadcasts, so it is rarely necessary to send out a broadcast with multiple packets. However, packets are still sent every ten seconds to keep up with changes in the status of the internet.

With split horizon, the only routing tuples sent by a router are those from its *backside*. In other words, a router sends an RTMP broadcast through Port 2 with all of the routes that it knows about from Port 1 and vice versa. It does not send the routes that it learned about from Port 2 back through Port 2.

Figure 11-5 shows a typical configuration with three LocalTalk networks attached to an Ethernet backbone. With split horizon, each LocalTalk-to-EtherTalk router puts out an RTMP Data packet onto the Ethernet with only the routing tuple from its own attached LocalTalk network. The router does not include routing tuples for the other LocalTalk networks in its RTMP Data packet to the Ethernet because it learned about these networks from the Ethernet (the same port in and out is not allowed).

How Phase 2 deletes a route

Phase 2 routing uses the same aging process as Phase 1 to delete invalid routes. But Phase 2 added a process called *notify neighbor*.

When a route's entry state in the routing table is set to bad, the notify neighbor process begins. Remember that the router itself is sending out RTMP Data packets every ten seconds. When the route's state is set to bad, the next RTMP packet sent by the router contains a special code to notify neighboring routers that it believes the route to be bad. This is done by setting the hop count for the bad network to 31. Routers that receive a tuple with a hop count of 31 can immediately set the entry state to bad without waiting for their own validity timers to reach 40 seconds. A router receiving a bad-entry tuple should invalidate an address only if its routing table shows that the sending router is the source router for that network. This is because there may be an alternate route.

How Phase 2 routes packets between extended networks

You may want to review the switching process described in the section "How Phase 1 routes packets between nonextended networks." The same process is used in Phase 2 to switch packets. The only difference is that with Phase 2 the router now recognizes destination networks that are identified as being within a network range.

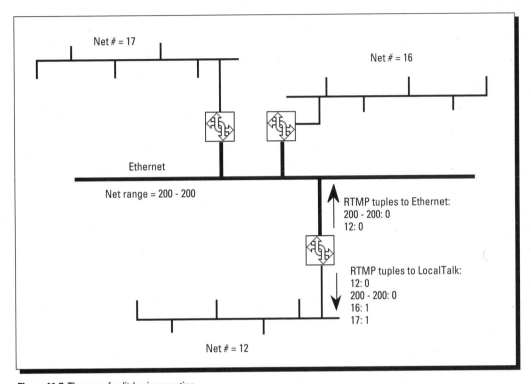

Figure 11-5: The use of split-horizon routing.

The AppleTalk Phase 2 nonextended network

Routing between LocalTalk networks, which remained nonextended network types, changed little with Phase 2. Split horizon, however, can be implemented by Phase 2 routers on nonextended networks, including LocalTalk. (Split horizon was described in the section, "How Phase 2 routers develop routing paths.")

The AppleTalk Zone System

Up to this point, the process used by AppleTalk routers to identify each attached cable is similar to that of other protocols, such as TCP/IP. Most protocols use a numbering system to identify the network and the network nodes. But asking the user to remember these numbers would be exceptionally unfriendly. And this is not the Apple way. So Apple developed a system for making networks as friendly as Apple's graphical interface operating system.

AppleTalk is unique among protocol systems in that it has zone names and node names, as well as network numbers and node addresses, to map to locations across a multinet LAN. The user selects a destination node name from a zone list from the

Chooser. AppleTalk routers pick up that request, convert the zone into a network number, and then forward the packet to its destination. This conversion process is done within the router by the Zone Information Protocol (ZIP).

ZIP (Zone Information Protocol) is the system that maps a zone name to one or more network numbers. In addition to its routing table, the router builds a *zone table,* called a *Zone Information Table,* or ZIT.

The ZIP procedure changes when it is applied to extended networks. We'll discuss this as we did with AppleTalk routing — explaining the simpler nonextended system first and then the more complicated extended system.

Zones in AppleTalk Phase 1 nonextended networks

Zones are logical areas that exist for the convenience of the user, not for the routing requirements of the router. This means that a zone, as a logical area where services reside, may extend across *multiple* nonextended networks, including LocalTalk. The fact that one zone may span several networks is commonly overlooked, so an administrator may attach a unique zone name to each network. These unique names create a lengthy zone list in the Chooser and are not necessary.

When you plan zones, divide your LAN into logical groupings of users. Are all engineering users on the fourth floor, which has three LocalTalk networks? Or do you have several islands of engineering groups that will want to exchange data? Either way, you can select the single zone name "Engineering" for all these networks. This way, all engineering users can find file servers, printers, and other network devices installed for their use, all within their local zone.

If your network configuration has dissimilar groups of personnel within one network, you'll need to choose a zone name that identifies some common characteristic of these people. You may need to choose less descriptive names. And you can keep the Chooser list to a manageable size by placing several areas in one zone. Suppose that you have four LocalTalk networks on the fourth floor with many groups in each. You don't need separate zones for each of the four networks; one zone called "fourth floor" will do. For less conservative companies, you can pull together disparate groups into one zone with an imaginative name — characters from a book, for instance, like "Gandolf" or "Bilbo." But keep in mind that nondescriptive zone names like these can make locating devices more difficult for the new network user.

How zones are identified on nonextended networks

The following sections explain the ZIP process in AppleTalk routers on nonextended networks. The information will help you plan zone locations and troubleshoot.

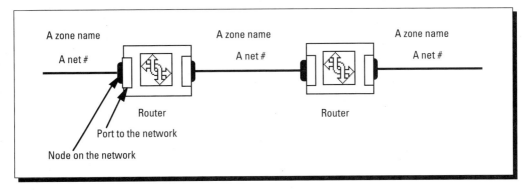

Figure 11-6: The zone name for each network segment.

Between two Phase 1 routers is one physical segment, identified as one network with its own network number. Each network is in one zone, but not more than one, although several networks can share a zone. Each router maintains a table, called a Zone Information Table, or ZIT, that maps a zone name to a network number for each of its ports. Figure 11-6 shows that each segment between two routers is identified with a zone name and a network number. Figure 11-7 shows how two networks can share a zone.

How zone information is maintained on a nonextended internet

Changes in the ZIT are based on information that the ZIP process discovers in the router's routing table. The ZIT is not independent; it is totally reliant on changes in the routing table to maintain its zone table.

When a router receives a new routing tuple that indicates a new network, the router's internal ZIP process (which has been monitoring the routing table), sometimes called a *scheduler,* starts up with the following exchange:

1. The ZIP process sends a ZIP Query packet to the source router of the new network number/range (the source router that sent the RTMP Data packet).

2. The source router sends a ZIP response that contains a zone *tuple,* which is a network number and zone name (net number: zone name).

To delete a zone, the route to the network numbers that are mapped to that particular zone must be deleted from the routing table.

To change a zone name, the route to the networks that are mapped to that particular zone name must be deleted and then reentered as new. When a network route is reentered in the routing table as new, the ZIP query process begins and the new zone name is added to the router's ZIT.

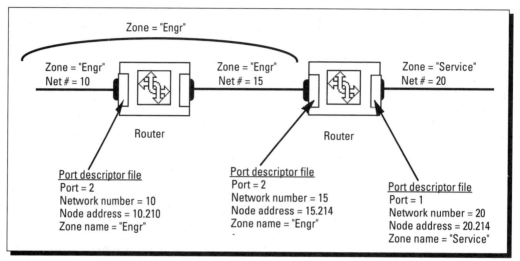

Figure 11-7: Two or more network segments can share a zone name.

To reenter a route as new, you must shut down the routers that are reporting the route and wait until the route disappears from all routers' tables on the internet. Then, restarting the routers when the routers were shut down causes the network number to be reentered as a new route (since it was deleted). This causes the routers' internal ZIP processes to query for the zone name for the "new" networks, which at this point is the new zone name that you've chosen.

Suppose that your internet has three LocalTalk-to-EtherTalk routers for three LocalTalk segments and one Ethernet segment. Your EtherTalk backbone is net 20, zone "Campus," and your three LocalTalk networks are as follows: net 12, zone "Engr"; net 13, zone "Marketing"; and net 14, zone "Marketing." You want to change the zone name "Engr" to "Engineering." You and the routers will need to go through the following steps:

1. Delete the route to net 12 from all of the routers attached to this internet. Do this by turning off the LocalTalk-to-EtherTalk router that is directly attached to net 12.

2. The ZIP processes of net 13 and net 14's routers are monitoring their routing tables and will see that the route to net 12 has been deleted by the RTMP process.

3. The ZIP processes of net 13 and net 14's routers will then delete from their ZITs the zone name associated with net 12.

At this point, any Macintosh issuing a GetZoneList packet (to obtain the internet zone list) will receive the following list: **Marketing, Campus, Engr** will no longer be displayed in any Mac Chooser.

4. Restart the router that is directly attached to net 12 with the new configuration of net 12, zone "Engineering."

5. Net 13 and net 14's routers obtain (again) the route to net 12 (through the RTMP process) and add net 12 to their routing tables.

6. The ZIP processes of net 13 and net 14's routers are monitoring their routing tables and will see that a new net has been added (by the RTMP process) to their routing tables.

7. The ZIP process of net 13 and net 14's routers send out ZIP Queries to the router that is listed in the routing table as the source router (or next router) for net 12. The ZIP Query requests the zone name associated with net 12.

8. The router that you just restarted (step 4) will respond with the zone name that is now in its configuration file — that name is "Engineering."

9. Net 13 and net 14's routers will receive the response and put "Engineering" into their ZIT.

Any Mac issuing a GetZoneList will receive the following list for display in the Chooser: **Engineering, Marketing, Campus.**

Note that the ZIP process doesn't send out a ZIP Query for new zones unless it sees a change in the routing table. This means that you can't add or change a zone without shutting down the router to remove the network route.

The standard recommendation is to wait ten minutes to ensure that all routes to the network have been deleted before bringing the router back up with the new zone name. Otherwise, one of the routers may still have the old zone tuple recorded, causing a conflict with your new configuration. (See "How Phase 1 deletes a route," for further information.)

AppleTalk Phase 2 extended zones

Recall from the section on AppleTalk network routing that extended networks allow multiple logical networks, grouped into network ranges, to exist on one extended network. The same idea applies to zones on extended networks that are grouped into *zone lists*. Each extended network can have from one to 255 zones.

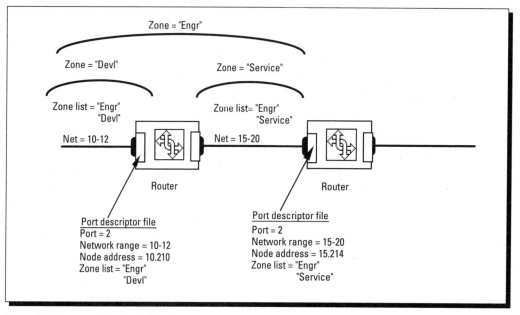

Figure 11-8: An extended network. Note that the zone "Engr" encompasses two networks.

How zones are identified on extended networks

Because zones are a logical convenience for the user and are not used by the router to track physical segments, the same zone name can occur in more than one network's zone list. Just as with nonextended networks, the user sees services in a zone that may actually be located over several networks (see Figure 11-8).

Overlapping zone names can make an AppleShare file server on the Ethernet appear in the same zone with LocalTalk network services. You can do this by

Future plans for ZIP

Yes, changing a zone is an unwieldy process for the network administrator. A more dynamic system had been planned, in keeping with the rest of the AppleTalk stack. This plan was to be implemented with the now-defunct AMP — the Apple Management Protocol. Bowing to the wishes of network managers of multiprotocol networks who don't want to contend with multiple management systems, Apple is pursuing SNMP. This protocol is increasingly becoming a de facto standard for network management in the Ethernet world. We hope that the ZIP process will improve in the evolving SNMP for AppleTalk specifications. But for now, AppleTalk network administrators must contend with this difficult ZIP internet process.

putting the LocalTalk's zone name in the Ethernet network's zone list. The file-server administrator must choose that zone name when configuring the server.

Just as with the network number range, the administrator has no control over which segment of the network cable acquires a zone name from the zone list. Each node, on startup, chooses a zone to place its services in. This is neither a dynamic selection nor a network administrator's selection, but is the choice of the node user. When the user selects the network icon in the Control Panel, the node acquires the list of zones from a local router and then displays it to the user. The user can then make a selection by clicking on the desired zone. Subsequently, the node uses this selected zone as its local zone.

Note that a node with multiple sockets for services, such as a server with multiple file-sharing volumes and a printer port, cannot place the services in different zones.

If no selection is made for the user's node to reside in, the node locates itself in the *default zone*. The default is set in the routers by the administrator as one of the zones in the zone list.

How zone information is maintained on an extended internet

To add, change, or delete a zone from the zone list, you must use the procedure that we described in the section, "How zone information is maintained on a nonextended internet."

The important point to note is that the router cannot merely add a zone to a zone list, but must completely swap out one zone list for another. Each pointer from the routing table refers to an entire zone list, not just one of the zones. Therefore, the entire zone list must be deleted and reentered via the ZIP query process. The new zone list may be the same as before, or have only one new zone, or be completely different. When the router records a change in the routing table, the ZIP process goes out to get an entirely new zone list to map to the new (or relearned) network number/range.

NBP — Working with ZIP and Routing Processes

NBP, or Name Binding Protocol, is the system that allows you to find the list of the devices in your Chooser and select a device to communicate with. When you open the Chooser and select the LaserWriter icon and a zone, you'll see a list of LaserWriters as the router for that zone responds with the list. When you highlight a particular LaserWriter, you select that printer to converse with and send your files to for printing. The request for retrieving the list of LaserWriters from another zone is done with a combination of NBP, ZIP, and the AppleTalk routing process.

In the Phase 1 code specifications, the NBP system consisted of three NBP packet types: the NBP BrRq (broadcast request), the NBP LkUp (lookup), and the NBP LkUp-Reply (lookup reply). Phase 2 added the NBP FwdReq (forward request).

How NBP works in Phase 1

To illustrate exactly how the name binding process works in Phase 1, we'll give a step-by-step example. Suppose that a Macintosh user wants to see all LaserWriters in a particular zone. This is the sequence of events that occur:

1. The Mac user selects a zone and the LaserWriter icon in the Chooser.

2. The Mac issues an NBP BrRq, asking to see all devices of the type "LaserWriter" in that particular zone. (The socket address in this BrRq packet is one that only routers will respond to.)

3. The local router receives the packet and looks at its ZIT to determine which network numbers are mapped to the requested zone. The router then looks in its routing table for the addresses of "next routers" in the path for those networks. (Remember that there can be several networks in each zone.)

4. Next, the local router prepares an NBP lookup packet (NBP LkUp) with the destination addresses of the next routers.

5. Routers that receive the LkUp packet from the originating router now broadcast to their networks their own NBP LkUp packets to locate all devices that match the device type.

6. Devices that match respond by sending an NBP lookup reply (LkUp-Reply) to the destination address of the Macintosh that originated the NBP process. Each router in the path forwards the LkUp-Reply until it reaches the originating router.

7. The originating router sends the LkUp-Reply to the Macintosh.

The Macintosh can now display the list of responding devices in the Chooser for the user's selection. Figure 11-9 shows this procedure in action.

How NBP works in Phase 2

For Phase 2, the process is the same as with Phase 1 routers, with one exception. The local router that sends the NBP packet to the next router over an internet now sends an NBP FwdReq (forward request) packet instead of an NBP LkUp. With the addition of the NBP FwdReq, there now is a distinction

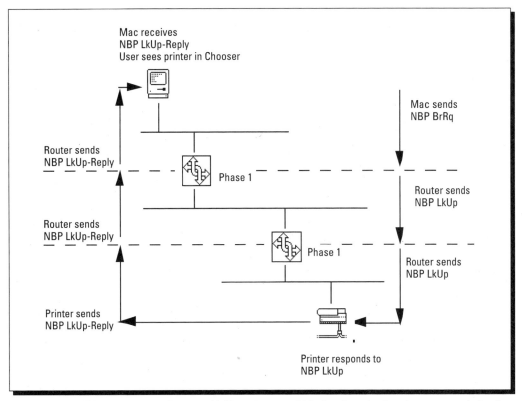

Figure 11-9: The NBP process over an internet with Phase 1 routers: A Macintosh sends a broadcast request; the local router sends an NBP lookup to the target network router; the devices respond with a LkUp-Reply.

between sending an NBP request from one router to another router (FwdReq is used) and sending an NBP request from a router to a device (LkUp is used). Figure 11-10 diagrams this procedure.

The AppleTalk Node Boot-Up Procedure

The following sections explain what happens when a node boots up. First, we'll describe how a node boots up on a nonextended network and then in the more complex extended network with multiple zones and networks. You'll see how a node chooses a zone from the zone list or a network from the network range.

First, however, you may need to review the AARP process. On Ethernet, an additional process called the AppleTalk Address Resolution Protocol (AARP) determines the hardware address if it has the AppleTalk node address. AARP

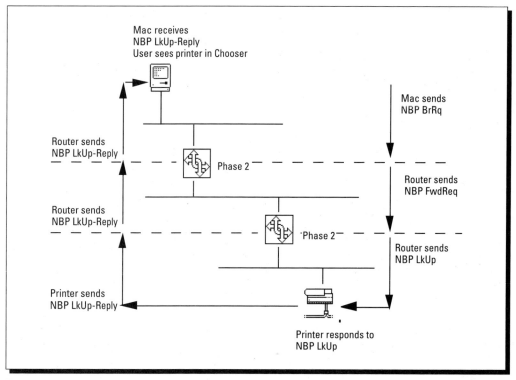

Figure 11-10: NBP over an internet with Phase 2 routers. A Macintosh sends a BrRq; the local router sends an NBP FwdReq to the target network router; the devices respond with a LkUp-Reply.

uses three packet types: probe, request, and response. The probe is used to verify a unique address on booting; the request is used to obtain the hardware address of a node; and the response is used to return the hardware address. The AARP process is required for Ethernet node compatibility with other Ethernet devices on the cable.

Nodes in nonextended networks

A node on a nonextended Ethernet cable starts up and then sends out an AARP probe packet. The AARP probe contains the tentative AppleTalk node address that the node wishes to use. The node either picks this number randomly or uses the same number that is saved in PRAM (non-volatile memory).

The node repeats the AARP probe every ⅕ second for ten times These probes are sent to the multicast hardware broadcast address **$090007ffffff**. Every AppleTalk node on the network receives this broadcast. Any node that already has the address given in the new node's probe packet returns an AARP response.

If the new node is on LocalTalk, it sends out multiple LLAP Enquiry control packets to the broadcast address (255) to verify that its node address is unique. If a node on this network is already using the address, it returns an Acknowledge control packet.

Nodes in extended networks

Nodes booting up on extended Ethernet networks also use the AARP probe to verify that their address is unique. Because the node address is now a combination of **net.node**, the node also needs to verify that it is using a valid network number (a net number within the range established by the routers). The node also needs either to verify that the zone name it chose from PRAM is still valid or to know what the default zone is.

Each zone on an extended network has a unique broadcast address, called a *multicast address*. Nodes can use this address to look up services within a zone without disturbing devices located in other zones. The booting node also needs to know the multicast address for the zone that it has chosen or for the default zone.

The multicast zone address, the validity of the network number, and the validity of the zone name are all verified by sending a GetNetInfo (GNI) packet. A router replies to the node with a GetNetInfoReply (GNIR) packet to verify or flag as invalid the node's assumptions. If the node has not chosen a zone, the GNIR packet provides the default zone name and its multicast address.

If the information that the node has chosen is valid, the following sequence occurs:

1. The node sends an AARP probe to the hardware multicast broadcast address to verify the uniqueness of its **net.node** address (ten times every ⅕ second).

2. The node sends a GNI packet containing its **net.node** address and desired zone to the hardware multicast broadcast address.

3. The router sends an AARP request to the hardware multicast broadcast address (a request for the hardware address of the node sending the GNI).

4. The node sends an AARP response to the hardware and node address of the router to return the node's hardware address.

5. The router sends a GNIR to the hardware and node address of the node (this packet validates the zone and network number and provides the zone's multicast address).

The following sequence occurs when the information chosen by the node is not valid because the node is from another internet:

1. The node sends an AARP probe to the hardware multicast broadcast address to verify the uniqueness of the **net.node** address (ten times every ⅕ second).

2. The node sends a GNI to the hardware multicast broadcast address (this packet contains its **net.node** address and desired zone).

3. The router sends a GNIR to the hardware multicast broadcast address; the router must use the broadcast because it has no route to the invalid network that the node is using as its address (the GNIR packet contains the valid network range and the default zone with its multicast address).

4. The node sends an AARP probe to the hardware multicast broadcast address to verify the uniqueness of its **net.node** address (this packet contains its new address selection with a net number in the valid range).

5. The node sends a GNI to the hardware multicast broadcast address (this packet contains its new **net.node** address and the default zone).

6. The router sends an AARP request to the hardware multicast broadcast address (this packet requests the hardware address of the node sending the GNI).

7. The node sends an AARP response to the hardware and node address of the router (returning the node's hardware address).

8. The router sends a GNIR to the hardware and node address of the node (validating zone and network number).

The following sequence occurs when the information chosen by the node is not valid because the node is new to any internet:

1. The node sends an AARP probe to the hardware multicast broadcast address (ten times every ⅕ second); the node uses a network number in the *start-up range* of 65,280-65,534.

2. The node sends a GNI to the hardware multicast broadcast address (this packet contains its **net.node** address and desired zone).

3. The router sends a GNIR to the hardware multicast broadcast address; the router broadcasts because it has no route to the start-up range network (this packet contains the valid network range and the default zone with its multicast address).

4. The node sends an AARP probe to the hardware multicast broadcast address to verify the uniqueness of its **net.node** address (this packet contains the new address selection with a net number in the valid range).

5. The node sends a GNI to the hardware multicast broadcast address (this packet contains its new **net.node** address and the default zone).

6. The router sends an AARP request to the hardware multicast broadcast address (requesting the hardware address of the node sending the GNI).

7. The node sends an AARP response to the hardware and node address of the router (returning the node's hardware address).

8. The router sends a GNIR to the hardware and node address of the node (validating zone and network number).

Non-AppleTalk Ethernet Backbones for Macintosh Networks

This chapter focused on AppleTalk routing as the mechanism for linking separate AppleTalk networks. Another method, sometimes referred to as KIP (for Kinetics-Star Internet Protocol), enables a backbone to route TCP/IP between individual LocalTalk networks. You can use this routing method when you want to keep all AppleTalk traffic off the Ethernet.

Do keep in mind, however, that this method restricts you to AppleTalk end nodes residing only on LocalTalk networks. As soon as you put a Macintosh with an Ethernet card on the backbone Ethernet, you'll need AppleTalk-over-Ethernet routing services for that node to share such AppleTalk services as file sharing with other networks, including other LocalTalk networks. This is because KIP does not enable AppleTalk routers to listen to AppleTalk traffic on their Ethernet side. In fact, no zones will be created for the Ethernet user. An Ethernet-connected Macintosh must use TCP/IP end-node software for network communications in a KIP environment.

To establish KIP, you must have a Unix host on the internet that is running the *atalkad daemon.* This daemon (a Unix background process) stores all configuration information in a static routing table database. By static, we mean that any new

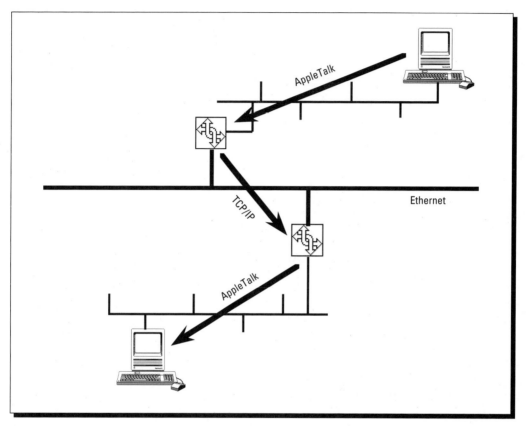

Figure 11-11: A KIP backbone.

networks must be manually entered into this file by an administrator. Then, each LocalTalk-to-EtherTalk router is assigned an IP address as well. These routers must have in their feature set the capability to do KIP routing. The LocalTalk-to-EtherTalk KIP router queries the atalkad daemon for information about the route a packet must take to access other LocalTalk networks (see Figure 11-11). All routing is done in IP between the LocalTalk-to-EtherTalk routers and the daemon.

The atalkad daemon

The atalkad daemon (pronounced a-talk-a-d) is a special Unix *daemon* that enables AppleTalk configuration information. A Unix daemon is a program that executes in the background, performing tasks independent of intervention by users or network administrators.

You can access the daemon via The Internet. For more information, consult a local Unix administrator; you will need some assistance in order to get atalkad up and running on your network.

Summary

In this chapter, we discussed in depth the AppleTalk routing and zone processes and showed you the start-up sequence for nodes in both extended and nonextended networks. We covered the following topics:

✔ LAN, MAN, and WAN are terms that describe the geography of a network's configuration.

✔ A collection of AppleTalk networks joined with routers is called an AppleTalk internet.

✔ The primary function of an AppleTalk internet router is to get data packets to their destinations.

✔ A Phase 1 router operates on a nonextended network; a Phase 2 router operates on an extended network.

✔ AppleTalk is unique among networking protocol systems in that it uses zone names and node names, as well as network numbers and node addresses, to map to locations across a multinet LAN.

✔ You can change, add, or delete zones from the zone list displayed in the Chooser.

✔ You can use a non-AppleTalk Ethernet backbone for your AppleTalk Network.

In the next chapter, you'll learn transition strategies for moving an AppleTalk Phase 1 network to AppleTalk Phase 2.

Chapter 12
Making the
Phase 2 Move

In this chapter . . .

✔ Four strategies for moving AppleTalk internets from Phase 1 to Phase 2

✔ The seven most common problems network managers have with transitions

✔ How to test for the common transition problems

✔ Why transition is more difficult for large internets

✔ Technical definitions of the terms Phase 1 and Phase 2; nonextended and extended

I n this chapter, we'll show you various strategies for the transition of a network from AppleTalk Phase 1 to AppleTalk Phase 2. Beyond explaining techniques and options, we'll list some problems that can occur during the transition. Some talented network managers unexpectedly experienced the seven technical problems we describe in this chapter, and we hope their experiences will sharpen your sense of caution.

This chapter underscores our two basic network management tenets: First, understand the network protocol as thoroughly as you can. Second, test every product before you put it on your production network.

We'll concentrate in this chapter on strategies for making a transition from Phase 1 to Phase 2 — not on the basics of how extended networking in Phase 2 works. Before reading this chapter, you'll need a clear understanding of the AppleTalk Routing Protocol, GetNetInfo packets, default zones, RTMP packets, network ranges, zone lists, and split-horizon routing. If you're not familiar with the concepts used in extended AppleTalk

networks, refer to Chapter 3, "Understanding AppleTalk Protocols," and Chapter 11, "Designing an AppleTalk LAN."

Although this book primarily covers LocalTalk and EtherTalk networks, many of the EtherTalk concepts for Phase 2 apply as well to other types of extended AppleTalk networks, such as TokenTalk.

We believe that network administrators should move their networks over to AppleTalk Phase 2. Phase 2 offers many advantages, such as split-horizon routing, and Phase 2 is the building block of many exciting new networking products. Just be careful and thorough in your transition plans. And we can't emphasize too strongly that you should test all products before releasing them on your production network.

The Basics of Moving to Phase 2

The basic task in changing your internet from Phase 1 to Phase 2 is actually quite simple — you change the configuration files of all your EtherTalk routers from nonextended network configurations to extended network configurations. (No change is needed for bridges, which don't have network numbers.) Then you reload any EtherTalk devices with Phase 2 drivers.

Recall that you cannot make a LocalTalk network into an extended network. When Apple wrote the protocol, the company decided that multiple zone names and networks were unnecessary on such a slow network. So, for LocalTalk-to-EtherTalk routers, you only need to change the configuration files of the ports that are attached to EtherTalk networks.

To change the port's configuration file to an extended format, you must change the router's format for information in the port's configuration file; the format will change from a network number to a network range and from a zone name to a zone list. A network range is an extended numbering scheme, and a zone list is an extended zone-naming scheme.

Defining terms: Phase 1 and Phase 2

Before going further, we need to clarify some terminology. As much as possible, we try to use the terms "extended" and "Phase 2" together to avoid confusion. To be absolutely precise, there are Phase 1 routers and Phase 2 routers. And there are extended networks and nonextended networks. But there are no Phase 1 or Phase 2 networks.

If this seems confusing, bear in mind that Phase 1 and Phase 2 are not networks — Phase 1 and Phase 2 are *specifications* for how to route and form packets. Routers *route* packets over and between either extended or nonextended networks. Software drivers *form* packets and then put them out over extended or nonextended networks.

The following critical distinction is most important to the network manager:

Phase 1 routers can route packets across nonextended networks, but *not* across extended networks.

Phase 2 routers can route packets across *both* extended *and* nonextended networks.

Note that many Phase 1 routers, such as the older Shiva FastPaths (Model 2), were built before the release of the Phase 2 specification. Phase 2 routers can recognize both the Phase 1 and Phase 2 specifications; a Phase 2 router can tell whether a packet is being sent from a Phase 1 or a Phase 2 router by looking at an embedded version number in the RTMP Data packet. In a later section of this chapter, you'll see that these routing decisions can sometimes lead to problems.

Moreover, some Phase 2 routers implement a portion of the Phase 2 specification even on ports the administrator has configured for Phase 1 routing on a nonextended network. For example, some vendors have chosen to implement split-horizon routing on both extended and nonextended networks. So even if you believe your internet is totally Phase 1 because you selected Phase 1 in your configuration file's dialog box, you may in fact have something more than Phase 1 on your internet. Unless you have only older routers on the internet, what you probably have is an internet that is using some newer Phase 2 technology to route packets over nonextended (Phase 1) networks.

As you can see, this terminology can be confusing. We don't want to be slaves to terminology, however, and for the most part the two sets of terms — Phase 1, nonextended, and Phase 2, extended — are used interchangeably. We'll continue to use the terms together where precise distinctions are not required.

Choosing an extended network configuration

In the next section, we'll discuss four methods for changing your internet from nonextended (Phase 1) to extended (Phase 2). With any of these methods, you'll have to devise a new numbering and zone-naming scheme.

To keep the implementation of the extended network configuration simple, you can even use the same network number and zone name you used for your nonextended (Phase 1) network. If, for example, your EtherTalk's network number was 45, the new network range can be 45-45, which is a network range of one network. Furthermore, the zone list can be a zone list of one, consisting of the same zone name you used before.

The rules for network numbers are the same for Phase 2 as they are for Phase 1: You cannot duplicate a network number on another network, even if the number falls within a range of numbers. If your nonextended (Phase 1) network number is 45, and this nonextended network is connected with a transition router to an extended (Phase 2) network, you cannot use the number 45 to make the Phase 2 network's range 45-45 or even 43-46. As long as two or more networks are connected, each network number can be used only once.

As you select network numbers for your extended (Phase 2) internet, remember to plan for the growth of your network. Try to estimate how many users you will have over the next five years and how many additional networks you expect to connect to your current AppleTalk internet. Is there a good possibility that you will be connecting more buildings or more remote sites to your internet? If so, plan a numbering scheme you can grow with.

For example, many large companies use a code, based on their building and floor numbers, for establishing network numbers. In such a system, the network range 1014-1014 can stand for Building 101, Floor 4. This type of code allows easy addition of networks to your internet numbering scheme.

When choosing a network-number range for a particular network cable, also consider how many users you'll have on the cable. Recall that in Phase 2, each network number allows 253 AppleTalk devices attached to an Ethernet cable. If you have selected a network range of 4-6 for a particular cable, for example, you have created networks numbered 4, 5, and 6 — three networks of 253 nodes each. You can therefore attach 759 AppleTalk devices to that Ethernet cable.

Most networks don't have more than 253 devices and therefore require only a one-number range, such as 4-4. This type of numbering means that a particular cable is identified by each attached router as network 4. In fact, we advise you never to set up more than one network for each cable. If more than 253 users are on a cable, we suggest that you install an EtherTalk-to-EtherTalk router to facilitate management control over your network. For more about managing your AppleTalk internet's configuration, refer to Part Three, "Managing an AppleTalk Network."

Although we recommend only one network number per network cable, we do advise the use of multiple zone names. Wise selection of zone names will help

Assigning zone names

Remember that zone names are intended as a reference for the user. As a result, zone names that simply match up with network numbers are of no help to the user who is trying to determine what is available in a zone.

Don't give each network its own zone name: This is not necessary and, in most cases, not desirable. In larger internets, such a numbers-oriented management strategy often results in huge lists of zone names that mean little to the user. Zone names like "Building 101 Floor 4" to match a network range of 1014-1014 do not indicate what network resources and devices can be found in the zone. As you choose zone names, also keep in mind that multiple network cables can share a zone name.

users navigate their way around the internet. Select descriptive zone names that will help users locate file servers, mail servers, and other multiple-user devices. Where appropriate, select zone names that describe the type of users who will have their Macs connected to the Ethernet. If your zone list includes an Engineering zone and a Marketing zone, for example, users who want to share engineering data can select to be in the Engineering zone, and users who want to share marketing data files can locate their Macintoshes in the Marketing zone.

The following example illustrates the use of helpful zone names. An AppleTalk internet at a certain company had an engineering program office, with Macintoshes on a LocalTalk network and file services on an EtherTalk network. (The network was set up in this way because the AppleTalk file server was on a VAX multiprotocol host.) To make it easy for Mac users on the LocalTalk network to find their server on the EtherTalk network, the zone name for the LocalTalk network was included in the EtherTalk network's zone list. In this configuration, a LocalTalk Macintosh would display both its LocalTalk zone's services and the EtherTalk file server in the same Chooser list because both LocalTalk and EtherTalk services were in the same zone. The user didn't need to be aware that two networks were involved.

Four Phase 2 Transition Methods

After you carefully choose a configuration for your extended network, you're ready to select a method for changing your nonextended (Phase 1) internet to an extended (Phase 2) internet. With any of the methods discussed in the next sections, be sure that all your devices and software drivers are Phase 2-functional and that you are prepared to install the new software at the same time you change the routers. If you still have devices or software drivers that can operate only as Phase 1 nonextended network nodes, you can use any of the first three methods to retain some Phase 1 functionality on your internet.

You can use any of several methods to accomplish the Phase 1 to Phase 2 configuration change. In the following sections, we'll discuss four of these methods:

1. The logical separation method

2. The physical separation method

3. The transition router method

4. The go-for-broke method

Each method has its advantages and hazards, and the size and complexity of your AppleTalk internet is a factor in deciding which is best for you. Keep in mind that the logical separation and the transition router methods are by far the most dangerous, especially in networks that have routers from two or more vendors. In fact, the logical separation and transition router methods led to most of the seven problems we'll describe later in this chapter. Yet hazardous as they are, the logical separation and transition router methods remain the most convenient for many network managers — especially those who need to quickly establish Phase 2 routing or who do not have enough personnel resources to use the physical separation or go-for-broke methods. We don't recommend the use of the logical separation or transition router methods, but the two methods are used so commonly that we are including them in our list of procedures so that you can be informed of all your options.

The logical separation method

With the logical separation method, you break your AppleTalk internet into two permanently separate, logically unconnected (no data throughput) internets. You do not have to physically separate the cables. With this method, the two internets will operate independently of each other, even though both are attached to the same physical cable.

The steps for the logical separation method are fairly straightforward. First, you choose the network cables that you want to upgrade — you may select, for example, one floor of a building to do first. Next, you shut off the routers that attach those networks to your original (Phase 1) internet and reconfigure their EtherTalk ports with an extended network format. When you reboot the newly configured routers, the networks attached to their ports will now make up a new Phase 2 internet.

If you plan at a later time to connect these logical internets with a transition router (described shortly), you must change the network numbers so that no duplication occurs. The logical separation method assumes that you will never connect the Phase 1 nonextended networks to the new, extended (Phase 2) networks. But if you do need to connect these internets at a later date as circumstances warrant, choosing new network numbers now will prevent potential duplications of network numbers later.

Each router you reconfigure to an extended (Phase 2) network format will function as if it were on a second and completely different cable running in a totally separate internet. Remember that an AppleTalk internet can be defined as a collection of networks joined with routers. Each separate internet is called a *logical internet*. The term *logical* differentiates between the functional type of network separation, which happens at the software level, and the *physical* type of network separation, where actual cables are separated. With logically

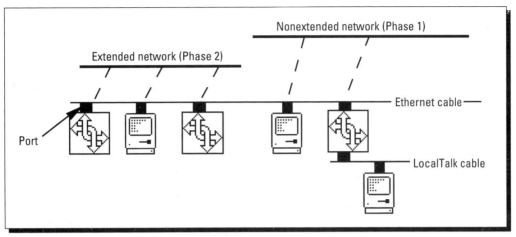

Figure 12-1: Two logical networks on one physical cable.

separated networks, the routers remain connected to the same physical Ethernet cable.

The Phase 1 EtherTalk network has a separate identity from the Phase 2 EtherTalk network because its Ethernet header is different. A device, such as a Macintosh running an AppleTalk Phase 1 driver (Ethernet version 2), ignores a packet with a Phase 2 header (Ethernet 802.3). Likewise, a Phase 2 device ignores packets with Phase 1 Ethernet headers.

Figure 12-1 shows two separate logical networks that exist on the same physical cable. The two Macintoshes are on separate networks even though they are attached to the same Ethernet cable. No router connects one network to another, so these Macintoshes have no path to each other and cannot communicate with each other for services, such as transferring files.

Note: In the figures of this section, a thick horizontal line represents the logical networks, and a vertical dashed line indicates the ports that are associated with each logical network.

Any LocalTalk network configuration stays the same because you do not reconfigure the port that attaches to the LocalTalk network — LocalTalk cannot be an extended (Phase 2) network. A LocalTalk network will be part of whichever of the two internets (extended or nonextended) the EtherTalk port of the LocalTalk-to-EtherTalk router is configured for. If the EtherTalk port of the LocalTalk-to-EtherTalk router is configured for Phase 2 routing and is therefore attached to the extended network, any network attached to the other ports of the router, such as a LocalTalk network, will also be a part of the extended network's internet.

Refer again to Figure 12-1, which shows a LocalTalk-to-EtherTalk router with a LocalTalk network attached. The EtherTalk port of the router is configured to attach to the nonextended (Phase 1) internet. Therefore, the LocalTalk network is also a part of the nonextended internet. Any devices attached to the LocalTalk network will *not* be able to communicate with devices that are part of the extended (Phase 2) network.

An advantage of the logical separation method is that you can complete the transition in stages, while your internet continues to run. This way you can pace yourself, devoting only a few hours at a time to the task of network transition. You may also find the extra time advantageous when you are caught in between trying to obtain upgrades for some of your network products that still run only Phase 1 software and having to use other, newer products that will only run Phase 2.

The logical separation method does have disadvantages, however. During the transition period, a device on the nonextended (Phase 1) internet cannot send files or communicate with devices on the extended (Phase 2) internet. If you have an e-mail system, for example, you will need two servers — one for each internet. Again, no mail will pass between these two internets. Another potential problem is that your router types will leak packets between Phase 1 and Phase 2. This problem is described in a later section.

The physical separation method

A second method is to physically separate your Ethernet networks and make the Phase 2 transition one network at a time. With this method, you reformat one router at a time to your new, extended (Phase 2) configuration. You do not, however, connect the newly configured router back to the same Ethernet segment. Instead, you start a new Ethernet segment that is physically disconnected from the Phase 1 Ethernet segment and attach the newly configured routers to the new segment. Of course, you won't have full connectivity until every one of your EtherTalk routers is reconfigured to Phase 2.

Figure 12-2 is an illustration of two physically divided networks during a transition to Phase 2. Note that the two networks do not share the same Ethernet cable as the logically separated networks in Figure 12-1 did.

A word of caution: Because you'll eventually connect all your networks back together, you must be careful during the transition not to duplicate your network numbers.

The physical separation method is similar to the logical separation method, but it is more cumbersome. And you must be careful not to attach Phase 1 internet cables or routers to your Phase 2 internet. You have the same disadvantage as

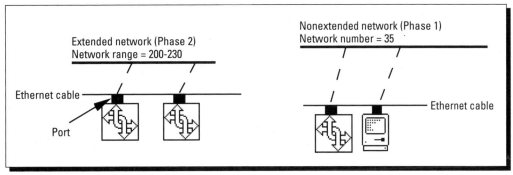

Figure 12-2: An example of physically divided networks.

you'd have with the logical separation method in that you lose communication between the two internets, for the obvious reason that the cables are physically disconnected. But just as with the logical separation method, you'll have the advantage of more time to upgrade your Phase 1 products to Phase 2.

The physical separation method does have several advantages over the logical separation method. You don't have to worry about any routers leaking packets, for example. In fact, the physical separation method, even though it is cumbersome and time-consuming, is one of the safest ways to move your AppleTalk internet to Phase 2. Also, with the physical separation method, Phase 1 packets will never pass into your Phase 2 internet. You can therefore safely use the extended features of Phase 2 and configure the new networks with network ranges of multiple networks (such as 4-6) and zone lists with multiple zones.

The transition router method

In the transition router method, you establish a connection between a Phase 1 and a Phase 2 internet by using a special router, commonly called a *transition router*. The transition router can route traffic between a nonextended (Phase 1) network and an extended (Phase 2) network.

To connect a Phase 1 internet to a Phase 2 internet with a transition router, you'll first need to create two separate logical internets, just as with the logical separation method. Then, when you configure the transition router, the router will have two logical ports attached to the same physical Ethernet cable. Both of these *logical* ports will attach through just one *physical* connection.

Configure one port so that it attaches as a router node to your Phase 1 internet, and configure the second port so that it attaches as a router node to your Phase 2 internet. The transition router will now route between these two logical internets, making them one internet.

The transition router sends out RTMP and ZIP packets in both an extended and a nonextended format, so that both Phase 1 and Phase 2 routers receive a complete picture of the internet's route structure. The transition router also translates data packets into the appropriate format. In other words, if the router receives a Phase 1 packet, the router translates the packet headers into 802.3 Ethernet format so that the Phase 2 routers can receive the packet.

If you plan to use a transition router, carefully observe the following rule: Configure your Phase 2 routers with a network range of one network number and a zone list of one zone name.

Recall that a single network range, such as 4-4, allows devices to select network 4 to reside in. On the other hand, with a multiple-net range, such as 4-6, devices can choose network 4, 5, or 6 to reside in. Because Phase 1 routers cannot map a route to a cable that has more than one network on it, however, a multiple-item network range is not allowed anywhere on an internet that has a transition router. The same logic applies to the zone list.

The following discussion may help you understand this important transition rule. Each entry in a Phase 1 router's routing table can hold only one number for identifying a network. The Phase 1 routing table has no capability for storing a range of numbers (*number-number*) as is the format of a Phase 2 router's routing table.

Figure 12-3 shows the type of network numbering you'll need to use with the transition router method. In this setup, the transition router has one physical port connection to the Ethernet cable and two logical network ports. Notice that the extended (Phase 2) network has a single-number network range of 200-200, whereas the nonextended (Phase 1) network has a net number of 35. Multiple-number network ranges are not allowed anywhere on this internet because of the presence of the transition router.

> If you use a transition router *anywhere* in your internet, every network range must consist of only one network number, and every zone list must consist of only one zone name. This rule applies even to internets that have multiple Ethernet backbones.

Suppose that you have on the network an Ethernet segment that is all Phase 2. If this Ethernet segment is connected to a mixed Phase 1, Phase 2 transition network, you must observe the transition rule of one net number per range and one zone name per list because a Phase 1 router on one side of the EtherTalk-to-EtherTalk router must have a listing in its routing table of the networks on the other side. The transition router must be able to translate this listing into the single-number format that the Phase 1 router can use.

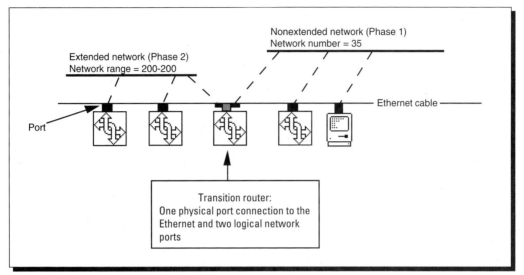

Figure 12-3: An internet configured with a transition router.

If you need more than one zone name in the zone list, which is quite likely on a large network, you cannot use the transition router method. You must change the network over all at once (the go-for-broke method described in the next section). Otherwise, your other option is to face loss of connectivity between network sections, as with the physical separation method.

The go-for-broke method

A fourth method for transition is to shut the entire internet down — in other words, "go-for-broke." With this method, you turn off AppleTalk on all of the routers, and then bring the internet back up, one router at a time, with the new Phase 2 configuration.

Although the go-for-broke method will require the most cooperation from your users because they will have to endure an extended downtime period, we recommend the go-for-broke method over the other three methods. If all of your routers and software drivers are Phase 2 capable, the go-for-broke method is the fastest, safest, and most efficient way of moving your entire internet to Phase 2.

If you are using multiprotocol routers, such as those from Cisco Systems, you need only to turn off the AppleTalk routing. The other protocols, such as TCP/IP or DECnet, will not be affected by this operation. It's also a good idea to shut down the rest of the AppleTalk nodes. Once you have all the routers on-line, you can bring these nodes back up again.

Shutting off all AppleTalk devices prevents any of the nodes from becoming confused by the change in zones. If you need to keep the devices running, you probably won't have problems, but shutting the devices off before you make the transition and then rebooting them after the new internet is up is a much cleaner process. With the routers turned off, devices won't be able to connect to devices on other cables.

With the go-for-broke method, be sure to schedule three times the amount of time you think the process will take. Turning off all of your routers, reconfiguring them, and then restarting them may take longer than you expect.

When planning how long the go-for-broke method will take, you might want to consider some of the following questions:

❖ How many *knowledgeable* people can help you?

❖ How long will it take you to walk from one router to the next?

❖ Do you have keys or access to all the locations of the routers?

❖ How long will it take you and your colleagues to reconfigure a router?

For example, ten minutes is a good estimate for the amount of time it will take you to reconfigure a router you are familiar with. As with any new configuration, we strongly suggest that you try out the configuration on a test network first so that you can iron out any difficulties with the use of the router's interface.

In a fast-paced weekend, a team of two colleagues (both of whom are familiar with configuring your types of routers) should be able to shut down and bring back up an AppleTalk internet of about 35 routers. We recommend, however, that you make contingency plans for Monday morning in case you run into problems. You should determine in advance whether you will switch back to Phase 1 or whether you will leave the internet down and continue working on the transition.

We feel that for many large networks, the go-for-broke plan is the only one that makes sense. The method allows you to take full advantage of the extended zone-list feature of Phase 2, and, if you complete the transition over a fast-paced weekend, you'll suffer the least duration of lost connectivity time. Also, as you'll see in the following sections, the go-for-broke method can help you avoid several problems that may crop up in a transition environment.

Seven Phase 2 Transition Problems

Somehow things went awry with Apple's first dreams of its Phase 2 specification. Apple envisioned an easy and quick transition for everyone; administrators who needed a little extra time to gather up the new code for all their devices could use Apple's internet router's "upgrade" utility. The utility would act as a transition router, allowing administrators to maintain both Phase 1 and Phase 2 networks in the same internet. Apple believed that developers would quickly turn out their new Phase 2 products, and any router developers having questions about implementation could observe Apple's example with the Apple Internet Router.

Now, over two years after Phase 2 was introduced, many networks are still not running in extended (Phase 2) network mode. Implementations of the Phase 2 specification were all a bit different from one another. Some vendors had trouble getting their new Phase 2 products to pass the stress test of busy or large networks, and network administrators were often forced to make large capital expenditures in order to upgrade their Phase 1 products to Phase 2 before they could complete the transition. Because of budget restraints, many administrators had to put off Phase 2 completely, or tried to live with a mixed Phase 1/Phase 2 transition internet.

The following sections describe seven technical problems network managers have encountered over the last two years. Software revisions fixed many of these difficulties, so be sure to check with your vendors to get the latest versions of their products. We present these problems so that you can see what types of things can go wrong and how important it is to test products and configurations before you put them on your production internet.

Routers that leak packets from Phase 1 to Phase 2

One of the first transition problems to be discovered was that certain routers *leak* packets. The leakage occurs when a router configured for a Phase 1 nonextended network sees a Phase 2 extended network packet and fails to ignore it as it should. Instead, the Phase 1 router accepts the Phase 2 packet and begins leaking the Phase 2 packet. In the worst cases, the router converts itself to a Phase 2 extended network router. In such a case, the router that formerly sent and received Phase 1 packets no longer acknowledges the Phase 1 packets, but simply drops them.

Because of this potential leakage risk, it is not a straightforward task to create two logically separated networks, with one network running in nonextended mode and the other in extended mode, as in the logical separation method. Theoretically, the logical separation method, which looks fine on paper, should work. In reality, routers that leak packets may not stay in the logical network where you put them.

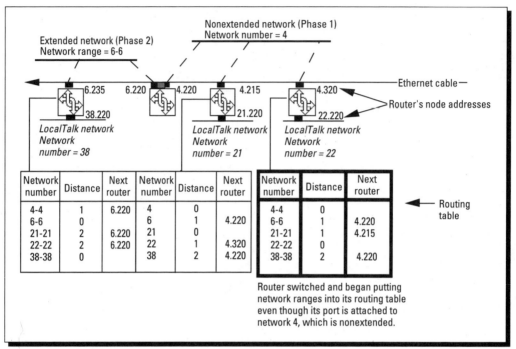

Figure 12-4: A router switching from Phase 1 to Phase 2.

This means that certain Macintoshes — those on the Ethernet or those that are behind the routers that were receiving zone information from the router that switched to become a Phase 2 extended network router — can no longer reach the services they could reach before the switch. The switched router not only changes its network routing to an extended (Phase 2) format, but it also begins sending out 802.3 rather than Ethernet version 2 packets.

Note the example shown in Figure 12-4. In this example, the original nonextended (Phase 1) network was configured with the network number 4, and an extended (Phase 2) network was configured with the network range 6-6. The switched router adds an extended network configuration of the range 4-4. When the switched router forwards a data packet from a node on its directly attached LocalTalk network (network 22), to any other node or network destination, the data packet is formatted into an 802.3 packet type.

When the data packet is destined to go to a node in network 38 or network 6-6, the switched router will look in its routing table and determine that the next router for networks 38-38 and 6-6 is reachable via node 4.220. When the data packet is destined for a node in network 21, the switched router will follow the same process and forward the packet to node 4.215. Likewise, when the data packet is destined to a node in network 4, it will send the packet directly to node 4. In all three cases, the receiving nodes (nodes 4.220, 4.215, or 4.x) are set up as nonextended (Phase 1) end nodes and should only receive packets in Ethernet version 2 format. These nodes throw away any packets sent to them in 802.3 format. Because of the packet type incompatibility, any nodes that are in networks behind the switched router (in this example, network 22) will lose connection to any devices beyond the switched router.

Servers that turn into routers

The problem discussed in this section certainly caught many AppleTalk administrators by surprise. Several manufacturers of AppleTalk Ethernet file-share servers changed their implementation dramatically when they added Phase 2 drivers. Instead of simply providing EtherTalk Phase 2 drivers for their servers, they added built-in AppleTalk routers as well. This situation was seen on AppleTalk servers that reside on non-Macintosh platforms.

Some vendors gave their new routers both seed and non-seed start-up modes, but others provided seed mode only. This means that when you reconfigure the seed-only router/servers for Phase 2, you also must add a network range and a zone list. The servers (which are now also routers) participate in the routing scheme of your internet: They issue RTMP packets, and they answer ZIP queries.

The server-turned-to-router turns into a problem when the server administrator, who in many companies is *not* the same person as the network manager, must configure the router properly to coexist on the network. The server administrator must be aware of the correct network range and zone list to use. At an even more fundamental level, the server administrator must know to ask the network manager for the correct network range and zone list. Experience shows that often the server administrator does not understand the importance of the addition of a router and merely types in the numbers provided by examples in the server's installation manual.

Incorrect network number and zone name entries cause the server to conflict with routers on the internet. The result is loss of connectivity. The users on the Ethernet, whose Macintoshes obtain their zone lists from the router in the file-share server, find that the Chooser list of zones that other users see (from properly configured routers) is gone. These unfortunate users see only the zone that the server administrator entered from the example in the installation manual. The users whose Macs are receiving the invalid zone list from the file-share server/router will not be able to connect to any of the network services that are in the "real" internet.

An added problem occurs if non-seed routers are coming on-line after the misconfigured file-share server/router is up. A non-seed router obtains its network range and zone-list configuration from the first router that answers the non-seed router's query. Because the misconfigured file-share server/router is not busy with real routing (unlike the properly configured routers), the misconfigured router will most likely be the first router to answer the new non-seed router. When a non-seed router takes its routing and zone information from the misconfigured file-share server/router, the connectivity problem is further compounded because the new non-seed router will display the invalid zone list to any networks that are behind the new routers.

Why *did* the vendors of AppleTalk file-share servers add routing capabilities to their servers? One reason may be historical. Because Phase 1 Ethernet networks were nonextended and allowed only one zone name per cable, several vendors' servers implemented an internal logical network to go along with their services as a convenience to users. This internal logical network, which had its own zone name, allowed the server to be found on a zone separate from the other devices. Many Ethernet servers had other services, such as spooled printers, and all services could be grouped together within one easily identifiable zone. But there was no longer a need for an internal, logical network of this type when Phase 2 was introduced. An extended (Phase 2) network allowed the administrator to add a special zone to the zone list for the Ethernet server and its services.

If you are a network manager, we advise you to monitor the installation of all AppleTalk servers on your internet, especially those that reside on non-Macintosh platforms. For example, we know of two non-Macintosh-platform servers that originally added routing to their Phase 2 implementations: TOPS on its Sun platform and Novell NetWare on its PC platform. Make it your responsibility to manage the installation of servers. Verify whether each server's configuration files do or do not require routing information (such as net-number or zone name) and verify the placement of the servers for best performance.

For more information on performance management, refer to Chapter 15, "Performance Management." For more information about how network-number conflicts can cause lack of connectivity, see Chapter 11, "Designing an AppleTalk LAN," and Chapter 14, "Fault Management." To learn more about non-seed routers and configuration management in general, see Chapter 16, "Configuration Management."

Routers that send Phase 2 packets to Phase 1 routers

Under some conditions, routers can send Phase 2 packets to Phase 1 routers. This problem occurs on internets that have multiple Ethernet networks still using the old Phase 1-only routers. You can suspect this problem when devices behind the older router don't show up in the Chooser for nodes on the other side of an EtherTalk-to-EtherTalk router (nodes on a different Ethernet cable).

When a router receives a packet type that it doesn't know about, it drops that packet as unreadable. Some Phase 2 routers send a new Phase 2 packet type called an *NBP FwdReq* (the Name Binding Protocol Forward Request) packet to Phase 1 routers. Because the code of the Phase 1 routers predates the existence of the NBP FwdReq packet type, the Phase 1 router throws the packet away. Because the Phase 1 router is unable to process the NBP FwdReq, any devices from the zone behind the Phase 1 router never respond. Note that these devices are invisible to the users behind the Phase 2 router. When a user clicks on that zone in the Chooser in order to see a device such as a LaserWriter, the user will not see the LaserWriter or any other device. In fact, the user will tell you that the zone is dead. The zone isn't really dead, however. The problem instead is with certain routers' interpretation of the new Phase 2 specification.

On a Phase 2 internet, when you open the Chooser and select a zone and the LaserWriter icon, you'll see a list of LaserWriters because the Phase 2 router for that zone is responding to an NBP FwdReq. In the original Phase 1 specification, however, NBP requests over an internet were made with an NBP LkUp (lookup) packet type. A Phase 1-only router expects to see the LkUp packet rather than the FwdReq. If the FwdReq is discarded, the list of available LaserWriters never appears in the Chooser. You can't see, or select, any devices from that zone.

The router type that exhibits this behavior decides that because it is attached to an Ethernet network in which all routers are newer, Phase 2-capable routers, all routers on the entire internet must be Phase 2-capable as well. The router therefore uses the new Phase 2 NBP FwdReq packet to send out NBP requests over the internet. And the router does this even if you selected Phase 1 in all your routers' configuration files.

The router's assumption is incorrect. The router decided that if all routers on its Ethernet are Phase 2-capable, all the routers on the other Ethernets in the internet are also Phase 2-capable. Recall that the router determines whether all

Testing for servers that turn into routers

To test whether a file-share server is behaving like a router, first start up another router and monitor the server's packets. If the server sends a GNIR (GetNetInfoReply) packet, you know that the server is operating in the mode of a router.

devices on its own Ethernet backbone are Phase 1 or Phase 2 by checking an embedded code in the broadcasted RTMP Data packets. But RTMP information from a second Ethernet backbone is regenerated by the EtherTalk-to-EtherTalk router (RTMP information is regenerated at each hop because broadcasts are not forwarded across routers). Therefore, if a Phase 1 router is on the other side of the EtherTalk-to-EtherTalk router, the router that is deciding whether or not all of the routers on the internet are Phase 2-capable does not know about the existence of the Phase 1 router. The RTMP information from the Phase 1 router will be regenerated by an EtherTalk-to-EtherTalk Phase 2 router and so the embedded code will be in a RTMP Data packet coming from a Phase 2-capable router.

So why doesn't the EtherTalk-to-EtherTalk router catch the NBP FwdReq packet and change it to a Phase 1 LkUp? At each hop, the NBP FwdReq is merely switched along its way. The intervening routers only regenerate RTMP and ZIP information because this information is sent to the broadcast address. All other data packets, NBP packets included, are simply routed according to the destination address inside the packet. The router looks at the destination address, which is in the **network.node** format, checks its port files to see which port file has a route for that network, and then sends the packet out that port. Checking each packet type to find those that are NBP packets would mean checking deeper within the packet structure — the process would slow down any router considerably.

This process is illustrated in Figure 12-5. The Macintosh shown at the top of the figure sends an NBP BrRq (Broadcast Request) to a Phase 2-capable router (Router A in the figure) that has been configured to route packets over a nonextended (Phase 1) network. The network manager selected this configuration — having the Phase 2-capable router route packets over a nonextended network — by selecting Phase 1 in the router's configuration dialog box.

When the Phase 2-capable router (Router A) receives the NBP BrReq, it forwards the packet toward its destination in the form of an NBP FwdReq packet. Recall that the NBP FwdReq packet is new to the Phase 2 specification and is used to forward an NBP request over an extended (Phase 2) network rather than over a nonextended (Phase 1) network. The Phase 2-capable router (Router A) has made the decision that all routers on the internet are Phase 2-capable because there are no Phase 1 routers on its network. Note that the Phase 1-only router is two networks away.

The next router (Router B) receives the NBP FwdReq packets and forwards it toward the destination. Unfortunately, the next router in line is a Phase 1-only router which does not recognize the NBP FwdReq (Router C) packet type. The packet is discarded, and the LkUp-Reply is never returned to the original Macintosh. Without the LkUp-Reply, the Macintosh will never see the printer from the

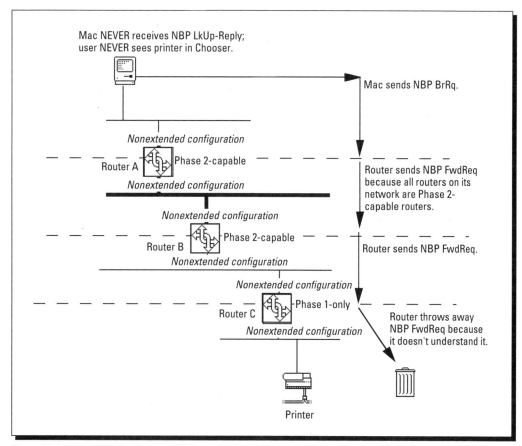

Figure 12-5: How an NBP FwdReq can fail on a multitiered internet.

Testing for misconfigured routers

You can test for a router that sends NBP FwdReq packets when configured as a nonextended network node. Attach to an isolated Ethernet cable one port of the router to be tested and a second Phase 2-capable router along with a network packet analyzer. Select Phase 1 (nonextended) mode for both routers' network configuration files. Attach a Macintosh to the other port of the router you are testing — this is usually the LocalTalk port. Attach a printer to the second (LocalTalk) port of the second router. While capturing packets with the network packet analyzer, open the Chooser and look for printers in the second zone. If the analyzer shows that the router sent an NBP FwdReq instead of an NBP LkUp packet, you've found a misconfigured router.

network behind the Phase 1-only router, and the user will never see the printer in the Chooser.

See Chapter 11, "Designing an AppleTalk LAN," for more about the NBP process.

Default zones that change

Another problem involves default zones that change. A default zone is set by the administrator in the router configuration file. Devices that don't select from the zone list a zone to reside in are placed in this default zone. Some server implementations are not zone-configurable and therefore always reside in the default zone.

With early implementations of Phase 2, some routers did not use the default zone that the administrator selected in the router's configuration file. These routers disregarded the administrator's configuration information and used either the last or the first zone in the zone list as the default zone.

If you are using a router model of this type, your only problem is that your default zone won't be the one you select, although it will be a stable zone. But if you use router types from several vendors, one defaulting to the last zone in the list, and another model using the default zone you select, you can have further difficulties.

One problem is that a device such as a server may reboot into a different default zone each time, depending on which router it heard from. Users are left playing a game of "where did the server go?"

A second problem occurs when you use seed routers that verify the network configuration before coming on-line to route. The routers will discover the conflict of two or more different default zones when they receive mismatched GNIRs (GetNetInfoReply) and won't route until the conflict is resolved. The zones that are behind them won't be visible in the Chooser. Although this process may sound unfriendly, having the seed router not come up and route unless the network is properly configured has its advantages. The system alerts you to the conflict *before* users complain that network devices are down. In this case, the devices are just rebooted into the other default zone.

An administrator can spend valuable time troubleshooting the specific operations of a device that keeps "disappearing." The administrator may, for instance, go through the routine of troubleshooting a server's operating system, only to find out that the disappearance resulted from the existence of two conflicting default zones.

Routers that restrict the number of zones

Several router vendors have developed Phase 2 routing software that allows only a limited number of zones. With these routers, the limit has been anywhere from 120 to 150 zones, although the AppleTalk Phase 2 specifications state that Phase 2 zone tables can include up to 255 zones.

With these routers, only a limited number of zones can be held in the ZIT (Zone Information Table). A network administrator may go over this limit when placing a large number of zones in the EtherTalk zone list and the number of zones in the ZIT already includes many zones from other nonextended networks, such as LocalTalk. Also, in larger internets, the administrator sometimes has more than one extended network and tries to give each one of these a large zone list, again adding to the number of zones in any of the internet routers' ZITs.

The problem takes a strange twist in an unstable internet, where routers restart themselves, or in a changing internet, where new routers are coming on-line. In this situation, a Macintosh receives a zone list from a router and selects one of the zones. But then the Macintosh is told that the zone is invalid for use when it sends a GNI (GetNetInfo) packet back to confirm the zone and receive the zone's multicast address. How did this happen?

Between the time the router sent the zone list to the Macintosh and the time it receives the Macintosh's GNI packet, its ZIT has changed. Because of its limitations, the router deleted the zone that the end node requested in favor of another new zone coming from a new router — recall that the router can hold only a limited number of zones. Two other signs of this problem are Macintoshes mysteriously moving back into the default network or entire zones appearing and disappearing from the Chooser list.

Devices that don't respond to a zone multicast

Another problem occurs with some early implementations of Phase 2 software device drivers that do not recognize a specific zone's multicast address. These devices recognize only those packets sent directly to their net.node address or

Testing for routers that limit the number of zones

To find out whether a router limits the number of zones in its zone information table, place the router and a Macintosh with an Ethernet card on an isolated test Ethernet cable. Configure the router with 250 zones in the zone list. Bring up the router first; then turn on the Macintosh. If the Macintosh is able to select from all 250 of the zones, the router does not have this problem.

those sent to the AppleTalk broadcast address, **$09:00:07:ff:ff:ff**, which is where all AppleTalk nodes will respond. However, when an NBP LkUp packet is sent to a zone, it is addressed to the zone's specific multicast address, which is different from the overall broadcast address for the entire EtherTalk network. These devices did not respond to NBP LkUps and therefore are invisible to the network user.

If several devices are on an EtherTalk network before a router is installed, and if one of these devices is of the type that doesn't recognize a zone's specific multicast address, the following events occur. At first, the devices will see each other. But none of these devices are using a zone multicast address, as this address is given out by a router; these devices are sending their NBP LkUps to the AppleTalk broadcast address. If, then, a router is placed on this network, the nodes will notify their users/administrators that they need to be rebooted. When the nodes are rebooted, they send out a GNI (GetNetInfo) packet, and the router returns a GNIR (GetNetInfoReply) packet containing the zone multicast address for the chosen zone.

The malfunctioning device, however, ignores the GNIR information and continues to respond only to LkUp packets sent to the broadcast address. Devices that previously could communicate are no longer able to do so because they are sending their NBP LkUps to the new zone multicast address that the malfunctioning device is ignoring. This problem may be mistakenly diagnosed as bugs in the router because the problem with network connectivity appears when a new router is brought on-line.

Start-up nodes that initiate a GNIR flood

The final Phase 2 transition problem we will discuss involves a flood of GNIR (GetNetInfoReply) packets. The flood results from an implementation of an end node's Phase 2 driver that flushes its **net.node** address from its memory cach time the end node starts. Normally, a Phase 2 end node will retain its **net.node** address in non-volatile memory and will use this stored number in the AARP probes that it issues upon startup. (AARP probes are used to verify that the **net.node** is unique. Please refer to Chapter 11 for a more thorough discussion of how AARP and GNI packets are used in Phase 2 end node startup.)

EtherTalk zone multicast addresses

An EtherTalk zone multicast address is computed by the ZIP process in a router and can range anywhere from $09:00:07:00:00:00 to $09:00:07:00:00:fc. The EtherTalk multicast broadcast address that is sent to all EtherTalk devices is $09:00:07:ff:ff:ff. This broadcast address is used by RTMP Data packets and AARP probe packets.

Because the driver flushed its net.node number, it must use a number from the startup range. After verifying that it has a unique address within the startup range, the end node sends out a GNI packet to obtain zone verification. Because routers do not have a route to the startup range network and therefore cannot respond directly to this end node, routers respond to the GNI by sending a GNIR to the broadcast address.

When the device broadcasts its GNI packet, every other device on the cable is interrupted once. Now, with every router replying to the device at the broadcast address, every AppleTalk device on the cable is interrupted as many times as the internet has routers.

If you are using a software driver, end nodes are not moved from one extended network to another. However, if you are using a software driver for an extended network that doesn't maintain the **net.node** in its memory, every time that node is restarted, your internet receives a flood of broadcast GNIR packets. If you use this software driver on many nodes, your problem compounds by the number of nodes that are restarting, a number that increases dramatically if the problem software driver is installed on your Macintoshes and your users habitually turn off their Macintoshes at night and restart them in the morning all at about the same time. The more Macintoshes with this forgetful software driver that are restarting, the more likely it is to be a problem.

Refer to Chapter 11 for more information on how a node starts up.

Is Phase 2 Worth It?

Is all this trouble worth it? Yes. There are potential hiccups and bugs in the implementation of a new Phase 2 network. But after you work through these difficulties, your internet will run much more efficiently than it did before. Split-horizon routing alone is reason enough to justify a move to Phase 2. Also, a zone-multicast system that restricts NBP LkUps to devices in a particular zone

Testing for GNIR flooding

An Ethernet packet monitor can help you detect the problem of GNIR flooding. Set up a test network with an Ethernet packet monitor, a router, and a Macintosh (or whatever platform the driver is on). Configure the router with a network range and zone list different from the internet where the Mac was located. Start the router. Load on this Macintosh any of the drivers you want to test. Reboot the Macintosh once. The Macintosh will come up with an invalid net number; reselect an appropriate address. Then reboot again and watch to see if it selects the same address.

reduces unnecessary traffic. Perhaps the most important reason of all is to be able to use new networking products built on the Phase 2 specification, such as System 7's file-sharing features. So go for it, and good luck.

Summary

In this chapter, we covered four methods you can use to change your AppleTalk Phase 1 internet to an AppleTalk Phase 2 internet. We included examples of problems that network managers have had with their Phase 2 transitions so that you can avoid such problems in your network.

In this chapter, you learned the following points:

✔ Phase 1 and Phase 2 are specifications for how to form and route packets on an internet.

✔ Phase 1 specifies a nonextended network configuration; Phase 2 specifies an extended network configuration.

✔ The four main methods for making the Phase 2 move are the logical separation method, the physical separation method, the transition router method, and the go-for-broke method.

✔ Many administrators experienced problems when making the transition to Phase 2 because products that implemented the Phase 2 specification often varied among vendors.

✔ As an administrator, you should plan to make the transition to Phase 2 — the advantages outweigh any potential hiccups in implementations.

In the next chapter, you'll learn the basics of AppleTalk wide area networks.

Chapter 13
Designing an AppleTalk WAN

In this chapter . . .

✔ How to put together a wide area network

✔ The building blocks of wide area networks

✔ The advantages and disadvantages of point-to-point circuits, X.25, Frame Relay, and other circuit types

✔ Issues in routing AppleTalk between two LANs

A WAN, or *wide area network,* is an internetwork that extends between two or more LANs, usually across long distances, such as between cities and even across continents. Wide area network connectivity for AppleTalk users means that when you, as a user, select any Chooser driver, such as a LaserWriter driver, you can use a device in a zone that is located miles away on the other side of a wide area link. Connectivity for the network means that routing information regarding zone names/lists and network numbers/ranges is communicated across the wide area link so that routing tables and zone information tables are maintained and packets are forwarded to their destinations.

In this chapter, we'll help you understand the basics involved in using and managing a wide area network. Note that the security issues involved in managing wide area networks are covered in Chapter 17, "Accounting and Security Management."

Building Wide Area Links

The full amount of information and background that you need to make decisions about setting up your WAN is beyond the scope of this chapter. We will, however, provide you with some of the basics so that you will be better informed when you begin considering the design of your WAN. For more detailed information, we suggest that you talk with carrier vendors and WAN router vendors. Both types of vendors have excellent literature available for the new WAN network administrator and designer.

Setting up WAN services

For best results, you need to select and integrate into your existing AppleTalk LAN topologies a WAN service setup that adds the most value to your LANs in the most cost-effective manner. Many choices are available for WAN services. You can build a WAN using phone or satellite links, but phone links are most commonly used because the satellite links are slower.

Following are some of your other choices:

❖ You can choose a private WAN that you manage yourself, or you can have the carrier you select manage your private WAN for you.

❖ You can choose a public Value Added WAN (called a VAN).

❖ You can choose from a number of carriers; AT&T, U.S. Sprint, WilTel, MCI, CompuServe, and BT (Tymnet) all have WAN offerings.

❖ You need to select one of the following circuit types: point-to-point circuits, circuit-switched service, or packet-switched services. This choice depends on how often you will use the line, whether occasionally or 24 hours a day.

❖ Finally, you need to select the amount of bandwidth you need: 56 kbps, 1.544 Mbps (which is referred to as T1), or 45 Mbps (sometimes referred to as T3).

To summarize your choices, you need to select between public or private services, and then select a carrier, the quantity of line usage, the circuit type, and the bandwidth.

Bridge versus Router

We recommend that for connecting AppleTalk LANs, you always use a router-to-router connection instead of a bridge-to-bridge connection. A router broadcasts one RTMP Data packet every ten seconds; a bridge forwards all broadcasted RTMP Data packets from *all* the routers on the LAN.

For example, if ten LocalTalk-to-EtherTalk routers are connected to an Ethernet backbone that has a bridge going over a wide area link, and ten LocalTalk-to-EtherTalk routers are on the other side, 200 RTMP Data packets will be sent every ten seconds. This type of overhead will drown your bridged wide area link at a certain point, especially if you are also bridging other Ethernet protocols, such as IPX, DECnet, or TCP/IP, over the same link.

The building blocks of a WAN

To explain all of your WAN options, we need first to describe how a WAN is put together. A router that connects a LAN to another remote LAN with a port attached to a wide area link is called an *exterior router,* or a *DTE* (Data Terminal Equipment). An exterior router is usually a router that is on an Ethernet cable (as opposed to LocalTalk). An exterior router then typically connects to a specialized high-speed modem called a CSU/DSU. The CSU/DSU is connected to a switch that brings the network into a carrier's system. At the destination or termination point, the carrier's switch is connected to a CSU/DSU and then again to an exterior router.

The exterior router must perform a specialized function called *packet encapsulation.* Because the data traffic in a WAN is leaving Ethernet's data link and physical characteristics, the data must be *encapsulated* into a data link format for the physical conditions of the wide area link. (*Encapsulation* is the sandwiching of a packet inside of a new type of header and trailer.) The most common encapsulation type for wide area links is HDLC (High-Level Data Link Control). LAPB is also used for the underlayer of a packet-switched network protocol called X.25, which we'll cover in an upcoming section. Data packets are encapsulated into either HDLC or LAPB by the exterior router and de-encapsulated by the termination end exterior router.

Point-to-point circuits

One of the most common ways to build an AppleTalk WAN is by using a *point-to-point circuit.* A point-to-point circuit is a permanently dedicated circuit between two end points. The carrier's equipment that constructs the circuit does not manipulate the data traffic in any way. The point-to-point circuit is therefore said to be *transparent* to the end LAN protocol (such as AppleTalk).

Point-to-point circuits are available in a variety of speeds, from 1200 bps to 1.544 Mbps (T1). Because AppleTalk routing currently requires constant broadcasting of RTMP Data packets (every ten seconds), we recommend that you do not connect two AppleTalk LANs with anything less than a 56 kbps line. Preferably, you should connect the LANs with a T1. For the sake of reference, a 56 kbps line is 0.05 percent of Ethernet's 10 Mbps bandwidth, and a T1 is 10.544 percent of Ethernet's ten Mbps bandwidth.

Note: A point-to-point circuit that you lease from a carrier is usually priced at a monthly flat charge. The cost is based on the distance of the circuit and its bandwidth.

Circuit-switched services

With a circuit-switched service, a fixed amount of bandwidth is allocated and reserved between two end points, but only for the duration of the call. This call can either be made automatically with software, or manually by a person dialing the phone line. *Dial-up service*, another name for circuit-switched service, is appropriate when you need to establish LAN-to-LAN connectivity only for short time periods. For example, you might use dial-up service when you need a connection only one day of the month, possibly to send sales reports to your corporate office.

The most common bandwidth available for a circuit-switched service is 56 kbps, although it is possible to find offerings of circuit-switched services at T1 speeds. Included in the speed factor is the call set-up time, which can vary from 10 to 30 seconds.

Note: The cost of circuit-switched service is based on bandwidth, distance, and the amount of connect-time during which a call is actually established.

Packet-switched services

Packet-switched services are quite a bit different from either circuit-switched or point-to-point. For packet-switched networks, you have a network-layer protocol: The three available today are X.25, Frame Relay, and SMDS. These protocols assess what is "real" traffic and make a connection only when there is actual data to transmit (RTMP, ZIP, and the other overhead packets of AppleTalk are considered data to the packet-switched protocol). Within a packet-switched network are store-and-forward switches that will send data traffic to its destination.

You can set up a packet-switched network to be *multipoint*, with one port on your LAN's exterior router connecting to multiple termination or destination points. For example, one port on an exterior router in Los Angeles may connect your LAN to a packet-switched network and send data to Chicago, New York, and Denver — one connection, three destinations. This setup can be very cost-effective because you don't need to purchase a port on your exterior router for every destination, as you would with point-to-point circuits.

The throughput of a packet-switched circuit cannot be equated to its bandwidth, as can point-to-point or circuit-switched links. Delay is incurred for processing at each store-and-forward switch, and, for X.25, delay is incurred for error-recovery and flow control. Bandwidth is also taken up by protocol information (X.25, Frame Relay, or SMDS) that must be added to the data packet. The bandwidth of a packet-switched circuit is therefore described in terms of the bandwidth for the area between the exterior router and the network switch that puts the data out over the wide area link, rather than the bandwidth between source to destination. The area between the exterior router and the network switch is referred to as the *access line*. Access line bandwidth for packet-switched networks is available at 300 bps to 56 kbps and T1 all the way up to T3 (45 Mbps), depending on which protocol is used.

Note: The fee for a packet-switched service is usually based on the amount of traffic, but distance and connect-time can also be factors in the cost. Note that the AppleTalk protocol has a great amount of overhead for routing and for NBP searches to zones. The pay-per-usage charge for a packet-switched circuit may be higher for an AppleTalk WAN than for multiple point-to-point circuits.

The next sections deal with the various types of packet-switched services: X.25, Frame Relay, and SMDS.

X.25

X.25 is a network-layer protocol that is used to connect two or more LANs. X.25 is a permanent, virtual-circuit type of packet-switched circuit, which means that with X.25, a network carrier administratively configures a path through the store-and-forward switches of the network. X.25 delivers packets in sequence and provides additional features, including flow control, and recovery and retransmission of lost or errored data. A LAN protocol, such as AppleTalk, is encapsulated into X.25 by the LAN's exterior router for transmission over the wide area link. Bandwidth for X.25 links is available at 300 bps to 2 Mbps.

Frame Relay

Frame Relay, a packet-switched protocol, is similar to X.25 in that it is also a type of virtual circuit. Frame Relay, however, is much faster than X.25 because it does not have overhead for providing flow control and error recovery of data. X.25 was built when terminal-to-host communications were the norm and such overhead was necessary. Now, with the proliferation of LAN protocols, such as TCP/IP and AppleTalk, the extra overhead is not necessary and is in fact redundant with the error-control features of LAN protocols. Bandwidth for Frame Relay is currently available at 19.2 kbps to 2 Mbps, and developers are working on making Frame Relay available at T3 (45 Mbps) speeds.

SMDS

AppleTalk applications of SMDS were shown for the first time in networking shows in early 1992. Like X.25 and Frame Relay, SMDS is a packet-switched service protocol, so you can configure an SMDS network to be multipoint. In a multipoint network, one connection can have multiple destinations; the data is sent through store-and-forward switches within the SMDS network. Like Frame

Relay, SMDS does not provide error control or flow control. SMDS, however, differs from both X.25 and Frame Relay in that SMDS is a datagram type of packet-switched circuit. A datagram service does not guarantee that packets will be delivered in the same sequence as they were sent. SMDS is fast, with bandwidth speeds available at a low end of T1 to a current high end of T3 and projections of future speeds of 150 Mbps.

Public and private WAN links

All the WAN circuits described in the preceding sections — point-to-point, circuit-switched, and packet-switched — are available from carriers, where your links share the circuits with other customers on a public network. Or, you can build your own private network.

A public network has the advantage of being controlled and monitored by the carrier. With a public network, you can concentrate on your business, not on your wide area network. Also, hooking up to a public network does not require a large capital expenditure in equipment that may soon become obsolete.

Public networks, however, have two drawbacks. One is that public networks are not as secure as private networks. With a public network, it is possible (although difficult) for an unauthorized entity to call into the network. (For more information on security procedures for networks, see Chapter 17, "Accounting and Security Management.")

The second drawback is that upgrades to new technology will take place at the carrier's schedule, which may not be as fast as you'd like.

Private networks commonly connect privately owned switching equipment to point-to-point circuits leased from a carrier. It is possible to build a completely private network if you can obtain your own right-of-way for installing circuits (possibly with satellite links). Private networks can be more cost-effective over time, when compared to the monthly charges of a public network. Also, with a private network, you can control the timing of any moves to a new technology, such as SMDS.

All these technologies — point-to-point, circuit-switched, and packet-switched — connect two or more AppleTalk LANs. But there are several ways to get AppleTalk out onto the WAN, as we'll describe next.

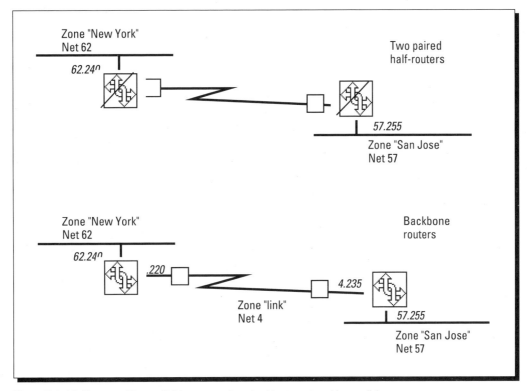

Zone "New York"
Net 62

62.240

Two paired
half-routers

57.255

Zone "San Jose"
Net 57

Zone "New York"
Net 62

62.240

.220

Backbone
routers

Zone "link"
Net 4

4.235

57.255

Zone "San Jose"
Net 57

Figure 13-1: A half-router wide area link is compared to a backbone router wide area link.

Routing AppleTalk across a Wide Area Link

There are two kinds of AppleTalk exterior routers: *half-routers* and *backbone routers*. Exterior half-routers differ from exterior backbone routers in that they don't expect the link between them to be configured with AppleTalk network number/range and zone name/list information. The backbone router, however, treats the link in the same manner as any other locally connected cable. See Figure 13-1 for a diagram that illustrates the difference between half-routers and backbone routers.

With both half-routers and backbone routers, a more sophisticated system is needed for wide area network routing. The major drawback to routing AppleTalk over a wide area link is the amount of overhead that occurs with the constant stream of broadcasted RTMP Data packets. Also, you must be careful not to duplicate network numbers when joining an AppleTalk LAN to another. In some cases, you must change all the router configuration files of one of the LANs to new, non-conflicting numbers. In addition, AppleTalk, as a purely hop-count-based protocol, has no way of establishing that one parallel path is better than another. Even if you have two point-to-point links, with one at 9.6 kbps and the other at T1, the AppleTalk protocol looks at these links as equal because both are one hop away.

The IETF (Internet Engineering Task Force) AppleTalk/IP Working Group is working with many ideas for enhancing AppleTalk routing capability. At present, we can describe only three publicly announced methods: tunneling, AURP (AppleTalk Update Routing Protocol), and network number remapping. Keep an eye open, though, for many changes in the next five years from the development work the IETF is doing for AppleTalk wide area networking.

The tunneling method

Cayman Systems and Digital Equipment have implemented a method that tunnels AppleTalk packets through a foreign network protocol's wide area link. Two currently used foreign protocols are IP and DECnet. Within an exterior half-router, the central routing process forwards all packets that are destined out of the exterior port into an encapsulation process. This process stuffs the AppleTalk packet inside a foreign protocol packet, which is then sent to the paired half-router on the other side of the link. At this router, the packet is de-encapsulated and forwarded to a normal AppleTalk network.

Figure 13-2 is a diagram of a tunnel process. Note that tunneling encapsulation occurs first. Then the AppleTalk-within-TCP/IP or DECnet packet is encapsulated into a form such as HDLC that is appropriate for the wide area link circuit type.

Tunneling AppleTalk through a foreign protocol data link has several advantages. Because the packet moves through the data link as if it were a packet from the

Load-Sharing

In the example shown in Figure 13-3, one router has two ports with two point-to-point circuits attached. In our discussion, we said that the foreign protocol specified that the slower link was a backup link. The foreign protocol had the capability to plot "cost" as well as hop count to make routing decisions.

Another way of distributing traffic load across two links is to use the software of a router rather than the software of the protocol. This technique is referred to as *load-sharing*. If a protocol, such as AppleTalk, does not have the capability to distribute data traffic evenly across two links, a router with two ports can maintain usage tables for each port to decide when to switch traffic out of one port over to the other. Note, however, that to do load-sharing by relying on the router rather than the protocol, both links must be attached to the same router.

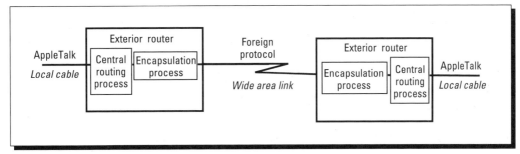

Figure 13-2: The diagram shows how AppleTalk is tunneled through the foreign network protocol's link.

foreign protocol, the packet benefits from any features that the system has as the packet travels between the two half-routers. For example, the packet benefits from the foreign protocol specifying a default route that is a faster link, while maintaining a redundant path in case of failure (see Figure 13-3).

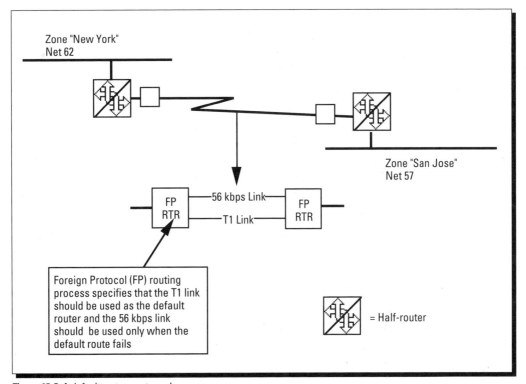

Figure 13-3: A default route on a tunnel.

The drawback to tunneling is that the administrator must maintain the foreign protocol network. If the site doesn't already have a foreign protocol link and must establish one, tunneling can require quite a learning curve for the administrator, who must learn all the intricacies of routing the foreign protocol.

The AURP protocol

Apple is working on a new protocol for AppleTalk wide area networks, called Apple Update Routing Protocol (AURP). Although it is not available as of this publication, AURP will interact with the current Phase 2 RTMP (Routing Table Maintenance Protocol) and take over for routing packets across a wide area link. Similar to tunneling, an exterior half-router will use AURP to route packets to the second half-router of a pair.

AURP is similar to RTMP in that it will use the split-horizon routing method (see Chapter 11, "Designing an AppleTalk LAN"). On discovery of a new exterior router, AURP will request complete routing information from that router. After it has received the full network number range and zone list, the AURP router can request one of two ways to be informed of changes. This is where AURP differs significantly from RTMP. The AURP router can request the peer exterior router to do either of the following:

❖ Send updates only when a change occurs and at a specified minimum interval (such as "send changes to me only once an hour")

❖ Never send updates, in which case the router polls its peer when it wants to receive up-to-date routing information

AURP will certainly help in reducing overhead, which can become an overload with the current RTMP requirement of sending a message every ten seconds.

Remapping network numbers

A problem of conflicting network numbers becomes more likely as the WAN grows larger. This is because it's highly probable that each LAN will be administered independently and coordination among the various AppleTalk LAN administrators to prevent overlapping network numbers becomes more difficult.

To solve this problem, Apple is working on a system for *network number remapping*. Current plans are to give an exterior router a range of network numbers to use for networks that come from other exterior routers. The router will create a map of the original network number to the given network range, and it will appear to the local cable that packets coming from these networks are originating from non-conflicting ranges.

This process may sound simple at first, but the more complex the wide area network becomes, the more intricate the process will need to be. For example, if a tunnel has several exterior routers, the network mapping process needs a method for identifying which network range originated from which exterior router, especially if two or more of these routers have the same network number or range on their locally attached internets.

Where To Obtain More Information

If you are interested in routing AppleTalk over wide area networks, we suggest that you pay close attention to the IETF AppleTalk/IP Working Group's findings. Let this group know what your wide area network's requirements are. Your chance to speak up is now, while solutions are still in the development stage.

Summary

In this chapter, you learned several ways to build a wide area network. You also learned about some issues regarding AppleTalk routing that Apple and the IETF committee are working on. We covered the following points:

✔ You can use three types of circuit services to build wide area networks: point-to-point, circuit-switched, and packet-switched.

✔ Three protocol types fall within the packet-switched category: X.25, Frame Relay, and SMDS.

✔ Speeds below 56 kbps are not recommended for connecting one AppleTalk LAN to another.

✔ When connecting two AppleTalk LANs together, you need to be careful not to duplicate network numbers. Apple is working on a network-number remapping scheme to solve this problem.

In the next chapter, you learn about fault management and how to set up a network disaster recovery plan tailored to your needs.

Part Three

Managing an AppleTalk Network

Part Three: Managing an AppleTalk Network

Managing a network is a multifaceted job, ranking right up there with Excedrin Headache number 79. Management takes in such tasks as finding bottlenecks in network traffic, learning why a user can't find the LaserWriter, seeing that servers are backed up properly, and checking that no more than the correct number of licensed software packages are running on the network.

One problem with defining network management is that there are so many aspects to it. Networks consist of wires and cables, computers, peripherals, file servers, and software. And don't forget the users. All these items are interwoven into the network environment.

It makes sense to break down the tasks of network management into groups of similar activities. Then you'll find that some tools fit better in one category than into another and that your own view of the management task may be clearer. In Part Three, we've chosen to subdivide the tasks (and chapters) according to a model that the International Standards Organization (ISO) has been developing for network management. The five categories, which have already been defined by the ISO in an attempt to standardize the functions of network management, are as follows:

- ❖ Fault management (Chapter 14)

- ❖ Performance management (Chapter 15)

- ❖ Configuration management (Chapter 16)

- ❖ Security management (Chapter 17)

- ❖ Accounting management (Chapter 17)

Another category of network management not defined by the ISO, which we call resource management, concerns the users, along with their Mac hardware and software, but not the network itself. We'll cover this subject in Chapter 18, the last chapter in this part.

Chapter 14
Fault Management

In this chapter...

✔ A description of fault management

✔ How to prepare a network disaster recovery chart

✔ Tools for monitoring and troubleshooting the network

✔ A step-by-step guide to troubleshooting your network

✔ Examples of network disaster recoveries

Fault management is often overlooked until too late. If you are a network manager, not only must you plan and design new networks as the company grows, but you must also maintain the smooth operation of the networks that are now in place. Fault management is absolutely critical to any network management scheme. If you are a network manager, fault management picks up at the point when your network management plans fail or the network has suffered some kind of failure and a swarm of angry network users is heading your way. This chapter helps you develop a well thought-out fault management plan that you can put into action as soon as trouble starts.

In this chapter, we'll discuss effective techniques for monitoring and troubleshooting networks, and we'll demonstrate how specific problems have been solved with these techniques. You'll learn the basic elements that should be part of a network disaster recovery plan and how to create a chart that ranks these elements by priority. Then after constructing this chart, you'll see how to review your own network environment and add any further elements appropriate to your needs. You'll probably have to do some research to complete the chart, but we urge you to take this time — it's well worth it to have a chart like this in advance of tragedy.

Preparing a Disaster Recovery Chart

The network disaster recovery chart (see Figure 14-1) has several purposes. After you draw up a list of features and users, you'll be ready to achieve an important goal of the chart, which is to establish priorities. Setting priorities is important when, for example, you are working on two or more hot projects and some part of the network fails. Your chart indicates which project takes priority. For such a plan to be effective, it's a good idea to have management in prior

Network manager	Group	Reaction time	Components	Repaired by
Nancy Jones	Program Office E-Mail Users	One Hour	Wiring StarController Router E-Mail Svr HW E-Mail Svr SW E-Mail Node SW	B. Turner N. Jones N. Jones J. Tice J. Maleski J. Maleski
Dave Kosiur	3rd floor AppleShare Users	Five Hours	Wiring StarController AShare Svr HW AShare Svr SW AShare Node SW	B. Turner N. Jones J. Tice J. Maleski J. Maleski

Group: <u>Program Office E-Mail Users</u> Representative signature: *L. L. Bartkowski*

Group: <u>3rd floor AppleShare Users</u> Representative signature: *Jean Harrison*

Figure 14-1: The network disaster recovery chart.

agreement on these priority settings. You may even decide that you need authorized signatures at the bottom of your chart.

Identifying the group

To create the network disaster recovery chart shown in Figure 14-1, you first need to know which features are in use on your network and who uses these features. By *network features,* we mean applications such as e-mail, Apple-Share, file-transfer applications, or workflow-database applications. Don't confuse network features with the topology and internetworking products that make up your network, such as bridges and routers. On the network disaster recovery chart, the combination of a feature and the users of that feature is called a *group.*

Identifying the network's users

The next step is to identify who is using the features that you've identified. In a large network, it is probably adequate to identify the users by departments and activity groups rather than as individuals. Yet even in a large network, it's important to keep in mind who the high-demand users are. Office politics is often an unavoidable part of the network manager's life. Our philosophy is to grin and bear it by balancing the needs of the high-demand users against the needs in the critical business arenas. After completing this chart, you should have an idea of how to apply this compromise to your situation and avoid the pendulum effect that the combination of politics and crises can create.

Remember that each feature and its set of users makes up a group. You can come up with descriptive names to label these groups. One group could be the "xyz program office e-mail users" and another group the "executive e-mail users." The division into groups should be made along organizational-chart lines and take into consideration who will require different levels of priority.

Determining downtime and reaction time

Next, you need to assign acceptable downtimes for each group. Determining downtime can be tricky, because downtime is not truly controllable. A network failure may be caused by a loose cable that you quickly locate, or it may be caused by a misconfigured router, which may take hours or even days to hunt down. Perhaps a better term than downtime is your *reaction* time. The question you are really asking is more like this: "How fast should you and your organization *react* to a failure of a particular group's network, such as the executive e-mail users?"

Planning a redundant communications path to solve a problem

How can using a redundant communications path help resolve a problem? Suppose that a particular program office's server fails. On this server is an application that the office depends on to plan meetings efficiently. A redundant communications path is in place if the program office can use its voice mail as an alternative method of scheduling meetings until the server is repaired. Of course, the program office won't be as satisfied with this method as with its primary tool, but the alternative method gets the office by until the repair is made.

To determine an acceptable reaction time, look at questions such as these:

❖ What impact will downtime have on the company's revenue?

❖ How will downtime affect the normal work flow of the office?

❖ What, if any, are the alternative methods, commonly referred to as *redundant paths*, for the user to reach the desired feature?

Obtaining authorized approval

Once a reaction time is established, it's best to get approval from a key person in that group. Again, it may be prudent to have this person's signature on your network disaster recovery chart.

Establishing network support

You now have a list of groups that define your network; each group has an assigned reaction time; and redundant paths are identified. Are you finished? Not by a long shot. You still need to do the planning that will get your organization ready to meet these goals. Identify which organizations and individuals play a part in the repair of your network. Don't stop at the hardware level of the network, but cover support all the way up to the people who support the end-node network feature applications.

The larger your AppleTalk internet gets, the more complex it becomes. Recall the principle that the universe constantly moves from order toward chaos. With the right planning, and a heap of diligence and responsibility, you can alter this course and avoid chaos on your network. In a small network, you may be the master of all: the cabling, the servers and their specialized applications, the bridges, and the routers. In larger networks, these tasks are more likely to be split among many individuals and organizations. So you'll need a well constructed plan to keep all these people on an orderly course.

Finding the individuals responsible for the repair of various components of the network is the next critical step in your fault management plan. You are responsible for staying on top of organizational changes that affect delegation of responsibilities. Get to know these people. They will be your lifeline. We suggest also getting to know the people in your human relations department so that they'll provide you with timely organizational charts.

At this stage of the planning, take some time to look over the list of network groups (features and users) that you have compiled. Then you need to establish who is responsible for the repair of the feature within the group.

Although each company has a different organizational plan, the following is an example of what this list may look like.

❖ Physical repair: cabling and wiring

❖ Hardware repair: servers and network devices (such as bridges)

❖ Software repair: Macintosh servers

❖ Software repair: VMS/AppleTalk servers

❖ Software repair: Unix/AppleTalk servers

❖ Software repair: network devices, such as bridges and routers

For each group on your chart, you can identify individuals, such as those who "own" the areas mentioned in the preceding list, who will be responsible for the repair of the hardware and software of individual features.

For example, in Figure 14-1, the group called "3rd Floor AppleShare Users," managed by Dave Kosiur, has different persons identified for various repairs. For example, J. Maleski is responsible for software repair on the Macintosh node and on the AppleShare server; J. Tice is responsible for hardware repair of the AppleShare server; N. Jones is responsible for hardware repair of the network device (the StarController), and B. Turner is responsible for repair of the wiring that goes to the 3rd Floor AppleShare server.

Be sure to include on your chart all the responsibilities needed for each group. You can then work with these individuals so that they agree to support the identified reaction times for each group and to make sure that they know the importance of their roles.

Reviewing the completed chart

Your chart will look complete now. You've identified features and users and split them into groups. You've found a key individual for each group, and you've agreed on specified reaction times. You've also made a list of all possible persons and organizations that may be called on for repair. Are you finished? Not yet.

One more item is needed for your list. Someone must be responsible for that first step — the discovery and inspection of the failure. This person will decide whether the disaster is more likely the result of a software crash or a broken-cable connection. We believe that this person should be the network manager.

In some companies, the person responsible for the wiring looks at all problems first and then hands the task off to another person, who manages the software. We believe that this approach has two major flaws: one is that no one "owns" the network failure, assuming responsibility from discovery to repair, and, second, no one takes a systems approach to look at the whole network and decide the most logical place to begin.

The network manager must remain knowledgeable, at least at some level, about all elements of the network, because that person is involved in how the network is designed and installed. The network manager is therefore the best person to look at the whole network to decide where to begin. The network manager should also "own" the problem and take responsibility for another key process in fault management — escalation. If a network repair looks like it is going to exceed an acceptable downtime, or if you're having difficulties getting the right people to work on the problem (perhaps because of other commitments), you need to escalate the issues to appropriate layers of management and to the key users. Keeping others informed of the progress of repairs can calm many nerves. Most users and managers simply want to know that something is being done and that someone has taken ownership of the problem.

Effective Network Monitoring and Troubleshooting

The term *proactive* has a special meaning for network managers. A proactive network manager has the right tools and skills to stay on top of a disaster. The best fault management plan enables the network manager to avoid noticeable network downtime by catching the problem before the users do. To do this, you'll need to monitor your network. Monitoring your network is also one of the quickest ways to know what changed — to determine what changed, you need to know how it looked before.

When your network monitoring shows that a failure has occurred, you will need good troubleshooting skills to get you through. Some say that troubleshooting is an art. But troubleshooting is also a skill that you can develop. Troubleshooting is the application of a logical, consistent, step-by-step analysis of the problem.

Before we get further into troubleshooting, consider the following network manager's classic mistake. The troubleshooter looks at a system, picks the area that the troubleshooter has the least contact with or understands the least, and then decides that this should be the starting point of the network repair, instead of following a logical, systematic approach, in which the starting point is always the same. Not only is this approach ineffective, but it can be somewhat threatening to the person who is responsible for and who does understand the chosen area. Thus, the network manager puts that person on the defensive, without a logical framework for the failure analysis. This approach can turn network repair into a quagmire of "who screwed up?" finger pointing.

Network repair should always be done logically. To keep your thinking along logical paths, the upcoming section, "Troubleshooting the network," will offer a series of steps you can follow. Even as top-level managers breathe down your neck — some companies claim that each minute of network downtime costs them as much as a million dollars — it is imperative that you remain unemotional. Don't panic. Take a few deep breaths and begin at the beginning. It may seem to go slower at first, but you'll almost always arrive at a solution faster by remaining calm and working through the problem step by step.

Also, as you are either monitoring your network or stepping through trouble-shooting a network failure, keep in mind that a network is a system of related parts. Each part or component can be described separately; however, in action, each integrates with other components to fulfill its function. In your mind's eye, you need to visualize these component relationships as you step through the problem.

Monitoring the network

You can monitor a network by using several sets of tools. The most predominant tools today are those that use NBP (Name Binding Protocol) and AEP (AppleTalk Echo Protocol). Also available are the diagnostic tool sets that come with most AppleTalk routers, bridges, and repeaters. Another set of tools uses a non-AppleTalk protocol called SNMP. Some of these tools now even implement features that send alarms to you via a modem or e-mail. For more information on NBP and AEP, see Chapter 3, "Understanding AppleTalk Protocols."

Because so many vendor offerings are available and because these offerings change over time, we'll list features that we think are useful, instead of citing particular products.

NBP and AEP diagnostic tools

A commonly used set of tools depends on NBP and AEP. AEP tools allow you to send an echo packet to a selected device; if the device is live, it will return an echo packet. These tools require AEP software on the clients that you want to *echo*.

NBP tools send out NBP LkUp (lookup) packets for various types of AppleTalk devices and processes. These devices then return a set of information to the requesting tool. The term for a network device or process within a node is a *socket*. Each node on the network has sockets within it that further address each network-aware process in the node. The format of an AppleTalk address is net.node.socket. In the address 3.128.142, for example, 3 is the network number, 128 is the node number, and 142 is the socket number.

A Macintosh can have several sockets. The Mac may, for example, have a socket for sending and receiving e-mail, and another socket for System 7's file-sharing feature. An NBP tool will return information regarding the type, quantity, and names of devices in a particular zone. An NBP tool may tell you, for example, that a zone has one FastPath router, two Apple LaserWriters, and ten Macintoshes.

Some NBP diagnostic tools enable you to send a query at specified intervals and also to maintain a log of *events*. (An event may be the addition or deletion of network services.) For example, you can ask the NBP diagnostic tool to produce a report that shows you when any of the FastPaths changed status. Some tools will even send you such a report instantly via modem or e-mail. Inter•Poll, made by Apple, is a popular tool that uses both NBP and AEP (see the sidebar "About Inter•Poll" in the section "The faulty cable disaster").

Like the AEP tools, NBP tools require that the devices you query have applications that will respond to NBP LkUp packets. These applications are called NVEs, or *Network Visible Entities*. AppleShare, for example, is an NVE and thus will respond to an NBP LkUp.

Because NBP is an essential part of the AppleTalk operation, most network services are NVEs. The router, however, is an exception because it does not *always* behave as an NVE. As a result, NBP-based diagnostic tools are currently not efficient at monitoring router activity.

Some routers will behave as NVEs only off one port; other routers will not behave as NVEs off any port. If, for example, you have a LocalTalk-to-EtherTalk router that is only an NVE on its LocalTalk port address, but is not an NVE on its Ethernet port address, any NBP query sent by a diagnostic tool to the zones on the Ethernet will not include this router in the reported list of EtherTalk devices.

Router diagnostic tools

Our favorite tool set for monitoring the activity of a medium to large size AppleTalk internet is the set that comes with AppleTalk routers. These tools can be found in routers that join two LocalTalk networks, as well as routers that join an EtherTalk network to a LocalTalk network or to another EtherTalk network. Most router tools allow the network manager to set the tool to monitor the network for almost every action or to monitor for only very serious actions. The tools can also provide messages that warn of unusual activity, according to the level of monitoring set. Such messages might warn you about unusual occurrences, such as a multitude of ZIP (Zone Information Protocol) GetNetInfoReply packets; ATP (AppleTalk Transaction Protocol) packet time-outs; or routes to networks going away or coming on-line.

Such messages should supply another important item of data — the time these events occurred. Many router diagnostic tool sets also include diagnostics that tell about network misconfiguration, including the Ethernet address of the misconfigured router and the specific nature of the misconfiguration. When you use these tools, you are seeing the network from the router's perspective. You may need to look at the diagnostic messages from other routers on your network, as well as to look at the network with other types of tools to gain a full perspective of the problem. Router diagnostics are great for quick check-ups on your AppleTalk internet to see whether anything is going haywire.

Bridge and repeater diagnostic tools

Many vendors' bridges and repeaters that are used to expand LocalTalk networks come with diagnostics. One difference between the diagnostics supplied with bridges and repeaters and diagnostics offered with routers reflects a primary functional difference of these devices. Unlike routers, bridges and repeaters do not keep track of network numbers or zone names. Note that bridges and repeaters come into play only in the first and second layers of the protocol stack — repeaters operating at the physical layer, and bridges at both the physical and the data link layers. These layers are concerned with the physical representation and formation of data packets, not with network numbering. Network numbering is part of the network layer and therefore is a concern of router diagnostics.

For more information on how bridges and repeaters work, see Chapter 2, "Understanding Networks." For information about protocol layers, refer to Chapter 3, "Understanding AppleTalk Protocols."

Bridges differ from repeaters in that they maintain tables of addresses for each cable that is attached to a port. This table helps the bridging software decide whether a packet should be forwarded to a destination address across the bridge, from one port of the bridge to another. Bridge diagnostics, therefore, can tell you things about the addresses on each port, and some diagnostics send NBP LkUps to compile a list of all devices by name.

Bridges and repeaters (such as Farallon's StarController) can tell you when they have shut down a port — a process called *jamming a port* — due to a bad signal. A bridge or repeater will jam a port so that a bad signal coming from a faulty end node does not propagate across the entire cable and take up the cable's bandwidth. Or, the diagnostics may tell you about a faulty physical cable on a particular port. So, if several users seem to be pushed off the network, check the diagnostic messages from your bridge or repeater to see whether the users are all on the same port. If so, see whether something is wrong with that port.

Another consideration for diagnostic tools, whether for repeaters, bridges, or routers, is the distinction between *in-band* and *out-of-band*. *Out-of-band* means that the diagnostics tool doesn't need to use the AppleTalk network to perform its diagnosis. Having some of the diagnostic information obtainable out-of-band is important when the network is malfunctioning. You can usually obtain out-of-band reports by plugging a Macintosh loaded with the diagnostic software into a special serial port on the repeater, bridge, or router.

SNMP tools

A third set of tools uses SNMP, the Simple Network Management Protocol. SNMP is a protocol to help manage networks that have several different protocol suites running.

Apple Computer supports SNMP, and plans are under way to develop SNMP strategies for all AppleTalk devices. We expect early releases of SNMP tools for AppleTalk within the year 1992. SNMP is not part of the AppleTalk stack, but is an open architecture protocol that was developed to operate over TCP/IP networks. *Open architecture* defines an architecture that is not the property of a particular vendor. Thus, the code for building an SNMP tool is freely available to developers. At the time of this publication, very little is available for AppleTalk network devices. Several routing vendors implementing both TCP/IP and AppleTalk routing supply in their boxes SNMP software that can be accessed via the TCP/IP port.

A MIB (Management Information Base) is like a database, in which certain information is stored after the device's SNMP software gathers it. An SNMP management station can send certain simple routines to access the information in a MIB and then present the information on-screen. This information is displayed as a graphical representation of the network, with lines indicating networks, and icons indicating routers, bridges, and other important devices, such as servers. In most implementations, colors are used to indicate whether devices are on or off; this information is valuable for fault management and configuration management. For example, the FastPath Kinetics MIB stores such read-only information as the count of the total number of alignment errors on the Ethernet interface. For further discussion of SNMP, refer to Chapter 16, "Configuration Management."

Troubleshooting the network

Suppose that you've been monitoring your network with your network diagnostics tool set and you've discovered a network failure. Or worse yet, a user has discovered one first — now *you're* on the defensive with the clock ticking. The following is a series of troubleshooting steps that can help you step through the problem.

The steps can be seen in two parts. The first part, comprised of steps 1, 2, and 3, is the phase of gathering information from the user to narrow your search by putting it within boundaries. In the second part, covered in steps 4 and 5, you use diagnostic tools and start looking at the components and relationships of the network. You'll start at the top layer of the protocol stack, where you look for possible problems with applications on a user's machine, and work your way down to the bottom layer of the protocol stack, where you look for problems with the cabling or other hardware components that make up the network.

1. Write down the user's statements regarding the problem, or, if you've discovered the problem yourself, write down the symptoms of the problem.

2. Write down all the components that could be involved. Don't forget application items, such as client/server software and the Chooser. And don't forget such simple physical items as transceivers and PhoneNet connectors.

3. Break the symptoms, or the user's statements, into small segments. Next, develop a series of either/or questions for each segment based on the user's statement (or your discovery notes) and the components of the network. These questions should give you the groundwork to begin either at or close to the top layer of the protocol stack when you use your diagnostics tools in the next series of steps.

4. Try to establish *what changed*. If the network was functioning before, something changed to allow the failure. Sometimes you can't establish this immediately, but ask yourself constantly as you work through the problem: "What has changed here?" Remember to refer to your monitoring tool set. If you have been monitoring the network, you should have some idea about what the tools told you previously as opposed to what they are telling you now.

5. Use your diagnostics tools to work through your list of questions. Continue to make new questions. This stage should be like stepping through a flow chart.

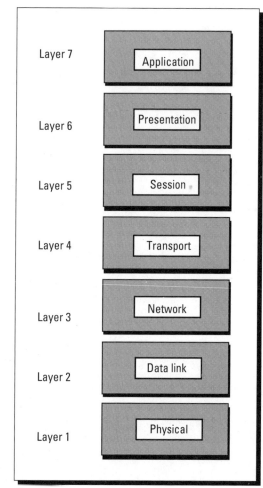

Layer 7	Application
Layer 6	Presentation
Layer 5	Session
Layer 4	Transport
Layer 3	Network
Layer 2	Data link
Layer 1	Physical

Figure 14-2: The OSI Reference Model.

As mentioned, steps 4 and 5 involve using the OSI Reference Model (see Figure 14-2). We believe that protocol layers provide an excellent mechanism for stepping through your network logically. Although it may take a little effort to discipline your thinking according to the protocol layers, if you stay with it, it will become a natural process.

After you use the first three steps to gather information, you should be able to narrow the problem to a group of devices, or even one device. If the problem seems to be narrowed down to an end node or a set of end nodes, begin at the top with layer 7, the application layer.

It may be that a problem is occurring with an application's interface to a network driver, which would mean that the problem is within the operating system of the end node and not actually out on the network. For example, the Scores virus can cause print jobs to abort from within several applications. If the Scores virus is corrupting the system software and preventing the user from using network services, you'll need to reinstall the operating system and any affected applications.

Look next at layer 6, the presentation layer, if the user is having printing or file-sharing problems — the AFP (Apple Filing Protocol) and PostScript are located in that layer. A problem at the presentation layer might be a misconfigured AppleShare server, where a user's account was not entered correctly in the server or the user's AppleShare client driver on the user's end node was not properly installed. Another example of a problem at the presentation layer is with the use of fonts, where a user did not select a PostScript font that the printer had in its memory and the user's file printed out in bitmap format.

Look in the network, transport, and session layers (layers 3, 4, and 5) for problems that stem from misconfigured routers, traffic overloads that don't allow sessions to be established, and problems with NBP (Name Binding

Protocol). An example of difficulty at these layers is the problem discussed in Chapter 12, "Making the Phase 2 Move," in which an NBP forward packet is sent to a router that recognizes only Phase 1 NBP LkUp packets. At this level, you can use the Chooser as a diagnostics tool for a perspective of what is visible on the network because the Chooser uses the NBP process.

Finally, work your way down to layers 1 and 2 — the data link and physical layers. By this time, you've gathered quite a bit of information and have the problem fairly well narrowed down. At the data link layer, you can use network packet analyzers to look at the packets on your network to decipher problems with the three layers just above the data link layer — problems that you didn't find with tools such as the Chooser and router diagnostics. A packet analyzer can also help point to the physical layer if you find that no packets at all are going between two points on your network. At the physical layer, you look for such mechanical problems as loose connectors and faulty cables.

Examining the network by using the OSI Reference Model may seem cumbersome at first, but the model does provide a useful theoretical base to help put boundaries around your network problems and attack them in a logical progression. Troubleshooting is often easier if you start from the top layers, where the examination techniques and tools are simpler to use, and then move down to the more technically difficult lower layers.

Examples of Network Disaster Recoveries

The troubleshooting process we've outlined may seem confusing at this point. So, to clarify these steps, the following section will walk you through a network failure caused by a faulty cable. You'll see how the five-step troubleshooting process led the troubleshooter to the problem cable. Afterwards we offer some short narratives of network disaster recoveries.

The faulty cable disaster

What follows is a walk-through of a disaster that can occur even on small LocalTalk networks. In this example, the user reported a network failure with this statement:

> **"No one can print in zone Alpha!"**

After the manager completed the first step — receiving the user's complaint — the next step was to identify the components of the network this user was on. In this case, the base of the network was a LocalTalk network created by a daisy-chain of AppleTalk shielded wires and connectors (see Figure 14-3). The AppleTalk connectors had built-in resistors, and the network included ten

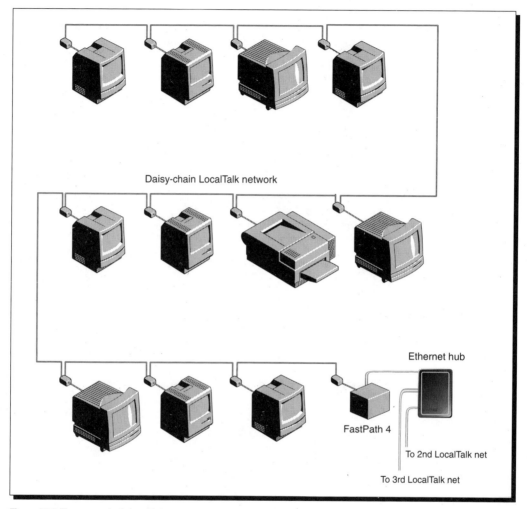

Figure 14-3: The network of zone Alpha.

Macintoshes, one Apple LaserWriter, and one Shiva FastPath 4. The Shiva
FastPath 4 was connected to an Ethernet cable with a thick-wire AUI connec-
tor. The Ethernet network was created by a Synoptics Ethernet hub. Two other
LocalTalk networks, each with its own zone name, were connected to this
Ethernet hub. All the Macintoshes in zone Alpha were supposed to be running
System 6.0.5 laser prep and LaserWriter.

Following the third step of our five-step process, the network manager divided the user's statement to form several questions for each part:

"... in zone Alpha"

A. Was the user who reported this statement located on the same network cable as the Alpha zone?

Or

B. Was the reporting user accessing the printer from another zone?

These questions led the network manager to the parts of the network that were involved. The larger the portion of the network involved, the more likely it is that the problem is caused by a single component that touches all the sections. Remember, too, that components can be software, as well as hardware. In this example, the components that affected everyone on the network were the set of laser prep drivers and the cable.

"No one ..."

This phrase always needs to be closely examined.

A. Was this a true statement?

1. For all users in Alpha?

2. For users of Alpha's printer from another zone?

Or

B. Did *no one* include a group of related users, but not all the users?

1. Were these users in a row on the daisy-chain?

2. Was one of the users who could print actually on the other side of this row, sending packets across this section of daisy-chain to get to the printer?

3. Or, was just one user involved?

". . . can print . . ."

This is probably the most important part of the statement to decipher.

    A. Could the users see the printer in the Chooser?

        1. Never?

        2. Sometimes?

        3. Always?

    B. If always, what happened when the user sent a print job?

        1. The light blinked on the LaserWriter, but no paper came out?

        2. The print job aborted, and the bomb appeared on the Macintosh screen?

With these questions, the network manager covered a lot of territory to pinpoint the problem, working from the network as a total entity and proceeding down to each end-user's machine. Next, we'll look at how the questions were answered and how the network manager used the information to expose the problem.

". . . in zone Alpha"

The user reporting the problem had one of the ten Macintoshes located on the Alpha network. This step located the problem within the LocalTalk zone, thus ruling out a malfunction with the LocalTalk-to-EtherTalk router or with the Ethernet hub. If the user had been on another network, the equipment between the two networks, and problems with the routers that use the protocols ZIP, RTMP, and DDP, from the network, transport, and session layers (layers 3, 4, and 5), would have also been suspect.

"No one . . ."

In this case, all ten Macintosh users on the network replied that they could not print either. If only one user had been unable to print, the next list of questions would have focused first on the operating system of that particular Macintosh. If the manager found no application trouble in the system, the manager would next check the physical layer — the LocalTalk connector. If only a certain segment of users, but not *all* users, could not print, the list of questions would possibly have traced the problem to the physical wiring, such as reflection caused by missing resistors.

"... can print ..."

In this case, no one could see the printer in their Choosers. If the users could see the printer appearing and disappearing, a resistor problem would be a strong possibility.

Always remember that even if you suspect that you know what the problem is, it is always important to step through the analysis. If the printer were appearing and disappearing in the Chooser, the problem could have been caused by a system virus. You would have found any virus problems when looking for application layer problems.

After working through a series of questions based on the user's initial complaint, the next step is for the network manager to see what changed. In this example, the network manager, who was unfamiliar with the day-to-day operations of this particular building's network, did not know of anything that had changed.

This brought the manager to step 5, where the manager was ready to select diagnostic tools to search for the problem. In this case, the network manager selected Inter•Poll, Apple's software diagnostics tool, to look at the problem at layer 4 — the transport layer. The network manager started at this layer because the user's inability to see the printer in the Chooser indicated no NBP traffic between the end nodes and the printer. As a result, problems at the upper layers were highly unlikely. The network manager selected Inter•Poll to confirm suspicions of trouble at the transport layer.

Using one of the ten Macintoshes, the manager tried to select the Alpha zone in the Chooser to see whether the LaserWriter would respond over the

---

About Inter•Poll

Inter•Poll, a software diagnostics tool sold by Apple, should be a staple item in your troubleshooting arsenal. For Macintoshes running operating systems prior to System 7, the Inter•Poll tool needs an INIT called *Responder* to be placed into the system folder of all Macintoshes on the network where you want to use this tool. With System 7, the Responder code is built into the operating system.

The Responder INIT and Inter•Poll work as a team. Inter•Poll sends out a query in the form of an NBP LkUp to a selected zone. All devices with the Responder INIT reply with some basic information about their status, such as the name that is in the Chooser window and what type of machine it is. In addition, Inter•Poll lets you send echo packets to each device with the Responder INIT. The INIT will return the echo packet. Apple LaserWriters have a built-in Responder that also replies to an Inter•Poll query.

network. But no zones showed up at all. The view from other Macintoshes showed the same result. This was indeed a dead network. The network users, of course, had determined the viability of the network based only on the printing feature. But results from Inter•Poll showed that other network features, such as file-transfer applications, wouldn't have worked either.

At this point, the network manager had several options:

❖ Use packet analyzer tools to examine layer 2 — the data link layer.

Or

❖ Use tools that examine layer 1 — the physical layer.

The network manager decided that if nothing could be determined by the Chooser, which uses the NBP (Name Binding Protocol), or by Inter•Poll, which uses the AEP (AppleTalk Echo Protocol), there was a good chance that no packets would be seen. The analysis strongly suggested a physical problem with either a component (in this case, the printer) or the cabling.

The LaserWriter was an easy place to begin looking. A built-in diagnostic feature of the LaserWriter is contained in a cover sheet that is printed when the LaserWriter starts up. If this sheet prints after the printer is restarted, you know that the internal mechanisms of the machine are working. In this case, the cover sheet did print. (Note that you can send a software command to the LaserWriter to prevent it from printing the cover page. If this command has been issued, printing the cover sheet to check the operations of the printer won't work for you.) The LaserWriter therefore appeared to be functioning perfectly.

The network manager next had to choose a method for examining the cabling and cabling components, such as the transceivers and AppleTalk connectors. Using an ohmmeter is appropriate if the problem appears to be caused by incorrect placement or breakage of resistors. But a resistance problem usually reveals itself as an intermittent network failure, with devices such as LaserWriters appearing and disappearing from the Chooser. Because this was not the case, the network manager chose another approach to examine the physical layer — the divide-and-conquer method.

The network manager split up the network into two small islands of users and moved the LaserWriter back and forth between the islands. At this point, the LaserWriter showed up in the Chooser for one group but not for another. By continuing to split the network this way, the manager found a faulty section of cable between the last Macintosh and the FastPath. Replacement of this cable restored the network back to full functioning.

Although this network failure and resurrection took several pages to describe, it took only a couple of hours to perform. One of the main reasons for quick success was a logical step-by-step analysis of the situation. All components were carefully considered. The diagnostic approach was top-down, working from the upper layers of the protocol stack down, and in this case, all the way down to the bottom — the physical layer.

This detailed example took you through the troubleshooting process to locate a faulty cable. The following sections show you some additional problems for which you can look.

Overloaded printers

Overloading an Apple LaserWriter is a common problem. With the profusion of sophisticated drawing packages that send huge files to the printer, network managers are seeing LaserWriter's "hung" more often. The problem can often be traced to insufficient memory in the LaserWriter. Upgrading to a LaserWriter NTX or replacing the printer with a high-end PostScript printer can solve the memory deficit.

Also, keep an eye on applications that send files to the printer in bitmap format. Bitmapped images require that each pixel on the page be given a definition of black or white. As a result, very large files are sent to the printer. The immediate solution is to shut off both the Macintosh and the LaserWriter to clear their memory buffers.

ZIP storms

The problem of ZIP storms has been seen on several large AppleTalk internets that are still using AppleTalk Phase 1. We cite the problem here as an example of how a network crash can occur, not by the failure of a component, but by the complex AppleTalk relationships among several components.

The disaster in this example is called a ZIP storm because a malfunction on the network causes an inordinate number of ZIP (Zone Information Protocol) request packets to enter and flood the network. A ZIP storm can flood an entire Ethernet backbone, halting processes by other protocols, including TCP/IP and DECnet.

ZIP storms have occurred only in networks that contain over a hundred zones and that have all the following devices in combination: LocalTalk-to-EtherTalk routers, EtherTalk-to-EtherTalk routers, and a Phase 1 Ethernet server/router.

The ZIP storm in this example was traced to a *runt* RTMP (Routing Table Maintenance Protocol) Data packet that also had a strange listing of network

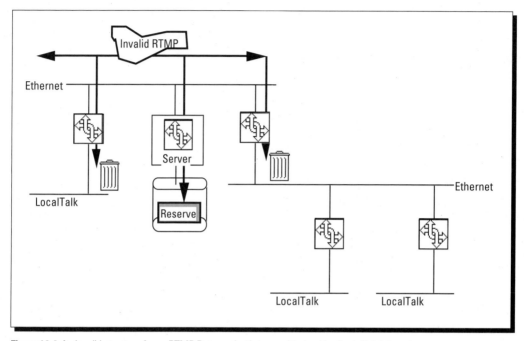

Figure 14-4: An invalid structure for an RTMP Data packet is transmitted on the AppleTalk internet.

numbers. (A *runt* packet on Ethernet is a packet that is smaller than 64 bytes, an illegal size to the Ethernet specification.) The strange network numbers turned out to be random garbage and did not identify actual networks on the internet. Because of their invalid structure, these runt RTMP packets with their bad network numbers were thrown away by both the LocalTalk-to-EtherTalk routers and the EtherTalk-to-EtherTalk routers. The Ethernet server/router, however, placed these invalid network numbers into a special holding buffer. In Figure 14-4, this buffer is labeled as "Reserve."

The Ethernet server/router then broadcasted its next RTMP Data packet. The RTMP Data packet coming from the Ethernet server/router had a valid structure, but it also now contained numbers (which it obtained from the runt packet and stored in the buffer) for routes to nonexistent networks.

All routers use the RTMP packet broadcasted from the Ethernet server/router to create new entries in their routing tables. However, because the invalid network numbers are also now found within the valid RTMP packet, all the routers will broadcast RTMP packets with the bad numbers until the routes are timed-out (see Figure 14-5).

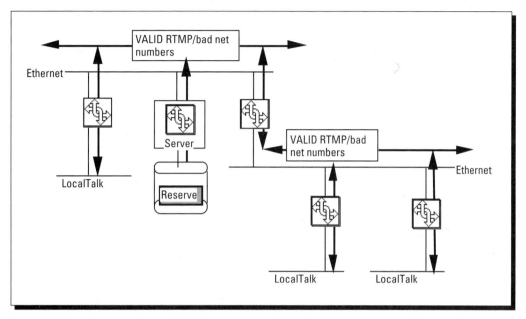

Figure 14-5: The valid structure for the RTMP packet is sent out by the Ethernet server/router and is absorbed into all routers' routing tables.

Note that timing-out routes in Phase 1 takes a long time because each router continues to validate the route until it is incrementally set to 15 hops. The process of deleting routes is described in Chapter 11, "Designing an AppleTalk LAN."

In the example network, on finding the new route in the routing table, the ZIP process in the router sent out ZIP Query packets to find out the zone name for these nonexistent networks. So many of these ZIP Query packets were sent out that layer 2, the data link layer of the Ethernet, was flooded (see Figure 14-6).

The network managers found the problem by isolating the network into segments and running network packet analyzers to find out what all the ZIP packets wanted and where the strange network numbers were coming from.

The networks in this example were down for several weeks. It took the calm step-by-step approach of some top-notch network managers and vendor technical support teams, but they eventually found the problem and got the network up and running again.

Note that this type of ZIP storm cannot occur in a Phase 2 network. In Phase 1, every router broadcasts an RTMP Data packet with all the network numbers it knows about — even those that are invalid.

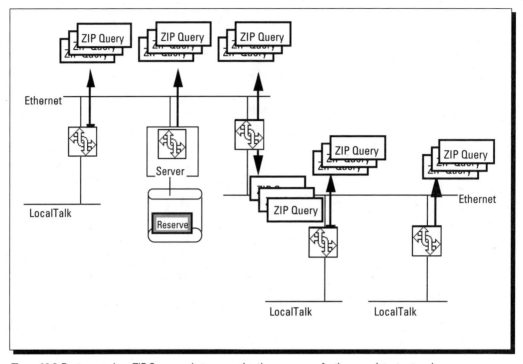

Figure 14-6: Routers send out ZIP Query packets requesting the zone name for the nonexistent networks.

In Phase 2, however, a router broadcasts an RTMP Data packet containing only the network numbers that are directly connected to it (split-horizon). For a typical backbone network configuration, the packet contains two network numbers — the LocalTalk network number and the EtherTalk network range. For more information on split-horizon routing in Phase 2, see Chapter 11, "Designing an AppleTalk LAN."

Black holes

Black holes are a network problem that can occur on an AppleTalk internet of any size. Black holes are caused when the network is misconfigured — specifically, when two or more routers have a different network number for the same cable. Routers can send packets only to networks to which they are directly connected or to which they have a route. For example, if network 3 sees a packet from network 2, network 3 discards that packet if it doesn't have a route for it. This procedure helps maintain legitimate route tables, preventing the ZIP storms described in the previous example. What happens is that the two routers build completely separate internets with no knowledge of the other's existence. If a user

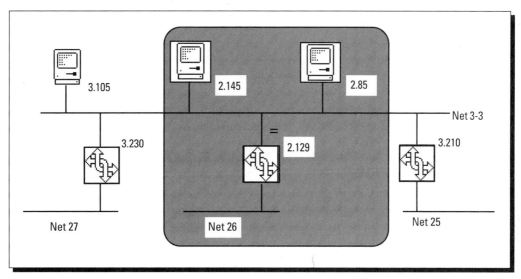

Figure 14-7: A black hole in the network.

is on one of these networks, it will seem as though the zones on the misconfigured router have simply disappeared into a black hole.

In Figure 14-7, the middle router has been misconfigured with net range 2-2 instead of net range 3-3. The other two routers have no route to network 2, so devices on the networks behind them, networks 27 and 25, will not see any devices on the network behind the misconfigured router, network 26. This problem is compounded when one of the Macintoshes on the Ethernet takes its start-up configuration (GNI/GNIR) from the misconfigured router and becomes a node in network 2.

Ethernet storms

Another common problem is an Ethernet broadcast storm caused by a malfunctioning device on the Ethernet. (The device can be either an AppleTalk device or any other type of node, such as TCP/IP or Novell.) In an Ethernet broadcast storm, the malfunctioning device floods the Ethernet with packets that are destined for the broadcast address. A router limits the extent of an Ethernet broadcast storm because a router will not forward packets destined for the broadcast address.

A bridge, however, will not limit the flood because a bridge will pass packets that are destined for the broadcast address across to any of the bridge's other attached cables.

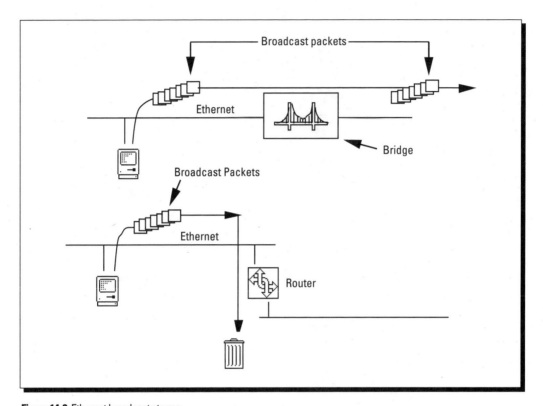

Figure 14-8: Ethernet broadcast storms.

In Figure 14-8, notice that the broadcast packets are passed across the bridge but are not passed across the router. The figure shows that the router effectively serves as a "firewall" to prevent the storm of packets coming from the offending device.

When you detect an Ethernet storm, remove the offending machine from the network. You will have to do some additional troubleshooting to find the malfunction, which can result from hardware failure or software misconfiguration. So that you can quickly isolate the offending device, it's a good idea to maintain a list of Ethernet addresses and their locations. Otherwise, you will have to use the divide-and-conquer approach and separate your network into smaller and smaller islands until you find the malfunctioning device.

Customer Service from Technical Hotlines

Suppose that you've tried everything you know about. You've carefully worked through the problem step by step. Now you're stuck, the network is still down, and your eye is twitching. It's time to call the folks who made the network products that you bought. A consideration in purchasing a product is the quality of service that the company provides. Investigate this service by asking the sales people specific questions and asking people in local Apple user groups about their experiences with different vendors.

However, good service is not 100 percent the responsibility of the vendor. Some of that responsibility is yours. For best results, be sure that you are prepared before you call. Have available the serial number of the product or the maintenance contract number, and remember that you will also need to provide configuration information.

Every network is unique. Maintaining an accessible list of components on your network is invaluable. Many vendors will request a packet trace (from a network packet analyzer). They will also request reports from their product's diagnostics. Don't make assumptions. After all, you were stuck, so be prepared to let someone else take a fresh look at the problem. Carefully explain to the vendor the events that you have seen on the network and the specifics of the failure. The vendor should then work with you to step through the problem.

Calling the vendor

Here are some things that you should expect from your vendor:

Courteous service: Number one is courteous service. You should never be treated as if you are too ignorant to understand the problem or the solution. The vendor should always take the time to explain everything to you.

Also, you should never be asked to accept inferior service because of a vendor's internal problems. If everyone is on vacation that week, this is not your problem.

Prompt reply: The vendor should return your call within a reasonable amount of time. Same-day response is reasonable for most calls, but calls that are flagged as emergencies should be returned even more quickly.

Knowledgeable technical support: The vendor should have reasonably knowledgeable people answering the hotline. These people may not know the immediate answer to your question, but they should have the resources available to find out. Realize that some problems are tricky and must be fielded back to the programmer who wrote the code.

Vendors working with other vendors

A vendor should be willing to work with you on a problem that may be caused by a relationship of their product to another vendor's product. For example, not too many networks of over 20 zones all have the same router type. Remember that a vendor may find that the problem is caused by someone else's product. The vendor you call should help you explain this to another vendor. Many companies will even look at your problem with a team composed of people from several companies. The repair of the ZIP storm described previously was done with such a team.

Some vendors have regional sales engineers who can come to your site to help out. If this is important to you, ask whether this service is available. All vendors should be willing to send someone to assist you if the problem goes *ballistic*. The slang word ballistic means that you and the vendor have been pounding your heads against the problem for some time and your company is losing serious amounts of money from having the network down.

With all these pointers in mind, take a look at the hotlines that support the components that you have. Call the vendor in advance of a network failure and find out how much support the vendor can give you and what is expected from you when you call with a problem. Some vendors even provide 24-hour support contracts. Also, many vendors prefer that you call their hotline before you make a major change or upgrade to your network so that the vendor's staff can review the configuration with you, especially if you are moving from Phase 1 to Phase 2. A good relationship between you and the hotline staff is critical to your fault management plans.

Summary

In this chapter, we explained the importance of having a fault management plan. We covered the following points:

✔ You need a plan for who will be responsible for the various parts of your network, from who will repair the servers to who will repair the wiring.

✔ The network manager should be responsible for escalating a "network down" situation to key users and management if the repair time is taking longer than expected.

✔ Many bridges, repeaters, and routers provide diagnostic tools that help you monitor your network.

✔ Network problems can be attributed to multiple causes; you'll need to stay calm so that you can approach a failure logically.

✔ Vendors' technical hotlines serve as important fault management tools; know the procedures of network device vendors in advance of trouble.

In the next chapter, you'll learn more about network management. We'll tell you how to tune your AppleTalk internet for best performance.

Chapter 15
Performance Management

In this chapter...

✔ How throughput and bandwidth affect the performance of your LAN

✔ Guidelines for how many services and users to put on a network

✔ How to configure an internet for the best performance

✔ Which topology is best for your size of network

P erformance management means getting the best throughput for each network service you have. Of course, *the best* for you must fall within your budget limitations. So we'll further define performance management as getting the *best throughput that you need* for each network service. This chapter suggests some ways you can get the most for your money through performance management.

An Introduction to Performance and Throughput

Throughput is one of those words born in the age of technology. Quite simply, throughput is the amount of data that can be transferred through a device. In discussions about performance, flashy terms like *packets per second, speed,* and *response time* are often tossed into the conversation. But before you go racing off in search of the *fastest* network, we should caution you that performance should never be obtained at the price of stability. A fast network that frequently crashes is not the gleaming achievement that you envisioned.

To examine the steps toward making your network a hot performer, we'll break the subject down into two sections: the first section deals with service ratios, some of which are based on traffic patterns and traffic volume. In the second section, we'll talk about network configuration.

We start with services first because services are the driving forces of your network. Just ask any network manager — does a manager hear from the users when a router slows down? Maybe. Ah, but does the manager hear from the users when a file transfer "takes forever"? You bet! After examining the needs of your network services, we'll look at ways to configure your network so that it is the strong framework you require.

We analyze the decisions you'll need to make about features by expressing them as three ratios:

❖ Services per network

❖ Services per device

❖ Users per service

After you determine these ratios, you'll know when it's appropriate to step a segment of your internet through this progression of possible setups:

❖ Build the network with a daisy-chain

❖ Build the network with a bus or passive star

❖ Build the network with a repeater

❖ Build the network with a bridge

In the section on network configuration, we'll discuss these options so that you can make a decision appropriate to your needs.

As your network grows and takes over more space, you'll also need to decide when to begin joining networks together with routers. These decisions will lead you to a plan for your internet configuration. A backbone internet, for example, is a popular choice. We'll also discuss how to plan an internet in a star configuration, a design popularized by the AT&T premises distribution wiring system.

Using Traffic Statistics To Determine Service Ratios

To make effective performance decisions, you need to know several important facts about your network services:

1. What network services are available?

2. Who uses these services?

3. How much traffic is generated between the users and the services?

If you completed the Network Disaster Recovery chart presented in Chapter 14, "Fault Management," you've already done most of the work to determine the location of both the services and the users. In the following sections, you'll learn about tools that gather traffic statistics. These tools will help you determine the volume of traffic between network services and their users.

In 1990, several traffic monitoring tools hit the market. Among the important features of these tools include capabilities for plotting the following aspects of network traffic:

❖ Traffic patterns established by the entire network over a period of time

❖ Statistics on the amount of traffic between specific nodes, such as individual workstations and printers

❖ The amount of traffic generated by specific services and measured against the network's full bandwidth

Over the next several years, vendors will undoubtedly introduce many more tools to enable you to monitor your AppleTalk network traffic. Instead of describing specific tools, we'll examine the important plotting capabilities just listed.

Statistics plotted over time

The capability for plotting statistics over a period of time is an important feature in a traffic statistics tool. A snapshot gives you an idea of what's going on at any given time, but it's even more important to determine the busy or peak times for each network service. An effective traffic statistics tool should enable you to establish the busy times during the day — and throughout the week. If your business uses projected monthly work schedules, these schedules may also help locate peak periods for your network.

Looking for traffic patterns

We suggest that you monitor your network traffic over a period of several weeks before deciding on a new network configuration. It's best to establish long-term traffic patterns than just rely on an occasional heavy week to make configuration decisions.

Statistics on specific node-to-node traffic

Another statistic you can gather with tools is a plot of usage between specific nodes. These tools will tell you which users and services are taking a specific amount of the bandwidth.

After running the statistics program, for example, you may see that the users Mary and Jon are using one of the LaserWriters at a rate of more than 60 percent of the total traffic going to that node. If the statistics tell you only about sending and receiving traffic in separate charts, rather than showing specific node-to-node usage, you would know only that Mary and Jon are busy users on the network.

That's why it is important to establish the correlation between users and services. Further investigation may show, for example, that Mary and Jon should either spool their print jobs for after hours or that a new high-end printer should be purchased for their needs. Or, perhaps the statistics will show that their heavy use was atypical, and that the extra usage resulted from an additional task added to that week or day. Determining these correlations is another important reason for plotting statistics over time.

Statistics plotted against full bandwidth

It is also convenient to be able to plot each service's traffic against the full bandwidth of the network. Some programs plot each node's traffic only against the total traffic, so you might see a node producing 20 percent of the total traffic on the network. Unfortunately, that statistic doesn't tell you whether that node is actually causing performance difficulties on your network. After all, the total network traffic may be low. If, however, you see that a service node is sending 20 percent of the network's total bandwidth, you can more readily pinpoint a performance problem.

As a rule, most EtherTalk and LocalTalk networks never exceed a 10 percent usage of their total bandwidth. If you have a busy network and see that the traffic rate is approaching 50 percent or more, you'll also notice that the collision rate has gone way up. Because packets must be re-sent after a collision, your network's throughput will decrease in proportion to an increase in traffic. So watch your network's traffic use, and be sure to watch the collision rate to get a total performance picture.

Using Service Ratios To Design Your AppleTalk Internet

After you obtain statistics about your network's traffic conditions, you can start making decisions about service ratios, according to the following categories:

❖ Services per network

❖ Services per device

❖ Users per service

Although these three ratios depend greatly on the amount of traffic the service receives, there are some general guidelines to follow. Keep in mind that sometimes a slowdown in response from a service is not network related. The culprit may be an improper balance of the system configuration, such as with INIT conflicts or insufficient RAM on the user's Mac. (See the *Macworld Complete Mac Handbook,* by Jim Heid, for more information on configuring a Macintosh.)

Services per network

Each network in an AppleTalk internet can have multiple services on it, including services that are distributed across all users' Macintoshes (or AppleTalk PCs). Remember that the more traffic you have on a network, the more collisions you'll have and, therefore, the less throughput. In any case, the user will perceive that the network is slow.

In the following sections, we offer some rules of thumb to help you decide how many services to place on each network. We'll divide this discussion into two groups of service ratios — those for LocalTalk networks and those for EtherTalk networks.

LocalTalk networks

If we define a LocalTalk network as a cable with its own network number, rather than a zone extending over several networks, we can say that the number of primary services on this network should not exceed three. *Primary services* can include central file servers, printers, and other devices that are shared by a significant portion of the network's users. Examples of *secondary services* are distributed file-share systems that see only occasional use, and file-transfer programs. For more information on file-sharing and file-transfer programs, see Chapter 20, "Moving and Sharing Files on the Network."

Even with as few as three primary services on the network, you should be vigilant in watching for traffic overload. Reduce the number of services as necessary to prevent network throughput from slowing down.

If you are using a LocalTalk bridge, you may decide to put heavily used primary services on their own segments and have users access these services across the bridge. Although this method docs cause some slowdown as traffic goes through the bridge, it does free up other segments for secondary traffic.

On LocalTalk, only *one* network conversation can take place on each network segment that is behind a bridge. (A multiport repeater does not create multiple segments that will allow separate conversations.) You may also want to split up the users into groups on different segments (see Figure 15-1). That way, when a user from one group accesses a primary service, other groups are not affected. For more about LocalTalk network segments, see Chapter 6, "Designing a LocalTalk LAN."

Figure 15-1 demonstrates that on a single LocalTalk network (top diagram), only one session can take place at a time. If Mac B is printing to the LaserWriter, Mac A and Mac C cannot communicate with each other. With a LocalTalk bridge, multiple sessions can take place, as in the lower diagram. In this example, Mac B is printing to LaserWriter A, while Macs C and D are exchanging information, and Mac E is using server E. All three network sessions are happening at the same time without interfering with one another.

When planning how many primary and secondary services to put on a network and how much traffic to load on that network, think about what the user sees. In the first example in Figure 15-1, only one user is able to access a printer. That user obtains the print job quickly. But if another user decides to print at this time, this second user sees only that it takes a long time to get the job printed. Behind the scenes, the AppleTalk software on the computer keeps re-sending until its packets get across the network. That's a good way to frustrate users. So keep your users' requirements in mind when you plan your network loading.

EtherTalk networks

EtherTalk networks are similar to LocalTalk networks in that they allow only one network conversation in an instant of time. The two networks differ greatly, however, in bandwidth. Ethernet at 10MB per second can complete a conversation much faster than LocalTalk at 230.4K per second (only 2.3 percent of Ethernet). And you can add many more services on an Ethernet network without seeing a significant performance hit. Because Ethernet cabling

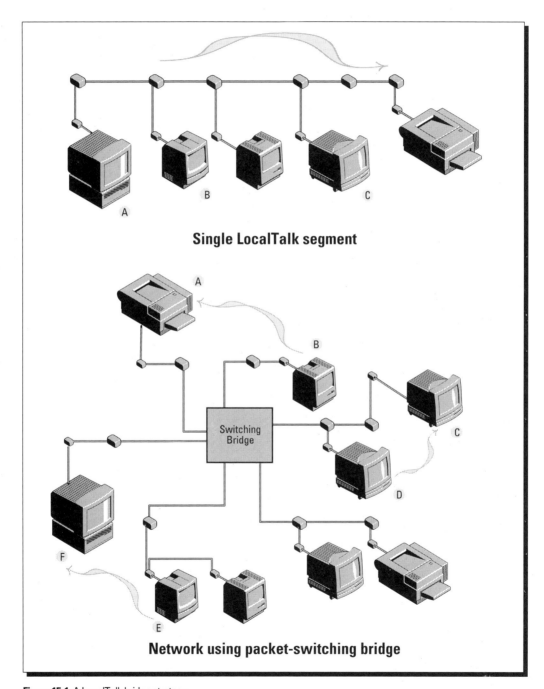

Single LocalTalk segment

Network using packet-switching bridge

Figure 15-1: A LocalTalk bridge strategy.

is a more expensive solution than LocalTalk, however, we suggest staying with LocalTalk as long as you have occasional or light usage and moving up to Ethernet only when you have a service, such as a file server, that accepts a significant number of large file transfers. Remember that graphics files are almost always big files, so Ethernet is a good idea for networks with servers that handle a large number of graphics files.

Even constant activity from a small group of users may justify the use of Ethernet. If possible, move power users and their servers onto EtherTalk networks in order to keep them on the same network. If you put a heavily used server on EtherTalk and keep the users on a LocalTalk network, all that traffic will need to be transmitted through a LocalTalk-to-EtherTalk router.

Services per device

Another consideration in your high-performance network design is how many services to put on one device. Many network server applications, including certain e-mail servers, file-share servers, and print servers, can be doubled up on a Macintosh. (Some applications that require servers are AppleShare, Meeting Maker, Microsoft Mail, QuickMail, and ODMS [Odesta Document Management System].)

Doubling up functions on devices is a popular cost-cutting strategy. You can, for example, run some of these server applications on Macs that individuals are using for personal workstation tasks, such as word processing and spreadsheets.

A similar strategy is to combine a software router application, such as Farallon's Liaison, and a server application on one Macintosh. Another alternative is to run a server application on a router that has its own hardware platform, such as GatorShare running on the GatorBox router.

Doubling up on services in this way will save money, but it will cost you in performance. Unless the usage of any of these server applications is minimal, we don't recommend these strategies. One service per platform (as in one server application per Macintosh) is a safe bet for getting the best performance out of that platform. It is also good fault-management practice, making it easier to detect the origin of errors. Moreover, a limit of one service per device minimizes the impact to your users when you must take down a device to work on it.

If your internet consists of more than a few networks, it's never a good idea to put anything else on a Macintosh that is running a software router. Keep in mind that if you put a software router on a user's Macintosh and if that user locks up the

Macintosh, the routes that the software router was advertising are gone and must be reestablished. After 80 seconds of silence, other routers will purge that route through the RTMP process (see Chapter 11, "Designing an AppleTalk LAN"). On the other hand, routers with their own optimized hardware platforms and operating systems (such as FastPaths, Ciscos, and GatorBoxes) can multitask several services. But, even as you load up these routers with different tasks, be sure to monitor their diagnostics for any error or buffer-overflow occurrences.

Users per service

The third service ratio listed in this chapter indicates the number of users per service. This particular ratio depends heavily on the type of traffic statistics you obtain. It may be fine for fourteen people to access the same file-share server if all are occasional users. Yet, for most work environments, fourteen active users to a printer is not a good number. We suggest that administrators of larger networks use a planning model for networks, allocating, for instance, four users per printer. Then, vary the model as conditions require. (Monitoring the network's collision rate can help you decide.) For example, you may want to share a higher performance print server among a larger group of users.

When looking at users per service, consider as well where those users are located in relation to services. A user shouldn't need to go through more than one bridge, router, or other network device to get to an often used service. In fact, going through *no* network device is best where possible. Printing services, usually the most burdened network service, should be placed within the same network as the user whenever possible. An exception to this is placement of a high-end Ethernet printer, such as a DEC LPS40, which prints 40 pages per minute. These are expensive items, so most administrators plan for sharing them with as many networks (or network segments) as possible. It is best to locate this kind of device centrally, spacing the majority of users an equal distance from this service. You'll find more information on this subject in an upcoming section, "Setting Up Internet Configurations."

Planning Network Configurations

Working with an area of about 1,000 square feet, you have several options for network configuration: the daisy-chain, the bus, and the passive star or the active star. Each of these topologies has pluses and minuses, as you'll see. Network length limitations are further discussed in Chapter 6, "Designing a LocalTalk LAN," and Chapter 8, "Designing an Ethernet LAN."

For very small networks, you may opt for the simplest network configuration, which is the daisy-chain. This topology, though, is fraught with performance pitfalls, notably bad crimps causing reflections (see Chapters 7, "Installing a

LocalTalk LAN," and 14, "Fault Management"). Consequently, we don't recommend daisy-chains of more than ten nodes, including printers and file servers.

The next step up is the bus topology. This configuration allows each node to be joined separately to the network cable so that disconnecting a node doesn't cause network failure (see Chapter 7). An Ethernet bus requires more planning than a LocalTalk bus because the Ethernet network can only be tapped into at specific distances (see Chapter 9, "Installing an Ethernet LAN"). For LocalTalk networks, you can also configure the network as a passive star, which is simply several bus segments joined in a star formation (see Chapter 6, "Designing a LocalTalk LAN"). However, a bus topology is still a simple style that allows for only minimal network traffic. Remember the rule of one network conversation at a time on a segment.

Once your network grows past ten nodes, you need to resolve two questions: which topology to change to, and whether you will use a centralized wiring closet. Wiring closets can be used for bus, passive star, and active star networks, as well as Ethernet star hubs, and are a more stable way to go if you can afford it. A wiring closet is similar to a phone closet in that it is a special room dedicated to switching equipment, and often the same room can be used for both data and phones. Pairs of wire are run from the office locations to the closet, where they can be cross-connected to the desired equipment (such as a LocalTalk repeater). For performance management, wiring closets are a definite advantage as they enable you to adapt the network quickly to new service needs by simply moving cross-connects.

With or without a wiring closet, you can install an active star repeater to strengthen your network. The repeater enhances performance by isolating signals that could disrupt the network. Each port on a repeater can isolate a signal that is perceived to be causing a problem. Further, the repeater amplifies the physical signal as it moves from one port to the next, a capability which allows for more than the 32-user limit on a simple bus LocalTalk network.

But the rule of one conversation at a time still applies to a network divided by a repeater. So be cautious about putting a large number of users on a network with a repeater. Look at the traffic statistics and decide how long your users will wait for a service. On a lightly used network, you can probably get away with more than 32 users.

The next step is to divide your segments with either a bridge or a router. Your choice depends on the type of use that your network sees. For a widely distributed traffic pattern, with many nodes exchanging packets and sending them often, a *packet-switched bridge,* such as the LocalSwitch (Tribe Computer Systems) is a good way to go. (In Figure 15-1, you saw an example of a LocalTalk bridge configuration.) On the other hand, dividing segments with routers makes sense when much of the traffic must travel across an AppleTalk internet because of expensive shared services or because a large number of users is tied into one service system, such as a corporate e-mail system. At this point, you've crossed into making decisions about internet configurations, which is the subject of the next section.

Also, after you decide to use routers, you still need a topology for the router-connected networks. Your networks can be bridged segments configured as a star, bus, or daisy-chain system, depending on your performance requirements, as you'll see next.

Setting Up Internet Configurations

An *internet,* a collection of AppleTalk networks joined with routers, can be configured in two ways. One way is to combine two or more networks serially in a row, and the other way is to connect them in a star layout with a center hub and one or more *legs.* We recommend the star topology if your LAN internet is a collection of networks at one physical site (an Ethernet or fiber-optic internet in one or multiple buildings, rather than extended across a city).

See Chapter 11, "Designing an AppleTalk LAN," for descriptions of LANs, MANs, and WANs. See Chapter 13, "Designing an AppleTalk WAN," for MAN and WAN configuration strategies.

A star topology offers several advantages over a serial approach. With a serial configuration, a packet may travel through several routers to get to its destination. This can be a serious detriment to your network performance. With a star topology, packets travel through a router to reach a backbone and then through another router if needed to reach a second network.

A typical serial network has three or four LocalTalk networks in a row connected with LocalTalk routers. To expand this serial network, the *leg* can be routed to an Ethernet, which may have other legs connected to it. This creates a combination serial/star topology. Any packet that needs to reach the Ethernet from the end LocalTalk network must travel through four routers. This brings up the problem of where to place centralized services, such as e-mail servers or high-speed printers. With a star topology, such services are easily placed on the backbone, which is central to all network users. Figure 15-2 compares a serial internet to a star internet.

In very large networks, you may need to place routers between sections of the Ethernet for better fault management. Should this become necessary, follow the star topology shown in Figure 15-3, and plan for an Ethernet backbone with the various Ethernet segments branching off of it. This arrangement still allows centralized placement of services.

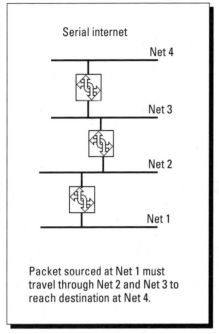

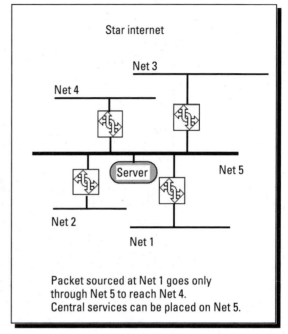

Figure 15-2: The star internet compared with the serial internet topology.

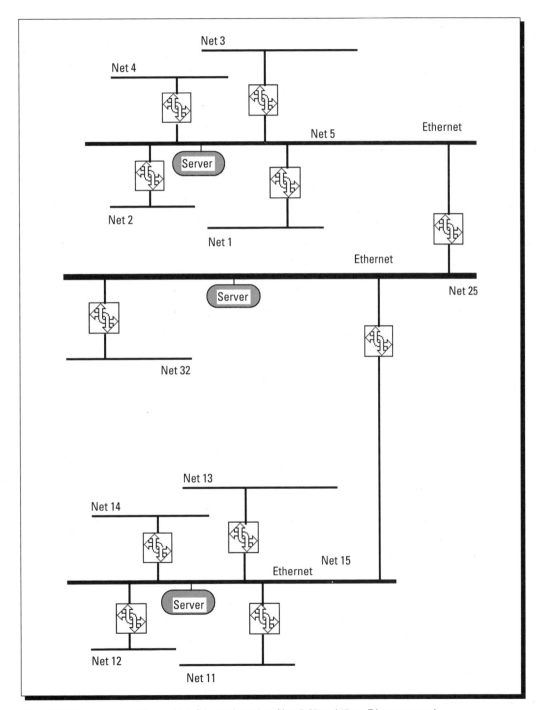

Figure 15-3: This star internet has multiple Ethernet branches. Nets 5, 25, and 15 are Ethernet networks.

Summary

In this chapter, you've learned various ways to improve the performance of your AppleTalk internet. We discussed the following topics:

✔ Performance management means getting the best throughput that you need for each network service.

✔ You should never seek network performance at the price of stability.

✔ Gathering network traffic statistics can help you determine service ratios for your users and their devices.

✔ LocalTalk networks should include no more than three primary services, such as file servers and printers.

✔ EtherTalk networks are more expensive to set up and maintain, but they do allow for heavier service usage.

✔ Depending on your performance needs, you can configure your network in one of the following topologies: the daisy-chain, the bus, or the active or passive star.

In the next chapter, we'll describe how you can best configure your network devices for both performance management and fault management.

Chapter 16

Configuration Management

In this chapter...

✔ A description of SNMP for AppleTalk

✔ Configuration setups for routers, servers, and bridges

✔ How seed and non-seed routers differ

✔ When to use seed or non-seed routers

✔ Configuration tips to avoid problems on your network

The discussions in the previous chapters, "Fault Management" and "Performance Management," were based on the OSI network management model, explained in the introduction to this part. This chapter and the two that follow are also based on that model.

The concept of fault management is self-explanatory, but the distinction between performance and configuration management can be confusing. According to the model presented in *The Simple Book,* by Marshall T. Rose, performance management is " . . . responsible for controlling and analyzing (the throughput and error rate) of the network (including historical information)" whereas configuration management is " . . . responsible for detecting and controlling the state of the network (for both logical and physical configurations)."[1]

Tools for configuration management can monitor, control, and report the configuration of any of the network devices. Properly managing the configuration of your network devices should yield good performance in throughput and lack of error (performance management), as well as a low incidence of network failure (fault management). In other words, performance management is primarily concerned with network configuration to achieve fast throughput, whereas configuration management is concerned with the proper configuration of network devices to achieve performance results, a low failure rate, and low security risk. This chapter provides an overview of the process of configuration management.

---

[1] Marshall T. Rose, *The Simple Book, An Introduction to Management of TCP/IP-based Internets* (Englewood Cliffs, N.J.: Prentice Hall, 1991), p. 17.

Open Network Management for AppleTalk Managers

Today, AppleTalk network managers must continue to manage their network configuration primarily with *proprietary* software tools. *Open,* the opposite of proprietary, refers to a set, published standard that everyone has access to and can implement. But open network management for AppleTalk is still chalk on the drawing boards, voices in meeting rooms, and bits on e-mail systems.

Why do network managers need open network management tools? Recall the discussion in Chapter 11 of all the processes that take place on the internet. ZIP, RTMP, and NBP all deliver an easy communications interface to the users of an AppleTalk internet. Remember that the workings of an AppleTalk internet can become highly complex, with multiple types of components: Macintosh and PC workstations, routers, servers, bridges, and repeaters.

Currently adding to this complex system are the many forms that vendors use for providing information on network statistics. With open network management, however, one device can monitor all network services, even those from different vendors, and then display the data all on one monitor. (See Chapters 11, 14, and 15 for the background concepts of network topology.)

Apple is currently pursuing a software tool set for open network management. The software is called SNMP (Simple Network Management Protocol), which is now widely used for TCP/IP networks and has become the standard for enterprise computing. SNMP is not yet available for AppleTalk devices, but soon will be, so we'll give you an overview of what you can expect from its features.

Two basic concepts of SNMP make it useful. First is its use of *agents* and *managers*. Second is its *extensible MIB* (Management Information Base).

With SNMP, each managed device, such as a router, bridge, or file server, has a piece of software installed called an SNMP *agent*. An SNMP agent relays specific information about its *owner* device, which may include such items as the date and time of the last reset, the routing table, or amount of available disk space. An SNMP-based network management system running on its own workstation uses the *manager software* to query these agents, collect the data, and present it to the network manager, preferably in the form of a graphical display of the network. The data that the network management system collects is maintained in a *network statistics database* on the management workstation. Figure 16-1 shows the relationship of the SNMP agents to the network management system.

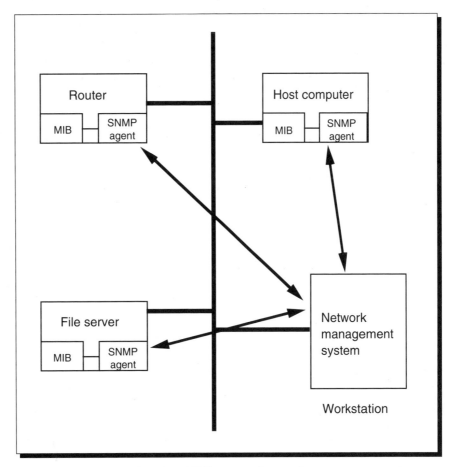

Figure 16-1: This schematic shows how SNMP agents and a network management system interrelate.

SNMP will also go beyond monitoring and reporting to provide actual configuration control of your network's various devices — all from the network management system. For example, from one monitor, you will be able to select and add new zones to several networks' zone lists.

Part of the SNMP specifications is the structure of the MIB. Certain basic information should always be a part of each device type's MIB. This includes such data as the network address, interface type, and certain counters (to monitor traffic conditions) and thresholds. Each device type has a MIB that tells the agent software what information to report, monitor, and control.

Earlier, we mentioned that a MIB is *extensible*. This means that a vendor implementing a MIB for a device can define new variables that can be reported by SNMP. The hitch here is that the vendor must let other vendors know what has been added to the MIB. If this doesn't happen, only that vendor's software (and hardware) will be able to use the added information in the MIB. And this is contrary to the idea of SNMP serving as a common network management scheme. Usually, vendors do readily publish information on their MIBs. Then it's up to the developers of network management systems to write their programs to acquire and use the additional data.

In 1991, Apple began to take an active part in defining an SNMP MIB that could be used with AppleTalk routers. The fundamental work in this effort was started at Carnegie-Mellon University. Some router manufacturers have already begun to experiment with their own MIBs. But, with all the router manufacturers, including Apple, now discussing this as a group, you can be sure that a standardized MIB for routers will appear before the end of 1993.

Apple's SNMP efforts probably won't end with the standardized MIB. It's just as important for network managers to obtain information about workstations as routers, so it's quite likely that Apple will also implement a MIB for the Mac itself, an effort that Apple discussed at the 1991 MacTivity Conference.

For now though, many sets of proprietary configuration management tools are available. The following sections of this chapter will show how you can use these tools to your network's best advantage.

The Configuration Management of Network Devices

For the present discussion, we'll treat configuration management with respect to the following types of devices: routers, Ethernet filtering bridges, and servers.

Managing the router configuration on your internet is the most critical element of configuration management. If the configuration of devices at the network layer is done incorrectly or inefficiently, the layers of applications above will suffer as they cross from one network to another.

The configuration of Ethernet filtering bridges is another important consideration. You can use Ethernet bridges to filter out or stop AppleTalk traffic from going across, which is an effective way to segregate one area from another.

Finally, we'll talk about the configuration of the server. As ADSP, a sophisticated data-transfer protocol, became available with the Macintosh operating system in version 6.0.4, many new server-based applications came to the

AppleTalk market. These applications also need to be configured correctly and efficiently for the health of the network.

The configuration of AppleTalk routers

You can break down the configuration management of AppleTalk routers into three facets:

1. Monitoring, or using software tools to view the configuration.

2. Reporting, in which software tools report the configuration to you along with any discrepancies or errors that the tool finds.

3. Control, in which you manipulate the configuration of the router.

You can perform all three activities by using various applications. As with other discussions of software applications, we'll concentrate on pointing out the features you should look for, rather than identifying specific applications.

Configuration monitoring tools

Monitoring is built into almost every router application we've seen. This feature may variously be called *diagnostics, error report,* or *debug.* Monitoring features enable you to view the condition of the router at any time, and these tools perceive and report certain errors or unusual conditions.

A typical condition identified by a monitoring tool is a multitude of GNI (GetNetInfo) packets being sent to the multicast broadcast address. This condition occurs when a node starts up on an extended network in the Phase 2 start-up network range (for details on GNI broadcasting, see Chapter 11, "Designing an AppleTalk LAN"). Well-written tools also tell you when a router is misconfigured in relation to the configurations of other routers on an internet.

Configuration reporting tools

Tools that report differ from tools that monitor. Reporting tools are self-initiating: They don't wait for you to open the software to look for errors, but send a report to you on their own. When SNMP for AppleTalk becomes available, a report, as gathered by the router's agent, will be sent via SNMP commands to a network management station. The central station can then present the network manager with up-to-the-minute conditions of an entire internet.

Configuration control tools

You're probably already familiar with tools that control configuration. These are by necessity built into every router. Configuration control tools are currently all proprietary software, but the future SNMP network management should offer control capabilities for AppleTalk. As an administrator, you must control two sets of information on the router: the zone name and list and the network number and range for each port.

See Chapter 11, "Designing an AppleTalk LAN," for information on selecting appropriate network numbers or ranges; see Chapter 14, "Fault Management," for the consequences of incorrect selection.

Controlling zone name changes

In addition to controlling the installation of new zone names and lists, the network administrator controls any changes to a zone name and list. Currently, there is no easy way to change a zone name or zone list on an internet. In the future, AppleTalk routers will have built-in SNMP network commands that have the capability of changing zone names.

For now, here's the method for changing a zone list. First, shut down all routers that are attached to the cable; if ten LocalTalk-to-Ethernet routers are attached to the backbone, you must shut off *all* ten. At this point, there is no established routing on the network. Traffic can occur locally, as between two Macintoshes with Ethernet cards, but no traffic can cross the routers into other networks. And users on this cable will see no zones showing up in Choosers.

Next, go to one of the routers and change the configuration by entering the new zone information. Reboot the router. This will be the first router on the network and thus will be the router that establishes the network range and number and the zone name and list. Continue around the network, rebooting each router with the new configuration.

This method won't work if you try to change the configuration only of the zone list while the network is running, because there has been no change in the network range and number. Remember that the router checks its routing table to make a change in the ZIT (Zone Information Table). Currently, no mechanism exists for dynamic zone list assignments across a network. And, if you try to change the network range while the network is running, the newly configured routers will conflict with the old routers. (For more information about how zone names and lists are generated across an internet and about shutting off routers for this process, see Chapter 11, "Designing an AppleTalk LAN.")

Controlling router start-up

Besides controlling network numbers and zone names, you also have control over the router start-up procedure. Specifically, you can select the start-up type to be *seed* or *non-seed*.

Seed routers *seed* the internet with the configuration information (network number and range, zone name and list) that the administrator enters. Non-seed routers will wait and listen for a seed router and then take this configuration information from the first seed router that they hear. Note that once a non-seed router obtains a network configuration, it begins to participate in the routing of the network, which effectively makes it a seed router for any new non-seed routers coming on line. What this means is that seed and non-seed determinations apply only as the router is starting up.

A router, whether non-seed or seed, first obtains a unique node address for each port through the AARP probe procedure (see Chapter 11). Next, if the router is non-seed, it begins a *discovery* process. A seed router, on the other hand, begins the process of *verification*.

These processes verify or discover the network number or range, the zone name or zone list, and, for extended networks, the default zone. Once this discovery and verification phase is complete, the router can begin the actual routing process by sending out RTMP Data packets every ten seconds, answering queries, such as those found in the ZIP protocol, and forwarding packets to their destination networks.

It is important that the process of verification or discovery be completed before the router begins functioning so that misinformation does not travel onto the internet. If the verification phase for seed routers is not completed correctly because of a conflicting configuration, Apple recommends that the router not use that seed information and alert the network administrator in some way. We've seen vendors use several methods for handling a seed router that attempts to start up in a network that has a configuration different from its own (whether a zone name and list or default zone or network number range).

Apple's recommendation is that the router alert the administrator when it detects a different configuration for either a network or zone on the network and to not

Choosing between seed and non-seed routers

Selecting whether to make a router a seed router or a non-seed router depends on two rationales. Making all routers except one non-seed makes certain that all routers will obtain the same configuration information, as this information issues from a single seed router. This is especially helpful if you are using a long zone list.

However, if you have power-failure problems, consider making most or all of your routers seed routers. Then, if two areas fail and only one comes back up, the area that is coming back up won't be waiting for the second router that contains the seed information.

route until the administrator has eliminated the disparity. Farallon, Cisco, Apple, and Digital currently take this approach. To eliminate the difference, the administrator may either change the configuration file to match the existing configuration or find the other router and change its configuration. Or the administrator can change the router to non-seed and let it discover the correct network and zone information.

A second method, first implemented by Cayman Systems, has been termed *soft-seed*. With this method, a router starts up as a seed router. But if the router detects a conflict during the verification phase, the router switches to discovery mode, thus acting as a non-seed router, and obtains the information from the other seed routers on the network. A drawback to this method is that the administrator loses control over network configuration.

A second problem is that an administrator may not discover an undesired configuration for some time. This is because most soft-seed implementations don't report to the administrator a changeover from the administrator's selected seed information to information from another router.

A third method, initiated by Kinetics in the FastPath and now copied by many vendors, is to circumvent the verification process and begin routing with the seed information found in the configuration file, regardless of the configuration in use on the internet. We consider this practice dangerous because it opens the possibility of loss of connectivity to parts of the internet. Even simple mistakes such as typos in the seed configuration can jeopardize the network (see Chapter 14). Also, without the verification phase, the administrator cannot be alerted to a configuration problem because the router has not checked for one.

The configuration of Ethernet filtering bridges

As network manager, you can also control the configuration of Ethernet filtering bridges. With Ethernet filtering bridges, you can filter the flow of packets based on the protocol type. The bridge discards packets of a type that you specify to be filtered. If you establish AppleTalk filtering, there will be no AppleTalk connectivity over that bridge. Some bridges also enable you to establish priority settings that take effect when their buffers become full and overflow packets have to be discarded. A low-priority packet type is discarded first.

If you decide on any of these configurations, carefully consider that the AppleTalk protocol needs timely AARP probes for start-up devices and RTMP Data packets to maintain routing tables. Never eliminate Ethernet broadcasts if you want to maintain AppleTalk Phase 1 connectivity over the bridge — or

AppleTalk multicast broadcasts if you want to maintain AppleTalk Phase 2 connectivity. Broadcasting is a critical part of the functioning of the AppleTalk protocol (RTMP for example). For this reason, we also suggest that you don't make AppleTalk packets a low priority. Making AppleTalk a low priority can result in zones disappearing and reappearing because of the RTMP time-out procedure.

To specify AppleTalk Phase 1 packets, you need to identify their type field. Two types of packets are available: 809b and 80f3. To specify AppleTalk Phase 2 packets, you need to identify in an 8-bit string that the packet is 802 LLC; then identify the vendor code and type. These two strings are **aaaa03080007809b** and **aaaa0300000080f3**.

The configuration of AppleTalk servers

A third type of device that you control the configuration of is the AppleTalk server. You can configure only a few settings with AppleTalk servers, and these settings are on servers that automatically establish network conversations, such as e-mail servers and workflow-management servers. For most e-mail servers, you can set the timing for the distribution of names lists. For most e-mail servers and workflow management servers, you can also establish the time for forwarding of data. The time interval that you set has a direct impact on the performance of your network. Check with vendors for their recommendations. Also, monitor your network and adjust these settings as necessary.

With some servers, you can determine security restrictions regarding passwords. Standard practice is to enforce the rule that all users have passwords of a certain length and that passwords must be alphanumeric. Whereas AppleShare servers are currently limited to eight-character passwords, other vendors' products permit longer ones. It's best not to use passwords containing less than six characters, or passwords that are composed only of alphanumeric characters. Such passwords are too easy to "spoof" or detect with the existing password-breaking software often used by computer hackers.

Other Tips for Configuration Management

Following are several tips to help you avoid problems on your network:

❖ Never test a new configuration on-line during normal business hours — this means that you test on a "lab network" first and then test on the real network after hours.

❖ Never test a new software version on-line during normal business hours.

❖ Make sure that you have tools to monitor your devices once they're on-line.

❖ Keep the vendor's tech support phone number and policies handy.

And, finally here's a tip from our technical editor with which we heartily agree: Never make a major change just before you go on vacation — you may not have a job to come back to.

Summary

In this chapter, you learned about the future direction of network management tools. We covered the following topics:

✔ Configuration-management tools can monitor, control, and report the configuration of any network devices.

✔ At this time, only proprietary tools are available for configuration management.

✔ Although SNMP (Simple Network Management Protocol) is not yet available for AppleTalk systems, Apple Computer is developing this protocol for use in configuration management.

✔ Configuration management involves the management of routers, Ethernet filtering bridges, and servers.

The next chapter will cover accounting and security management procedures. We'll provide background information and give you some important tips.

Chapter 17

Accounting and Security Management

In this chapter . . .

✔ Tracking printer usage on the network

✔ Keeping track of networked modem usage

✔ How to restrict usage of network resources

✔ How to control shared workstations

✔ Keeping viruses off your network

✔ Restricting zone access

A number of casually designed AppleTalk LANs have come into existence, mainly because small AppleTalk networks are relatively easy to install. But as these LANs grow larger or become incorporated into standard corporate networks, the network manager soon finds a need to account for resources and provide for security. It's one thing to total up the cost of the hardware and software comprising the network and yet another to continually monitor usage of the resources (such as laser printers, servers, and color printers) so that users are properly charged for the resources.

You may have thought that moving to a LAN from a mainframe or minicomputer would make all these accounting problems go away, or that such problems can be blissfully ignored. Remember, though, that companies still have to think about the bottom line. For complex network systems, bottom-line accounting entails a detailed breakdown of usage. That's where accounting management comes in.

Managing security for larger internets is also more complicated than managing security for a small network. Some companies have long practiced some measure of computer security; if you've worked with a mainframe computer, you'll remember logging in with a password. The step of logging into shared resources can extend to networks as well.

Two areas of security must be managed on networks. The first area is at the level of network management. This level involves restricting LAN access to network managers for such activities as configuring routers and assigning file-server passwords. A second level involves maintaining the security of the users and their data. We'll look at both of these security areas in the second part of this chapter.

Accounting Management

There comes a time in every network's life when you have to pay the piper. You just spent a lot of money setting up a network, buying computers, and installing software, and maybe everything's running smoothly. Now someone with a ledger or spreadsheet in hand wants to know how much it cost. Was it worth it? How often will you have to upgrade the network hardware and software? Are you planning to enlarge the network? Are the departments being properly charged for their use of special printers and slide makers? And so on . . . .

Accounting management is simply a means of answering these and other questions that may relate to network usage. Sometimes, pertinent questions don't have a dollar sign in front of them. You'll find, however, that the tools of accounting management help you plan for future network expansion and perhaps even help sell company management on the effectiveness of current and future network plans.

Should you really bother with the accounting management of your network? If your network is small and you can see all your network users by looking down the hall or glancing around the room, maybe not. You know the costs of your network, probably because you installed it yourself, you put paper and toner in the laser printer, and you're the one who sees requisitions for new Macs and software.

> You may not need accounting management for a simple network where you're in touch with costs and maintenance. But as your network grows and you need usage details to manage costs and justify new equipment, you may have no choice but to practice accounting management.

But if you have a larger network, one comprised of a few workgroups or possibly one extending across several buildings — if not counties or states — you may have no choice but to try accounting management for your network. Under these circumstances, you may well be asked for usage statistics on laser printer output, perhaps even broken down by department or workgroup so that the costs of the network (particularly the operating costs) are properly distributed among profit centers. Or, if your phone bills go through the roof, you may need to determine who's using the networked modems or fax modems so often.

As mentioned, accounting management can provide you with ammunition for network expansion. By auditing usage of laser printers, modems, or file servers, you may be able to spot problem areas and point out what network equipment needs to be upgraded or replaced, or what new equipment might help. Having usage statistics (and perhaps even related costs — don't forget how much your co-workers' time is costing the company) can help determine if your network is maxed out and needs to be expanded.

Unfortunately, there aren't many tools available to handle the accounting management of AppleTalk networks. Perhaps this stems from the individualism of microcomputer users in general, and Mac users specifically. But there are a few steps you can take to audit resource usage on your network. We'll cover these in the following sections.

Auditing printers

The most commonly audited device is a networked printer. We're not talking here about tracking the amount of paper or toner used. Printer auditing involves keeping track of print jobs according to the paper used (plain paper vs. transparencies, for example), the number of pages, and who printed the file. Armed with that type of information, you can bill the appropriate department in your company for using a specific printer. This type of auditing can be especially important when you've installed costly printers, such as for larger page sizes, special paper, or color output.

Ordinary print spoolers (including Apple's own AppleShare Print Server) don't tell you much about usage, especially on a user account basis. Instead, you have to devote a machine (Mac or PC) to act as a print server for one or more printers and run special spooling and auditing software to track the jobs sent to each printer. A noteworthy program that includes audit logs as well as calculation of printing costs per user is Print Central (Compumation Inc.).

Auditing file servers

You wouldn't normally think of monitoring file usage on a file server in the same way as auditing a printer. What may be more important is tracking the amount of disk storage that each person is taking up on the server. Discovering that a person hasn't used any of the files he or she has stored on the server in six months is a good reason to talk to the user about removing the files and freeing some of that space for others. Or you may wish to monitor disk-space usage by department in order to justify a new server specifically for one department's use.

None of the Mac-based file servers offers much of anything in auditing. Apple's own AppleShare 2.0 has a pitifully small report that shows little detail about server usage. It doesn't, for instance, break down file usage by users or by age of the oldest files or folders. Apple's newer AppleShare 3.0, which just shipped as we wrote this book, doesn't offer any expanded reports; the new version does at least include the hooks so that developers can write their own report generators. Distributed, or *peer-to-peer,* file servers like TOPS (Sitka Corp.), or System 7's File Sharing feature stress the individual's control of the sharing process and offer no logs at all.

Auditing telecommunications devices

Telecommunications costs are a significant item in most every company's budget. Call-tracking on an employee-by-employee basis is common, but how do you handle a phone line used for a modem shared by networked users? That's when you turn to network tools for logging modem usage. Maintaining logs of modem usage for outgoing calls can tell you who is using the modems; you can then use the information for billing purposes. Logging incoming calls to a modem will also tell you if an unauthorized user is attempting to call into the network.

Auditing the usage of networked modems and other telecommunications devices on AppleTalk systems is a mixed bag. Most e-mail systems that offer telecommunications links don't offer auditing of calls, either incoming or outgoing; QuickMail is the exception. And if you're connecting two remote networks with half-routers (see Chapter 13), the routers don't support call logging either. Apple's new personal link for connecting a Mac to an AppleTalk network, AppleTalk Remote Access (ARA), does allow the receiving Mac to maintain a log of callers who are using ARA.

As we've said, auditing the device usage on an AppleTalk network is problematical. You can get some reports, but for now, you're on your own when it comes to compiling those reports into a spreadsheet to calculate usage and chargeback costs for various users.

Security Management

Network security is an important aspect of managing a network, whether to limit usage of certain devices or to prevent unauthorized traffic on the network. Currently, there is no overall security application for AppleTalk networks, nor is it an easy task to monitor your network's security. One reason for this difficulty is the variety of services that a network can provide. Little has been done to standardize all the security features needed to encompass networks that have more than one type of service (printing, file-sharing, telecommunications) to which access should be controlled. Also, many Macintosh users tend to be casual with their computing resources, both hardware and software, and think nothing of sharing those resources. These users may resent having security restrictions placed on them.

Security experts tend to identify five major areas of security for networks. The following is a list of those areas as well as some security techniques associated with each area.

1. Physical security

Techniques that emphasize physical security include locating your file servers in locked rooms, using Tempest technology to prevent the broadcasting of errant data signals, or keeping high-risk network activities within a shielded room.

2. Authentication of users

Using passwords as well as magnetic cards, voice prints, or other technology are all ways to control access to resources.

3. Definition of privileges for users

You can define user privileges by assigning only the basic access rights to each user as needed and not providing network management rights to all users.

4. Encryption of data

You can secure data by using DES (Data Encryption Standard) encryption schemes for the transmission of electronic messages or other confidential files.

5. Maintenance of audit trails

Logs that track attempts to dial into a network modem or to track usage of secure files on a user-by-user basis are effective ways to maintain audit trails for future reference.

The following are some additional practices which will help you maintain network security on AppleTalk LANs:

❖ Restrict users from routinely using certain output devices, such as high-resolution imagesetters or slide makers.

❖ Subdivide the network so that one workgroup's resources cannot be accessed by users in another workgroup.

❖ Allow only certain users to send faxes or to use special e-mail services (MCI Mail or CompuServe, for example).

❖ Limit dial-in access to the network via modem to certain callers.

❖ Control user privileges on shared workstations.

❖ Conscientiously apply passwords to file server and e-mail accounts.

Additional security techniques are discussed in the upcoming sections.

Controlling zone and device access

An effective method of managing security involves restricting certain areas of your AppleTalk internet. Just as areas of your company or university may be off-limits to certain users, you can restrict access to certain areas in your LAN.

Of course, to provide the ultimate in security, you must physically disconnect the designated area from the rest of your internet — and in extreme cases, put this physically disconnected network into a shielded room so that radio frequency signals from the computers cannot be detected. (Did you know that each tap on your keyboard emits a signal that powerful spy technology receivers can pick up?) For most security needs, however, you can use a technology called *filtering* to restrict access.

Filtering is optional software that is provided with most routers. The implementations of filters from each router vendor all vary somewhat, but we can outline here the three basic methods used by router vendors:

❖ GetZoneList packet restriction

❖ NBP LkUp-Reply packet restriction

❖ RTMP packet restriction

We can further subdivide filters into two types of access restrictions:

❖ one-way access restriction

❖ two-way access restriction

NBP and GetZoneList filters restrict access in one direction and allow access in the other direction, but RTMP filters only set up two-way access restrictions. One-way access restricts either incoming access or outgoing access. For

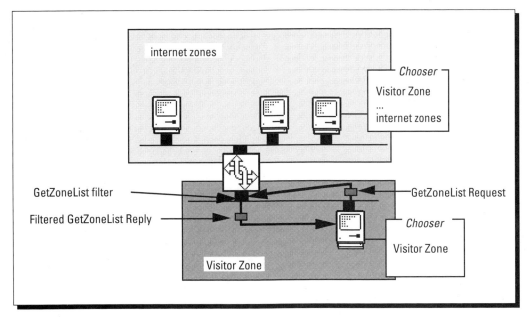

Figure 17-1: A GetZoneList filter.

example, in a one-way access restriction, a filter restricts all users of Zone A from accessing any network services outside their zone. The filter, however, would allow all incoming traffic into Zone A. With an RTMP filter's two-way access restriction, users from one network are restricted from accessing services in a second network — and users from the second network are restricted from accessing services in the first.

GetZoneList filters

A GetZoneList filter is useful when you want to restrict a certain set of users from accessing your internet. Suppose that you want to set up a zone for visitors' use but do not want the visitors to be able to access the internet. You can set up a GetZoneList filter to restrict the visitors' use of the network. This setup is depicted in Figure 17-1.

In Figure 17-1, the GetZoneList filter is set up in the configuration of the router's port that is attached to the Visitor Zone. When any Mac from within the Visitor Zone boots up and sends a GetZoneList packet to the router (to obtain the internet zone list to display in the Chooser), the

NBP LkUp-Reply packet restriction is an intensive operation for a router to perform. Note that the operation will seriously impact the router's ability to quickly switch data packets. Other filter types also impact the performance of a router. With today's technology, speed and security do not necessarily go hand in hand.

router returns a "filtered" zone list, and the Chooser displays only the Visitor Zone. Because the visitor sees only the filtered zone rather than the complete list of internet zones in the Chooser, the visitor is less likely to become frustrated with not being able to access services in other zones.

The router, however, *will* send out the full zone list to any Macintoshes that request the GetZoneList through the router's other port (refer again to Figure 17-1). Users on the internet will therefore be able to access any services that were set up for the visitors in the Visitor Zone. This may be a desirable situation if you have installed expensive special services, such as high speed printers, for visitors' use.

NBP LkUp-Reply filters

NBP filters work by restricting the passage of NBP packets across the router. Although it is possible to set up a filter that restricts NBP BrRq (Broadcast Request) packets, most router vendors implement an NBP filter that uses NBP LkUp-Reply packet restriction. With this type of restriction, some implementations allow the filter to search all NBP LkUp-Reply packets for a particular type of reply.

Consider the example shown in Figure 17-2. Suppose that you set up a zone for desktop publications (the Publication Zone) and that the LaserWriters in the Publication Zone are all heavily used. You can set up an NBP filter that restricts users who are in zones outside the Publication Zone from accessing the LaserWriters in the Publication Zone. In the example in Figure 17-2, the router checks all packets against the filter and then discards any NBP LkUp-Reply packet that has the NBP device type of LaserWriter. Any users from outside the Publication Zone, such as users from the Engineering Zone, will receive no entries in the Chooser for LaserWriters in the Publication Zone.

The NBP filter allows for partial communication to a network area. Because the filter restricts only a particular device type, users can still access other device types in the restricted area. For example, users in an Engineering Zone can log onto an AppleShare server in the Publication Zone (see Figure 17-2) to send rough drafts to the editors.

RTMP filters

RTMP filters are useful for segregating your AppleTalk internet into restricted areas. Suppose that you have three separate areas in your internet: Marketing and Sales, Engineering and Development, and a shared area with AppleShare servers. In this example, you do not want the users in the Marketing and Sales zones to be able to access the Macintosh file servers in the Engineering and Development zones. Figure 17-3 illustrates this type of RTMP filtering process in an example network.

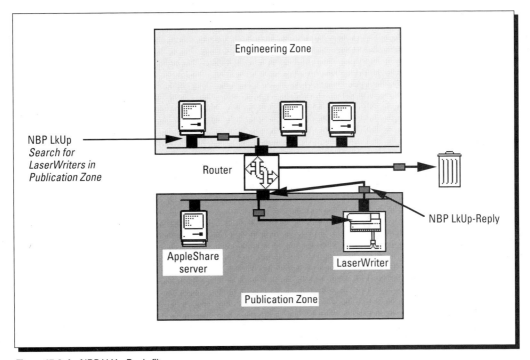

Figure 17-2: An NBP LkUp-Reply filter.

In Figure 17-3, an RTMP filter is used to set up the three distinct areas. First, a separate network cable is installed; the AppleShare file servers are installed on this cable. In the example, this zone is called the Share Zone. Next, two routers are set up; one router is placed between the Marketing and Sales Zone and the Share Zone. Note in Figure 17-3 that port A of router 1 is attached to Marketing and Sales's networks, and port B is attached to the Share Zone.

The second router is placed between the Share Zone and the Engineering and Development Zones. Note that port C of router 2 attaches to the Share Zone; port D attaches to Engineering and Development's networks.

With this physical configuration in place, RTMP filters are set up in the router's configuration software. All zones associated with Engineering and Development are listed and placed into the configuration file of port A, where the router requests "which zones to discard/filter?" (This request can come in many variations depending on the router manufacturer's implementation; "deny . . ." or "don't listen to . . ." are two possible wordings.)

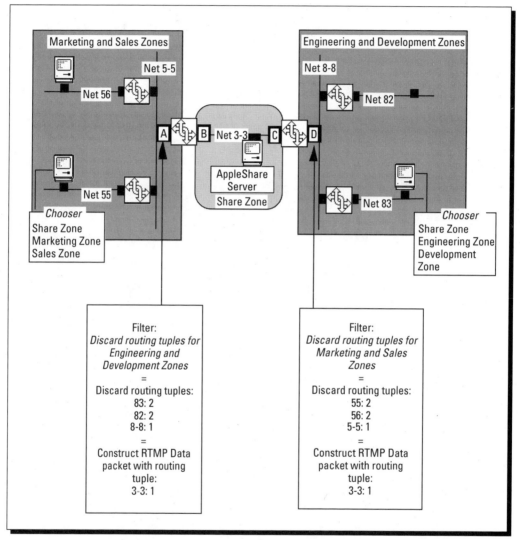

Figure 17-3: Setting up an RTMP filter.

The same process is repeated for port D: All zones associated with Marketing and Sales are listed and placed into the filter for port D. These actions properly set up a two-way RTMP filter.

The RTMP filter looks at the zone names and matches the names to their network numbers. (Remember that routers use network numbers for routing packets; the zone names are for user convenience.) When composing the

RTMP Data packet that the router will broadcast out of the port, the router filters out the routing tuples associated with the zones to be restricted. Without these routing tuples, any routers that are also attached to the same network will not learn about routes to the restricted areas. Because they do not learn about the routes, the ZIP processes in these routers never request the zone names for these routes. Because the users will not see the zone names for the restricted areas in their Choosers, the users will not search for services in the restricted zones.

In addition to the RTMP filter, the router should also run a GetZoneList packet filter. Then any Macintoshes that are directly attached to the same network as the port with the filter (rather than behind another router) will receive a filtered zone list that will not include the restricted zones.

It is important that you set up any RTMP filter on two ports as in this example. If not, the AppleTalk protocol will stop communication from going in both directions anyway; however, the result will not be very friendly. Figure 17-4 is an example of this situation.

In this example, the RTMP filter was set up only on port A to discard routing tuples related to Engineering and Development; no RTMP filter was set up on port D to discard routing tuples associated with Marketing and Sales. With this setup, you might think that Engineering and Development would still be able to reach services in the Marketing and Sales network areas. After all, access was restricted just to Engineering and Development — it didn't matter whether Engineering and Development could access Marketing and Sales. And, in fact, Engineering and Development users will be able to see zones in the Marketing and Sales network area since their routers will receive full routing and zone information.

If, however, an NBP search (NBP BrRq packet) is sent to a zone in Marketing and Sales (from a Macintosh in the Engineering and Development network area), the NBP LkUp-Reply packet will never make it back. The routers in the Marketing and Sales network area will not have a route to return the NBP LkUp-Reply packet because the routers did not receive routing tuples for the Engineering and Development network areas. As shown in Figure 17-4, the router would not know where to switch a NBP LkUp-Reply packet that is destined for return to network 82; the router would have no "next address" for network 82. Therefore, the router would discard the NBP LkUp-Reply packet. The users in the Engineering and Development network areas would have a list of zones in their Chooser in which *no* services were reachable — not a very friendly situation.

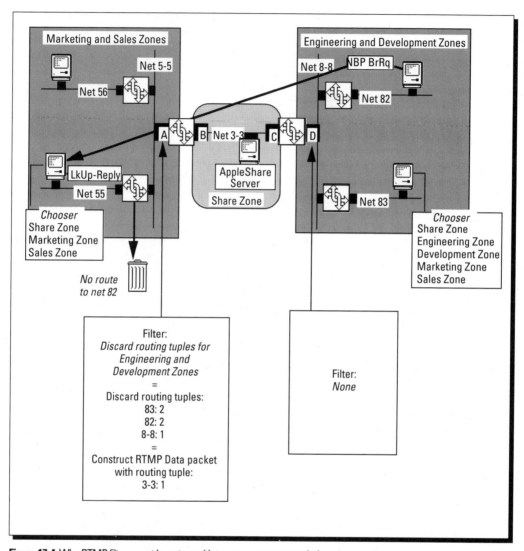

Figure 17-4: Why RTMP filters must be set up with two-way access restriction.

Controlling telecommunications access

Another important area of network security involves telecommunications access. If you permit remote access to the network by modem, you can choose either of two levels of access control: password security or call-back control.

The simplest to set up is password security. In such a system, each user is assigned a password that must be entered correctly as part of the dial-in process. NetModem and NetSerial (Shiva Corp.) both offer password options, as do the R-Server and C-Server (Solana Corp.). Because it is so easy to set up, however, password-based security is also easy to break. Many companies, therefore, don't consider password security to be adequate.

If a simple password scheme isn't secure enough for your purposes, you can use what's called *dial-back,* or *call-back* control. With call-back, you call the device and give it your name. Once you've done this, the device breaks the connection. The device then looks for your name on its list of permitted callers and calls you back at the phone number it has listed for you. The one difficulty with this type of security is its assumption that you always use the same phone number to call in. If you're on the road or call from a variety of regional offices, you have to list a separate entry for each of your phone numbers, including different names for each one.

PhoneNET Liaison (Farallon Computing Inc.), a software router, is the only program that offers call-back control for dial-in network access; Shiva has now added call-back security to its EtherGate and NetModem/E hardware. Liaison can also log all calls, both inbound and outbound; the program further lets you control the zones that a dial-in user can access. Microsoft Mail 3.0 (Microsoft) has a limited version of call-back security for remote users who want to access the mail server via modem. Even if you don't use the call-back option, the mail administrator can determine which mail users can call into the server. QuickMail controls dial-in access from individual users only by the user's name and password, and anyone with a mail account can dial in to the mail server.

If you're using e-mail gateways with your LAN-based e-mail package, you may also have control over which e-mail accounts can use the gateway services. This control covers such options as access to MCI Mail and CompuServe via modem, as well as the capability to send faxes.

So far, we've discussed products that were developed specifically for use with AppleTalk networks. But you should be aware of other products on the market for modem security that function independently of the network protocols. These products usually take the form of some modem-related hardware device (a multiplexer, for instance) that includes authentication and dial-back features.

Some V.32 modems now include security features such as the storage of user passwords and callback numbers within the modem, so that you don't need special software on a Mac for these features; the CXR Telcom/Anderson Jaconson 9653-MM2, MultiTech Systems MultiModem V32, and Telcor Systems Accelerator V.32 are examples. Other modems, such as the NEC America N9635E and Telenetics OZ Guardian Modem, also offer audit trails to display all authorized and unauthorized attempts to access the system. The N9653E can also be programmed to restrict access to specific times of the day or specific days of the week.

Some companies offer other means of caller authentication. For example, Millidyne's Auditor uses a call-back strategy, but requires a special access identification code, as opposed to a simple password, in order to complete the connection. LeeMah Datacom Security Corp. offers the InfoCard personal authentication device, which requires a to enter their user personal ID number, into a small hand-held device in order to make a connection via a modem.

Very few modems that we know of offer built-in data encryption, which will improve the security of your transmissions. Cylink offers the STM-9600 modem, while Racal-Datacom markets the Omnimode and RM series of encrypted modems.

Controlling file access

File server software, such as AppleShare, DataClub, and TOPS, includes simple security provisions, such as passwords for user accounts. Users are owners of either the disks or the folders on disks that make up the file server. But the security of the data is only as secure as the passwords. If you, as the server administrator, want a secure server, you'll have to make certain that users guard their passwords and routinely change them to prevent unauthorized file use — and it's never a good idea to assign blank passwords for anything.

AppleShare 3.0 has a new feature to enhance its password security — you can now set up AppleShare to require a minimum password length, and you can *age* passwords, a system that requires users to select a new password after a set time period.

Password security takes on a more personal face in System 7.0's File Sharing; users take responsibility for creating accounts and passwords for people they want to share files with. When users are cavalier about the security of their Macs and its files, you, as network manager, should make it clear that they'll have little recourse if something goes wrong. A word to the wise . . . .

Controlling shared workstations

Whereas many of us enjoy offices where we each have our own Mac, many schools and companies must use shared workstations. The shared workstation is especially prevalent in schools, where sharing resources in classrooms and labs is desirable. But many companies also set up special workrooms for communal use by members of a group. Inevitably, the users store their files on these workstations rather than keeping them on their own floppies or removable cartridges. As network manager, you have the problem of ensuring the privacy of those files if they're left on the Mac. Another concern is when not all users merit the same printing capabilities or use of such network resources as modems.

Quite a few programs on the market now require users to log on to a Mac, and folders are locked to all except their rightful owners. Among programs of this type are Advanced Security, A.M.E., Camouflage, DiskLock, EmPower, FileGuard, MacSafe, and Sentinel. Many programs even maintain an encrypted audit trail to log both legal and illegal access, but few go beyond file and folder protection to restrict access to networked resources. One program that does this is Access Managed Environment, or AME. Beyond setting different levels of protection for users or groups of users, you can also control on a user-by-user basis which desk accessories and networked resources each user can access. Another program, Authenticator, originally developed for Harvard University, has some of these features, such as controlled access to a work-station and both controlled and logged printer usage on a user basis.

With the inclusion of the File Sharing feature in System 7, everyone can now make their Mac a shared computer. Users should be informed of the danger of activating File Sharing and allowing all users access to their files. We recommend that users only implement File Sharing when they have a need to share files with another user or group of users and also that they keep the number of users who have access to their Macs to a minimum.

Whenever possible, do not enable guest logins under System 7's File Sharing. Especially, do not enable guest privileges for your entire hard disk! If you do, anyone who logs in as a guest can delete any or all of your files.

Recognizing that Apple's File Sharing feature did not include adequate monitoring of remote user access, TriK Inc. offers Nok-Nok as an added security product for File Sharing. Nok-Nok allows you to be notified any time a remote user connects to your computer; the product also can maintain an activity log. Each entry in the log contains information about the user who attempted to connect, including the time and date of the attempt. Nok-Nok also lets you decide how long a connection can be maintained.

Dealing with viruses

Viruses of any kind can be nasty. Certainly, enough has been written about computer viruses in the last few years to convince people that viruses are a problem. Whether or not viruses actually disrupt your daily work, you should guard against them. Some viruses, such as the WDEF virus, attempt to infect other workstations over the network and can lead to horrible workstation and network performance.

Like their biological counterparts, computer viruses are designed to spread easily. A virus contains software instructions that enable it to copy itself into legitimate files. Some viruses infect only application files, but others can invade document files or the Mac's system files. In addition to replicating itself, a virus can also inflict unique symptoms on the infected computer. Often these symptoms are relatively harmless and just a nuisance, but some viruses are maliciously designed and will cause serious trouble to your Mac.

How can you combat viruses? The best bet is a three-pronged approach — education, isolation, and eradication. First, educate the users of your network about the potential problems that viruses cause and how they spread by sharing software (and, in some cases, data). Take care before any new software is run on a networked Mac.

Second, create an isolated workstation, not connected to the network, for running *any* new program before you distribute the program to others. Run the program while using one of the available virus detection/prevention programs. You may also choose a virus-scanning program that runs *after* the suspect program to search your system for viruses. If your virus detection/ prevention programs are up to date and if they don't detect any viruses, you can go ahead and distribute the program.

Using an isolated workstation, however, doesn't always work. This approach has its best chance of succeeding when your company strictly enforces a centralized method for distributing software to employees. Even then, remember the *personal* in personal computers — users often like to acquire and install their own software, either for business or non-business uses. If you can't be sure that only software that is company purchased and distributed is installed on each Mac, you should make sure that each Mac has its own virus detection programs and that the users know how to use them. This forms the third step — eradication.

> You can't be sure that your users aren't installing their own software for business or personal use, so it's a good idea to provide each Mac with its own set of virus-detection programs.

Several effective anti-virus programs are available (SAM and Virex among others), as well as one excellent public-domain package (Disinfectant). All are kept up to date for detecting viruses and preventing them from infecting your machine. Every Mac should have at least one such program installed.

A final comment about viruses — users often mistake other system problems for those caused by viruses. This often happens when viruses are foremost in their minds, especially when another new virus article has appeared in the press. It's amazing how many things viruses have been blamed for. The best way to counteract paranoia is with training. Make sure that your users know what viruses do; also make sure that the users know how other problems are caused, such as INIT conflicts, insufficient system heaps, and so on. The more you educate your users, the fewer problems you'll have later.

Summary

This chapter introduced you to the concepts of accounting and security management for networks and for individual Macs. Although no comprehensive, do-it-all accounting or security programs for AppleTalk networks are currently available, we reviewed the tools currently available for managing accounts and security on your network.

In this chapter, you learned the following points:

- ✔ A print server is your best tool for keeping track of printer usage.

- ✔ You can use AppleTalk routers to secure either zones or individual devices from unauthorized access.

- ✔ Using dial-back options for modems on a network is one of the most secure ways to prevent unauthorized access to the network via modem.

- ✔ You should use an isolated (non-networked) Mac to check all software for viruses before the software is distributed on the network.

In the next chapter, we'll discuss how best to manage your network's resources.

Chapter 18

Resource Management

In this chapter . . .

✔ Software tools for scanning Macs for hardware and software

✔ Software for controlling multiuser access to licensed applications

✔ How to update software over the network

✔ Privacy issues

Even a smoothly running network can give the network manager headaches. There's always the problem of distributing product upgrades or system software. System 7.0, for example, promises to bring a full cascade of program upgrades with it in 1992. And this is the area where resource management tools take over. This chapter introduces you to the types of tools available and shows you how to use these tools effectively.

The Elements of Resource Management

Resource management typically isn't included in the definition of network management. Yet resource management makes extensive use of the network and often falls within the job description of the network manager, so we include this management concern as part of our coverage of network management.

Varied activities fall under the heading of resource management. You may be concerned with installing the proper system files on everyone's Mac or checking that everyone is using the latest version of a software package. Ensuring that all copies of the software are properly licensed is another aspect of resource management. So, too, is updating software over the network. Resource management has become one of the fastest growing areas of Mac application development over the past two years. Thanks to that fast growth, you can now pick and choose among a variety of programs to cover every aspect of resource management.

Our opinion of resource management is that it's good for some environments, but useless in others. Small networks probably don't need specialized resource

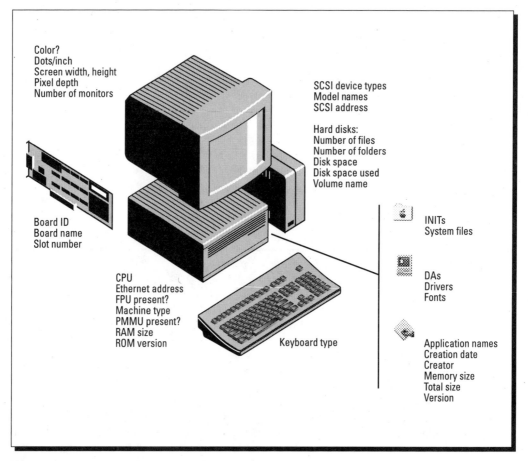

Color?
Dots/inch
Screen width, height
Pixel depth
Number of monitors

SCSI device types
Model names
SCSI address

Hard disks:
Number of files
Number of folders
Disk space
Disk space used
Volume name

Board ID
Board name
Slot number

INITs
System files

DAs
Drivers
Fonts

CPU
Ethernet address
FPU present?
Machine type
PMMU present?
RAM size
ROM version

Keyboard type

Application names
Creation date
Creator
Memory size
Total size
Version

Figure 18-1: The types of data that you can acquire with resource management programs.

management. Even some large networks of over 100 Macs cannot use resource management. Some companies don't have a centralized person or department for maintaining software upgrades and the like. In such systems, individuals order their own upgrades. We don't condone this approach, but some companies still operate this way.

The way you manage your network and related resources is a matter of personal and corporate style. The tools we'll describe offer varying degrees of flexibility, allowing you to customize them to your own needs. This flexibility applies both to collecting information and to reporting it.

The data that you collect to maintain users on the network falls into two basic categories (see Figure 18-1). First, you need data about the hardware and software each computer, and, second, you want location or user data. The slate of programs currently offered can all use Apple's built-in system support, now called Gestalt, to learn which NuBus cards and monitors are installed, as well as how much RAM and disk storage are available.

Defining resource management tasks

Before we review the programs for collecting system and application data over the network, we've put together some illustrations of how these tools can be used.

Situation 1: Users have more than one Laser Prep file.

Problem: Users are complaining that they're always resetting the laser printer when they print because someone on the network is using a different Laser Prep file.

Solution: Use software such as Inter•Poll, GraceLAN, or Status*Mac to scan the users' disks. Find out who has an out-of-date Laser Prep file or who has installed a new one that other users don't have yet. Decide which version should be used, and either update the problem Macs manually or use network-wide software-updating software like NetDistributor.

Situation 2: You need to distribute fonts for desktop publishing.

Problem: Not all the users have the proper fonts for printing their reports.

Solution: If you already know which fonts are needed, use software-updating software to distribute the missing fonts. If you don't know who has which fonts, scan the users' disks with a program like GraceLAN or Status*Mac to identify the fonts each user has, and then update the users' Macs.

Situation 3: You're planning to upgrade to System 7.

Problem: It's time to upgrade all your Macs to System 7, but not everyone has sufficient RAM or the right hardware (a PMMU, for instance) to use all of System 7's features.

Solution: Use GraceLAN or Status*Mac to scan each user's Mac for RAM and needed hardware (PMMU); check to see if users have sufficient disk space for added files. Then either use Apple's Installer program and the System 7 files on a file server, or use updating software like NetDistributor to update each Mac over the network.

Situation 4: You're planning for a new version of a word processor.

Problem: This is similar to the System 7 upgrade situation, but this time you need to find out who has the program and what the version is.

Solution: Use GraceLAN or Status*Mac to scan each user's disk for the program to be upgraded. Then use a program like NetDistributor to update each user's version.

Situation 5: Users have multiple system files on the same Mac.

Problem: Some users may complain that they don't see the same fonts or desk accessories when they use their programs. This may be because they've installed more than one system file on their Mac.

Solution: Use a program like GraceLAN or Status*Mac to scan the users' disks for multiple system files; then ask your users to remove all but one.

Situation 6: The company is moving to centralized control of licensed software.

Problem: Rather than let each user keep a copy of a particular application on the Mac's hard disk, your company wants to keep a copy on a file server and control access according to the site license.

Solution: Scan everyone's hard disk to see which users have a copy of the program; then work with them to remove it. Now install KeyServer or Quota on the file server and use it to keep track of the number of legal simultaneous users for the licensed application now installed on the server.

Situation 7: Management wants an audit of all Mac hardware.

Problem: Your company management wants to know the serial numbers of all Macs and what hardware is installed in, or attached to, them.

Solution: Use a program like GraceLAN or Status*Mac to scan each user's Mac for the hardware configuration. Unfortunately, the Mac doesn't electronically encode its serial number anywhere. If you planned ahead, you entered the serial numbers when you installed the GraceLAN or Status*Mac responders; if not, each user will have to relay the serial number to you. With the data in hand, create a custom report.

Collecting system data

What kinds of information can you acquire with resource management programs? The simplest programs, such as Inter•Poll, Radar, and TalkManage (see Table 18-1 for vendors and features), collect the version of each Mac's System and the Finder and LaserWriter files, as well as the zone, network, and node numbers. The more sophisticated programs, such as GraceLAN, Status*Mac, and Network SuperVisor, collect much more information about a Mac, including the types of cards and disks installed, type of monitor, the desk accessories, the fonts and INITs installed, as well as the applications residing on each hard disk. GraceLAN can also acquire data from MS-DOS computers that have an AppleTalk-compatible adapter installed — in this case, GraceLAN lists the type of processor, the version of DOS, the amount of regular and extended memory, and other information about hard disks and video adapters, as well as serial and parallel ports.

Table 18-1: Overview of Features in Resource Management Programs

| Product | Vendor | Software updating | Reports | | | Logs | Internal data-base | Data export-able | Special work-station software req'd. |
			Printed	Save file	Custom				
Administrator's Aid	ICATT	✔							
Aperture Net & Res. Mgr.	Aperture Technology		✔	✔	✔		✔	✔	
GraceLAN	Technology Works		✔	✔	✔			✔	✔
GraceLAN Asset Manager	Technology Works								
GraceLAN Updater	Technology Works	✔	✔	✔		✔			✔
Inter•Poll	Apple		✔	✔	✔				✔
NetDistributor	TriK Inc.	✔	✔	✔	✔	✔			✔
NetOctopus	MacVONK	✔	✔	✔	✔	✔	✔	✔	✔
NetUpdater	MDG Comp. Serv.	✔				✔			
Network SuperVisor	CSG Technologies		✔	✔	✔		✔	✔	✔
Radar	Sonic Systems		✔	✔	✔			✔	
Status*Mac	ON Technology		✔	✔	✔	✔	✔	✔	✔
VersionTerritory	SoftWriters	✔							

How do you collect and store all of this information? The amount of information you can collect from a node is directly related to the software that you install on that node. Inter•Poll and TalkManage depend solely on Apple's Responder INIT to get their information. Remember, in System 7.0, the functions of the Responder INIT are now handled directly by the System file; there is no longer a separate Responder file. All other programs require you to install a special cdev on each Mac for obtaining more than just the basic system information. Using the master program (or administration program), you then query each Mac on the network for its information and wait for the answers (see Figure 18-2). Some queries can be issued and stored for later processing on the Mac at the user's convenience, and the results are forwarded later. Status*Mac and Network SuperVisor require you to import the results into their databases. GraceLAN, on the other hand, stores the data internally while the program is active. If you want to store the data for analysis at a later date, you must export the data to a text file, which can then be imported into any database of your choosing.

The success of these programs depends on the active participation of each network user. Usually, the individual Mac user is responsible for running the profiler that collects the information. Users should be aware that if they don't send a profile to the network manager, they risk not getting an update to a needed software program because the network manager may not know that the program is there.

Tracking software licenses

Controlling access to properly licensed program copies is another facet of facilities management. KeyServer and Quota are two programs designed to control networked access to applications.

KeyServer can be especially useful because it maintains a queue of users waiting to use an application that's already been signed out for use. Furthermore, because KeyServer passes only a key from the license server to the user for legitimate program use, the amount of network traffic generated by this form of access control is small.

Quota differs from KeyServer in its design because Quota depends on an INIT on the user's workstation for authentication and permission to use an application. Application usage is then relayed to a status database on a file server. The database is accessible to every user, but modifications such as changing access rights can be made only by the Quota Admin application.

Both programs maintain logs of application usage so that you can determine who's been using what software. You can review the logs to see if you need more copies of a particular program. Conversely, if a licensed program is not

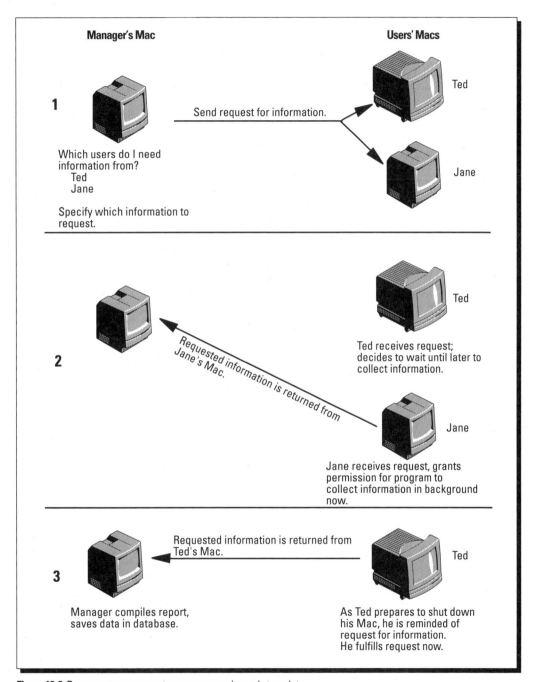

Figure 18-2: Resource management programs acquire and store data.

heavily used, you may want to reduce the number of licensed copies when the next version is ordered.

AppleShare 3.0, the latest version of Apple's file-server program, also includes a software control feature. As long as the program you want to control has been written as a multilaunch program, you can set AppleShare to allow a maximum number of simultaneous users for that program. For example, if you're licensed for ten users of FileMaker Pro, you can install one copy on the server and set the limit to ten. When the eleventh user tries to launch File-Maker Pro from the AppleShare server, the user is informed by an AppleShare message that the program is unavailable at this time. Unlike KeyServer, though, AppleShare does not log all uses, legal or otherwise, of the program.

Updating software

Merely being able to collect system and application data isn't enough to solve workstation- or usage-related problems. If possible, you want to correct conflicts caused by different versions of software by upgrading software over the network. For instance, you may want to send a new version of the LaserWriter Prep file to certain users. GraceLAN Updater (Technology Works), NetDistributor (TriK Inc.), NetUpdater, and VersionTerritory are designed with this form of management in mind.

NetUpdater uses HyperCard and a custom stack to define scripts for certain actions, such as "update QuickMail address books" or "delete Compactor 1.0." You can apply these scripts to selected Macs on the network. Any file can be replaced on the user's workstation. But all replacement files and installation scripts must be located on a file server that the users can access.

Counting program copies for site licenses

You might think that programs like GraceLAN or Status*Mac are perfect for counting the number of copies of a program so that you can order a site license. However, you'll soon discover that most, if not all, vendors will not accept a number from these utility programs as an accurate count for site licensing.

Vendors commonly view these numbers as suspect because users often think nothing of

copying an upgrade from someone else if they already have an older version, despite the fact that the vendors charge for such upgrades on a copy-by-copy basis.

One possible solution to this problem is for the program vendors and the developers of GraceLAN and Status*Mac to cooperate on using registration numbers to track legitimate copies of each program.

VersionTerritory follows a similar procedure, but it is a stand-alone application, not a HyperCard stack. Once sets of update instructions are created, they can be executed in the background from the administrator's workstation. You can also choose to monitor the progress of an upgrade on a user-by-user basis, learning, for example, that someone's hard disk doesn't have enough room for the new software.

GraceLAN has a complementary program, GraceLAN Updater, which gathers data about software and hardware installed on everyone's Mac; the program also can poll DOS machines for certain configuration information. GraceLAN Updater uses some of the data acquired by the GraceLAN Responder to determine whether software updates can be installed on the user's Mac. For instance, a user's hard disk may have insufficient space, or the Mac may be lacking a memory-management unit, even though the user wants to run System 7's virtual memory.

NetDistributor performs similarly to GraceLAN Updater. It, too, can use information from the GraceLAN Responder to determine whether all installation rules, as set by the network manager within NetDistributor, are met prior to installation.

User Privacy and Network Management

How much information should be private? The currently accepted guideline for resource management programs apparently is to leave user files alone. Thus, these programs focus on data collection about fonts, desktop accessories, INITs, cdevs, and applications, but not about an individual user's files. Application data usually includes the version number, which is handy for tracking up-grades. The latest versions of these programs give the user control over what information is sent back to the administrator. For instance, you can choose not to have information on your DAs or fonts relayed back to Status*Mac or Network SuperVisor.

Although each user may feel more comfortable with individual control, administrators and users must reach an understanding about what this control means to system maintenance. If the users don't relay information on their INITs, for example, they cannot expect the network administrator to solve the problem easily when their Macs crash, perhaps due to an INIT conflict.

How you collect data is something that affects both you, as network administrator, and the users on the network. Two factors are involved. First, there's the question of how quickly and how often you want data from the users. Second, do the users you support want to be interrupted from their own work to provide system information? Or would they rather do it at their own convenience?

Our opinion is that if you're going to monitor the network and the users' workstations at regular intervals for any reason, inform the users of that activity. Set the ground rules up front.

If your users object to *any* type of monitoring, we offer the following points as ammunition in favor of monitoring and "intrusive" network management. Answers to these questions may convince the users that monitoring offers them a benefit as well:

❖ Does the monitoring ensure continuous or improved uptime of the network?

❖ Does the monitoring ensure that the users receive software updates in a timely fashion?

❖ Can you solve the users' problems more easily because of the added information you have?

And this question relates to secure networks:

❖ If the systems are not secure from unauthorized use, how much time (and corporate funds) would the users have to spend in order to get back to square one?

Network Management vs. Privacy

A raging controversy continues about the seemingly irresolvable problem of network management versus the users' perception of the privacy of their computers. After all, don't we still call them "personal computers"?

The central issue is this: How much information should a network manager, or boss, or whoever be able to obtain about what's on your Mac or about how you use your Mac? Further, how much of that information should this person be able to acquire without your consent?

We offer no panacea for this dilemma. We bring up the issue here because it's likely to involve you at one time or another if you're a network manager, even if you're only monitoring traffic and analyzing packets.

Summary

In this chapter, we presented an overview of the types of problems you can solve with resource management tools and how these tools work over the network.

In this chapter, you learned the following points:

✔ You can install a license server to control multiple-user access to site-licensed software.

✔ Many resource management tools allow you to find out what hardware and software is being used on anyone's Mac.

✔ Network updaters let you create scripts for updating different versions of software on users' Macs over the network.

In the next chapter, we discuss printers and how best to use them on the network.

Part Four

Using an
AppleTalk Network

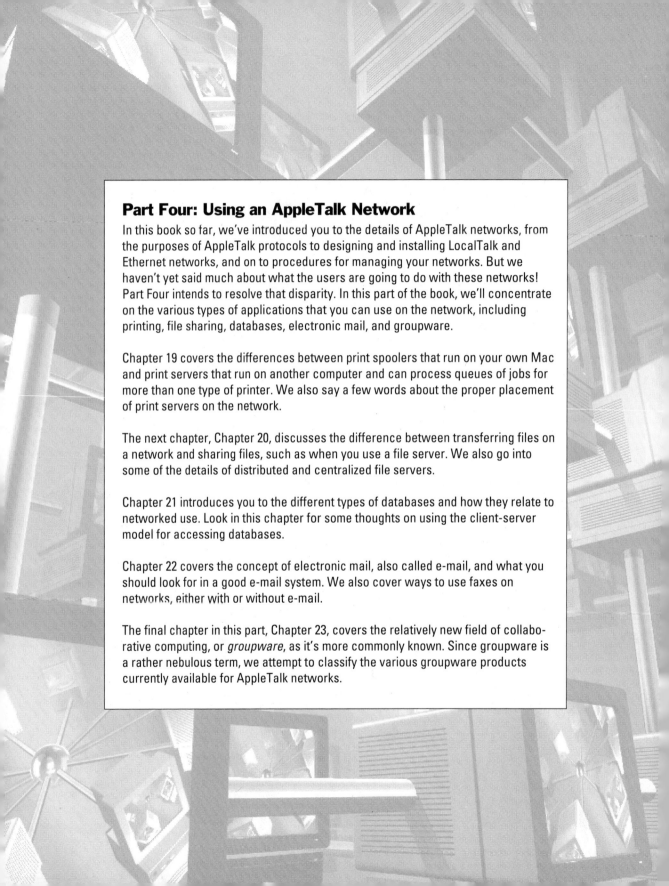

Part Four: Using an AppleTalk Network

In this book so far, we've introduced you to the details of AppleTalk networks, from the purposes of AppleTalk protocols to designing and installing LocalTalk and Ethernet networks, and on to procedures for managing your networks. But we haven't yet said much about what the users are going to do with these networks! Part Four intends to resolve that disparity. In this part of the book, we'll concentrate on the various types of applications that you can use on the network, including printing, file sharing, databases, electronic mail, and groupware.

Chapter 19 covers the differences between print spoolers that run on your own Mac and print servers that run on another computer and can process queues of jobs for more than one type of printer. We also say a few words about the proper placement of print servers on the network.

The next chapter, Chapter 20, discusses the difference between transferring files on a network and sharing files, such as when you use a file server. We also go into some of the details of distributed and centralized file servers.

Chapter 21 introduces you to the different types of databases and how they relate to networked use. Look in this chapter for some thoughts on using the client-server model for accessing databases.

Chapter 22 covers the concept of electronic mail, also called e-mail, and what you should look for in a good e-mail system. We also cover ways to use faxes on networks, either with or without e-mail.

The final chapter in this part, Chapter 23, covers the relatively new field of collaborative computing, or *groupware*, as it's more commonly known. Since groupware is a rather nebulous term, we attempt to classify the various groupware products currently available for AppleTalk networks.

Chapter 19

Using Printers on the Network

In this chapter . . .

✔ How the Macintosh sets up a printing job

✔ The differences between print spoolers and print servers

✔ Ways to connect serial and parallel printers to the network for sharing

O riginally, AppleTalk networking assumed that a laser printer would be shared over a network. In fact, a shared printer service is still a common task on AppleTalk networks. After all, you don't see LaserWriters on everyone's desk, even if prices have dropped since their introduction.

Setting up laser printers and other shared printing devices, such as imagesetters and slide makers, on a network requires a balance of wants and requirements. Users demand printing speed and expect minimal interference on their Macs and network traffic. In this chapter, we'll discuss these issues.

Reviewing the Mac Printing Process

As you work with a file on your Mac, the document is represented internally as a series of QuickDraw commands. QuickDraw is Apple's imaging model and is built into the Mac's ToolBox, or operating system. When you select the print command from your application, the QuickDraw representation is sent to the printer driver that you select in the Chooser. When you select the LaserWriter II icon, you indicate to your application that you ultimately want to print to a PostScript printer. The printer driver has the task of translating the QuickDraw page description into the PostScript commands required by the printer (see Figure 19-1).

If you're working under the Finder, or using MultiFinder with background printing turned off (an option in the Chooser when you select the LaserWriter icon), you're stuck for a while. You now wait for the Mac and the LaserWriter to complete their cycle of exchanging data and printing all the pages you requested. Only when the laser printer has completed your job will it relinquish control to your Mac so that you can go to your next job.

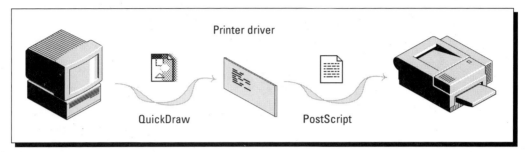

Printer driver

QuickDraw   PostScript

Figure 19-1: A page destined for a PostScript printer follows this route in the Mac printing process.

If you're on a network with a busy laser printer, your wait may be long. That's because laser printers can deal with only one job at a time; they can't store information for the next job. If someone is already printing on the laser printer, your Mac simply sits there, polling the laser printer to find out when it's ready to print your job. And you can't do anything else with the Mac while it's waiting.

But there are ways to deal with this problem and get back to using your Mac. Two selections ease those seemingly interminable waits for the printer: *print spoolers* and *print servers.*

A print spooler is software that intercepts your print job and stores it on your Mac. When the laser printer is ready for your job, the spooler sends the printing commands to the printer, just as your Mac would control the job, and without interfering with whatever you're doing at the time. Apple's Print Monitor in System 6.0.x and System 7 and Fifth Generation's SuperLaserSpool are two examples of such spoolers.

Print servers operate similarly to print spoolers, except that they're run exclusively on another computer. One reason for using a print server is that it can process print jobs from a number of users, sending them to more than one printer. Another advantage of print servers over spoolers is their more sophisticated logging and queue control, as you'll see shortly.

Using Print Spoolers

Various print spoolers differ primarily by the manner in which they intercept printing commands on your Mac (see Figure 19-2). Some spoolers, like Apple's own Print Monitor, grab the QuickDraw output directly from your application. Others, like TurboSpool (Peripheral Land Inc.), wait for the printer driver to perform its translations and then intercept the resulting data, either as a PostScript or a bitmap file.

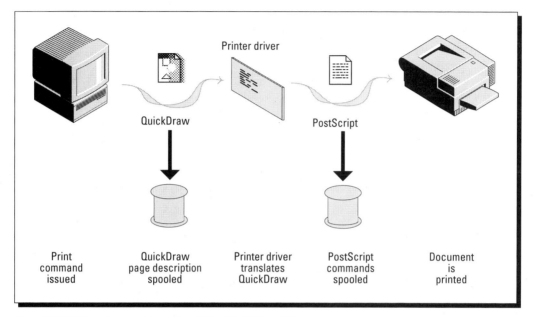

| Print command issued | QuickDraw page description spooled | Printer driver translates QuickDraw | PostScript commands spooled | Document is printed |

Figure 19-2: Print spoolers can intercept a printing job at different stages.

In the first case, with output taken directly from the application, the spooler takes less time to create the printing file, so control is returned to your Mac sooner. The second approach tends to take a bit longer because the printer driver must make its translations before the spooler file is created. In both cases, remember that you'll need some spare room on your hard disk for the spooler to store its temporary files.

After the spoolers create their spool file, they work in the background to send the file to the printer. This background process can be bothersome at times; communications between the spooler and the printer occasionally require extensive data transfers and take almost full control of your Mac before finishing. Erratic cursor movement in any program and slow character drawing in a word processor are indicative of the background spooler exerting control over your Mac.

What are the benefits and drawbacks of print spoolers? The main advantage is obvious — you can work on your Mac while the spooler sends your print file to the printer. Also, without the spooler, you'd wait for the laser printer to finish another job before you could send yours; the spooler patiently waits for the printer to become available, allowing you to do other work.

The spooler's disadvantages are relatively minor. First, the spooler does require some RAM to function in (usually less than 100K), and it also requires disk space for storing the spool files. From a management viewpoint, spoolers are meant for individual Macs. The spooler won't allow you to control the printer's queue — there's nothing you can do if Joe is printing the latest revision of his book while you're waiting to print a rush two-page memo.

Using Print Servers

As stated previously, print servers are designed to operate on a central computer, from which they control one or more printers. Usually, print servers also offer some sort of queue control for each printer, as well as the logging of all print jobs. Print servers are thus a network-wide service, rather than a service designed for individual Macs.

Understanding the operation of print servers

Whereas the print spooler intercepts a print job and sends it to the printer in the background on your Mac, the print server acts just as though it were the printer, accepting the incoming print jobs as quickly as possible. A print server usually receives print files and stores them on a hard disk, directing them to the appropriate printers as they become available.

Because print files are stored on the server before they're printed, a manager or a user can review the queue of waiting jobs and alter the order or even delete certain waiting jobs. Of course, the capability to change the status of other users' print jobs is in the hands of the server's manager and is subject to some type of security control. Users, however, can review their own queue of jobs and delete some of their own files if they want to.

Because print servers can service more than one printer, they often can be instructed to redirect jobs automatically to the next available printer (as long as paper and other requirements are identical). Also, print servers customarily can

Spooler or server?

Spoolers are best for individual Macs, where you are controlling your own print jobs.

Print servers work well as a network-wide service, because they are designed to queue print jobs from a number of computers.

handle serial, parallel, and AppleTalk interfaces to printers, making available some printers that normally aren't available on networks.

In Chapter 17, we discussed aspects of accounting management. Print servers help with accounting because they normally maintain a log of all jobs processed through the server. Full-featured print servers, such as Print Central (Compumation Inc.), enable you to assign users' names by department or category, as well as to sort out costs for each printer. These options make cost control and chargebacks easier.

Because print servers are rapidly writing your print file to their disk and not actually processing the print commands until later, they are faster than a laser printer at receiving your print file and turning control back to your Mac. The main disadvantage with a print server is that it can actually increase network traffic if it's improperly located on the network with respect to the printer that it serves. (See Chapter 15 and the following section for some tips regarding layout.) Another possible disadvantage is that a print server requires a computer to perform the server's functions, although sometimes this computer can provide more than one network service, such as acting both as a file server and a print server.

Setting up a print server

If you're going to use a print server with a networkable printer (such as a LaserWriter II), you should locate the server and the printer carefully. In particular, don't place a router between the server and the printer (or printers). Also, don't place the server and its associated printers in a single network that's separated from all the users by a single router — the router will become a definite bottleneck as all users send their jobs through it.

Consider the role the server plays in handling your print job (see Figure 19-3). First, you send a print file to the print server over the network. Then, in turn, the print server sends the file to the designated printer, which is a second transmission of the file on the network if it's a networked printer rather than a printer that's directly attached to the server. The print server just doubled the amount of network traffic associated with printing — we're sure that this is not exactly what you had in mind.

If you're using a print server with a networked printer, try to keep the server-to-printer traffic isolated from the user-to-server traffic. Segregating traffic is not always possible, but one approach is installing a LocalTalk bridge (such as the LocalSwitch) and placing the print server and its printers on one port of the bridge. With this layout, users send their jobs through the bridge to the print server, but any traffic between the server and its associated printers is isolated

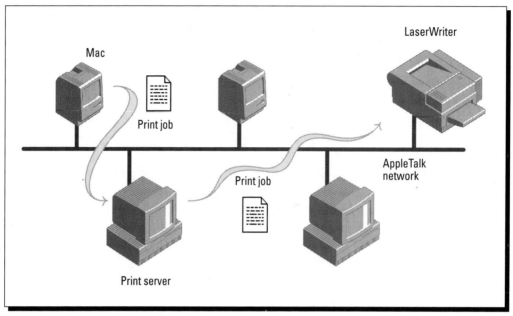

Figure 19-3: Note that the print job is transmitted on the network twice to get to the networked printer.

from the rest of the network. The only problem with this arrangement can be with throughput — if a number of users are sending jobs to the server, the bridge can turn into a bottleneck. If this happens, you're probably better off to do without the bridge and connect your printers to Ethernet to take advantage of the network's greater bandwidth.

Another remedy is to keep *all* the printers off the network. Although most of us think of LaserWriters as printers that are networked via AppleTalk, such printers also have a serial port. Other PostScript printers also have parallel ports for faster data transfers than a serial port provides. In these cases, you can use the serial or parallel ports to attach the laser printers to the server and thereby eliminate some network traffic (see Figure 19-4). This technique also works when a computer running a different operating system acts as the print server, which we'll describe in Chapter 25, "Sharing Printers and Files with Other Platforms."

Using Non-AppleTalk Printers

Attaching a LaserWriter to an AppleTalk network has always been a relatively simple task because of the LaserWriter's built-in networking support, first for LocalTalk and now for Ethernet. The problem, as we said before, is to get the print job done and off your Mac so that you can turn to other tasks.

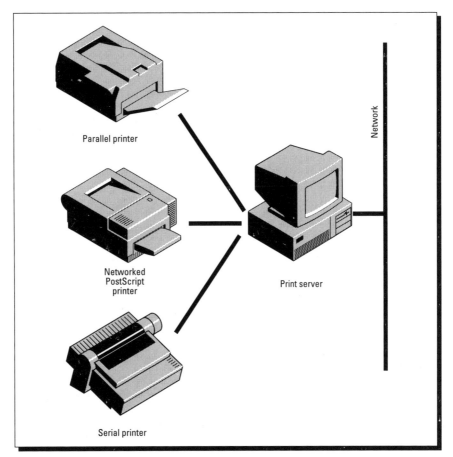

Parallel printer

Networked PostScript printer

Serial printer

Print server

Network

Figure 19-4: Print servers can handle print jobs for both serial and parallel printers, as well for networked printers.

But what about other printers that don't have built-in networking support? A great many printers have only serial or parallel ports. If these printers offer features that you can't find in networkable printers, such as high-speed multi-form printing, you can still set them up for sharing among networked users.

As described previously, one way to do this is to attach these printers to a print server that is part of the network. Two other approaches are possible (see Figure 19-5). First, you can install a device like the NetSerial (Shiva) or the C-Server (Solana) to act as the interface between your serial or parallel printer (or plotter) and the AppleTalk network. You may need a special printer driver to make this work, but most of the drivers necessary for serial and parallel printers are available from either Insight Development Corp. or GDT Softworks, Inc.

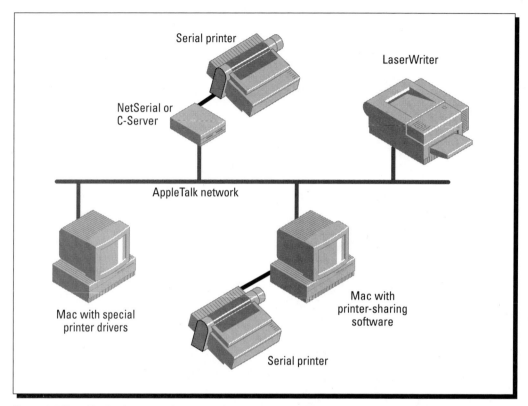

Figure 19-5: Use either hardware or software to make a non-networked printer or plotter available to networked users. Special printer drivers must be installed on the user's Macintosh.

The second approach is to turn someone's Mac (or a server Mac) into an interface between a printer and the network; the software you need for this is ShadowWriter (Gizmo Technologies). This second approach can be less reliable than our suggested hardware-interface solution because you will lose contact with the printer if the Mac serving as the interface is unavailable.

Summary

We've used this chapter to show how the Macintosh printing process takes place and how print spoolers and print servers make use of that process to reduce your wait while printing.

In this chapter, you learned the following points:

- ✔ A print spooler operates on an individual Mac, whereas a print server works on another net-worked computer.

- ✔ Some print spoolers work with the QuickDraw representation of a print file, but others work with a PostScript representation of the file.

- ✔ Users can track the progress of or delete their print jobs, even when using a print server.

- ✔ Print servers can accommodate many different interfaces to printers — AppleTalk and serial, as well as parallel.

- ✔ You can keep a print server and its associated printers on the same network side of a router to reduce traffic.

In the next chapter, we'll tell you about many options for moving and sharing files on your network.

Chapter 20
Moving and Sharing Files on the Network

In this chapter...

✔ The difference between file transfers and file sharing

✔ When to use file-transfer utilities instead of file servers

✔ The difference between centralized and distributed file servers

✔ Details of Apple's AppleTalk Filing Protocol (AFP) for standardizing file sharing

✔ How to set up an AppleShare file server

✔ How to set up fault-tolerant file servers

✔ Server backup strategies

Information justifies the network. More precisely, sharing information is the prime reason for installing a network. Most of us deal with information on our Macs in chunks called *files*. Whether they come from a word processor, page-layout program, spreadsheet, or drawing program, the least common denominator in all these applications is the file.

So how do we share file-based information on a network? Two basic methods for sharing files are available to upgrade the old sneakernet system of trading floppies between machines. One way is to move a file from my Mac to your Mac over the network — I send you a copy of my file, whereupon you can hack away at it to your heart's content. If you want me to see what you did with my file, you can return a copy of the modified file to me. We refer to this process as the *file-transfer method* throughout the book.

The second method for sharing information is to use a file server to share files. Suppose that I put a file of interest on the server so other users can see the file without copying it to their Macs. We refer to this process as *file sharing*. Or, if they want, users can copy a file from the server to their Macs to modify it.

The two methods may sound fairly similar — after all, isn't the file server just another means of transferring the file to other users? Not exactly. The file server can be used that way, but file servers incorporate features for protecting and

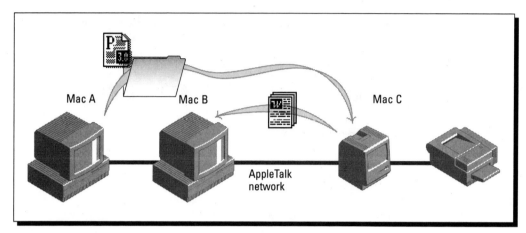

Figure 20-1: A file-transfer utility used on an AppleTalk network.

controlling access to the files that file-transfer programs don't have. When you use a file-transfer program to send a file to other users, you lose all control over what happens to that file once it's sent. On the other hand, when you copy a file to a server, you can set access privileges for the file so that it cannot be modified or copied.

Moving Files on the Network

There are a few file-transfer utilities that work on AppleTalk networks, such as Flash (Beagle Bros.), LapLink Mac (Traveling Software), Mac-to-Mac (Caravelle Networks), and Send Express (Gizmo Technology). Using one of these utilities is similar to the sneakernet method of putting the file on a floppy and taking that floppy over to the other user, except that with the networked versions you don't have to get out of your chair (see Figure 20-1). These utilities require that both machines be up and running at the same time for the transfer to be completed; otherwise, the destination Mac cannot receive the files that you're sending to it.

File-transfer utilities are a quick and easy way to share files or entire folders over an AppleTalk network; however, they do not permit simultaneous multiuser access to a file. Note that in Figure 20-1, Mac A is sending a Page-Maker document and folder to Mac C; Mac C, meanwhile, is sending a Word document to Mac B.

You can also use any of these network programs when you need to distribute files to more than one other co-worker. Many of the file-transfer programs allow you to define groups of users as named workgroups. You just select the name of the desired workgroup when you're sending a file, and a copy will go to everyone in that list. But watch out: When you're working with more than one person, problems can arise with keeping track of files and their changes.

When you transfer files around the network using a file-transfer program and expect to get the files back (after changes are made, for example), you'd better set up some kind of system for renaming the returned files. This is especially crucial if you want to keep track of both the old and new versions. For instance, you might call your original file "JAN92 REPORT(original)," and then call the edited one that comes back from Jane "JAN92 REPORT(Jane)", and the one that comes back from Don "JAN92 REPORT(Don)."

Even if Jane sends you the edited file back with the original name of "JAN92 REPORT(original)," the file-transfer programs we've discussed here don't automatically overwrite your copy of the file with the incoming file. Each of the programs allows you to select where these files are to be stored (a different folder, for instance) and how they're to be named — this is the point when you can rename the incoming file from Jane as "JAN92 REPORT(Jane)."

Although we'll cover electronic mail, or *e-mail*, in Chapter 22, note that you can use an electronic mail system in much the same way as any of these file-transfer programs. You simply enclose the files in a mail message and send the message off to the desired recipients.

E-mail has a distinct capability over most of the file-transfer programs. This capability is called *store-and-forward*. Many of the file-transfer programs require that both Macs be running at the same time in order to send or receive a file. But, because most e-mail systems store all messages on an e-mail server, you need only a connection between your Mac and the server to send or receive a file. Because of the store-and-forward architecture of an e-mail server, I can send a message or file to you even when you're not on the network; the server stores the message until the next time you're on the network. Then, when you log on to the e-mail system, my message (or file) will be transferred to your Mac, even if I'm no longer on the network. This makes information exchange much easier.

File-transfer programs are good for small workgroups where you need to occasionally transfer a file between users. We wouldn't recommend using a file-transfer program to send a copy of a file to 100 users, for instance. Nor would we recommend that you use one of these programs to send a copy of the stock inventory report every day.

Sharing Files on the Network

Whereas file-transfer utilities are good for transferring a small number of files among small workgroups, file servers are better suited for sharing files among large workgroups. File servers also have built-in mechanisms to assist you in controlling multiuser access to folders and files on the server, making use of databases easier, for example. We'll next look at what kinds of file servers are available and how they differ.

Understanding file servers

Because file-transfer programs perform a very basic action, that of moving a copy of a file from one Mac to another, these programs don't require any special understanding of new concepts, such as folder- and file-access rights. On the other hand, file servers offer services that make use of some new concepts.

File servers are comprised of a main processor unit (a computer) connected to a series of one or more hard disks or similar storage media (such as a CD-ROM or WORM drive). Each disk is usually called a *volume,* which is mounted by the file server. The file server then controls access to each of the mounted volumes, first at the level of the entire volume, then at the level of individual directories (or *folders,* with the Mac interface), or in some systems, at the level of individual files.

Each user of the file server has a designated log-in name/password pair. A file server stores this name/password pair in a special file on the main server volume and relates access privileges to that name. On the simplest file server, the access privileges define your ability to use a given volume and what you can do with files on that volume — whether, for example, you can add or delete files or copy files.

One of the file servers that we'll concentrate on in this chapter is AppleShare, which controls access to files in a slightly different way from file servers found on other networks. AppleShare (and other servers using the AppleTalk Filing Protocol) controls access to files at the folder level, rather than at the individual file level. This means that all files within a folder are treated equally; they can all be copied or deleted, for example. If you want different controls for the various files, you must place these files in folders with separately defined access privileges.

Furthermore, AppleShare's control over access privileges isn't limited to folders at the level of individual users. AppleShare uses the concept of *groups of users* and allows owners of folders to grant access to those folders to a group, rather than to an individual. This means that when you create a folder on an AppleShare file server, you can allow another person to use that folder if this user is also a member of an AppleShare group to which you belong. All members of that group will have the same access to the folder. If you want only one other user to have access to a folder, your only choice is to create a group of two, comprised of you and the other user, and allow access privileges to this group. You can also sidestep the group-based security and allow everyone to have access to the folder.

Because servers can control single-user and multiuser access to files in different ways, developers can use these access features to create *multilaunch applications*. These applications allow more than one person to use the program at the same time. The relations between single-user and multiuser applications are categorized in Table 20-1.

Table 20-1: Network File-Sharing Applications

	File-sharing mode center	
	Single-user mode	Multiuser mode
Single-Launch	❖ One user per application ❖ Only one user at a time can modify a file	❖ Only one user per application ❖ Two or more users at a time can modify a file
Multi-Launch	❖ Two or more users per application ❖ Only one user at a time can modify a file	❖ Two or more users per application ❖ Two or more users at a time can modify a file

Classifying servers

The field of file servers is far more complicated than that of file-transfer programs. That's because servers can be either *centralized* or *distributed*, which means that they can function either within a *client-server* or a *peer-to-peer* framework. We'll take a brief look at what all this means before we head on to the specific uses and features of each kind of server.

Centralized servers are reminiscent of the earlier days of mainframes, with all data of interest stored on one computer in a central location. You log on to the server whenever you want to access the data there or to add files to those already stored there. This is a relatively convenient setup, especially for large workgroups, where administration of the server is centralized and can be handled by one person, at least in theory. Also, this setup makes security a bit easier: You can lock up the server machine in a closet or computer room to prevent unauthorized access to the hardware.

Centralized servers are usually computers dedicated to the task of file services. In most cases, the centralized server is the best choice for such access-intensive applications as multiuser databases. For these situations, you want only one copy of the file to exist on the network, but you want more than one user to be working with the database at one time (see Figure 20-2). The security- and file-access options of a server make this possible, and the dedicated resources of a centralized server allow most databases to perform better than if they were installed on a distributed, or non-dedicated, server.

Macs other than the server can act only as clients. In Figure 20-2, three types of files are stored on the centralized server. Mac A, running PageMaker, is working with a PageMaker file on the server as if it were on a local disk. Mac B and Mac E, both running 4th Dimension, are simultaneously accessing the same 4D database file from the server. This is possible because both 4D and the server support multiuser access. Mac C and Mac D (both running Microsoft Word — an application that doesn't support multiuser access) are working with two different Word files on the server.

Distributed servers are a newer networking concept. With distributed servers, rather than storing all shared files on a single computer, the users store files on their own Macs and allow other users on the network to have access to those files. Each Mac can then function both as a file server and as the client of other file servers. The administration of such a system is more of a headache, however, because it requires that each "owner," or individual user, of a file server be responsible for that server. Also, finding files can be a hassle when a user isn't certain which server contains which files. There are ways around this difficulty, however, as you'll see shortly.

Distributed servers, such as Sitka's TOPS and Apple's File Sharing feature in System 7, seem to work best for small workgroups. One reason for this limitation is that your Mac is operating both as your personal workstation as well as a file server to other users. There's bound to be competition for your Mac's resources in this situation, and you don't want too many people using your Mac's disk space and processor just for sharing information (see Figure 20-3). Under such conditions, you wouldn't get much work done on your own

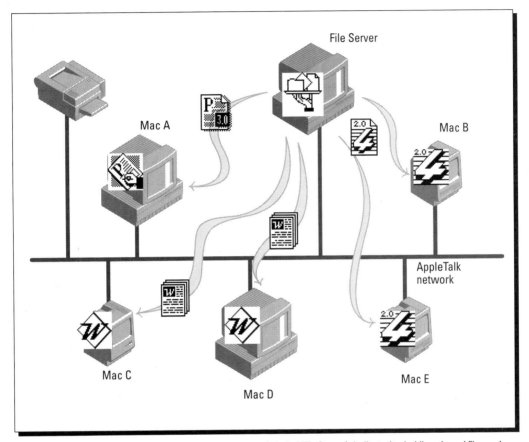

Figure 20-2: A centralized server system, with one computer (labeled File Server) dedicated to holding shared files and information for all users on the network.

Mac. As a rule of thumb, Apple recommends no more than 10 users for System 7's File Sharing feature. Many TOPS installations that we've seen tend to max out at 12 to 16 users.

In Figure 20-3, Mac D, running PageMaker, is a client of Mac A. Mac D is also acting as a server to both Mac E and Mac C (both running 4th Dimension, a multiuser application). If the distributed server supports multiuser access, Mac E and Mac C can be accessing the same 4D file on Mac D. Mac C is also a server for Mac B (running Microsoft Word).

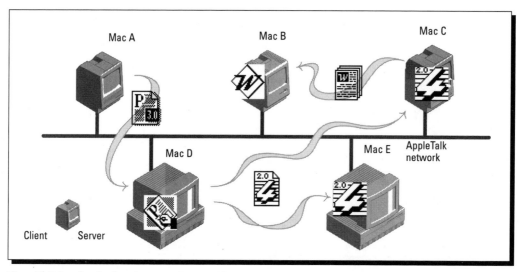

Figure 20-3: Running distributed server software, a Mac can simultaneously function as a client and a server.

Another reason that you want to keep a distributed server system relatively small is one mentioned earlier, that of finding files easily. As Figure 20-4 shows, many more interactions between users and servers can be required just to find a file in a distributed system, as compared to a centralized server.

DataClub is a distributed server program for Macs that successfully deals with many of the problems we've outlined here. DataClub doesn't distinguish among individual Macs as servers and clients. Instead, it combines the storage space of all available users into what appears as a single shareable volume on the network. You have only to log on to a single server to use any of the files on the participating Macs; finding files is just as easy — using the standard Find File DA (now a function listed under the File Menu in System 7) is all you need to do.

Unfortunately, the biggest drawback to DataClub also stems from the way it combines all available resources into a single volume. DataClub remembers where files are located, which means that you can find a file, but it may be stored on a Mac that's currently not part of the network. In this event, you must find out where the file is and start searching for the Mac's owner to get that Mac turned on. But this may or may not be a major problem, depending on the size and physical layout of your network.

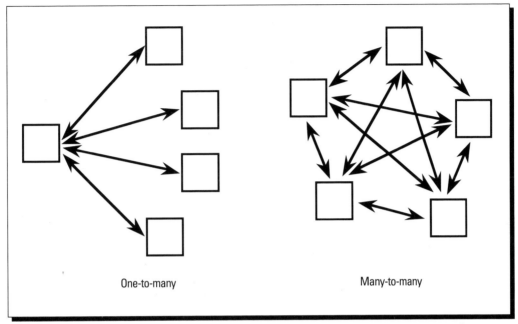

One-to-many   Many-to-many

Figure 20-4: This schematic shows how the number of interactions increases dramatically when you change from a centralized server to a distributed server.

System 7's File Sharing feature

With the introduction of System 7, Apple has made network-wide file sharing a part of the Mac's operating system. What Apple has done is to offer a feature called File Sharing that allows you, as the owner of your Mac, to make folders available for use by other users on the network. These folders can hold files that users can modify or delete, or they can add new files, according to the privileges you grant each user.

While your Mac with the File Sharing option is acting as a file server to other users, you can use the AppleShare client software on your Mac to access files on other Macs also running File Sharing. As your Mac is now acting as a file server and a client, we call this a *peer-to-peer,* or *distributed,* file server system.

How does the System 7 File Sharing feature work? The setup of File Sharing is covered in detail in the Networking Manual of the System 7 documentation, so we'll only summarize here.

The contents of any folder on your Mac can be shared with other network users. This is a two-sided process; you enable File Sharing on your Mac to make it a background file server, and the other users each log on to your Mac to see which folders and files you've made available for their use. To control access to the folders, you must add the names of users who should use your files; for added security, you can create passwords for each user.

You don't have to install special software to use File Sharing; it's part of the system software installed on your Mac along with System 7. All you need to do is turn on File Sharing and create your list of users. If you want, you can organize your users into groups and then assign access privileges to your folders for groups rather than for individuals.

The sharing options for any folder on your Mac allow you to set the access to **Everyone**, so that all users have access to your files. (See Chapter 17 for a discussion of the related security problems of this situation.) Or you can restrict folder use to one group or to an individual. If you want more than one individual to have access to a folder, you must define a group made up of those individuals.

System 7 arranges for the desktop to offer visual feedback about shared folders and to show whether they are currently being accessed. If a folder is set up for sharing but is not in use by someone on the network, its icon looks like the left-hand icon in Figure 20-5. But, if someone is using a file within the folder, the icon changes to the right-hand icon in Figure 20-5.

You can also monitor the file-sharing activities with an option from the Special menu. The Monitor window includes an activity bar and a list of shared folders and connected users. The File Sharing Monitor window can also be used to disconnect users from your Mac. If you choose to disconnect a user, you'll be asked how long the Mac should wait before the disconnection. Give the person at least a minute's warning to make a clean exit from the file. "Do unto others . . ." is a good precept to follow when sharing files.

Next we'll look at the AppleTalk protocol that is crucial to the workings of both AppleShare file servers and System 7's File Sharing — the AppleTalk Filing Protocol.

The AppleTalk Filing Protocol (AFP)

In Chapter 3, "Understanding AppleTalk Protocols," we covered each of the protocols that Apple has defined for its network operating system. One of those protocols is the AppleTalk Filing Protocol, or AFP. This protocol defines how file servers are supposed to handle file access by computers running Mac OS, DOS, or ProDOS. The first implementation of AFP was Apple's own AppleShare file server; many other servers, including ones running on Intel 80x86, DEC VAX, and Unix computers, are now available with AFP support.

Figure 20-5: Folder icons change when users are accessing folders with System 7 File Sharing.

The AFP specifications are concerned primarily with user access privileges at the folder (that is, directory) level and how these privileges are presented to the user at the desktop level. Another important feature of AFP is its control of how file names are mapped between the supported operating systems: Mac OS, DOS, or ProDOS.

As noted previously, AppleShare employs the concept of groups in defining access privileges. AppleShare has, in fact, three user categories for assigning access — **Owner**, **Group**, and **Everyone**. As owner of a folder on an AppleShare server, you can assign to each user category any combination of the following privileges: **See Folders**, **See Files**, and **Make Changes**. The first privilege lets someone see what other folders, if any, are contained within the folder you created. The second privilege allows users to not only see files within the folder, but also to open or copy any of those files. **Make Changes** allows users to create, move, or delete files and folders located in the folder you created. File Sharing within System 7 offers the same user categories and access privileges as AppleShare does.

The combination of these access privileges can lead to a unique folder, called the *drop folder*. To create a drop folder, you allow users (a group or everyone) to make changes, but not to see folders or files. Your users can add files to the folder, but they do not see what's in the folder. This is a simple way to enable users to send files to you and ensure the privacy of what they send you, as only you as the owner of the folder can manipulate the files within a drop folder.

On a Mac, AppleShare uses icons to display your access rights to each folder on the desktop (see Figure 20-6). In addition, every folder that you can open on an AppleShare file server has a set of small icons in the upper-left corner of the folder's window to indicate your access privileges within that folder (see Figure 20-7).

In Figure 20-6, note the AFP folder icons; these icons are generated by AppleShare, System 7's File Sharing feature, or any AFP-compatible file server. The differences in the folder icons depend on whether you're using the AppleShare client software under System 6.0.x or System 7.

Apple included two unique features in the Mac's file structures when it designed the Macintosh operating system. One is the capability for 31-character file names; the other is the division of a file's contents between the *data fork*

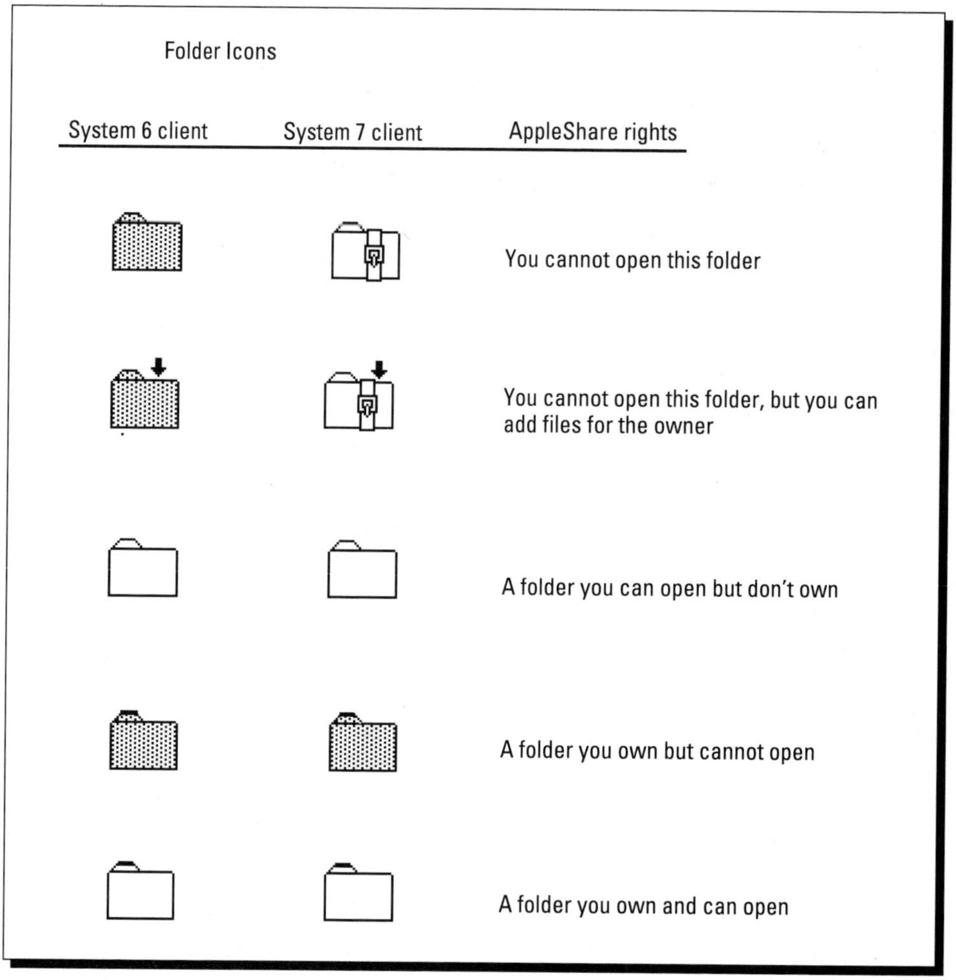

Folder Icons

System 6 client	System 7 client	AppleShare rights

Figure 20-6: The AFP folder icons and the access rights they represent.

and *resource fork*. Both of these file attributes can cause problems when you're trying to exchange information with other, non-Mac, systems, which is one of the capabilities AppleShare is designed to have. In part, the AFP specifications are rules that define how file names are mapped between the three supported operating systems: Mac OS, DOS, or ProDOS (for Apple II computers). Here we'll be concerned only with the Mac and DOS operating systems.

The Macintosh operating system lets you assign file and folder names of up to 31 characters; you can use any character except a colon in those names. On the other hand, MS-DOS limits file names and directory names (the equivalent

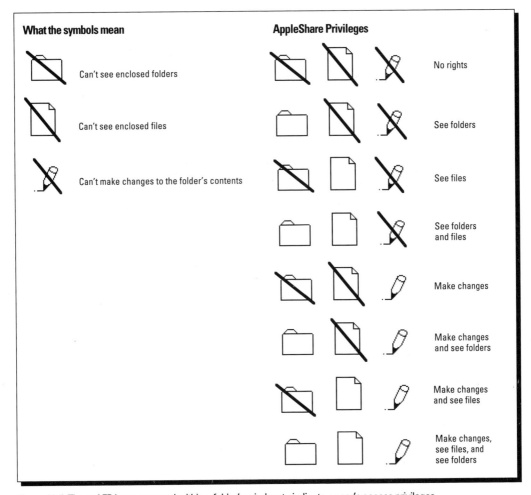

What the symbols mean

Can't see enclosed folders

Can't see enclosed files

Can't make changes to the folder's contents

AppleShare Privileges

No rights

See folders

See files

See folders and files

Make changes

Make changes and see folders

Make changes and see files

Make changes, see files, and see folders

Figure 20-7: These AFP icons are used within a folder's window to indicate a user's access privileges.

of a Mac folder) to a maximum of eight characters, followed by a period, then followed by one to three additional characters for the file extension. Many special characters — such as [,] , / , " — cannot be used in MS-DOS file names. AFP deals with these naming problems by maintaining multiple names for each directory and each file on the server and by following special rules for converting one name into another. To support Mac and DOS, an AFP server stores both a long name of up to 31 characters and a short name of up to 12 characters for a file. The manner in which file names are translated depends on which operating system (Mac or DOS) was used to create the file on the server.

If a Mac user creates a file name more than 12 characters long, AFP translates the file name for an MS-DOS user with the following changes and adjustments:

1. Spaces and periods are removed.

2. All alphabetic characters are changed to uppercase.

3. The first 11 characters are used to create the DOS file name.

As an example, the Mac file name **Project Overview**, which includes a space and upper- and lowercase letters, changes to **projecto.ver**. Likewise, the Mac file name **junk.c.o.**, with its mix of periods and lowercase letters, becomes **junk.co**.

4. The special characters of the following limited set are converted to the underline character:

(= + [ ] ; " * , < > / ? \ |)

As an example, a Mac-created file named **Facts+Figures** will appear to a DOS user as **facts_fi.gur**.

Note that when a Mac user creates a file following the normal DOS naming conventions, no changes are made. Thus, a Mac file named **MARKET.WKS** will keep the name for both types of users.

AFP introduces one other translation rule to avoid creating files with duplicate names. For instance, it would be a simple matter for a Mac user to create two files, one called Regional Data-East and one called Regional Data-West. Following the above rules, both names will be translated to the DOS file name of regional.dat, which won't work if you try to keep both files in the same directory. So, according to AFP, the first file stored in the directory is named regional.dat, as expected. However, if you save another file with a similar

File types in the Macintosh's operating system

The Macintosh operating system is unique in that files are composed of two parts rather than the more traditional single part. These two parts are known as the *data fork* and the *resource fork*. The data fork usually stores only the ASCII text and format information, such as you'd find in any regular word processing file on other systems. Mac applications store their program code in the resource fork, where you find such items as window and menu definition, as well as the program's icons.

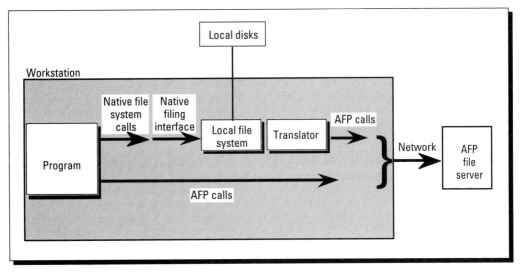

Figure 20-8: The AFP file access model.

name, as Regional Data-West in our example, this file is assigned the DOS name **regiona0.dat**. If a third file named Regional Data-South is created in the same directory, it becomes **regional.dat**, and so on. And, if you really like starting all your Mac file names with the same eight characters, the twelfth file starting with Regional will be renamed **region01.dat** (the zero is inserted in place of the seventh character) for the DOS user.

Even though the translations may be straightforward (at least to an AFP server), the rules can make it difficult if Mac and DOS users want to communicate with each other. DOS users actually have it easier because the files that they create on a server will display the same name for the Mac users. On the other hand, if a Mac user creates a file for DOS users to access on the server, the user should keep in mind these translation rules and try to name the shared files according to the DOS conventions.

The file-access model that is part of the AppleTalk Filing Protocol is designed so that a user's application program issues file-system calls found in the native operating system, but an AFP translator on the user's workstation translates those calls into AFP file-system calls that the AFP file server understands. This approach allows the user to access both local disks and any AFP file-server volumes as if they were all local disks (see Figure 20-8).

A program can directly issue AFP calls, or the AFP Translator can translate the native file system calls to AFP calls. Only AFP calls, however, are transmitted on the network to the AFP server.

On the receiving end, at the file server, another AFP translator takes over and converts the AFP File System calls into file-system calls of the file server's operating system. This conversion is necessary because AFP servers now run on a variety of operating systems (NetWare, Unix, and VMS, for example). The workstation-based AFP translators are needed because Mac, DOS, and Apple II workstations can use an AFP-based file server.

Managing a Centralized Server

If you look back to our discussion of System 7's File Sharing feature in this chapter, you'll see that the administration of a distributed file-server system such as File Sharing (and Sitka's TOPS) is mostly left up to the individual. Centralized file servers not only offer more power for networked applications, such as databases and e-mail, but also consolidate management responsibilities. Usually only one person needs to take the responsibility of maintaining a centralized server.

Because centralized servers are so important to networks, we'll give you some tips next for setting up and maintaining a centralized AppleShare server. We'll also use this example server to illustrate some server features and issues that can be applied to all types of servers, namely, fault-tolerant server design and making server backups.

Setting up a server

Apple has worked hard to make installation of the AppleShare software as simple as possible. AppleShare uses the same Installer program you find with system upgrades and other programs from third-party vendors — it's familiar to many network managers, as well as individual users. All you have to do is select the Mac hard disk that you want the AppleShare software installed on and click the OK button, and the server will be ready to run the next time you restart that Mac.

In order for users to access any files on the AppleShare server, you have to create accounts for them. Partly because both AppleShare and System 7's File Sharing are based on the AppleTalk Filing Protocol, the procedures for setting up users and groups of users are almost identical. Refer to our previous description of File Sharing in this chapter to review the concepts of users and groups.

Rather than merely repeating Apple's instructions for installing the software, we'll explain some ways to make your AppleShare server more efficient.

First, use as powerful a Mac as possible for the AppleShare server. Remember that a centralized file server is going to be accessed by many users at the same time, and a more powerful Mac, such as the IIci, IIfx, or a Quadra, is better equipped to process the server's requests because of the faster microprocessor found on those machines.

If you're working on the low end of the Mac line and must decide between a Mac SE and an SE/30 for your server, pick the SE/30 — you'll see a marked difference in performance.

Second, buy a big (100MB or larger) and fast hard disk for your server. Again, remember that many users will store files on this system, so you'll need the larger hard disk. And a faster access time will also make the server more efficient when many users are accessing it.

But there's a caution to observe here — because of the design of the SCSI software in the Mac's operating system, you may not see any increase in performance if you use a server that has a disk with an access time of less than 10-12 milliseconds. The Mac Quadras may be a different story, but we haven't had the opportunity to try a Quadra-based AppleShare server with many fast hard disks.

Finally, allocate the RAM on your server wisely. With AppleShare 2.0.1, the server software used up to a maximum of 2.5MB of RAM for a RAM cache to improve performance. Installing more RAM than that on an AppleShare server didn't make sense because the software wouldn't use the extra RAM. You should add more than 2.5MB of RAM to a server only when you plan to install other server-based software, such as electronic mail or a print server.

Things have changed with the introduction of AppleShare 3.0, which requires System 7 to run. With 3.0, AppleShare doesn't automatically allocate a large RAM cache to support more users. As manager of the server, you'll have to manually select a larger RAM cache so that your server can efficiently handle a large number of users.

Fault-tolerant servers

We discussed fault tolerance previously in the context of network design (see Chapter 5, "Network Design 101"). For file servers, the concept is the same: Fault tolerance means that the system can continue functioning when a component fails.

If you're dealing with a single file server, fault tolerance focuses on the hard disks attached to your server. This capability is often called *disk mirroring*. The idea is to install a second (backup) disk on the server for each primary disk. Then use hardware or software that automatically writes a copy to the backup disk of everything that's sent to the primary disk.

Two types of disk mirroring are currently available. The more common type is to write to both disks sequentially. Disk drive vendors such as Storage Dimensions are now offering disk mirroring with their larger disk drives for use with servers. The other type, which is more correctly called *disk duplexing,* writes to both disk drives simultaneously. The Disk Twin card from Golden Triangle is an example of a disk-duplexing interface for use with a Mac-based server.

If you're willing to treat power outages as a "fault" that needs to be guarded against, you should consider purchasing an uninterruptible power supply (UPS) for your file server. The UPS is designed to provide battery power when the normal power in the building is disrupted. UPS battery life is a consideration when shopping for a UPS — shorter UPS lives are designed to give your server enough time for a standard shutdown; a longer life UPS lets you keep on working with the server as if nothing happened. But we must warn that if you do install a UPS for your server, make it a regular practice to check the battery. There's nothing more embarrassing than to find out that the battery is dead when the building power dies.

Backing up servers

The more often people use a server to store their crucial files and applications, the more they expect the data to be undamaged. But let's face it — no computer's perfect, and they do crash occasionally. Then there are always the users who delete the wrong files. A solution to all these problems is the habit of making regular backups of the server.

Following are the most common ways to back up a file server:

1. You can select all the files on the server disk and use the Mac's drag-and-copy procedure to copy all the files to another disk attached to the server.

2. You can select all the files on the server disk and use the Mac's drag-and-copy procedure to copy all the files to a disk attached to your own Mac.

3. You copy all, or selected, files from the server to another disk or tape drive attached to the server, using software that backs up files at preprogrammed intervals.

4. You copy the files from the server to your own Mac, using software that backs up files at preprogrammed intervals.

We'll next look at the advantages and disadvantages of each approach.

The drag-and-copy approach is the simplest method, and it has the advantage of preserving the native format of the Mac files. No encoding or compression of the files into special proprietary formats are involved. There are, however, two potential problems with this approach. First, unless you're the network manager or another user with access privileges to all files on the server, you won't be able to copy all the files from the server. Second, if you want to also copy the server's system folder, you'll have to disconnect all the users from the server, shut down the server, and then restart the server with the AppleShare Admin program before making the copy.

The second approach is basically the same as the first; you're just using a different hard disk to copy to. This method has three disadvantages. The first disadvantage is the same as for dragging and copying to a disk attached to the server: You may not be able to access all the files. The second disadvantage is that the system folder on an AppleShare server is invisible and cannot be selected for copying on the Mac desktop. This means that if you have special files or INITs in the server's system folder, they won't be backed up. Third, copying files from the server to your Mac's disk will create a great deal of network traffic — the only time you may be able to back up an entire server is at night, which is no fun. That's why backup systems that can be preprogrammed to run on their own are better, as you'll see next.

One of the most popular ways to back up a file server is to use a tape drive with special backup software, such as NetStream (PCPC, Inc.) or Retrospect (Dantz Software). These systems can be programmed to run in the wee hours of the night, when no one else is likely to be using the server. Usually, though, these systems are capable of recognizing if someone is using a file and will skip that file in the backup. However, with AppleShare 2.0.1, many of these systems are limited to copying visible files and folders, which means that they, too, are unable to back up the server's system folder, just as with the previous methods. Also, because e-mail programs like QuickMail keep the master database file open or busy all the time, the backup software cannot back up that file while the e-mail server is running.

At least one program, SafeDeposit (Terranetics), can now back up busy files, such as those from your e-mail server, while they're in use. If you use such a program, however, use it with caution. You can be sure that the backup file isn't exactly up to date, because you are backing up a busy file that may have been changed. Also, AppleShare 3.0 includes a new programming interface for developers to create software for such tasks as unattended backup; look for these types of programs for AppleShare 3.0 some time in 1992.

The fourth approach listed is to have a preprogrammed system copying files over the network to your Mac. This suffers from the same disadvantages as the second and third approaches. However, because you can preprogram the system, at least you don't have to be around in order to make the backup.

Of all the approaches, which do we prefer? To us, the third approach seems the best. When you're planning your file server, try to buy another disk drive or tape drive that is compatible with AppleShare and set up a regular schedule of backups using programmable backup software. If you have files within the server's system folder that change with use, plan to shut down the server occasionally to back up those files — weekends are a good time for this.

Finally, no matter which backup system you use, always use three sets of backup media. By using three backup sets, you'll ensure that you have two sets to fall back on if one set goes bad.

Summary

This chapter explained the differences between file transfers and file sharing. We described the two types of files servers — distributed and centralized. We also covered the ways that file servers can control user access to files and how the AppleTalk Filing Protocol works for different types of computers.

This chapter covered the following points:

✔ File-transfer utilities may be adequate tools for sharing files when you're working in a small workgroup.

✔ Distributed file servers are good for small workgroups, but they bog down with usage of more than 10-12 users.

✔ Centralized file servers are best for large databases.

✔ The AppleTalk Filing protocol includes rules for translating file names between the Mac OS, DOS, and ProDOS conventions.

✔ Disk mirroring is a good way to protect your data on a file server because this technique duplicates the data automatically.

✔ File servers should have uninterruptible power supplies.

✔ Not all files on an AppleShare server can be backed up while the server is running.

In the next chapter, we'll discuss networked databases. We'll give you an overview of the types of databases currently available so that you can decide which is best for your network.

Chapter 21
Using Networked Databases

In this chapter...

- ✔ The differences between flat-file and relational databases
- ✔ Points to consider when installing a database on a network
- ✔ How multiuser databases control access to data
- ✔ The benefits of using client-server databases on a network

We've mentioned time and again that one of the main purposes of networking is to share information. The common application for working with shared data on a network is the *multiuser database*. Such applications as inventory control, order accounting and fulfillment, subscription data, and personnel data use databases to maintain up-to-date information for your business. The variety of databases is almost mind-boggling, but all have one thing in common: Each database provides the designer with the tools to create a specific structure for storing and reporting data to the users. We'll look at the concepts of databases before we move on to how databases can be set up and used on networks.

A Database Primer

What is a database? Simply stated, a database is a collection of information with a road map, or series of rules, stating how the varied pieces of information relate to one another. The information may be text, graphics, numbers, and even sound or animation. A simple example of a database is an address book application, which stores the names, addresses, and phone numbers of your friends and clients. A more complicated example is a sales and inventory system, which stores a catalog of your company's product numbers and descriptions along with records of what products are in stock, what's been ordered, and what's back-ordered.

In classifying microcomputer databases, four terms are commonly heard these days:

❖ Flat-file

❖ Relational

❖ Quasi-relational

❖ Object-oriented

We'll introduce each type in the next sections.

The flat-file database

A *flat-file*, or single-file, database is the simplest database. All the data that you want to work with is contained within a single file on your computer. From this file, you can perform searches for particular data using rules that you set up yourself, and you can create reports based on selected data. An address book is an example of a flat-file database.

The two basic building blocks of a flat-file database are fields and records. A *field* is a single item of information, such as your name. A *record* is composed of a series of fields, such as name, address, city, state, and phone number.

The relational database

A *relational* database is composed of a collection of tables, or *relations*. These tables consist of rows, and each row contains columns, or *fields*. When you search for data by criteria that you've selected, the data that meets those criteria may come from different tables, which are interrelated in some way. Where two or more database tables share a column, the information in the tables can be combined in a relational *join*.

Suppose that a report you generate contains data on employee names and addresses from one table. The employees' pay scale comes from another table, and their sales performance for the last four quarters comes from a different table entirely. Each of these tables can be altered separately from the others, and the relational database can maintain links between the entries.

One purpose of relational database design is to free the user from needing to know about the structure of the database. All the user has to do is construct appropriate queries and report formats. Although this is the avowed purpose of relational databases, not all such databases actually meet the goal of *data independence,* as it's called. Examples of Mac-based relational databases are

4th Dimension (Acius) and FoxBase+/Mac (Microsoft). Apple's Data Access Language (DAL) gives you access to relational database systems that run on VAX and IBM systems.

We can use an example of a sales and inventory system to set up a relational database. One way to do this is to create a table for all your customers, storing the company names, ordering contact, accounting contact, and the address, phone number, and fax number for each company that orders products from you. You'll also need a table of all orders for products, which we'll call the *order table*. Then you define another table that we'll call the *product table;* this table will contain the product numbers, descriptions, and prices for each product that you manufacture. Last, you define an *inventory table* that stores all your product numbers along with the number of products available in each warehouse. To place all these tables together in an operational system, you'll need to *join* the contents of each table. One way to do this is to have common entries in each table that need to be joined. Thus, your order table will be joined to the customer table by a customer number and to the product table by product numbers. The inventory table can also be joined to the product table by product numbers.

What do you gain from this setup? To see the advantages, we'll walk through placing an order using this system.

First, you create a new order and enter the proper number for the customer; the database finds that customer's number in the customer file and fills in the order form with the customer's address and other related information. Next, you start entering the details of the order, selecting products by number and entering the quantity for each. The database system can enter the product description into the order form by referring to the product list; it can also compare the quantity being ordered to the inventory file for that product — if insufficient quantities are available, the product will be listed as back-ordered. The order is now ready for processing.

We should stress one additional aspect of this database system. Because the files largely contain independent information, they can be updated independently of each other. For instance, you need only to update the product file to change the price of an item. Also, every time an order is placed, only the inventory file has to be updated with the change in number of items in stock.

The quasi-relational database

As you'd expect, *quasi-relational* databases offer some of the features of relational databases. The main purpose of quasi-relational databases is to provide the user with a means for constructing links between database files. This makes it easier to maintain database files independently of one another, as with relational databases, but the structure of the database and the links usually needs more careful definition than with relational databases. One reason is that the links are usually one-way. This means that the data in file A can be called from file B via the link, but the reverse request, from B to A, cannot be processed. FileMaker Pro (Claris) is an example of a quasi-relational database for the Mac.

The object-oriented database

The *object-oriented* database is a fairly new type and has only recently appeared on microcomputers. The major feature of an object-oriented database is its capability to represent and manipulate complex objects which include both data and procedures. What this means is that the database can store objects that have certain properties associated with them, and that these properties are maintained as the object is manipulated by a database operation.

To understand the object-oriented database, consider the following example. A database object named "Employee" is defined to include first and last name, address, company, and salary information. Then, if your database defines a subclass called "SetOfEmployees," any reference to SetOfEmployees carries with it the information defined in the object Employee. You don't need to ask specifically for each employee's name, address, and salary, as that information is already part of the object Employee. Object-oriented databases thus make it easier to create modules of data that are automatically available when you want to build bigger modules, which is the essence of the object-oriented approach to most things. An example of an object-oriented database for the Mac is GemStone, from Servio Corporation.

Now that we've given you a brief overview of the types of databases, we'll move to a discussion of how you can set up and use databases on a network.

Designing a Networked Database

Installing a database for use on a network is a balance between the users' demand for speed and ready access to data. This means that you not only have to consider what kind of network you'll use (LocalTalk vs. Ethernet, for example) but also where the database will be stored and maintained. In addition, you'll have to keep in mind who has access to the database at any given time.

When you install a multiuser database on your network, you need to consider these issues:

❖ How will you control access to the database information?

❖ What kind of server should you use for the database?

❖ Who (or more correctly, what kinds of computers) will access the database?

Single-user databases usually don't have any type of access control because they're designed for use by an individual. A password may be used to prevent unauthorized access to the database, but that's about the extent of control. But when you're working with a multiuser database system that is set up for more than one user at once over a network, certain control mechanisms must be introduced to protect the data and the users from one another.

Because a single-user database allows only one user at a time, you'll rarely find these on networks. Instead, the network manager will ordinarily install a multiuser database file or files on a file server so that an individual user can access the database while others are using the files. This method provides a ready separation of function, with the database application doing the processing as one function and the files holding the information as another function. So it often makes sense to install the database application on each user's Mac and keep the database files on the file server.

There can be more to it, though. The more complex databases separate their information into more than one file. For example, an index file may be used for sorting and another file may be used for the actual data. In these cases, it may be best to store some of the database files, such as the indexes, on the individual user's Mac rather than on the server. You may want to consider this option as you design your database setup.

Finally, although this book has focused on Mac-only networks, a large percentage of current LANs are *heterogeneous,* which means that they support more than one type of computer. LANs, in particular, generally combine both Macs and DOS-based computers. This means that you may be faced with selecting a database that can be accessed by both Mac and DOS clients. So another consideration when you design your database will be compatibility across computing platforms.

Controlling access to data

Multiuser access controls fall into categories called *file-locking, range-locking,* and *byte-range-locking.* The locking mechanisms are usually the responsibility of the file server on which the database is installed. Most Mac database products implement file-locking and byte-range-locking. Apple's AppleTalk Filing Protocol (AFP) includes specifications for both file-locking and byte-range-locking; a database that uses the AFP locking mechanisms can then run on any AFP-compatible file server, whether the server is on a Mac, PC, VAX, or Unix computer. With more than one set of locking rules in existence, database vendors must choose which mechanisms to support when they design their products.

File-locking is a straightforward concept. If a file is locked, no one can alter it. Many single-user programs lock a file when it's been opened by the application; if that file is located on a file server and someone else tries to open it and change the contents, this user will most likely be warned that changes cannot be saved in that file. Application programs often tell you that the file is a read-only file if it has already been opened by someone else; to save any changes you're planning, you have to save the file under a different name. This is the most basic level of change protection within a file. In the absence of file-locking, when a file is opened and changed by more than one user, the last user to save changes is the "winner," meaning that only that user's changes are saved in the document.

Byte-range-locking controls access only to parts of a file, rather than the entire file. Consequently, this control mechanism is better suited for use with databases. The range defined for locking can be a database record or a series of records. With other multiuser programs, such as a shared word processor (or groupware), you may choose to lock a range of words or characters. In either case, byte-range-locking allows each user to make changes to a file and preserve those changes independently of what's happening to the rest of the file. This is ideal for multiuser databases.

As an example, we'll return to our sales and inventory system. Should you happen to change a product price in the product file, that record can be locked so that anyone currently placing an order for the product must wait until you finish updating the file before the order is completed. And when the order is complete, the product will reflect the new price.

Selecting a server for the database

We've said that multiuser databases are installed on a file server. More often than not, this server should be a dedicated, or centralized, file because of the processing power that large databases demand. You can install a multiuser database on a non-dedicated file server, but problems usually arise in the conflict for computing resources between the database and the owner/user of the Mac that's acting as the server. Thus, as your databases get larger, it's a good idea to migrate them from a non-dedicated file server to a dedicated server. Any database that's larger than a few megabytes in size should probably be installed on a dedicated server.

Supporting clients for the database

By far the majority of databases on LANs are those from the DOS world; the most popular are dBASE (Borland) and FoxBase. And the majority of clients using these databases are DOS-based, although Mac support is now often available. Vendors of some of the popular Mac-based databases have plans to release Windows versions of their software, but none has been shipped as of this publication.

We've spoken to some clients who have inherited custom databases written to reside on NetWare servers. Once the network has been converted from DOS-only to combined Mac and DOS workstations, the clients usually want to preserve their investment in the custom database, while allowing Macs to use it as well. This frequently poses a problem, as the database often relies on NetWare and requires workstations to use NetWare's IPX protocol to communicate. (Macs normally use AppleTalk protocols to communicate with a NetWare file server.)

A new product called SoftNode (Insignia Solutions) offers one solution to this dilemma, because it allows Macs to emulate DOS computers (actually the related SoftPC product does this) and speak the IPX protocol (by using SoftNode) as well. If you're faced with a similar problem, take a look at SoftPC and SoftNode. Since SoftPC is a software emulation of a microprocessor and its operating system, you'll find that screen displays and general performance will

System 7's File Sharing feature

Note that System 7.0's File Sharing feature has two limitations that have a bearing on using file sharing as a server for databases. First, there's the limit of ten simultaneous users for your Mac under File Sharing. This limit may not be sufficient for your database. If this isn't enough, you should probably be thinking of a dedicated file server for your database anyway. Second, File Sharing in System 7.0 and 7.0.1 does not fully support all of the AFP features. A Mac running System 7.0 can act as a file server for a database, but the user of that Mac cannot access the database properly. This problem may be fixed by Apple in a later release of System 7.

be slower than that of the equivalent PC/AT that the program is emulating. Even then, SoftPC and SoftNode are simple, elegant solutions to multiplatform computing.

For readers concerned with accessing databases on other platforms, we'll cover some of the ways to accomplish this in the next section, as well as in Chapter 26.

Working with client-server databases

Much has been written about client-server systems over the last few years. In the past, a database was designed as a monolithic program, although there may have been logical divisions between client and server processing. Usually, both programs ran on the mainframe or minicomputer. Now, however, with increasing power on the desktop, interest has turned toward distributing the processing power for a database between the database server (the mainframe or minicomputer) and the client (your Mac or DOS computer).

Working with a client-server architecture allows you to formulate queries and examine data on your Mac as the client, while searches for appropriate data, along with data updates and related tasks, are handled by the larger computer as the database server. In the old days, a common approach to viewing database information on a microcomputer was either to generate a report on the mainframe and then download it or to copy the entire database to your micro (see Figure 21-1). In the latter case, this often wasn't even possible because of the lack of sufficient storage space on the micro.

Setting up a client-server database can reduce the amount of network traffic significantly. A major reason for this is that the server has sufficient intelligence to process queries and related procedures on the server and then transmit only the requested data (see Figure 21-2). If you compare Figures 21-1 and 21-2, you can see where regular and client-server databases process queries and how this affects the data transmitted over the network (the arrows and file icons in the figures). Also note that users can create procedures for a client-server database at any time (steps 1 through 3 in Figure 21-2) and store them on the server for later execution.

The Mac can become a client for many common large database systems in a number of ways. Vendors such as Oracle, Informix, Ingres, Digital, and Sybase all now provide some kind of client software for Macs to access their databases on other computers.

In addition, Apple developed a superset of SQL (a common query language for databases), originally called CL/1 and now DAL, for Data Access Language. Written to work within a client-server architecture, DAL enables you to formulate queries on your Mac and have those queries sent over the network to the appropriate databases on other larger computers (see Figure 21-3). The amount of network traffic is

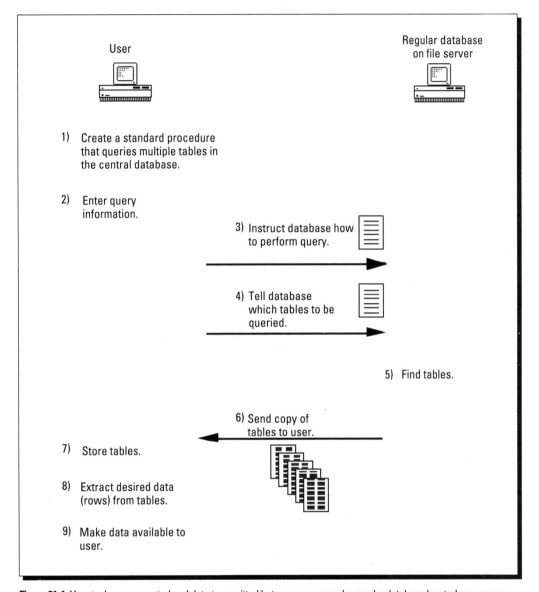

User

Regular database
on file server

1) Create a standard procedure
   that queries multiple tables in
   the central database.

2) Enter query
   information.

3) Instruct database how
   to perform query.

4) Tell database
   which tables to be
   queried.

5) Find tables.

6) Send copy of
   tables to user.

7) Store tables.

8) Extract desired data
   (rows) from tables.

9) Make data available to
   user.

Figure 21-1: How tasks are executed and data transmitted between a user and a regular database located on a server.

minimized, as you're not attempting to transmit the entire database over the network.

If you're going to work with DAL, you should understand that this is a query language based on SQL. You still need to provide some type of front-end, or interface, for constructing the queries. Many programs, such as 4th Dimension,

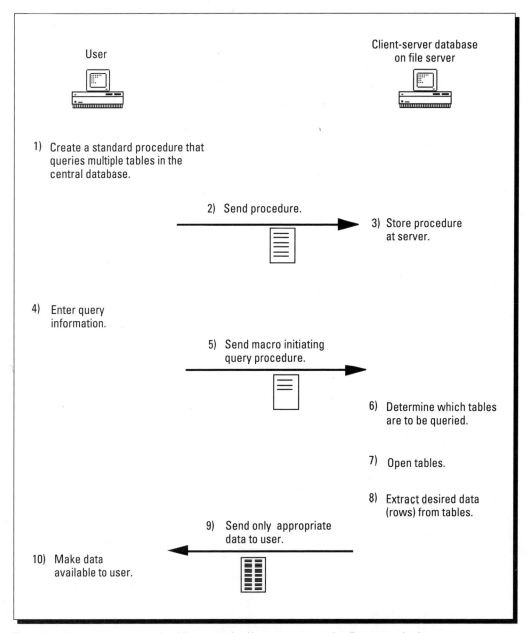

Figure 21-2: How tasks are executed and data transmitted between a user and a client-server database.

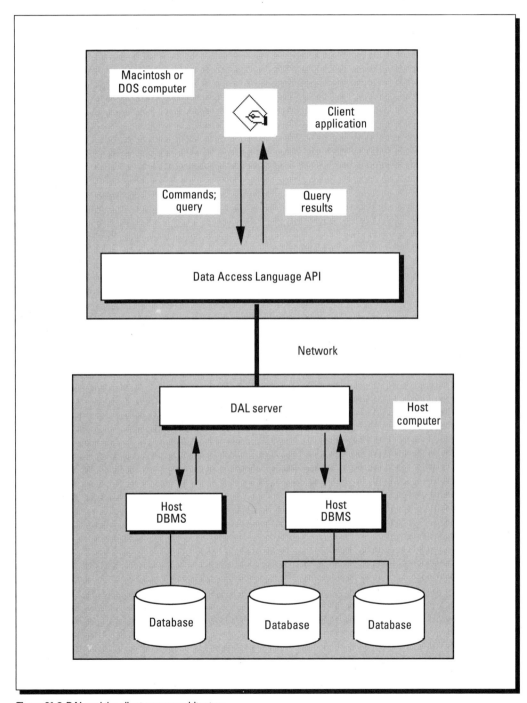

Figure 21-3: DAL and the client-server architecture.

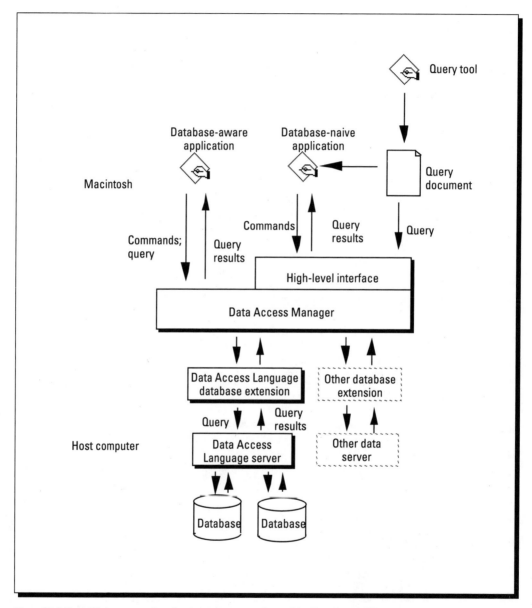

Figure 21-4: How different types of applications can use queries and the Data Access Manager.

Omnis (Blyth), Excel (Microsoft), and Wingz (Informix), offer DAL support so that you can create queries within them and then view the reported data in the same application. Other products, such as DataPrism (Brio Technology), GQL (Andyne), and ClearAccess (Fairfield Software), are designed to make query construction easier, not demanding extensive knowledge of either SQL or DAL. Last, remember that you require a DAL server on the mainframe or minicomputer for each type of database that you want to support (see Chapter 26 for details).

Query languages are special programming languages designed to enable users to construct requests for data from relational databases. In addition to allowing users to select columns and rows from tables that they select, query languages include conditional statements, such as IF . . . THEN, WHILE . . . and many of the other control statements found in programming languages. Such statements enable users to construct complex procedures for retrieving data.

Apple has also extended the capabilities of DAL by including many of the client capabilities within System 7, in the form of the Data Access Manager (DAM). The major change is Apple's definition of a system resource that can store any DAL query. By supporting queries at the system level as a resource, System 7 allows you to create and share any query. For instance, you can create special queries within DataPrism, GQL, or ClearAccess and then transfer those queries as resources to someone else using Excel with DAL to gather data. Even better, you can use these query resources within a program that by itself cannot create queries but does accept and manipulate data, as, for example, a word processor with a table function (see Figure 21-4).

Summary

We've devoted this chapter to a brief overview of the various types of databases that exist for the Mac. The descriptions of database types should help you decide which types are best for your network.

After reading this chapter, you should understand the following points:

✔ Flat-file databases are easy to construct, but relational databases provide more flexibility and can be easier to update.

✔ Databases using AFP's access control mechanisms employ byte-range-locking to control access to records.

✔ Client-server databases perform much of the query processing on the server and reduce network traffic because they send only the requested data to the user, not the entire database.

✔ DAL is an example of a query language for the client-server model and can be used with many SQL databases on other platforms.

In the next chapter, we'll cover electronic mail, describing its effective use on a network.

Chapter 22

Using Electronic Mail

In this chapter...

- ✔ What features to look for when shopping for e-mail
- ✔ How e-mail stores and processes your messages
- ✔ How to link LAN-based e-mail to other mail systems
- ✔ How to use facsimiles with e-mail

Electronic mail, or *e-mail,* is rapidly becoming one of the major uses of networked Macs. Already, over 500 thousand Mac users are taking advantage of e-mail on AppleTalk networks. In this chapter, we'll first look at the features that make up a good e-mail product and then explain some of the things you can do with e-mail.

What Is E-Mail?

Simply put, electronic mail is a network application that enables you to send messages to other users over your network. These messages may include text, graphics, or sound and may have other files enclosed with them.

Every e-mail user has a unique name or address. This address is used for routing messages, just as the postal service uses your home address to deliver mail to you. The network equivalent of the post office, where postal workers store and sort your mail, is the *e-mail server.*

Just as with a letter sent through the U.S. Postal Service, when you want to send something to someone on e-mail, you decide on the format for your letter, write the letter, and then address it to the intended recipient. Clicking the Send button is the same as taking your letter to the nearest mailbox. It's probably this similarity between the postal service and e-mail that has made e-mail so popular. The basic concepts are easy to grasp, making it simple for users to become comfortable with using e-mail.

Another reason for the popularity of e-mail is its convenience. This is primarily because of what's called *store-and-forward* architecture. This capability allows you to compose e-mail messages at your Mac and then send them to your list of

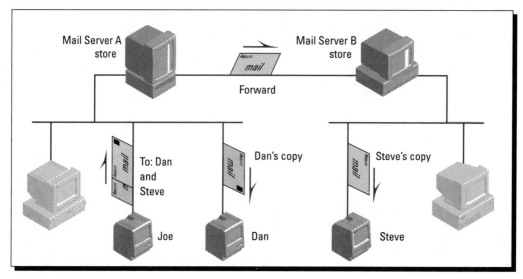

Figure 22-1: A diagram illustrating the store-and-forward process.

addressees, even if the intended recipients are not currently a part of the network (see Figure 22-1). Using store-and-forward, e-mail servers store pending messages until the intended recipients log on to the network, at which time the server can send, or *forward,* the mail.

Imagine a postal system where the post office refuses to accept a letter unless you guarantee that the recipient will be home when the postman plans to deliver it. That's what would happen without the store-and-forward architecture.

We'll offer an example to take a closer look at how the store-and-forward system works (see Figure 22-1). Joe, who is logged on to Mail Server A, sends mail to Dan and Steve. In a store-and-forward e-mail system, Server A stores mail for both Dan and Steve until it can deliver that mail. Dan receives his mail when he logs on to the network and Server A. Steve's copy gets forwarded from Server A to Server B whenever Server A connects to Server B. That could be immediately, if both servers are on the same network. Or this will happen later if the connection is made by modem. Server B then stores Steve's copy until Steve logs on to that server.

Selecting E-Mail Features

Although most e-mail products share relatively the same architecture with respect to the store-and-forward capability, each e-mail package brings with it a variety of distinguishing features. Some of these features considerably affect

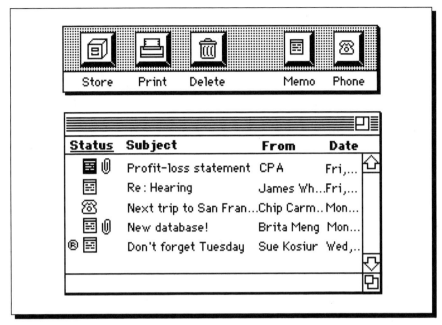

Figure 22-2: The InBox mail interface is the simplest available, showing buttons for only two forms, Memo and Phone. The lower window shows the list of waiting messages, with icons for message type, reply requested (®), and enclosures (paper clip).

the way you use your e-mail service, so we'll devote some time next to consider the more important choices to be made.

User-related features

Personal tastes get involved when dealing with the user interface on the Mac; individual customization is as much the rule as the exception. All currently available e-mail programs for the Mac have reasonable user interfaces, but they do vary in complexity. (See Figures 22-2 and 22-3.) Some programs display all their bells and whistles at once. Other programs, such as cc:Mail (Lotus) and InBox (Sitka), keep the fancier user options — custom forms and the like — to a minimum; this way the interface can remain simple. What is food to one is poison to others; and so it is with e-mail interfaces (although none has been found to be poisonous!).

If you're in the process of selecting an e-mail program, you'll have an array of user-related features to consider. Most of these features focus either on message sending and receiving or on handling address lists.

Sending messages is at the heart of the e-mail system. First, you'll want a program that makes it easy to compose a message and find the proper

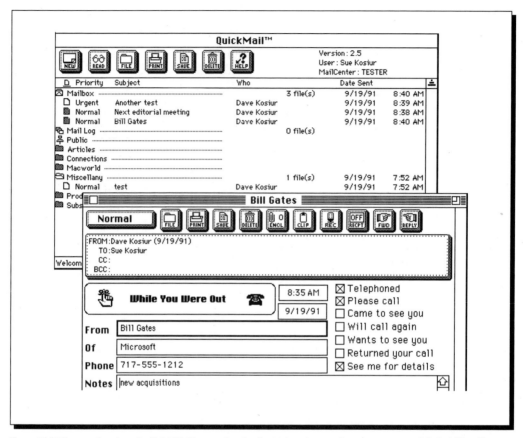

Figure 22-3: The user interface for QuickMail is more involved, with icon buttons for message types (labeled "New") as well as actions for any message. Messages are stored in folders, with waiting mail in the MailBox. The front-most window shows a typical message form, in this case for recording a phone message — note the large number of options available on the form, represented by the row of icons.

addressees. And then you probably want a program that lets you send multiple file enclosures along with the message — you shouldn't need a program like StuffIt to create a single package of the many files you want to send just because your e-mail program has a single-enclosure limit.

Users may not always be connected to the network, yet want to prepare messages to send at a later time. For these occasions, it's important that your program provides off-line support, either directly within the e-mail application (or DA) or by importing files into the message. You should be able to compose your messages in a word processor, for example, and import them later. Few programs work off-line — QuickMail and WordPerfect Office allow you to compose and address messages if you're not connected to the server.

Received messages may call for either formulating a reply or forwarding the message to other readers. The best programs let you send a reply to a subset of the original address list (a selected few on the cc: list, for example). Also, a good e-mail program lets you add comments to a received message before you forward it to someone else. Unfortunately, no e-mail program that we know of lets you specify a forwarding sequence so that a certain addressee will see the message before another does.

Two further issues pertain to organizing the received messages — first is filing the messages in the native e-mail format for creating later replies, and second is saving the messages as files on your disk. Almost all e-mail vendors have adopted a folder-like paradigm for filing messages. Some applications let you drag messages to the folders just as you would on the Mac desktop, but with others, you pick the folder's name from a pop-up menu.

More important is where these messages actually reside once they're filed. Programs like Microsoft Mail, cc:Mail, and WordPerfect Office have you file messages on the server. QuickMail is the only program that files messages on your local hard disk (cc:Mail has an archive function that also works this way). Filing on your local hard disk saves the server's hard disk space, which most mail administrators will appreciate. But local hard disk filing does make it more difficult for users on the road or those accessing mail through more than one computer to review past mail when needed.

Every e-mail program lets you save the contents of a message to the disk of your choice, so that's not a distinguishing factor. But a related feature that we've found useful is the capability to append a message to one that was previously stored. This is a great way to maintain a history, often called the *thread*, of an important series of communications.

As touched on previously, you want to make it easy for users to find and use e-mail addresses when it's time to send a message. One way to simplify this routine is to allow all users to create and maintain their own address books. All Mac e-mail programs let you create at least one personal address book, which can contain a subset of the master directory maintained on the server, as well as individually entered custom addresses (we'll get to this shortly). Personal address books are especially handy when you're working on a large e-mail system, where the entire system may contain a network-wide directory of 10,000 or more names.

Selecting each addressee's name from a list can be a pain when the number of intended recipients reaches ten or more. And if you mail messages to the same group more than once, you'll appreciate a mechanism that saves this group list for later use. E-mail programs usually offer two options to assist with group lists. First, the e-mail administrator can set up groups of addressees on the server for everyone's use. Second, you should be able to create your own groups much as you would your personal address book.

While we're on the subject of creating personal address books and groups, the question of updating these addresses is worth noting. E-mail systems customarily offer some mechanism for exchanging the directories on each mail server to maintain a network-wide directory. In some cases, you must purchase additional software to compile this global directory. The next step is to propagate any changes to the user. With applications like Microsoft Mail, this is done automatically; in other cases, as with QuickMail, you're prompted to verify the changes manually for each altered address.

These updates don't apply to the custom addresses that you create in your personal address book. Suppose, for example, that you know the address for Joe Sender, a special correspondent who uses MCI Mail. Rather than having the mail administrator insert Joe's address on the MCI Mail gateway for your system, you can enter it in your own address book. But this address won't be updated by the mail system's directory service because it doesn't know about Joe. Most LAN-based mail systems propagate all addresses to all servers. While this works well for small- to medium-size organizations, it is unwieldy in large ones.

Another feature concerning users deserves mention here: custom message forms. QuickMail started the trend toward user-defined forms that could include both graphics and text; Microsoft Mail and WordPerfect Office also support custom forms. Note that these forms are defined within the e-mail system, not by a forms-based front-end to a database. Using custom e-mail forms is much like using personalized stationery — they both help get a point across effectively and say something about you.

One last comment about user-related features concerns the option of remote access to the server. With the increased popularity of laptop and notebook computers, more users are taking their computers with them on the road. While away, they want to communicate with the home office and use the e-mail system as well. Being able to make direct calls to the mail server with a modem is an attractive feature, and this option usually includes the basic security measures, as with a password-based log-on. Microsoft Mail also lets you restrict dial-in privileges to specific users so that all mail users cannot simply dial into the server. The common problem with remote access is that only one user can dial into the server at any time. Where access is available to many users, people may become frustrated by repeated busy signals.

An alternative plan does not rely on direct dial-in to the mail server, but offers your users dial-in access to the network. If you maintain multiple modems or a modem server for the network, more than one remote user can join the network and access the mail server. While on the network, this user can also access other network services, such as printing and file servers.

Server-related features

Until now, we've talked about the features that keep the users satisfied with their e-mail service. But this is all for naught if the e-mail server isn't reliable or lacks some important features. We'll guide you next through some server-related features to look for.

Previously, we mentioned the store-and-forward architecture that's so important to today's e-mail systems. Not only is it useful for client-to-server communications to send mail to someone who's currently not connected, but this capability also enhances server-to-server communications. If you're on a network that's large enough for more than one server, the e-mail system needs a channel for passing messages to users of other servers. Again, just as it does for users, the store-and-forward architecture lets servers hold messages meant for other servers that may be down or disconnected. Message storage is particularly valuable if you have e-mail servers that are connected by modem lines, where each server can hold messages destined for the other and exchange them when the modem link is established.

Two further aspects of server architecture come into play when you consider an e-mail system. One is the method that the server uses to store its messages. The second is the location of most of the server's intelligence.

An e-mail server can store one copy of a message for each of the intended recipients; or it can store a single copy of the message independent of the number of addressees. The latter approach is preferred because it reduces the space required on the server's hard disk. Naturally, this method also applies to enclosures included with a message.

With respect to location of the server's intelligence, the early e-mail programs used a file-based system. This system relies on a file server to store files containing all e-mail messages, directories, and other necessary files. The e-mail application on the user's computer contains all the intelligence needed to store a message in the appropriate file on the file server, as well as to retrieve messages addressed to the user (see Figure 22-4). The computer acting as the file server doesn't hold an additional application designed specifically to assist the e-mail program; the server's operating system handles multiuser access to e-mail files just as it would control a multiuser database file, which is essentially what an e-mail server's main file is.

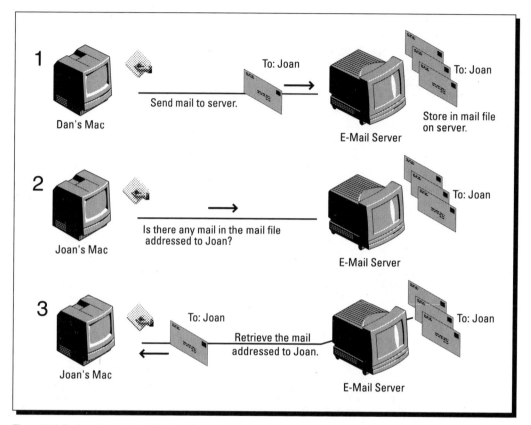

Figure 22-4: Exchanging mail via a file-based system.

More advanced e-mail systems use a client-server architecture that distributes the system's intelligence between the user's computer and the server (see Figures 22-5 and 22-6). Thus, when you use a program like QuickMail or Microsoft Mail, you have to install a program on the mail server to make everything work. This program usually assumes the tasks of notifying each user when mail is waiting, monitoring each log-on to the system, and updating directories. The client software (your DA or application) has only to worry about composing, sending, and receiving messages, as well as responding to the server's alerts.

For most environments, the client-server architecture is preferred. Yet there is an advantage to the file-based system; this system can be used on a variety of file servers and doesn't require specially written server software for each server's operating system.

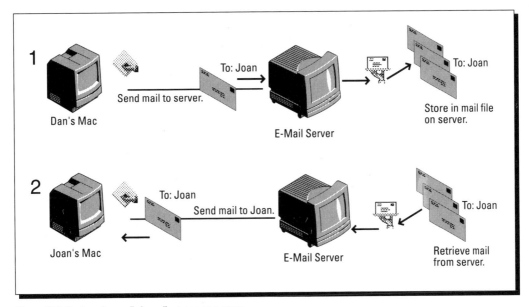

Figure 22-5: Exchanging mail via a client-server system.

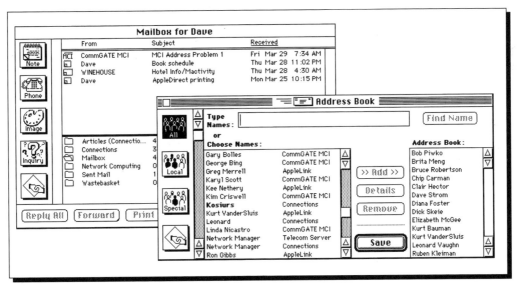

Figure 22-6: Microsoft Mail uses icons (left-hand side of rear window) to indicate what forms are available. Messages are shown in the upper-half of the window, while folders for storing those messages are in the bottom half. The front-most window shows the user's address list, which, in this case, includes addresses for the network (Connections), MCI (CommGATE MCI), and AppleLink (AppleLINK).

cc:Mail and InBox let you install their system files on practically any file server, and only the client software is system-specific. But when you get to complicated multiserver systems, you must purchase additional software to get the servers to exchange e-mail. That's less of a problem with the client-server architecture.

The Administrative Issues of E-Mail

Each e-mail system depends on a centralized e-mail server, so e-mail requires some administration. At the most basic level, this means assigning names and passwords for the users and perhaps assigning dial-in privileges. More complicated systems may require you to determine routes between servers, diagnose server problems, set times for server-directory updates, and select gateway configurations (discussed later in this chapter). And don't forget backing up the mail server's files.

Diagnosing e-mail problems is perhaps the one administrative area not yet adequately addressed by most e-mail programs. With the one exception of Microsoft Mail, the reporting options available to server administrators are quite limited, offering data on disk usage, number of messages transmitted, date last used, and the like. Microsoft Mail does include more options in its reports, some of which can be used to gauge server-to-server traffic and other performance issues that may prove useful for reconfiguring your e-mail system. Microsoft Mail is also the only program with customizable server reports.

You must exercise some care when you're ready to back up a mail server. Most vendors advise you to be sure that all mail users are logged off before you back up the server files; otherwise, the files may be altered and subsequently damaged during the backup process. Again, Microsoft Mail is the exception — it includes a special cdev for scheduling mail-file backups on the server.

Host-Based E-Mail and Gateways

Although we've concentrated on LAN-based e-mail systems, many of the concepts and features we discussed also apply to larger e-mail systems, which we'll call *host-based systems* because of the larger computers that they normally run on. In fact, host-based e-mail systems long predated LAN-based systems.

If your company has Macs either with mainframes or minicomputers, designing an e-mail system for a LAN can take one of three directions:

1. With the *host-centric* approach, you use the host computer's e-mail with some connection between the Macs and the host (see Figure 22-7).

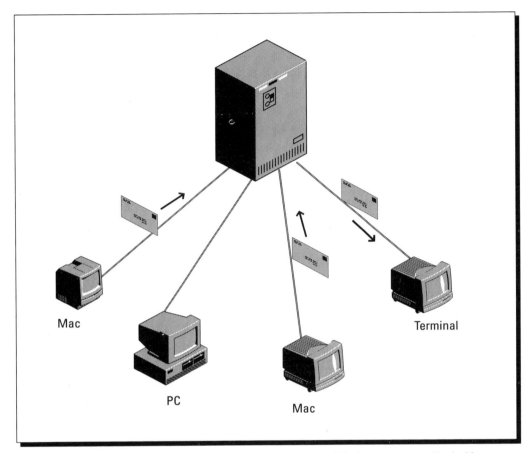

Figure 22-7: In the host-centric mail system, mail is processed on the host and the messages are read by the Macs, acting as terminals.

2. With the *mixed client-server* approach, a host computer runs an e-mail server application and client Macs on the LAN communicate with the host server (see Figure 22-8).

3. With the *LAN-centric* approach, you use a LAN-based e-mail system and link it to the host-based system via an e-mail gateway (see Figure 22-9).

When you use a host-based e-mail system exclusively, each Mac user needs to have an appropriate terminal emulator to communicate with the host (for details, see Chapter 26, "Running Applications on Other Platforms"). In these cases, the Mac is little more than a smart terminal (or *dumb terminal*, depending on the software), and the user has to learn the procedures of the host's operating system.

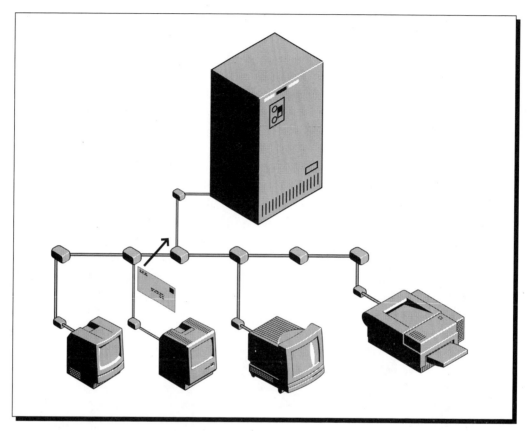

Figure 22-8: In the mixed client-server mail system, both the host and the Mac share in the processing of messages.

Another way of using the host's intelligence to process mail is to share the tasks, as in a client-server mode. In this case, the host acts as the mail server and also performs some of the mail processing, such as notifying users of pending mail. But the Macs on the network also perform some of the processing tasks, such as creating and storing mail. This approach doesn't limit you to the use of a terminal emulator and provides more Mac-like front-ends to the host's mail services.

Usually, setting up a mixed client-server system requires running the host's network protocols on the Mac (DECnet, for instance) or installing a gateway between the two network protocols (for example, AppleTalk for the Macs and DECnet for a VAX; see Chapter 24, "Using Non-AppleTalk Protocols").

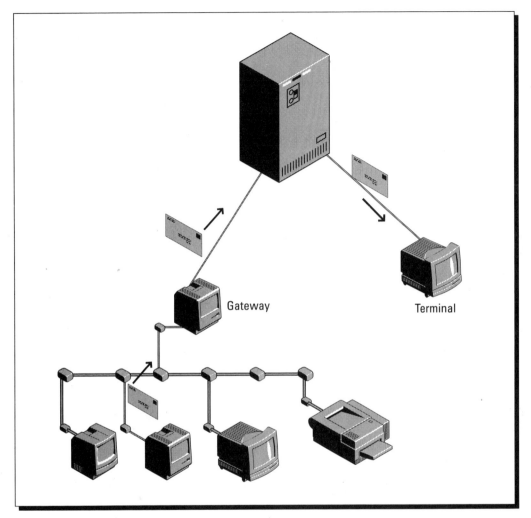

Figure 22-9: In the LAN-centric mail system, an e-mail gateway converts message formats and addresses between the LAN-based e-mail and the host-based e-mail.

A LAN-based system also lets you use more of the Mac's interface and intelligence to process e-mail. The crucial link here is the e-mail gateway. This gateway provides translations of both addresses and messages between the formats used by the e-mail systems on the host computer and on the LAN. Gateways can also be used to provide translations between two different LAN-based e-mail systems.

Selection of a LAN-based e-mail system with a gateway as opposed to a host-based system is a difficult choice. And this choice is often determined as much by corporate politics as by suitability to your needs. Bear these factors in mind while you're planning:

❖ A LAN-based system with gateways gives the user a single interface to a multiple mail system.

❖ LAN-based e-mail can help distribute the e-mail load, but the system may not be powerful enough when the numbers of users reach into the thousands.

❖ Gateways don't necessarily transfer all information in both directions; some may not forward or translate enclosures or handle graphics and sound.

❖ Host-based systems usually carry with them company-supported automatic archiving and backup of files.

❖ In the absence of universal directory services (something still on the horizon), employment of varied e-mail systems usually means maintaining redundant user directories.

Other Gateways

A diverse assortment of e-mail gateways is available beyond those meant for connecting host-based e-mail. Various other gateway designs hook up to national or international service providers, such as AppleLink, CompuServe, Genie, MCI Mail, EasyLink, and the Internet. These gateways usually connect to the larger system via a modem.

Should you plan to use a gateway to connect to one of these services, be aware of the limitations these services may impose on your e-mail. As an example, some services don't provide for file enclosures; some services do, but permit only one per message, which is not the norm for most LAN-based e-mail systems. If a service provider does not support multiple file enclosures, make certain that your gateway can translate one of your messages containing multiple enclosures into multiple messages, each with one enclosure.

Many foreign (that is, non-LAN) mail systems use such complex addressing schemes that a gateway must map to the LAN-based e-mail scheme. A good technique for coping with complicated addresses is to have them created and stored on the server that includes the gateway and then to designate simpler aliases for these addresses.

The X.400 messaging standard put forth by the ISO promises to reduce many of the problems found in current e-mail gateways. Just bear in mind that few, if any, current mail systems use X.400 as their native protocol and thus are translating between their own proprietary protocols and X.400. When e-mail systems switch over to X.400, the number of translations (of messages, addresses, and enclosures) will be reduced, making interoperability between mail systems simpler.

Using Facsimiles with E-Mail

Facsimile transmission, or fax, currently enjoys an international popularity that overshadows that of e-mail. The primary reason is that more people have fax machines than computers. But it's possible to combine e-mail and fax transmissions to expand the reach of either service.

All LAN-based e-mail systems offer some type of gateway to fax-transmission facilities. The normal process is for you, as an e-mail user, to select the address of an intended fax recipient and next create your message. Then the gateway converts your message to a form suitable for fax transmission and dials the phone number of the addressee's fax machine. You can usually specify a cover sheet, stored electronically on the server, for use with the outgoing fax as well. One nice feature of a fax gateway is that it can automatically dial the phone numbers of all addressees, even though you created only a single message (with an address list) in your e-mail program.

Whether you use the fax system alone on the network or via an e-mail interface (that is, a gateway), there are a few things that you should be aware of. First, fax images are bitmapped images. Standard resolution for a Group 3 fax is approximately 200 dots per inch, which can lead to large files that must be stored on your fax or e-mail server. Then consider that the time to convert text and/or graphics to a bitmapped fax image can be extensive — good fax systems let you perform the conversion at your Mac or at the server. The better procedure is to schedule the conversion at the server; locating conversion here reduces the amount of data to be transmitted over the network and also releases the Mac back to the user more quickly.

When setting up a suitable configuration for a fax server, the size of the stored images will be a paramount consideration, as all fax images are stored as bitmapped graphics. For example, a 10-page MacWrite file (text only, no graphics) takes up 24K on a hard disk, whereas the fax image created from that MacWrite file requires 737K of disk storage. Similarly, a scanned image that we saved as a PICT file took up 450K of storage on the disk, but the fax image created from that PICT file was 1.2MB in size. Most sites we've consulted prefer to devote a Mac with a large hard disk to act solely as a fax server — with a gateway in the case of an e-mail connection.

For the time being, you'll find that it's much easier to use a fax gateway to send faxes than to receive faxes, especially over a network. That's because incoming faxes aren't like e-mail, as they don't contain any electronic addressing information. Fax gateways usually deal with this by accepting all incoming faxes and sending them to one designated user, perhaps the mail administrator. That person then has the responsibility of reviewing each fax and forwarding it to the appropriate e-mail user. Technologies are being developed to overcome this problem — one is known as DID, or Direct Inward Dial, which requires a special phone line and phone number for each user. Another method encodes the address of the recipient in the fax message header itself, but requires matching systems. Other approaches append a user ID via touch tones after the fax modem's number is dialed, but a single solution hasn't been accepted by fax vendors.

Actually, you don't need a fax gateway to send and receive faxes. Service providers such as CompuServe, EasyLink, and MCI Mail all offer fax transmission to their users. Of course, this service is limited to text-only faxes, but these may be sufficient for some users' needs. Using an e-mail gateway to these services can get you both e-mail transmissions to other computer users and fax transmissions to customers who don't have a computer.

We'll offer here a few last thoughts about working with faxes on computers. Combining a fax modem and fax gateway with e-mail is a good way for your users to send faxes. But, often, it's not optimal for receiving faxes. If a fax has to be signed and re-sent, you'll go through the bother of printing the received fax, signing it, and then scanning it back in or sending it via a regular fax machine. Remember that the fax is a bitmapped image and that many of these faxes take a long time to print. Also, faxes are received as 200-dpi bitmapped images, so they're not of a high-quality; if you intend to use artwork that has been faxed to you, you're better off arranging for the other party to send a file to you via a regular modem.

Fax or modem?

When two computers communicate with each other over a modem, arrange to transfer electronic files; if the other person doesn't have a computer, use a fax. If you send a computer-generated document to a fax machine, it will almost always look better if you send it through a fax gateway or modem than if you print it and then scan it in through a fax machine. This is because a fax machine never has perfect registration of the scanned image, whereas the computer-generated fax does.

Expanding the E-Mail Interface

Even though e-mail already offers great communications flexibility for net-worked users, the marketplace promises even more changes and advantages in the not-too-distant future. Many of these improvements derive from the idea that e-mail's message-handling system can be used for more than personally generated messages, particularly for application-to-application transfers of data and commands. Thus, we'll see new systems that use message-handling and directory services as e-mail does, but with different interfaces on the front-end.

The first move in this direction has offered *Application Programming Interfaces*, or APIs, to existing e-mail systems. These APIs allow developers to provide direct support for e-mail within their applications. For example, Microsoft Word and Excel enable you to send and receive documents via Microsoft Mail while you're within those applications; Aldus PageMaker lets you place received mail documents as stories within a page-layout file.

Apple is already moving up to the next step by developing what it calls the *Open Collaboration Environment* (OCE). Apple's OCE will provide a foundation of directory, security, and transport services for developers to create collabora-tive applications, independent of existing electronic mail systems. Coupling OCE with some of Apple's new features in System 7, such as AppleEvents, should make it easier for Mac applications to exchange data and commands over the network.

And what about multiplatform support? Most of the popular LAN-based e-mail systems offer support for both Mac and DOS clients, as well as for Mac and DOS servers. In some cases, the problem is just to decide which products are appropriate; working your way through the list of selections is like ordering a meal at a Chinese restaurant. But it can be rewarding.

These new steps toward message handling within applications are even crossing platform boundaries. Of possible significance is Lotus' development of the Open Messaging Interface (OMI), now already superseded by VIM, or Vendor-Independent Messaging, and Microsoft's Messaging Application Programming Interface (MAPI). Both are designed to provide APIs for using common message-handling services across computing platforms. Apple has stated that its Open Collaboration Environment will support VIM, which should mean interoperability with DOS and possibly even Unix platforms. Although MAPI was designed initially to work with Windows on MS-DOS computers, Microsoft intends to extend MAPI to Mac-based applications as well. Only time will tell which of these interfaces will be the dominant one.

Summary

In this chapter, we discussed the important features of electronic mail, pointing out what to look for when shopping for and installing a LAN-based e-mail system. We also discussed ways to connect a LAN-based e-mail system with a host-based e-mail system. The following points were covered:

✔ File-based e-mail is good for multiplatform server networks.

✔ Client-server e-mail systems reduce the amount of processing over the network.

✔ An e-mail gateway is useful for exchanging mail between LANs and larger host computers.

✔ Networked fax systems (with or without e-mail support) require large amounts of storage and are better suited for sending faxes rather than receiving them.

In the next chapter, we'll address the issues of groupware.

Chapter 23
Using Groupware

Considering the relative ease of networking Macs, one would think that collaborative computing, or *groupware,* would have come early to Macintosh networks. That didn't happen, possibly because of the relative abundance of DOS computers as compared to Mac computers. Significant groupware applications, such as group scheduling, planning, and editing programs, showed up on DOS platforms first. However, an impressive array of groupware applications for the Mac has finally appeared. This chapter presents a brief overview of the field known as groupware.

Categorizing Groupware

Groupware, or *collaborative computing,* is a difficult field to define, mainly because groupware programs encompass a large variety of tasks, unlike programs that focus on a single activity, such as page-layout, word processing, or spreadsheet programs. When we think of groupware, we visualize systems that allow groups of workers to share information over a network. Further, we assume that the shared information is enriched, supplemented, or controlled by computer intervention. A file server, for example, is not considered groupware because it simply makes a file available for sharing among users. The server itself does nothing to the file; the server only controls access to the file and ensures that no more than one user is working with the same part of the file. On the other hand, some groupware programs keep track of user modifications to a file and notify users of the changes, as well as resolve differences among the various users' changes.

As the market currently stands, a wide variety of groupware programs is available. These programs are designed either to handle a specific group-related task or to provide a broad-based tool that can be modified to meet the workgroup's (or company's) needs. In the first case, programs are available for such tasks as scheduling meetings or co-authoring documents. In the second case, broad-based programs such as networked bulletin board systems are available. On reviewing the slate of Mac-based groupware and the functions of these programs, we find it convenient to adopt the organization proposed by Susanna Opper and Henry Fersko-Weiss in their book *Technology for Teams* (Van Nostrand Reinhold, New York, 1992). These authors recommend subdividing groupware by the type of application the programs are designed to perform. The result is the following four categories:

❖ Administration

❖ Information management

❖ Communications management

❖ Real-time meeting facilitation

We'll next examine what the Mac has to offer in each of these categories.

Administration

Groupware products that fall within the administration category are those designed to automate what we do in our offices every day. This includes such activities as sending messages via e-mail, scheduling of meetings, and simple document control.

E-mail

Although we devoted an entire chapter to e-mail (see Chapter 22), it's worth noting here that e-mail is currently considered the most successful groupware application. E-mail is more of a tool for groupware activities than a product that fills a specific niche. You can use e-mail to exchange important information about meeting agendas, reports, travel itineraries, and other business-related activities. A particular advantage of e-mail is that the products allow you to compose your messages and replies to other people's messages as your schedule allows. Because of its store-and-forward architecture (see Chapter 22), e-mail doesn't limit your communication with another user to times when both of you are available.

For those of you looking for real-time conferencing capabilities, QuickMail (CE Software) includes a QuickConference feature; a similar public-domain add-on for Microsoft Mail is available. Each of these products is rather limited and isn't meant to replace more sophisticated conferencing systems, as you'll see next.

Meeting schedulers

Meeting schedulers on the Mac are relatively new. Prior to the availability of these programs, people used e-mail, or even the telephone, to schedule meetings and distribute agendas.

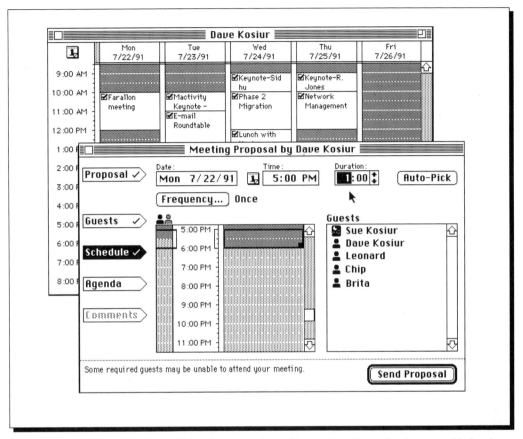

Figure 23-1: This example from Meeting Maker shows a user's weekly calendar, with meetings in separate blocks. The front window shows the user attempting to set up a meeting for 5 p.m. among five participants. One participant, Sue Kosiur, is listed as unavailable (moon icon) because she leaves work at 5:30 p.m.

The meeting schedulers currently available work in the following manner. First, as convener of a meeting, you send out a notice of the meeting, including the proposed date, time, and agenda, to all of the expected participants. Each participant then replies electronically (with a preformatted message form) whether or not he or she can attend; comments on the agenda may also be enclosed. Your meeting scheduler then displays the status of the proposed meeting, indicating who has confirmed attendance, who hasn't replied yet, and who can't make it. If the meeting is confirmed, each user's calendar on the computer will show the time period for that meeting blocked out (see Figure 23-1). Some meeting schedulers can automatically scan for an open time period for the requested meeting, but, as you'll see, this can be misleading when all users haven't kept their calendars up to date.

The meeting schedulers use either their own transport mechanisms or are layered atop e-mail. Programs like Microsoft's Schedule+ and WordPerfect Office's Calendar DA share resources with e-mail. The advantage of using an existing e-mail system is the consolidation of user accounts and directories — you don't need to set up and administer a new server just for the scheduler program. On the other hand, the *stand-alone schedulers*, as we'll call the rest, can offer special printing options and other features that users may find lacking in the e-mail-based system.

No matter what platform a group scheduler runs on, all the schedulers have inherent problems. The most prevalent problem is that *everyone* must use the product for it to be successful. If you don't properly block out your schedule or log on to the server periodically, you will either get incorrectly scheduled meetings or not learn of an important meeting. And then, of course, there are the users who don't want to be bothered by some meetings, so they block out a large portion of their day, even if they're available at that time. Research has shown that this is a common practice among daily users of group schedulers.

One difficulty in encouraging the use of group schedulers is the same one that faces users of individual scheduling programs. You're not always in front of your computer. Properly designed schedulers have to take into account ways of easily adding appointments to your DayTimer or Sharp Wizard or other means for carrying your schedule around. Some programs solve this problem by offering specially formatted printing output. Others offer an import/export program for electronically transferring your appointments.

Another aspect of group schedulers that has yet to be addressed is the reminder option. Just how do you get the user to pay attention to the reminders that flash across the screen or beep the user's computer speaker? That's not easily answered. One suggestion we've heard is to increase the belligerence of the reminder, perhaps by raising the volume of a particularly annoying sound when you should have been at that important meeting ten minutes ago. Perhaps a recording of your boss? And, of course, since we're being user-friendly, the developer will have to provide a way of disabling such a feature. Which puts us back to square one.

Document control

We're not sure that many people would include document tracking in groupware, but it seems to us that this category has one of the greatest potentials for success in networked offices. Moving around documents and files on the network is one thing — it's wholly another task to track where the documents are going, who's done anything to them, and who is on an electronic distribution list.

One of the prime movers in this category is ODMS, or Odesta Document Management System (Odesta Corp.). ODMS allows you to store files in a central location and create distribution lists for viewers of the files. ODMS can keep track of who has seen the file, or altered it (if allowed), and so on. If some people have been tardy in reviewing a file, you can alert them to the fact. MarkUp has similar features, but ODMS is more configurable to the work requirements of a company and runs on VAXes and computers other than the Mac that offer a broader market for the product.

Information management

The products in this category are those that relate more to managing task-specific information for a workgroup. This includes such items as document editing, project tracking, and information filtering (usually used with e-mail systems). Unfortunately, there are no Mac-based products for either group-based project tracking or filtering of e-mail, so we'll discuss only document editing here.

Document editing

Group-based document editing is often mentioned as a prime application of groupware. It makes some sense to have a computer system distribute documents for comment and then collect the comments in one place for presentation to the document's owner. One reason that this type of software succeeds is that it supports a well defined task that many people can relate to.

The major difference among the group-editing programs that are currently available is the *time-sense,* or *interactivity,* of the program. MarkUp (Mainstay) (see Figure 23-2), for example, lets the document's owner pick the reviewers and monitor their progress, after which the document reviewers can work on it at their leisure. The reviewer does not see what the other reviewers are doing. Each reviewer's comments are then returned to the document originator, who is responsible for consolidating the changes and corrections.

Aspects (Group Technologies) (see Figure 23-3) and Instant Update (ON Technology) are more attuned to the *real-time editing* of a document, whereby the changes are rapidly sent among the users. A problem with Aspects is that the program expects all users to be logged on and using the program at the same time. Currently, no provision is available for users to work on the same document at different times and have the changes sent back to other users of the document, as Instant Update does. A problem common to both programs is that neither contains a built-in mechanism for version tracking, which would enable you to revert easily to a previous document version.

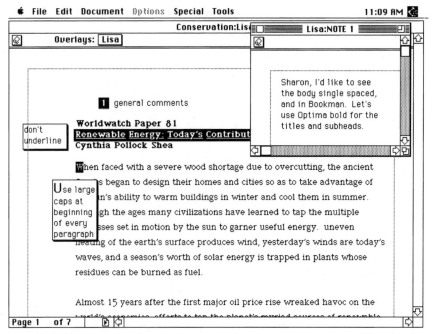

Figure 23-2: This example from MarkUp shows one reviewer's comments on a report. The editorial comments in small boxes are directly attached to text within the report. The other window, named Lisa: NOTE 1, contains a general note attached to the entire document.

Each approach has its own uses. Our own preference would be for a program that supports real-time usage among a group of users but allows some type of off-line editing as well. Also, it's important in some instances for each reviewer not to see what the others are doing.

Real-time usage in a group-editing program offers interesting possibilities for a group to brainstorm an idea, either when the participants are together in a meeting room or scattered across the country. What's lacking now is a full range of tools within the existing programs to take full advantage of brainstorming results. Neither Aspects nor Instant Update includes an outlining option to order groups of ideas into categories subsequent to brainstorming.

Group information retrieval

One asset of a workgroup or company can be the information that it generates. Compiling this information and making it available to networked users are the tasks of group information retrieval products. These products differ from a

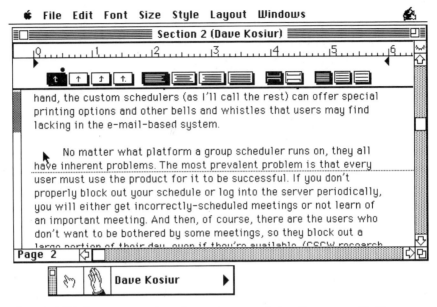

Figure 23-3: This Aspects screen shows the word processor feature. The uppermost text has a gray bar to the left of it, indicating that someone is editing that paragraph. In the meantime, Dave Kosiur has indicated that he is waiting to edit some part of the article (see the "Raised Hand" icon in the window at the bottom of the screen).

networked database in that they allow storage of free-form, or unstructured, data and generally don't provide the formatted reporting features normally found in databases. The search features in information retrieval software are very similar to those found in database software.

Marco Polo (Mainstay) is designed to serve as an information center for groups, wherein different users can be assigned separate privileges. Both text and graphics files can be stored, retrieved by keywords, and viewed from within the Marco Polo application. Sonar Professional does a similar job for text files only. MARS (Multi-User Archive and Retrieval System) also offers a special networked system for information retrieval from text and images.

Communications management

This category of groupware focuses on providing a communal work space for gathering, presenting, and viewing information. You might consider these products as replacements for, or supplements to, face-to-face meetings. Computer conferencing products fit into this category; for the Mac, the currently available products are networked bulletin board systems.

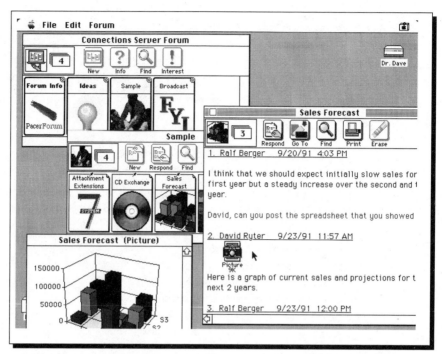

Figure 23-4: These windows are the interface to Pacer Forum's networked bulletin board system. Sales Forecast is a topic within the Sample board on the Connections Server Forum. The window labeled Sales Forecast displays the messages within the topic, with a camera icon showing that an image is attached to message #2.

Bulletin board systems are another way of exchanging and finding information. Mainly, these systems encourage "free" opinions and offer message threads as a way of tracking comments about other statements. Similar to this idea is a group-based decision support system called gIBIS, which has been used to propose discussions and track the various sides of an argument over a network until a "proper" conclusion is reached. A modified version of this concept for Macs, called hyperIBIS (public domain), allows you to set up and track arguments. Bulletin board systems, or BBSs, have now progressed from relying predominantly on telecommunications to systems that can be used entirely over an AppleTalk network, making them more convenient for in-house corporate use. In this class of bulletin board systems are PacerForum (Pacer Software) (see Figure 23-4), inForum (MacVONK), TeleFinder (using NetConnect from Spider Island Software), and hiBBS (T.I.C.). Some of these programs can also combine networked and modem access.

Real-time meeting facilitation

This category of groupware is primarily designed to support users in a face-to-face meeting; the most frequently used name for this class of products is *group decision support systems* (GDSS). Whereas no Mac-based product is specifically written to act as a GDSS, some products can be used to facilitate real-time, face-to-face meetings.

As an example, some groups have used Aspects with a Mac-controlled projector or large monitor in a room to display ideas and reports for a consensus of those present in the meeting. Other groups have used outliners like MORE II with Timbuktu to allow more than one person in the room to make changes to an outline as it's being developed.

What's missing from these attempts at using a program for meeting support is access to corporate databases and other information sources, such as e-mail and BBSs. A full-featured GDSS incorporates not only screen sharing and brainstorming support, but also immediate access to networked databases and, in some products, e-mail as well. Such a GDSS has yet to appear for Mac networks.

Looking Ahead

What does the future hold? Networked information exchange is going to get easier, thanks to wider implementation of electronic mail, System 7's IAC (Inter-Application Communications), and AppleEvents. With easy-to-use propagation mechanisms in place, especially at the system level, chunks of data both large and small will be easy to disseminate on the network. Passing data via IAC will allow better modularization of tasks — while you're using your word processor and we're using ours, we'll still be able to work together to create the final report. The major stumbling block here is the lack of common file formats for all necessary files — spreadsheets, project management, outlines, word processing files, and graphics. Within some standardized formats, sharing information will be difficult, even on the same Mac platform. One alternative is a set of built-in translators, such as the XTND technology developed by Claris, but even that hasn't been taken far enough, nor has it seen as wide an implementation as we'd like.

It's obvious that Apple has committed resources to enhancing collaborative computing. The company has been working on the system-based tools for collaborative computing for over two years and has publicly acknowledged the project by defining specifications for developers in the Open Collaboration Environment (OCE). OCE should make it easier for developers to tie together Mac (and later other) users over a network to work together within an application.

Workgroups using networked Macs will probably be on the forefront of those learning the advantages and disadvantages of groupware. This is because Mac users seem to embrace networking more readily, and because the cost of implementing a groupware system is less for Macs than for other platforms.

Summary

In this chapter, we've categorized groupware according to the following tasks: administration, information management, communications management, and real-time meeting facilitation. In reviewing the products currently available for the Mac, we've found that the bulk of the products fall into the first three categories.

After reading this chapter, you should remember the following points:

✔ Groupware is designed for networked users to share information over the network that is partly controlled or supplemented by computer intervention.

✔ Meeting schedulers are a common groupware product and can be used to supplement e-mail systems.

✔ Group editing of documents can be handled either as an interactive, real-time task or as a task that's passed sequentially from user to user.

✔ Bulletin boards can be run over a network to provide users with another means of storing and trading information.

In the next chapter, we'll begin our discussion of working with other computer platforms, and we'll start with the use of non-AppleTalk protocols.

Part Five

Working with Other Computer Platforms

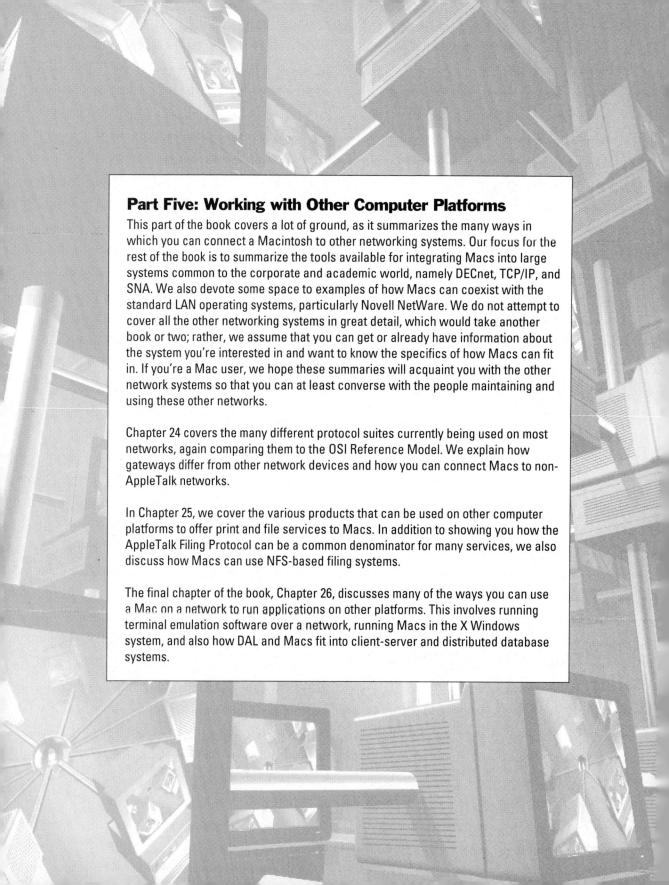

Part Five: **Working with Other Computer Platforms**

This part of the book covers a lot of ground, as it summarizes the many ways in which you can connect a Macintosh to other networking systems. Our focus for the rest of the book is to summarize the tools available for integrating Macs into large systems common to the corporate and academic world, namely DECnet, TCP/IP, and SNA. We also devote some space to examples of how Macs can coexist with the standard LAN operating systems, particularly Novell NetWare. We do not attempt to cover all the other networking systems in great detail, which would take another book or two; rather, we assume that you can get or already have information about the system you're interested in and want to know the specifics of how Macs can fit in. If you're a Mac user, we hope these summaries will acquaint you with the other network systems so that you can at least converse with the people maintaining and using these other networks.

Chapter 24 covers the many different protocol suites currently being used on most networks, again comparing them to the OSI Reference Model. We explain how gateways differ from other network devices and how you can connect Macs to non-AppleTalk networks.

In Chapter 25, we cover the various products that can be used on other computer platforms to offer print and file services to Macs. In addition to showing you how the AppleTalk Filing Protocol can be a common denominator for many services, we also discuss how Macs can use NFS-based filing systems.

The final chapter of the book, Chapter 26, discusses many of the ways you can use a Mac on a network to run applications on other platforms. This involves running terminal emulation software over a network, running Macs in the X Windows system, and also how DAL and Macs fit into client-server and distributed database systems.

Chapter 24
Using Non-AppleTalk Protocols

In this chapter . . .

✔ The protocols used by DECnet, SNA, TCP/IP, NetWare, VINES, and LAN Manager networks

✔ How Macs can be set up to use non-AppleTalk protocols

✔ The differences between routers and gateways

✔ How MacIP and IPTalk work

Recall that we introduced you to the OSI Reference Model for network protocols in Chapter 3. So far, we've concentrated on how the various AppleTalk protocols work within that layered model. Now it's time to see what other networking protocols are out there and how Macs can be used on these other networks.

Many network protocols are currently in use. Books that just summarize all of the protocols get thick quickly or even turn into multivolume sets. And wall charts covering more than a few network operating systems look like a cat's cradle gone awry. Such expansive treatments make interoperability look like the quest for the Holy Grail.

But don't dismay. The interoperability scene has been improving over the last few years. And Macs are becoming usable clients for many of the popular network operating systems, as you'll see in the various chapters of this section of the book.

Protocols, Protocols, and More Protocols

We won't attempt to cover all the networking protocols currently available. Rather, we'll take you through a quick summary of some of the more important protocols so that you'll have some understanding of how they relate to one another when we start talking about Macs.

We chose to subdivide the networking protocols into two groups. In the first group are the large system protocols, or those often used for creating large

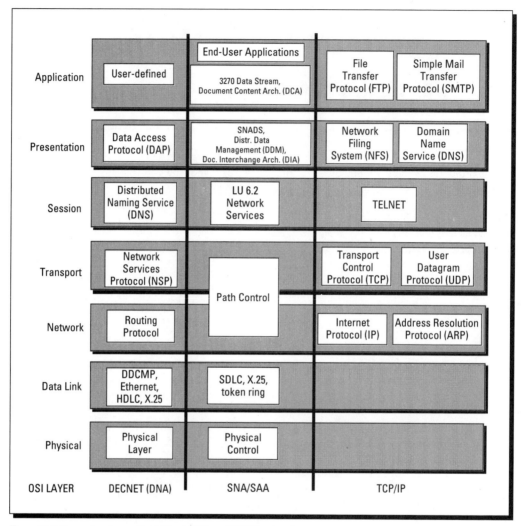

Figure 24-1: The protocols used for DECnet, SNA, and TCP/IP networks.

networks, including mainframes and minicomputers. In the second group are the LAN protocols, or those used for setting up a LAN of PCs and/or Macs. The dominant large system protocols are Digital Equipment Corporation's DECnet (or DNA, for Digital Network Architecture); IBM's SNA (System Network Architecture); and TCP/IP (named for the dominant protocols in the suite: TCP, or Transmission Control Protocol; and IP, or Internet Protocol).

Figure 24-1 arranges the large system protocols according to the OSI Reference Model. Figure 24-2 shows you the primary LAN protocols (except AppleTalk,

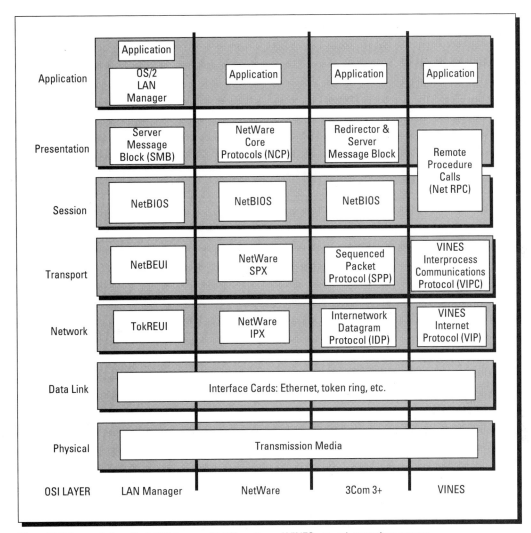

Figure 24-2: Protocols from the LAN Manager, NetWare, 3+, and VINES network operating systems.

which is diagrammed in Chapter 3). The LAN operating systems of interest here are LAN Manager, NetWare, 3+, and VINES.

One thing you'll notice right away in Figure 24-1 is that these protocols often can use the same data link and physical layers — the interface boards and transmission media. That's partly because the IEEE has created a series of standards for the physical and data link layers (see Figure 24-3), and it's hardly necessary to reinvent this wheel. Each protocol stack usually includes options for other transmission media and interfaces (such as ARCnet) as well.

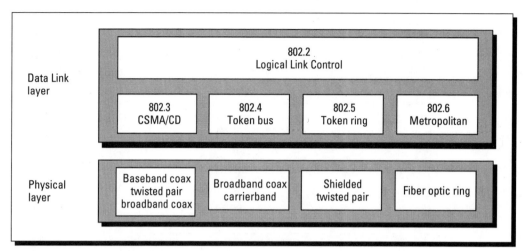

Figure 24-3: IEEE network standards.

Using Macs with Non-AppleTalk Protocols

You can link a Mac to any of these networking systems in one of two ways. You can choose either to run the protocols native to the other networking system on your Mac or to use a gateway between AppleTalk protocols and the foreign protocol suite.

A limited number of protocol suites can be run on the Mac. Of particular note are DECnet (also called DNA, or Digital Network Architecture) and TCP/IP. Both of these protocol suites can run on your Mac simultaneously with AppleTalk, allowing you to use your LaserWriter or AppleShare server at the same time you access a VAX or Unix computer.

Gateways can provide even more flexibility for your network because they don't require you to install the second protocol suite on each user's Mac. These devices operate in the lowest two or three layers of the OSI model. A gateway, however, uses from four to seven layers of the OSI model, as it must handle translations among more of the protocols in each suite (see Figure 24-4). We'll say more about the various types of gateways shortly.

How do the two approaches to using other protocols differ? If you run the foreign protocol suite on your Mac, you can get better performance than by running the same protocols through a gateway. That's because, in the latter method, you're competing with other users for the gateway's resources. On the other hand, if you're already running your Macs on a LocalTalk network and your users require only occasional access to the non-AppleTalk resources, a gateway can make a great deal of sense.

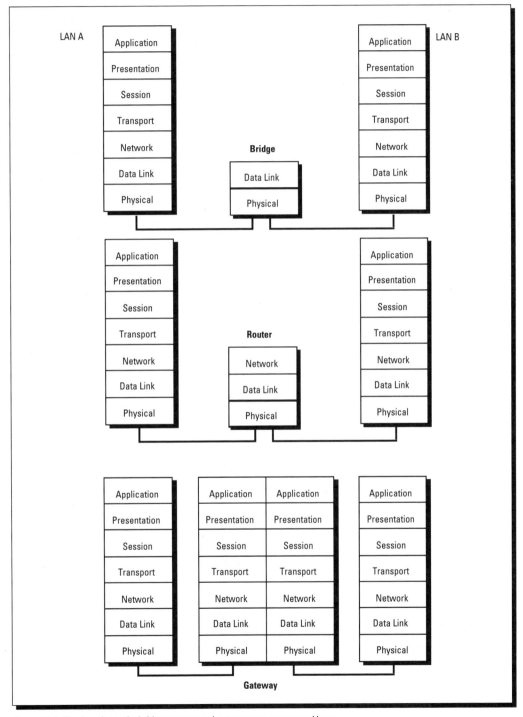

Figure 24-4: The functions of a bridge, router, and gateway are compared here.

Running Other Protocols on Your Mac

If you choose to run another suite of protocols on your Mac without a gateway, you can often use the same medium that you'd use for your AppleTalk network. In the case of TCP/IP and DECnet networks, you can use Ethernet cabling that's shared with EtherTalk. For SNA protocols, you can use either coaxial cabling for direct connections to an SNA host or controller, or token ring cabling that can be shared with TokenTalk. If your Macs are running on LocalTalk and you want to use one of these protocol suites over the same network, you'll have to turn to a transport gateway, which we'll discuss in the next section.

TCP/IP

The most popular way to run TCP/IP protocols on a Mac is with Apple's own MacTCP. This driver is frequently packaged with many of the TCP/IP-based programs, such as TELNET, X Windows, and NFS, currently available to provide additional services to a Mac user. MacTCP conforms to various Internet standards and provides the basic IP-related protocols (TCP, UDP, and IP). MacTCP allows you to run both TCP/IP and AppleTalk processes at the same time, for example, simultaneously running a TELNET session and printing to a LaserWriter on LocalTalk. With the introduction of MacTCP 1.1, which is compatible with System 7.0, you can use alternate Link Access Protocols (see Chapter 3 for a discussion of Link Access Protocols), such as token ring, PPP, and SLIP; formerly only Ethernet was supported. As you'll see in Chapter 26, "Running Applications on Other Platforms," a number of applications have been written for the Mac to take advantage of TCP/IP-based network services, such as virtual terminal emulation, printing, and file services.

DECnet

Software currently is available to convert your Mac into a DECnet end node, which allows you to send and receive data over the network. By being an end

MacTCP and the Mac Plus

If you're planning to use MacTCP 1.1 with a Mac Plus running System 7, be sure to use Apple's MacTCP+ Tool to patch Mac TCP. If you don't, a TCP connection might not work or will slow down network performance considerably. The Mac TCP+ Tool is available directly from Apple.

node rather than a DECnet routing node, your Mac is unable to route traffic between other nodes in the network, which is usually not important for an end user. The basic software found in Digital's PATHWORKS package for the Mac allows you to use serial communications, AppleTalk, or Ethernet to access a DECnet network. All DECnet network applications are layered atop the selected communications interface.

SNA

You run a subset of SNA protocols on your Mac when you're using terminal emulation software with an associated interface board to emulate either IBM 3270- or 5250-style terminals (and associated local printers). In such cases, you may not be using the same cable as for AppleTalk because the SNA protocols are most often run on non-Ethernet networks — coax, twinax, or SDLC (Synchronous Data Link Control) networks. This usually means that your 3270 emulator board attaches to a coaxial cable that feeds into an IBM communications controller. (A 5250 emulator usually uses twinax cable, which is a coaxial cable with two conductors in the center.) Those emulator boards that also come in token ring varieties allow you to run SNA and TokenTalk sessions on the same cable.

Using a Gateway

What is a gateway? The word *gateway* actually encompasses more than one type of networking device. In networking today, there are three devices that are routinely called gateways; to distinguish among them, we'll refer to them as encapsulating routers, transport-level gateways, and application-level routers.

Encapsulating routers do just what their name implies — they take packets from one network system and enclose them in packet formats for transmission on a second network system. These routers also perform the reverse process; that is, they can process the encapsulated packets, stripping away the second system's packet information and send the packets to the first network (see Figure 24-5). Some common examples of encapsulating routers are the Shiva FastPath and Cayman GatorBox when they're set up to connect AppleTalk and TCP/IP networks using MacIP, which we'll discuss later in this section.

The *transport-level gateway* performs a function similar to that of an encapsulating router. The distinguishing factor between the two devices is that the transport-level gateway uses protocols at layers higher in the OSI Reference Model (see Chapter 3) than does the encapsulating router. We'll cover a detailed example of this in the following section on IPTalk.

Note here that Digital chooses to call the gateway between AppleTalk and DECnet that they provide with PATHWORKS a *transport gateway*. It's not

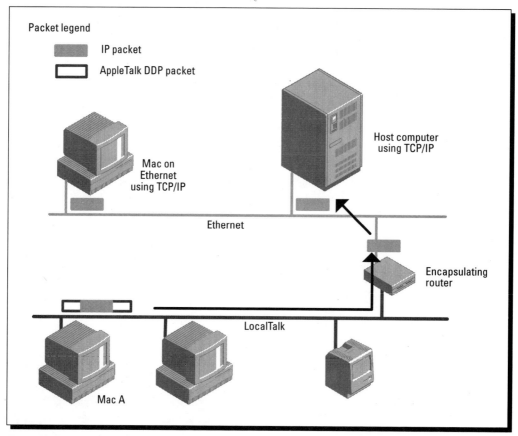

Figure 24-5: Packet encapsulation using MacIP.

simply a *transport-level* gateway because the PATHWORKS AppleTalk-DECnet gateway uses protocols above those in the OSI transport layer (namely ADSP in the AppleTalk stack).

Last, we come to the *application-layer gateway*. This is the type of gateway we briefly described when we said that all seven layers of the OSI Reference Model are needed to translate data between two network systems (see Figure 24-4). A good example of an application-level gateway is an e-mail gateway, such as the gateways offered for CE Software's QuickMail and Microsoft Mail to exchange messages with X.400 (Touch Communications), VAXMail (Alisa Systems), and PROFS (Soft•Switch Inc.).

Gateways (the generic, all-encompassing term here) exist between AppleTalk and three major protocol suites: DECnet, TCP/IP, and SNA. In some cases, such as for DECnet and TCP/IP, the gateways are usually stand-alone hardware devices (like the FastPath and GatorBox) that can translate between AppleTalk and the desired protocol suite. Software gateways are available for DECnet and TCP/IP as well. Many of the SNA gateways are software packages that are installed on another computer on the network, either a Mac or DOS, and provide SNA services to the Macs over AppleTalk.

TCP/IP

Perhaps because of the large number of TCP/IP networks throughout the world, there's been a great deal of interest in connecting Mac networks via TCP/IP backbone networks. Gateways are a good way to do this, and the various AppleTalk-TCP/IP gateway manufacturers have recognized this by offering two ways of tying together AppleTalk and TCP/IP networks. MacIP is meant primarily for providing IP services for LocalTalk networks, whereas IPTalk helps Mac users communicate with other AppleTalk networks over a TCP/IP backbone network without putting AppleTalk directly on the IP cables.

MacIP

Although IP packets cannot be transmitted directly on LocalTalk, they can be encapsulated in AppleTalk DDP packets. Adding and removing the DDP headers is done by both the MacTCP driver (on the Mac) and the IP router (see Figure 24-5), which also provides many supporting services. For example, the router manages a block of IP addresses and assigns them either dynamically or statically to the client Macs. The router can also perform a proxy ARP so that the rest of the IP network thinks that the Macs are directly attached to Ethernet. (This is *KIP-style* IP addressing.) The router can also be used to create an IP subnet for each LocalTalk network, which is a better approach.

We noted earlier that devices supporting MacIP should be called *encapsulating routers* because the process of encapsulating the packets occurs at the network layer in the OSI Reference Model. Figure 24-6 shows the flow of packet data through the protocols of the AppleTalk and IP stacks during encapsulation.

IPTalk

The IPTalk service is the opposite of MacIP. IPTalk encapsulates AppleTalk packets in UDP headers, which can be useful for sites that are IP-only and do not allow other protocols on the internetwork (see Figure 24-7). All LocalTalk traffic can be converted by the router to IPTalk instead of EtherTalk, although there is a performance penalty because of the additional processing that must be done by the router.

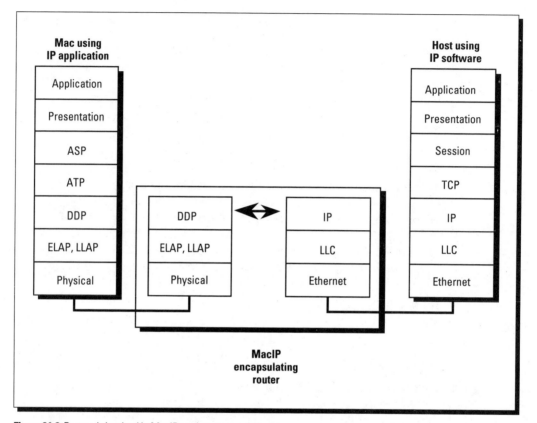

Figure 24-6: Protocols involved in MacIP packet encapsulation.

This approach also enables you to access CAP (Columbia AppleTalk Package) servers. CAP is public-domain software that allows Unix hosts to act as AppleShare file and print servers to Mac networks (see Chapter 25). CAP can use EtherTalk on the local cable, but commonly uses IPTalk for connectivity across IP-only backbones.

Devices supporting IPTalk packet encapsulation should be called *transport-level gateways*, in keeping with the terminology we defined earlier. Figure 24-8 makes the reason clear, as you can see that the UDP protocol used to encapsulate the AppleTalk packets is located in the transport layer of the OSI Reference Model.

DECnet

Some of the same hardware routers that provide access to TCP/IP networks can also become DECnet routers. In these cases, Macs running DECnet

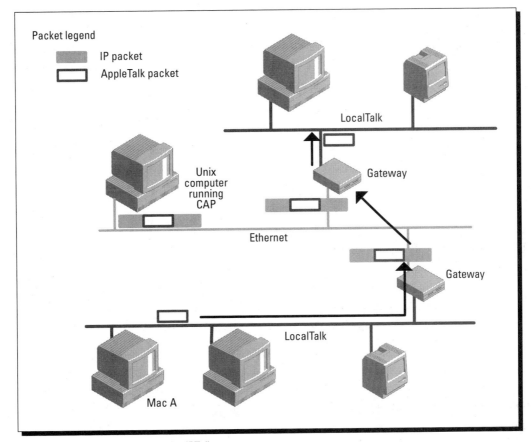

Packet legend

IP packet
AppleTalk packet

LocalTalk

Unix
computer
running
CAP

Gateway

Ethernet

Gateway

LocalTalk

Mac A

Figure 24-7: Packet encapsulation using IPTalk.

software on LocalTalk networks use LocalTalk as the transport mechanism to the router, which in turn connects to Ethernet and maintains a connection with DECnet. Encapsulation here uses the same approach as MacIP.

Digital's PATHWORKS for Macintosh includes software that provides gateway functions between AppleTalk and DECnet networks. With this software, the gateway process runs on the VAX, and AppleTalk users access the router via AppleTalk for VMS (also a part of PATHWORKS). As this gateway is only at the transport and session layers (see Figure 24-9), applications on the Mac would need to use the same higher-layer protocols as those on their VAX servers. X Windows, MaxNotes, VTXpress, ALL-IN-1 Mail, and ACMS Desktop are some examples of existing applications that do this.

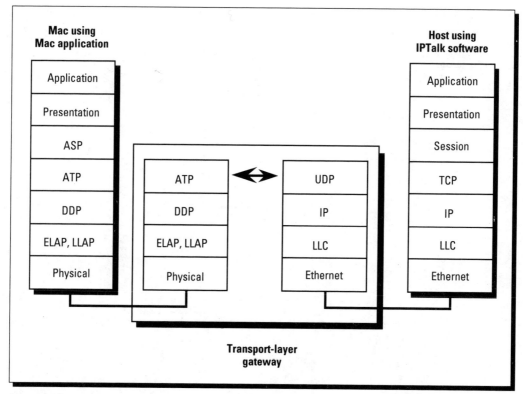

Figure 24-8: The protocols involved in IPTalk.

SNA/SAA

As mentioned previously in this chapter, the SNA/SAA gateways are mostly combined hardware-software packages. These products include an appropriate network interface board for the Mac or DOS computer that serves as the gateway machine as well as the software to control the gateway processes. One product, the Netway 2000 (Avatar Corp.), is a SPARC-based hardware gateway. Common configurations of these gateways include coax, SDLC, or token ring network interfaces.

By and large, the majority of gateways are designed to provide SNA connectivity, that is, 3270 terminal emulation and Type 1 and 3 printer emulation, to Macs running on AppleTalk networks. However, IBM's major direction in distributed computing and networking revolves around a strategy called SAA (Systems Application Architecture), which includes an interface defined for peer-to-peer communications, called APPC (Advanced Program-to-Program Communications). APPC runs on the LU6.2 protocol (see Figure 24-10). You

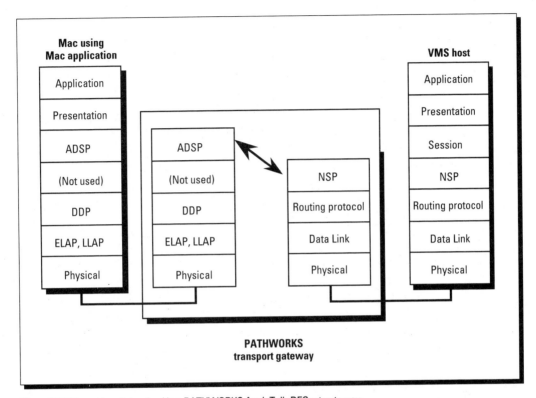

Figure 24-9: The protocols involved in a PATHWORKS AppleTalk-DECnet gateway.

can expect many of IBM's future network services to concentrate on APPC and LU6.2. Apple's new gateway, SNA*ps, provides both SNA and SAA/APPC connectivity in the same product and runs on a Macintosh.

Using other LAN Protocols

Until now, we've concentrated on the large system protocols: DECnet, TCP/IP, and SNA. But, as mentioned at the beginning of this chapter, there's a whole series of LAN protocols that should be considered when integrating Macs into heterogeneous (multiprotocol) networks. These network operating systems include LAN Manager, NetWare, 3+, and VINES (refer again to Figure 24-2).

One rarely sees protocols that are native to a non-AppleTalk network operating system running on a Mac. The original version of 3Com's 3+ ran some of the 3+ protocols on the Mac, but when 3Com switched to 3+Open (which has since reverted to Microsoft as part of the Microsoft LAN Manager), the system

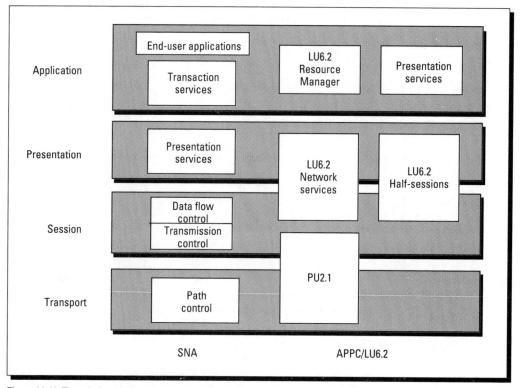

Figure 24-10: The relationships between LU6.2 (from the SAA suite) and SNA protocols.

was redesigned to support the AppleTalk stack on the Mac. One program that does provide non-AppleTalk LAN protocols on the Mac is the SoftNode module for the SoftPC DOS emulator package. This module handles normal IPX and SPX protocols through an Ethernet card and runs simultaneously with AppleTalk protocols on the same Mac.

The standard approach for supporting Macs on non-AppleTalk LAN systems is to incorporate the AppleTalk stack within the server. Thus, systems like NetWare (Novell) and LAN Manager (Microsoft, Digital) run multiple protocol stacks in parallel on the server, handling translations between the protocol stacks according to the client's needs (see Figure 24-11). This method allows the server to be the integrator for multiprotocol networks and lets each client computer run the protocol suite best suited for it. So a DOS computer would run NetWare's IPX/SPX protocols, but a Mac would continue to use AppleTalk.

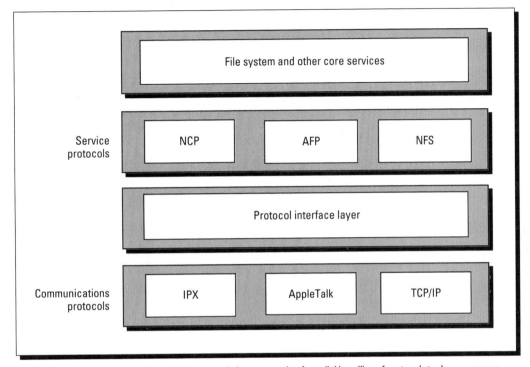

Figure 24-11: NetWare support for multiple protocols is an example of parallel handling of protocol stacks on a server.

Summary

We used this chapter to introduce you to the myriad protocols found in other, non-AppleTalk, network systems. In addition to running some of these protocols directly on your Mac, you can use either an encapsulating router or a gateway to link an AppleTalk network to many of these other networks.

In this chapter, you learned the following points:

- ✔ An encapsulating router doesn't change the contents of your AppleTalk packets.

- ✔ A gateway will most likely alter the contents of packets to conform to the other network system's requirements.

- ✔ Macs can run DECnet and TCP/IP (and some SNA) protocols either directly or via a gateway.

- ✔ MacIP encapsulates IP packets within AppleTalk DDP packets for transmission on LocalTalk networks.

- ✔ IPTalk encapsulates AppleTalk packets within TCP/IP UDP packets for transmission on TCP/IP networks.

- ✔ DEC's PATHWORKS gateway can convert between AppleTalk ADSP packets and DECnet NSP packets.

- ✔ NetWare systems allow access to more than one protocol stack.

In the next chapter, we discuss sharing printers and files with other platforms.

Chapter 25

Sharing Printers and Files with Other Platforms

In this chapter . . .

✔ Which print and file servers on other computer platforms support Macs

✔ Why AFP is a common denominator to many file servers

✔ How to use NFS for file sharing

✔ How to share printers with DOS, Unix, and IBM 3270 users

We discussed print services and file sharing for AppleTalk networks separately in Chapters 19 and 20. But as we deal with other protocols and other types of computers, we'll discuss print and file services together. These subjects are best treated together because the products available for installation on other computers usually include both print and file services in one package.

A number of products that run on other computing platforms provide print and file services for Macs. Table 25-1 lists these by product, vendor, and platform. We've subdivided the products into two categories, those based on microcomputers and those installed on larger computers, such as minicomputers and mainframes.

Table 25-1: Servers Running on Non-Mac Computers

Product	Vendor	Platform
Microcomputer-based		
3+	3Com	Intel 80x86
LAN Manager	Microsoft	OS/2
MACLAN Connect	Miramar Systems	Intel 80x86
NetWare	Novell	Intel 80x86
StarGroup Server	AT&T	Unix

Table 25-1 (continued)

Product	Vendor	Platform
TOPS	Sitka	DOS, Unix computers
VINES	Banyan	DOS, OS/2, Unix
Large system-based		
AlisaTalk		
AlisaPrint		
AlisaShare	Alisa Systems	VAX/VMS, Unix
Columbia		
AppleTalk		
Package	Columbia Univ.*	Unix
EtherShare	Helios USA	Unix
K-AShare, K-Spool	XINET	Unix
MacRAF**	Datability	VAX/VMS
PacerShare		
PacerPrint	Pacer Software	VAX/VMS, Unix
PATHWORKS	Digital Equip. Corp.	VAX/VMS
Sun-Partner	Info. Present. Techn.	Unix
uShare	Info. Present. Techn.	Unix

Notes:
  *Columbia AppleTalk Package (CAP) is freely distributed via the Internet.
**MacRAF is a disk server, not a file server.

Sharing Files and Printers on Microcomputer-Based Systems

In this section, we'll tell you about systems that use microcomputers, namely, NetWare, LAN Manager, TOPS, VINES, and 3+. We'll give you an overview of how users can print and share files when they're working on a multiprotocol, multiplatform local area network. Because the focus is on microcomputers, we'll cover combined Mac-PC networks. In the next section, we'll get to the systems that use large network protocols, such as TCP/IP, DECnet, and SNA.

The ideal network operating system supports all microcomputer clients and allows the exchange of files in both directions, from Macs to DOS computers, as well as from DOS computers to Macs. Although this is the general intent of most systems, you'll see that they don't always meet this goal.

Novell NetWare

Two versions of Novell NetWare are currently available: NetWare 2.x and NetWare 3.x. The earlier system architecture, 2.x, was originally written to support 80286-based servers; the newer architecture, 3.x, was written to take advantage of the architecture of 80386-based computers and subsequent systems, such as the 80486. Both versions of NetWare support Mac and DOS clients, and both are reasonable server systems for combined networks of Macs and PCs.

If you're looking for a server and considering NetWare, you should be aware that most of Novell's development efforts are focused on the 3.x line. Only with version 3.x, for example, can Mac clients make use of additional Novell products, such as SAA services and remote access. NetWare 2.x is an adequate server system for small- to medium-size workgroups, where only file sharing and printing are important to Mac and DOS users. If you need, or will later require, the services available in NetWare's add-on products, and if you want both Mac and DOS clients to use those services, you should concentrate on NetWare 3.x.

Both versions of NetWare support the AppleTalk Filing Protocol (AFP) for Mac access to files stored on the server. This means that NetWare can handle the longer Mac file names (and related conventions) and will translate Mac file names to standard DOS file names when a DOS user accesses the files (see Chapter 20).

As usual, when you're working in a multiplatform environment, you should exercise some care in naming the files that you, as a Mac user, intend to share with DOS or other users, as you will have much more flexibility than your co-workers. That flexibility in file naming, when translated by the AFP process, can lead to unnecessary confusion among non-Mac users if you don't name your files suitably.

The two versions of NetWare offer slightly different capabilities for printing. Both versions let the system administrator set up print queues for the printers on the server; both Mac and DOS users can then send print jobs to those queues, just as with any networked printer. With NetWare 2.x, however, print queues can be established only for printers that are directly connected to the print server. This means that serial and parallel printers are supported, but if you want to use a LaserWriter as a spooled printer, you must install a LocalTalk board in the NetWare server and attach the LaserWriter to the server via that interface board.

NetWare 3.x offers both Mac and DOS users more flexibility in accessing printers, as well as in controlling their queued print jobs. First, you can use NetWare 3.x to set up print queues for LaserWriters located anywhere on accessible AppleTalk networks, rather than for only those directly connected to the server. Second, Mac users can now view their print queues and change the status of waiting jobs, either deleting or holding jobs in the queue; this capability was previously limited to DOS users. Third, system administrators can choose to hide AppleTalk-based printers from users and can assign print queues on a zone-by-zone basis or by type of user, according to Mac, DOS, or OS/2 usage.

If you're concerned about which version of NetWare to install for supporting a mixed network of DOS and Mac computers, you should consider what expansions you may be planning for your network. Novell has stopped all development on NetWare 2.2 (the last version of 2.x) and is adding new features only to NetWare 3.x. NetWare 2.2 is less expensive than 3.x and can be used to create a reasonably performing server for Mac and DOS computers, especially for workgroups of 10 to 20 users. If your workgroup is larger than that, or if you'd like to take advantage of other NetWare options, such as SNA or TCP/IP connectivity, you'll have to install NetWare 3.x.

Microsoft LAN Manager

Microsoft LAN Manager's support for Mac clients became available only at the close of 1991, much more recently than NetWare's support. From the user's point of view, the features offered by LAN Manager for Mac users parallel those offered by NetWare.

LAN Manager also uses the AppleTalk Filing Protocol to handle files shared between Mac and DOS users, and it has the same naming restrictions that NetWare has. Also, as with NetWare 3.x, LAN Manager allows Mac users to print either to printers that are directly attached to the server or to AppleTalk printers on the network. In both cases, the LAN Manager server can maintain queues for the printers, and the Mac user can direct print jobs to those queues.

A product related to LAN Manager is the StarGroup Server (AT&T). This product offers file and print services for Mac as well as DOS clients. StarGroup Server uses a version of LAN Manager written for the Unix operating system and is designed to run on certain Unix computers.

Banyan VINES

Like LAN Manager, Banyan VINES only recently began to offer direct support for Mac clients within its operating system. The basic services offered by a VINES server are print and file services, just as with NetWare and LAN Manager. And again, as with the other two products, a VINES server uses the AppleTalk Filing Protocol to provide Mac access to files and can also maintain queues for printers.

3Com 3+

3Com's 3+ network operating system is an older system, originally scheduled to be replaced by 3+Open, 3Com's implementation of LAN Manager. But this system has since been frozen in time, as 3Com redefined its role in the network market. We don't expect to see new versions of 3+, and 3+Open has reverted to Microsoft under 3Com's LAN Manager licensing agreement.

Although 3+ does not directly implement AFP, this system does support Mac clients and provide AppleShare-compatible features, such as file-locking. A unique feature of 3+ is its use of a naming service to define user names, domains, and organizations. The two naming features, domains and organizations, can make it easier to organize groups of servers and printers and to restrict access to them as needed. Because of the added features of the naming service, 3+ uses its own Chooser document (an rdev in Mac terminology) to control access to file and print servers.

Sitka TOPS

One other network operating system supports both Mac and DOS clients, and that is TOPS (Sitka Corp.). TOPS is different from the other systems we've mentioned so far, in that it's the only peer-to-peer server system that supports both Mac and DOS clients. What this means is that for file-sharing, a computer can be both a file server in itself and a client of another file server at the same time.

TOPS operates as a presentation-layer protocol, just as AFP does, intercepting file calls from an application and redirecting them to the correct system as required. In order to work across platforms, TOPS has its own language for describing file access and related operations. This language is the same for all platforms; for TOPS to work with a particular operating system, software must be written to translate that system's file calls into the TOPS language.

Because TOPS is a peer-to-peer, or distributed, network operating system, you do not need a centralized server as a file or print server. Instead, the TOPS package includes a print spooler for your Mac and some print utilities for sharing printers among DOS computers.

TOPS Netprint allows DOS users to print to networked printers, such as a LaserWriter, directly from within an application. For the DOS user to print to a LaserWriter on an AppleTalk network, the DOS computer must have an appropriate interface board (LocalTalk or Ethernet) along with the TOPS software. TPRINT is a utility that allows some access to network printers from the DOS prompt; a DOS user can make a locally attached printer available to networked DOS users, who can direct TPRINT jobs to that printer. Unfortunately, Mac users cannot access that printer, there being no Mac version of TPRINT.

Servers Running on Other Systems

Although Novell NetWare is the most popular network operating system for microcomputer LANs, many corporations also have large minicomputers and mainframes that store corporate data and need other server software to share data with networked clients. Next, we'll take a look at the services that are available for Mac clients who access VAXes, Unix computers, and IBM mainframes.

VAX/VMS systems

A strong synergistic relationship has been built between Macintosh and VAX computers over the last few years. Early on, a great deal of Macintosh networking was driven by VAX users who wanted to link their Macs with their VAX computers running VMS. A number of products providing both print and file services have been the outgrowth of that synergy, with even DEC now offering its PATHWORKS product.

Most systems currently available for use on a VAX computer running the VMS operating system provide file services as well as print services (for VAXes running Ultrix, see our description of Unix systems). These are the products from Alisa Systems, Pacer Software, and Digital Equipment Corp. (Some products, such as the one from Digital, include additional items, such as e-mail and X-Windows support; Alisa and Pacer offer similar added products, but they must be purchased separately.) Another product, MacRAF from Datability Systems, is a disk server that allows users to share a virtual disk (a specially segregated section of a VAX's disk) among networked users.

All the file-server products that we've mentioned support the AppleTalk Filing Protocol, so standard AppleShare access privileges are maintained and filename translations are provided. Each product maps the AppleShare privileges to the requisite user privileges of a VMS user, although each product doesn't do it in the same way. Facilities are usually included for the automatic translation of text-file types and mapping of file extensions to icons. (VMS has more types of text files than the Mac; the differences usually relate to the line length and line termination — that is, carriage-return and line-feed combinations.) The latter feature of extension mapping enables users to define icons (displayed on the Mac desktop), which will be assigned to particular VMS files according to the three-letter extension of those files.

The VAX-based products provide print services in much the same way as the microcomputer-based systems discussed previously. The products spool jobs for laser printers on the server computer. The print queues can be directed either to laser printers directly attached to the server via a serial connection or to those connected to an accessible LocalTalk network. Because the print spooling and queue management are VAX processes, accounting records can be generated for later chargeback to users.

Unix systems

The functions provided by Unix-based server products are the same as those described for the VAX/VMS-based servers: A computer running Unix can spool print jobs and maintain print queues, as well as provide AppleShare-compatible file sharing for Mac clients. But, in this case, the products are written to run on a particular brand of the Unix operating system, rather than VMS.

As with the VAX/VMS-based products, the Unix-based servers implement the AppleTalk Filing Protocol to control Mac access to files and provide translation facilities for stored files so that both Mac and Unix users can use the same files — at least text files and other files compatible with applications running on both platforms. Unix-based print services include handling queues for both serially attached printers and laser printers attached via AppleTalk networks.

IBM mainframe-based systems

At the time of this publication, no products were available for IBM mainframe or midrange computers that provided file services to Mac clients. If you want to use files stored on an IBM computer, you have to transfer the files from the IBM to your Mac using one of the standard file-transfer procedures found in 3270 and 5250 terminal emulation software (see Chapter 26). However, the lack of IBM-based file services for the Mac may change in the not-too-distant future, now that Apple and IBM have started to work together on some networking projects. It's likely that at least some of IBM's midrange computers (the AS/400 series) will offer file services using the AppleTalk protocol stack and particularly the AppleTalk Filing Protocol before long.

File Sharing across Platforms

If you want to share files among different operating systems, there's more than one protocol that you can use to handle file formats. So far, we've concentrated on identifying platforms that act as AFP servers. Now we'll look at how you can use AFP on non-Mac clients and how you can use NFS, a popular Unix-based file-sharing protocol, on your Mac.

The AFP: The least common denominator

You probably noticed that most of the file server products we described in this chapter use the AppleTalk Filing Protocol (AFP) to provide Mac access to files. In a heterogeneous network with a number of different server platforms, this use of AFP enables you to have a common interface to all file servers, regardless of the machine they're running on. In fact, you don't have to use a Mac to benefit from this common interface because any DOS client running PhoneNET Talk (formerly known as PC AppleShare from Apple Computer) can also access all the AFP-based file servers with a similar standardized interface.

File sharing with NFS

We've said much about using the AppleTalk Filing Protocol, Apple's standard for file sharing. Another popular protocol has been implemented for file sharing: NFS, or Network File System. NFS was originally developed by Sun Computer and has since become available on a number of computers. NFS runs on Unix computers, as well as computers running non-Unix operating systems. Aside from its implementation on a large number of platforms, the key advantage of NFS is that it hides the differences between local and remote files, much like the AppleShare interface used by AFP.

Mac users can access NFS servers in three ways: They can install PathWay Client NFS (Wollongong Group) or NFS/Share (Intercon Systems) software on their Mac, or they can use GatorShare software (Cayman Systems) installed on a GatorBox router.

If you plan to provide NFS access to your Mac users on a LocalTalk network for light to medium usage (up to five or six users), GatorShare is a sensible solution, especially if you're already using a GatorBox as router. GatorShare takes care of mapping NFS rights to AppleShare and presents mounted NFS volumes as AppleShare volumes to the Mac users, making it simpler for them to deal with these foreign volumes.

On the other hand, if you're looking for heavy-duty access to NFS servers, you're better off selecting the PathWay Client NFS or NFS/Share software for direct installation on each client Mac. NFS/Share presents a more familiar interface to Mac users because it uses a Chooser device to present the NFS servers, whereas PathWay Client NFS uses a control panel.

Regardless of which NFS client software you install, you should be aware of the different methods your NFS server may use for user authentication. The three common mechanisms are **pcnfsd**, NIS (formerly called Yellow Pages), and direct user/group lookup. GatorShare uses any of the three, but NFS/Share automatically uses the first two, and PathWay Client NFS can use only the first method. However, as new versions of these products become available, this may change. In any case, in order to configure your NFS client properly, you may need to check into whether your NFS server is using **pcnfsd** for user authentication or another program that's a superset of it, such as **bwnfsd**.

Other file-sharing considerations

Macintosh files have two *forks* (or parts): the data fork and the resource fork. Thus, your Mac files can't be stored "as is" on foreign file systems, which have only one part for each file. Apple has defined two standard file formats to handle this problem: AppleSingle and AppleDouble. As the names imply, AppleSingle is a format for storing both the data and resource forks within one file, and AppleDouble is a format for storing each fork in its own separate file. Many file servers support the AppleDouble method for storing Mac files, which allows you to share files with non-Mac users. With this method, other users simply access the data fork of a Mac file stored in the AppleDouble format.

Even if you use the AppleDouble format to resolve file-exchange or file-sharing problems, there's still the Pandora's box of file translations between applications running on different platforms. For some applications, such as Aldus PageMaker, Microsoft Word, and Lotus 1-2-3, the vendors built in options for reading files from the program running on another platform (in this case, Macs and DOS computers). But many programs either do not store files in these ad hoc standard formats or cannot read these formats. This lack of standardization is likely to haunt users on multiplatform networks for some time to come. Translation tools for the Mac, such as MacLink Plus (DataViz) and Software Bridge (Argosy Software), and embedded technology like XTND (Apple) can make it easier for Mac users to translate between a variety of file formats. But none of these tools will provide the final solution for easy information exchange between platforms.

One last suggestion here — if you know you'll be sharing files with non-Mac users, keep them in mind when you're naming the shared files. Table 25-2 shows some of the naming conventions for files (see Chapter 24 about file-name translation for AFP-based servers). And don't forget that some programs, particularly those on DOS computers, often will not recognize a legitimate file unless it has the proper three-letter extension (such as WKS for Lotus 1-2-3).

Table 25-2: File-Naming Conventions for DOS, Unix, and Macintosh

DOS	Up to 8 characters, optional 3-character extension
	No blank spaces; can't use " / \ [ ] :	< > + = ; , *?
Unix	Up to 256 characters
	Blank spaces acceptable; cannot use /
	Avoid $ ' * ? ! # { } [ ] " ( )
Mac	Up to 31 characters
	Blank spaces acceptable
	Cannot use colon

Sharing Printers across Platforms

When it comes to sharing printers on a network that has more than one type of computer, you can take one of two approaches. First, you can set up your printers on the network so that both types of computers can access the printer with equal facility; this setup usually requires a print server that all users can access. Second, you can make the printer attached to your Mac available to other users, even if they're not using Macs. We'll address sharing printers in the following sections according to whether you are working with DOS, Unix, or IBM users.

Sharing printers with DOS users

We've already described a number of products that allow non-Mac clients to access AppleTalk printers. These products have one feature in common: All use a printer queue on a server to intercept printer requests and route them to the appropriate AppleTalk printer. But there are ways for DOS users to access an AppleTalk printer without a centralized server on the network. To accomplish this task, you'll need appropriate software and a proper network connection.

If you're working without a print server, you can usually use software on DOS-based computers to print to the printer. Many of the newer DOS and Windows applications can generate PostScript output that can be directed to a laser printer. For hardware, you usually have to install a LocalTalk interface board in the PC or use an Ethernet or token ring board with an AppleTalk driver, such as the one provided by PhoneNet Talk (Farallon). This will enable you to access LaserWriters on LocalTalk networks. Obviously, if your DOS computers are on Ethernet or token ring networks and the LaserWriters are on LocalTalk networks, you'll need a router to attach the two networks.

Sharing printers with Unix users

Unix users often use the lpr command for printing. These users can also access LaserWriters on LocalTalk if you install special software on the AppleTalk network to mediate between the lpr jobs and the LaserWriters. There are two ways to do this. First, Pathway Client NFS (Wollongong Group) includes an lpr server that runs in the background on the Mac, enabling Unix users to send lpr print jobs to any LaserWriter that they can access from their Macs. Second, you can install similar software (GatorPrint CS) on the GatorBox CS router (Cayman Systems). With this software, the translation of lpr arguments to PAP commands for the AppleTalk printers is done within the GatorBox CS, rather than on the Mac.

Sharing printers with IBM 3270 users

Users of SNA networks can also access LaserWriters on AppleTalk networks. Much like the lpr server approach for Unix users, products like MacMainFrame (Avatar) and MacIRMA (Digital Communications Associates) allow your Mac to designate an AppleTalk printer to support IBM 3287 printer sessions. The Mac running the MacMainFrame or MacIRMA software then accepts the 3287 sessions and redirects the output to the designated printer. Although you won't want to set up one of your LaserWriters as a high-volume printer for SNA sessions, you may want to use this option with a local LaserWriter so that you or your workgroup can redirect occasional SNA print jobs to a conveniently located printer.

Summary

In this chapter, we gave you an overview of the many file and print servers that run on non-Mac computers but support Mac access. Many of these servers use the AppleTalk Filing Protocol for Mac file services.

The following points were covered:

- ✔ All of the popular server platforms, NetWare, VINES, and LAN Manager, support file and printer access for Macs.

- ✔ Computers running either VMS or Unix can also serve as file and print servers for Macs using AFP.

- ✔ Macs can also become NFS clients for file sharing with NFS servers.

- ✔ The Mac file-naming conventions are much more flexible than those found in most other operating systems, and some care should be exercised when naming files to be exchanged with users on other operating systems.

- ✔ In addition to Mac users accessing other print servers, DOS and Unix users can access printers attached to Macs.

In the next chapter, we'll pick up the thread by showing how to run applications on other platforms.

Chapter 26

Running Applications on Other Platforms

Using the resources attached to other types of computers on a network isn't limited to exchanging files or using shared printers. If you're working in a large corporation, you'll probably find that important databases and applications are located on other minicomputers and mainframe computers. In this chapter, we'll examine some of the ways that your network can use applications and databases located on other computers.

While looking over the available options for running applications on other platforms, we'll start with the simplest method, that of emulating a terminal on your Mac. Then we'll move on to some of the newer techniques, such as client-server setups for X Windows and other applications on your Mac. Finally, we'll discuss the use of distributed processing to share tasks over the network.

With the most basic method, *terminal emulation,* your Mac, as a terminal client, sends your commands to another computer, just as a normal terminal would. Most current emulation products enable you to take advantage of your Mac's intelligence for scripting control, file transfers, and cut-and-paste operations while acting as a terminal to the other system.

The second method involves *client-server systems.* These systems allow you greater flexibility when using your Mac because they make use of the processing power on both your Mac and the host computer. Client-server systems also make it easier to support multiple platforms because the same server system can support different clients; all you need to do is buy the proper client software. Systems like X Windows and certain e-mail programs use client-server architectures.

The third method is *distributed processing,* which is a step beyond the client-server relationship. Distributed processing means just what the term suggests: An application and its data are distributed to run different parts of a program on the various networked computers. Rather than having one program on the server in control, and another program as the client accepting commands and data from the server, as in client-server systems, distributed processing treats each computer as a peer to the other computers. For example, with a distributed system, you might use a Mac to generate an image containing polygons, circles, and other graphic objects. But then a more powerful computer, such as a Cray supercomputer or Silicon Graphics workstation, performs the ray-tracing calculations for the scene you constructed and returns a fully shaded, colored image.

Understanding Terminal Emulation

The first terminal emulators were found on computers running independently of a LAN, connected to the host computer through an asynchronous RS-232 cable or a coaxial cable. But emulators and networks have evolved to the point where terminal emulators are now routinely run over a LAN. Our focus in this chapter is the use of terminal emulators over LANs rather than non-networked usage. We'll introduce you to the types of terminal emulation software and how to connect a Mac to other networks to run such software.

A definition of terminal emulation

As we said previously, terminal emulation is probably the simplest way to connect a personal computer to a computer that is using another operating system. Terminal emulation is a straightforward process — the terminal emulation program on your Mac converts your typed characters and mouse movements into characters and commands that the other computer's operating system can understand. When the other computer, commonly called a *host,* responds by sending commands and characters, these are converted into actions that the Mac can understand.

Prior to the availability of personal computers, the only way for users to interact with minicomputers and mainframes was to use a terminal that had little, if any, intelligence of its own. This terminal transmitted keyboard characters to the host for further processing. Now, personal computers run terminal emulation programs to do the same tasks formerly performed with dumb terminals. (The term *dumb terminals* arose to describe terminals having little computing intelligence built into them, doing little more than sending and receiving characters at the command of the user or the host computer.)

Running a terminal emulator on a personal computer (PC) brought the advantage of also being able to capture data from the host as it scrolled across the PC's

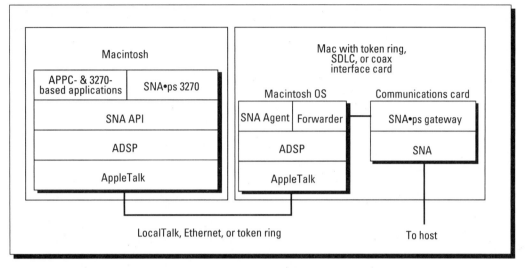

Figure 26-1: An example of an SNA-AppleTalk gateway.

screen for later manipulation on the PC. Eventually, even file transfers were made easier, as terminal emulators included file-transfer protocols for automatically transferring and translating files between the host and the PC.

Before we delve into software that you can use for terminal emulation with other computers, we'll look at how you can connect your Macs on one LAN to the host computers running on another network.

The physical network connection

Two approaches can be taken to physically connect a Mac using a terminal emulator to the host computer: The Mac can be directly attached to the same LAN as the host, or a gateway can link the Mac's network to the host computer's network.

A direct LAN connection is possible for all the network types discussed in this chapter, whether SNA, DECnet, or TCP/IP. For SNA networks, the choice is limited to a token ring LAN, using any of the many token ring interface cards available for Macs. (Individual, non-networked connections can also use cards with an SDLC or coax interface.) Both DECnet and TCP/IP LAN connections use Ethernet interface cards.

You'll maintain a more flexible network, however, if you install a transport-level gateway between AppleTalk and the host's networking system. Transport-level gateways are designed to use the AppleTalk LAN connections to the workstations and a regular connection to the host (see Figure 26-1).

One advantage to using a gateway is the consolidation of wiring required for communications. Instead of using one cable (twisted-pair, for example) for your LAN, and another cable (probably coaxial) for connection to the mainframe, you can use the same wiring for your LAN and the connections to the gateway. You'll have to run only one coax (or token ring or other type) connection to the front-end processor that's connected to the host computer. This capability can be particularly appealing when most of your users run sessions infrequently and don't require a dedicated connection to the host all day. A second advantage is that the gateway can perform some of the session-related processing that used to be done by the host computer, reducing demands on the host and enabling it to either handle more users or spend more time executing programs, or both.

The main disadvantage of a gateway is its limited processing capability. If you do have a number of heavy users of the host, chances are good that the gateway won't handle all those users' communications needs. For heavy usage, you'll probably do better with a dedicated connection for each of your power users.

Gateways can be divided into four major categories according to their hardware, as shown in Table 26-1.

Table 26-1: Gateways Between Macs and Other Network Systems

	SNA	DECnet	TCP/IP
Mac-based	MacMainFrame series	TSSGate	MultiGate Mac
	SNA•ps		
DOS-based	IRMA series		
	NetWare SAA Services		
Standalone	Netway	MultiPort Gateway	MultiPort Gateway
	FastPath	FastPath	
	GatorBox	GatorBox	
	EtherRouter/TCP		
	ComTalk		
	other routers		
Other platforms	VINES SAA Services	PATHWORKS	

All of the SNA gateways support the standard physical links to IBM networks: token ring, SDLC, and coaxial cable. Any of the standard AppleTalk media can be used to link to the gateway: LocalTalk, EtherTalk, and TokenTalk. At this time, the MacMainFrame and SNA•ps gateways support only Mac clients on AppleTalk, while the other gateways support either Mac or DOS clients.

Both the DECnet and TCP/IP gateways support Ethernet media on the foreign (non-AppleTalk) protocol side and any of the AppleTalk media on the other side. All these gateways are meant only to support Mac clients, mainly because DOS-based terminal emulators have not been written to run over AppleTalk.

Partly because SNA networks handle terminal sessions differently than do DECnet and TCP/IP networks, the AppleTalk-SNA gateways are sold on a per-session basis, starting with the relatively small number of 5 sessions and working up to a maximum of 128 sessions. AppleTalk-DECnet and AppleTalk-TCP/IP gateways are sold on a per-gateway device basis, where one computer is licensed to be the gateway, regardless of the number of sessions that will use the gateway. The hardware gateways are handled in the same way.

We'll now leave the world of hardware and move on to the software that you can use to emulate terminals on a network.

Terminal emulation software for networks

Although there are many ways to connect a Mac running a terminal emulator to a host — coaxial cable to an IBM mainframe or an asynchronous RS-232 cable to a Unix minicomputer, for instance — we'll concentrate on how you can use terminal emulators on a Mac over a network. Terminal emulation over a network can be classified into three main types of systems: SNA/SAA systems, DECnet systems, and TCP/IP systems. We'll look at each of these systems in turn.

SNA/SAA networks

Macs are capable of emulating either IBM 3270-style terminals or 5250-style terminals. The first style of terminal is predominantly used to communicate with IBM mainframes, whereas the second style is limited to communicating with IBM's minicomputers, the AS/400 series.

IBM 3270 terminal emulation products for the Mac can support either CUT-style (control unit terminal) or DFT-style (distributed function terminal) emulation. The evolution of 3270 terminal emulation for the Macintosh from CUT to DFT support offers the user more flexibility in operations, allowing multiple sessions per terminal and background printing, for instance. DFT terminal emulation also reduces the demand on the mainframe's resources for a user's sessions by requiring less computation and control by the mainframe.

Each DFT session is contained within its own resizable window with automatic font scaling, making it easy to zoom in on an active session and reduce other background sessions to smaller windows. Other features, such as host-addressable 3287 printer support on a networked printer, clipboard-based copy-and-paste to other applications, and graphical representations of the 3270 function keys in a floating window, are now standard items in all of the emulators.

Although the Macintosh has been a graphically oriented computer from day one, the 3270 terminal emulators did not initially support mainframe graphics. Now both Avatar and DCA offer graphics capabilities in their emulators, although each company takes a different approach. In the case of DCA, the MacIRMA product supports APA (all points addressable) graphics via IBM's PC Link (PCLK), which requires some graphics processing on the host. On the other hand, Avatar's MacMainFrame Graphics module supports APA directly, allowing graphics processing to occur locally on the Mac. The latter approach enables users to have up to five graphics sessions (atop DFT), whereas PCLK supports only one session at a time; direct APA support also reduces the load on host resources. Apple's 3270 emulator, formerly called MacDFT and now known as SNA•ps 3270, does not include graphics support.

Apple's SNA•ps 3270 can use either Apple's token ring card to provide 3270 terminal emulation, or it can be used over an AppleTalk network in conjunction with the SNA•ps gateway. Avatar has also designed its MacMainFrame software to be compatible with either token ring or gateway links for connecting to SNA networks. Avatar's software can now be used with other manufacturers' cards, such as Asante's MacToken token ring card for the Mac SE.

SimMac (Simware) includes 3270 CUT terminal emulation, along with on-screen buttons on the Mac that can be used to trigger user-defined scripts. Part of the program's appeal stems from the commonality of scripts between PC and Mac workstations, making it easier for managers to use the same software to maintain scripts for remote users, regardless of the computer used. SimMac can also be used with other manufacturers' boards, notably the Apple, Avatar, and DCA coax boards, as well as the Netway (now Avatar) gateways.

The most common IBM terminal type is probably the 3270-style terminal. However, many users of IBM's midrange computers, the older System/3X series and the newer AS/400 series, use the 5250-style terminal. Most of the products available for the Mac to emulate a 5250-style terminal are designed for point-to-point connections between the Mac and the host computer, not for networked use.

However, TwinAxcess ApLINK (Andrew/KMW) enables Macs on a LocalTalk network to share an interface board in a Mac II for connecting to an IBM midrange computer using 5250 terminal emulation. TwinAxcess ApLINK can be used with either Andrew/KMW's own twinax board or the Apple Coax/Twinax Board and should work with Apple's new SNA•ps gateway by the time of this publication.

DECnet networks

As with IBM mainframes, a common form of terminal communications is for the Mac to emulate one of the vendor's primary terminal types. Digital Equipment

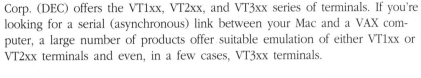

Corp. (DEC) offers the VT1xx, VT2xx, and VT3xx series of terminals. If you're looking for a serial (asynchronous) link between your Mac and a VAX computer, a large number of products offer suitable emulation of either VT1xx or VT2xx terminals and even, in a few cases, VT3xx terminals.

When you're working on a network but require terminal services, you'll probably want to take advantage of virtual terminal services over the network. What this means is that an agreed-upon format (a protocol) is available so that the computer can transmit the characteristics of a true terminal (clearing a screen, scrolling, character deletion, for example) to the host computer over a network connection. The main advantage is to provide you, the user, with a way to run applications requiring terminal input or control from your Mac while your Mac is a part of the network, without requiring a separate asynchronous connection.

One way of doing this in the DECnet environment is with the CTERM protocol. CTERM, however, is a character-based protocol (that is, it stuffs only one character from the terminal display into a packet for transmission on the network) and thus isn't optimal for LAN use.

A better transport architecture for terminal-based sessions on DECnet networks is Local Area Transport, or LAT. The LAT architecture *multiplexes,* or combines, user data headed for the same destination into a single packet. It also reduces the terminal services management function of the host computer. Bear in mind, though, that LAT is a nonroutable protocol, as it bypasses the network and data link layers.

Some terminal emulators, such as Mac241 (White Pine), PacerTerm (Pacer Software), and VersaTerm PRO (Synergy Software), can use either CTERM- or LAT-based communications on a network. LAT can be more easily used with certain terminal emulators because a LAT driver is now available from DEC as part of the PATHWORKS package. The LAT driver works with Apple's Communications ToolBox, which is available for System 6.0.x and is an integral part of System 7.0 (see Figure 26-2); emulators written to use the Communications ToolBox can then use the LAT driver for terminal sessions over Ethernet.

TCP/IP networks

Terminal services for TCP/IP-based hosts follow the same approach as for DECnet, using a virtual terminal mechanism. In the TCP/IP protocol suite, the protocol defined for this task is called TELNET. Products for the Mac include support for both TELNET and FTP, the TCP/IP file-transfer protocol, in the same package. Many of these products use MacTCP to provide the basic TCP/IP services (see Chapter 24), but some also include a version with their own proprietary TCP implementation for the Mac, usually to provide some features that MacTCP currently lacks, such as SLIP (Serial Line IP) support.

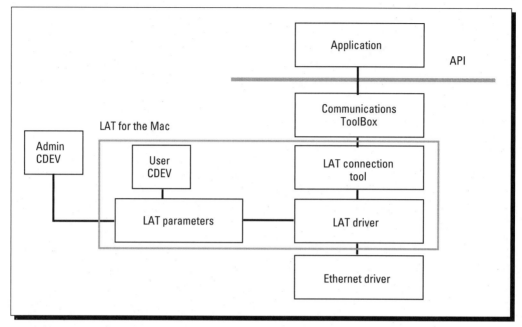

Figure 26-2: The relationship between the LAT driver on the Mac and the Communications ToolBox.

The majority of TCP/IP hosts are Unix computers. However, TCP/IP can also be used to access IBM mainframes, using what is known as the TN3270 emulation mode within TELNET. For instance, Intercon Systems' TCP/Connect II terminal emulator includes a TN3270 option, which handles 3270-style terminal emulation over TCP/IP networks. Similar options are available from the Brown University version of NCSA TELNET.

Before we leave the world of terminal emulation, we should mention that it's not uncommon to use a device known as a *terminal server* to connect terminals or microcomputers running terminal emulation software to a network and the host. Much like the SNA gateways we discussed, the principle behind a terminal server is to provide a set number of sessions that are shared by the terminal's users. The data generated by these sessions is often combined into packets for transmission on the LAN to make communication more efficient — LAT is an example of a protocol designed to do this.

In the TCP/IP world, software is available that allows your Mac to act as a terminal server for TELNET sessions. This software, part of the VersaTerm-PRO package from Synergy Software, is called VersaTermServer and runs in the background on your Mac. The Mac running VersaTermServer will have an Ethernet card installed for connection to the TCP/IP network, whereas other Macs running VersaTerm-PRO as a TELNET emulator can be on a LocalTalk network. Using VersaTermServer, you can allocate up to 24 ports for TELNET sessions, and the users on the LocalTalk network can then access a TCP/IP-based host on the Ethernet network.

The majority of terminal emulators mimic what you'd expect to see if you were using a dumb terminal, namely a character-based interface with the prompts and menus found on the host's operating system. This can be inefficient and confusing for users who only occasionally use the host or may not be familiar with the host's commands. In such cases, it's preferable to mask the operating system's commands by changing the interface on the Mac for displays that are easier to understand. This procedure, called *front-ending,* will be discussed next.

Front-ends for terminal sessions

Simplifying a user's access to the arcane world of another operating system can be of prime importance in setting up networks. Usually, two main benefits result from simplification: First, the users can be more productive by staying within their normal computing environment; and, second, support requirements can be reduced if all users are presented with the same interface. Although the focus of this section is largely on interfaces to IBM operating systems, some of the products can also be used with computers running either VMS or Unix.

You can provide a Mac-style interface to an IBM mainframe application in many ways. Apple, Avatar, and DCA provide a standard application programming interface (API) for developers to write programs that use their hardware. But, until a single API is offered for all the hardware (as intended by Apple's 3270 API, which has been endorsed by the other vendors), developers must write different code for each vendor's interface boards. Most of the APIs revolve around IBM's specifications for HLLAPI (High-Level Language Application Programming Interface). Apple's own 3270 API is an extension of HLLAPI, offering some features unique to the Macintosh; however, it should still be a straightforward matter to port a PC-based HLLAPI application to the Mac. To simplify the development process somewhat, each vendor's API includes support for Apple's HyperCard. This feature makes it easier to prototype interfaces and applications.

APIs aren't the only means of providing Mac interfaces to mainframe applications. Other tools that fill this need are MacWorkStation (United Data Corp., formerly available from Apple), Apple Terminal Services (ATS, formerly available from Apple), MitemView (Mitem), and BOTH (formerly called Masquerade 3270, Connectivite). These tools are more user-adaptable, making them easier for both system programmers and end users to work with.

With MacWorkStation (MWS), a host application that's been compiled with the appropriate MWS library will issue commands that relate to the user interface. Those commands are in turn received by the Mac, where a Mac application accepts them and converts them into the typical Mac interface elements of windows, menus, and dialog boxes. The host-application commands are still all character oriented, but the resulting display on the Mac uses the standard elements of the Mac interface. Because both computers share in the processing load — the host runs its application, and the Mac runs its application — and because the two applications communicate with each other, MacWorkStation is an example of a distributed-processing approach to connectivity.

In some cases, MIS departments hesitate to employ MacWorkStation because it requires recoding on the mainframe as well as on the workstation. But often the benefits outweigh the added work. PCs running Microsoft Windows can also execute MacWorkStation scripts by using ALAC (United Data Corp.), thereby extending the use of MacWorkStation beyond Macs.

Apple has also worked to expand the base for use of MacWorkStation. This is especially true for the client side with the introduction of ATS, or Apple Terminal Services. ALAC is an example of the application of ATS (and therefore MacWorkStation support) to a non-Mac client. X Windows support for ATS (from Integrated Solutions Inc.) makes it possible for X Windows servers to use mainframe code that supports MacWorkStation. A driver is now available to use ATS over TCP/IP networks as well. Thus, MacWorkstation can be used with IBM, VMS, or Unix operating systems. (As we went to press, Apple had just sold MacWorkStation and ATS to United Data Corp.)

MitemView makes maximum use of HyperCard as the development environment, using the vendors' APIs for controlling communications with the IBM. Mitem adds a series of XCMDs (external code modules) to a HyperCard stack to enable the developer to define character patterns from the mainframe that the stack will recognize and respond to. The patterns and responses can be stored in the HyperCard stack and then used to control various HyperCard displays that are shown to the user. Standard log-on procedures can be enabled by a button labeled **Log On** that brings up a dialog box asking for the user's account and password. In 1991, Mitem also added support for MacWorkStation and ATS, thereby extending its use to other (non-SNA) systems.

BOTH offers another approach to creating Mac applications that communicate with an IBM mainframe. With BOTH, the user controls the design process by relating IBM screens to Mac interface items, such as dialog boxes and icons. The first step is to have BOTH save all the IBM 3270 screens from a session. Then you can define the appropriate inputs to those screens, such as name and password for the log-on screen, and create dialog boxes for entering those inputs. BOTH

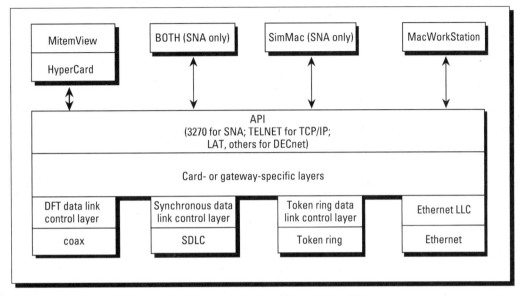

Figure 26-3: The relationship between the different front-ends and the underlying APIs.

even enables you to design special icons for functions or windows for entering such other data as a mail message, and then to combine those icons and windows in a stand-alone application.

When should you use these tools? MacWorkStation is probably the most powerful tool for creating a Mac interface to mainframe programs, but it requires writing code on both the Mac and the mainframe (see Figure 26-3). Many IBM shops are reluctant to modify all of their existing programs in order to support MacWorkstation. From this point of view, MitemView and BOTH are better solutions because no modifications need to be made on the main-frame side. The need for additional programmer support also decreases as you move from MacWorkStation to MitemView and on to BOTH.

Understanding Client-Server Systems

We mentioned client-server architecture in Chapter 21, where we discussed databases, and in Chapter 22, where we discussed electronic mail. Client-server systems offer two advantages to users and managers alike. First, with both the client and the server doing some of the processing, the amount of data that must be relayed between them over the network can be reduced (see Chapter 21 for an example). Second, the client and the server don't need to be the same types of computers running the same operating systems, which makes it easier to support the heterogeneous multiplatform networks so often found in corporations these days.

We'll look briefly at a few client-server systems involving the Mac. First, we'll look at the X Windows system, in which your Mac is actually the server (called the *display server*) rather than the client. This setup is the opposite of the way other client-server systems are set up. After that, we'll go over some of the multiplatform e-mail systems, and then we'll discuss a unique client-server system that lets Macs run DOS applications.

Macs and X Windows

In the last few years, the X Windows system has become quite popular, partly because so many types of computers, including the Mac, can act as X Windows servers. Because of this wide variety of available servers, developing an X Windows application for a given host computer (in the case of X Windows, an X Windows client) means that you can ensure a common user interface at different workstations. Large-scale developers, such as those working in corporations, are obviously looking for leverage to create useful applications that are easier to use than past ones, yet can also run on the variety of computers within their shops. X Windows provides such capabilities.

The client-server system of X Windows may seem a bit backwards when you try to define who's the client and who's the server. In client-server systems, a workstation such as your Mac is usually the client, and another, more powerful (or specialized), computer is the server. In X Windows, your workstation is actually the X Windows server. To help clarify this difference, we choose to call it the *display server* because the workstation draws a display according to the commands issued by the other computer — the X Windows client. Another way of looking at this relationship is to remember that the X Windows client runs the application that your workstation tells it to.

Note, however, that X Windows is not a panacea. For one thing, X Windows is a means of providing bitmapped graphical displays on a workstation, but it's not a graphical user interface (GUI) (see Figure 26-4). X Windows has only two basic components: The Xlib is a graphics subroutine library for your workstation, whereas the X Server portion is the system code designed for the server machine. XLib passes screen-display information from the host application to the X Server and passes user-input information from the X Server back to the host application. The X Server component interacts with the screen, keyboard, and mouse of the display server (your Mac) to create screen displays and translate your mouse and keyboard actions for the Xlib and the host application. If you're developing an X Windows application, you can either write code that uses the Xlib calls directly, or purchase one of the commercially available X tool kits, many of which provide some kind of GUI support. The tool kits make application design easier.

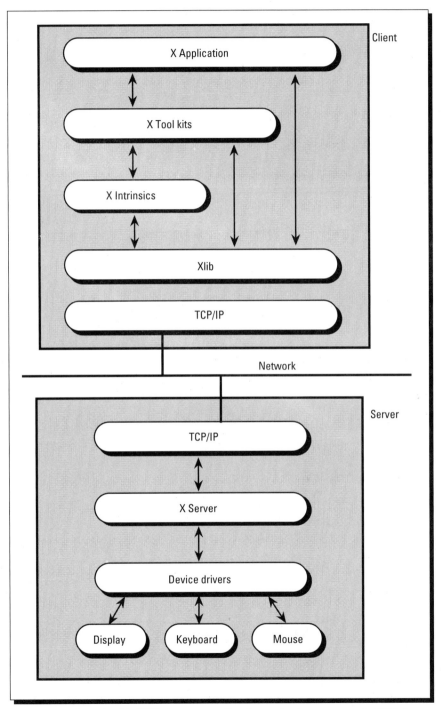

Figure 26-4: A schematic of the X Windows system. Note that applications are run on the X Windows client, and the results are displayed on the X Windows server.

If you've already selected an appropriate tool kit to create an X Windows client application and are using X Windows, you can use Macs as X Windows servers, either with Echo X (Alisa Systems), eXodus (White Pine Software), or MacX (Apple). All programs currently support TCP/IP, DECnet, and AppleTalk transport protocols, so you can use a transport-level gateway between your Mac on AppleTalk and hosts running on other network systems, such as Ethernet.

An interesting sidelight is that Macs can now also act as X Windows clients. This capability, something rather new for microcomputers, enables Mac users to display Mac application windows on non-Mac workstations and X terminals. The two products supporting Macs as X Windows clients are Planet X (Intercon Systems) and XGator (Cayman Systems).

Client-server e-mail

In Chapter 22, "Using Electronic Mail," we explained that the best LAN-based e-mail systems use a client-server architecture, which lets the Mac user compose and address mail, while the server takes care of storage and routing of mail. This same approach can be extended to multiplatform e-mail systems that use a computer other than the Mac to be the mail server.

Three e-mail systems that work this way are WordPerfect Office (WordPerfect Corp.) and Digital's two e-mail programs, VMSmail and ALL-IN-1 Mail. At the moment, WordPerfect Office lets you install your mail servers either on Macs or DOS computers; both Mac and DOS clients can use either type of server. Before long, WordPerfect Office servers will also be available for VMS systems and will support Mac and DOS clients from VMS servers as well.

Digital supports two types of mail systems in its PATHWORKS package for Macs. First, there's a simple VMSmail client that allows users to send and receive text-only messages using a VMS-based mail server. Then there's the ALL-IN-1 Mail client, which supports binary file enclosures, allowing users to send applications as well as other Mac files with a message. Properly formatted binary files, such as spreadsheets or documents created in a word processing program, can be exchanged between Mac and DOS users by means of ALL-IN-1 Mail. With both VMSmail and ALL-IN-1 Mail, Macs can either be directly connected to a DECnet network or they can be on an AppleTalk network and use a PATHWORKS AppleTalk-DECnet gateway.

DAL and client-server databases

In Chapter 21, "Using Networked Databases," we described Apple's Data Access Language, or DAL, which is a query language designed to work with many types of databases. The DAL system uses a client-server architecture (see Figure 26-5). Next, we'll review how DAL works.

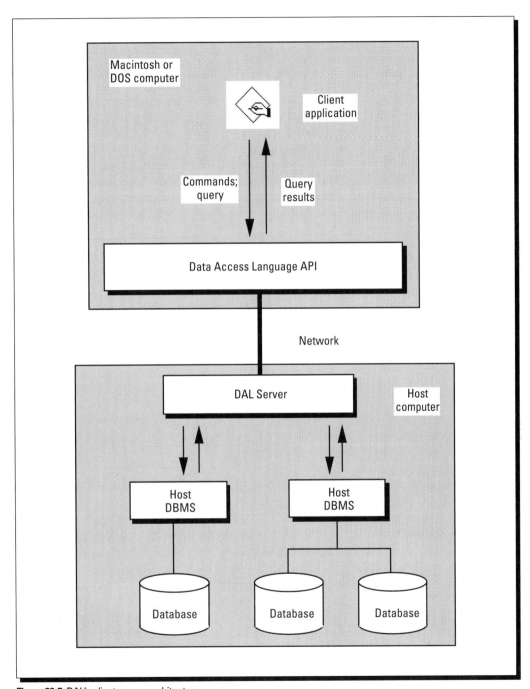

Figure 26-5: DAL's client-server architecture.

Mac, DOS, and Windows clients can construct queries requesting data from a database; then the DAL client software transmits the request over the network to the database server. The database server, which may be a minicomputer or a mainframe storing large corporate databases, also runs a DAL server, which takes care of translating the DAL commands into the command language of the particular vendor's database that's installed on the database server.

DAL was primarily designed to allow Macs to access data stored in databases located on other types of computers. Thus, Apple developed database servers for databases running on VAX computers using the VMS operating system, IBM mainframes using VM/CMS, MVS/TSO, or MVS/VTAM, and Macs running A/UX. Apple's VMS DAL Server supports the following databases: Informix, Ingres, Oracle, Rdb/SQL, and Sybase SQL Server. The MVS/VTAM DAL Server supports both IBM Database 2 (DB2) and Teradata DBC/1012 databases. The VM/CMS DAL Server supports SQL/DS databases, and the MVS/TSO DAL Server supports DB2.

Third-party vendors have also developed DAL servers. Pacer Software offers a DAL server for HP/UX, and SunOS on the Sun SparcStation; databases supported are Ingres, Oracle, Informix, and Sybase. Pacer also has plans for a DAL server for Ultrix and a DAL server for the IBM RS/6000 platform to be released sometime in 1992. Tandem Corp. has a DAL server for databases running on its Tandem computers, and Novell recently released the NetWare SQL 3.0 NLM (NetWare Loadable Module), which now includes DAL server support. The NetWare SQL NLM allows communications between DAL clients and applications built on Btrieve, Novell's record management software.

You see that DAL can be used as a common query language for a variety of host-based databases. Therein also lies the problem with DAL — DAL incorporates the query commands common to all of the databases and doesn't include database-specific commands. Thus, if you're looking to use some of the specific features that your database has, such as special query controls, DAL may not support them.

To get around the problem of database-specific command support, you can use any of the other available client-server database systems for the Mac. SequeLink (TechGnosis) is designed similarly to DAL, but the SequeLink servers are written specifically for each database they support, including all the database's special features. This approach gets you all the database features that you paid for, but it may cause problems on the client side, as you'll now need to know what kind of database you're querying. Other databases, notably Oracle, Ingres, and Sybase, each offer client software specifically for the Mac, but, in each case, the software is designed to communicate only with that particular vendor's database. Note, however, that Oracle and Sybase both offer host-based links that can connect their databases to other vendors' databases, making multivendor environments a bit easier to deal with.

Next, we'll take a look at a unique client-server system, the application server.

DOS application servers

An application server is somewhat similar to the X Windows system that we described in a previous section. An application server is composed of two programs. One program is installed in the DOS computer (the server) and intercepts all of the commands generated by the computer to create the screen display; the program then duplicates the screen display and relays it to the client program to create a copy of the screen display on the client. The second program resides in the client, receiving the screen-drawing commands from the server and drawing the appropriate display on the client. As you'd expect, the client program also accepts keystrokes and passes them to the server program, which feeds them back to the server's operating system as if they were generated locally.

What can you do with such a system? Well, thanks to a few programs that work over a network, you can use a Mac to control a DOS computer and run any of the DOS programs on that computer. The software sees to it that the screen displays are relayed to the Mac and displayed in a Mac window.

The two major programs that enable you to perform such feats of legerdemain are pcANYWHERE, coupled with PC MacTERM (Dynamic Microprocessor Associates, or DMA), and RunPC/Network (Argosy Software). The programs are related because both use pcANYWHERE as the server software on a DOS computer. DMA originally developed pcANYWHERE for other DOS users to control a DOS computer over an asynchronous connection, but then DMA extended the technology to support control by either Mac or DOS clients. DMA offers versions that run over either an asynchronous connection or a network. RunPC/Network is designed to work over an AppleTalk network only.

As added features, both of these programs allow a client to transfer files from the server to the client in the background and to redirect DOS print commands to any printer that the Mac client can access.

In our work with these programs, we found that these *application servers,* as we call them, provide a unique and useful way to maintain connectivity between DOS and Mac users. These programs are especially useful if you have custom-developed programs that run only on DOS platforms. One problem we've run into with these programs is the usual "RAM-cram" problem caused by DOS's 640K limit (at least, prior to DOS 5.0). Occasionally, programs could not be run on the DOS computer while the server software was active. Also, you'll probably find that displays of higher resolution than CGA, such as EGA and VGA, are displayed with seemingly interminable slowness at the Mac client if you're using a LocalTalk network. Running higher resolution server displays will require Ethernet for reasonably quick displays on the Mac client.

We'll now leave the arena of terminal emulation and client-server systems and move on to that of distributed applications.

Understanding Distributed Applications

The basic concept of distributed processing is to let each machine on the network do what it does best. Workstations can act as front-ends that control the user interface and support rules for data selection or data entry. On the other hand, you let the supercomputers and the mainframes do what they do best, which is crunching numbers and managing large databases.

Think of distributed processing as consisting of three main components: cooperative processing, distributed data, and distributed services.

Distributed processing is more than just the assignment of cooperating tasks to different machines and having them churn out results in concert. Distributed processing also includes the concept of distributed data — data can reside in a variety of physically separate locations. And then, of course, to make all this work properly, both the distributed processes and the distributed data must be transparent to the user.

Distributed services are often the most difficult to implement on a network. On a network, you're concerned with programs that monitor and control data transfers and other programs. Thus, if you're interested in having different processes on physically separate machines act in concert, you need distributed services. An example is monitoring the availability of data tables to determine where a user's request for data can be fulfilled, especially if there is data redundancy in the data tables.

The concept of distributed processing appeals particularly to corporations, as corporate databases typically reside on large mainframes, whereas the corporate users usually work on PC (or similar) workstations running such programs as Lotus 1-2-3 or Excel. Distributed processing enables the corporate MIS departments to tie together these two disparate camps, preserving the maintenance and security of the mainframe databases, while enabling users to analyze the data on their local machines.

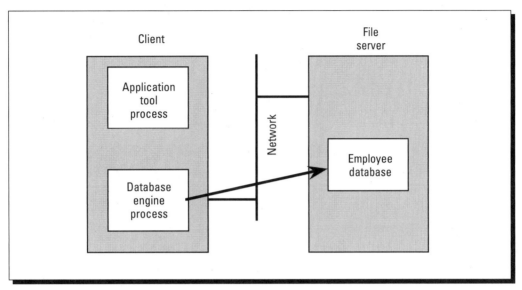

Figure 26-6: A database running on a file server.

Three main architectures are available for distributed processing: X/Open, IBM's SAA (System Application Architecture), and Digital's NAS (Network Application Support). Each uses SQL as a database language; the first two use LU6.2 as the communications architecture, but NAS uses DECnet. But you'll see that there are other ways of implementing parts of distributed processing, even on the Mac.

An example of distributed processing

As an example of how distributed processing differs from other network uses, we'll examine how a networked database can be created, starting with the standard file-server-based model and working our way to a distributed database system.

First, in Figure 26-6, you see a typical file-sharing scenario, in which a client machine contains the database engine and simply requests data from the database, which happens to be located on a networked file server. A database like 4th Dimension running on an AppleShare server is an example of this setup.

Next, in Figure 26-7, you see the client-server model. Instead of merely allowing client machines to share information, the system distributes the processing of the information, keeping a front-end process on the client machine and a back-end process on the server. The two processes communicate with each other (often by means of SQL statements) and make sure that only the requested information is

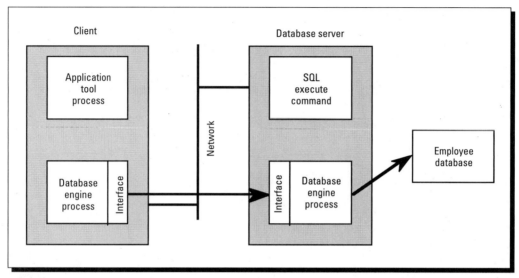

Figure 26-7: A client-server database.

passed on the network back to the client. DAL, SQLnet, and SQL server are examples. See Chapter 21, "Using Networked Databases," for more information on client-server databases.

The last figure in this trio, Figure 26-8, shows you the distributed database. In this case, the database back-ends, running on the database servers, can communicate with each other and exchange data from their respective tables to fulfill the request generated at the client's workstation. In this way, the client process does not specifically have to address each database server to get the data. Rather, it needs only to send the request to one database server, and that server will retrieve any additional needed data from other servers. This is often called data *transparency*. Digital's Desktop ACMS is an example of this approach.

Distributed applications for Macs

Because distributed processing is still a fairly new field, not many products are available for any computer, let alone Macs. The major product thrust in distributed processing has been the development of distributed databases. The one distributed database that now includes the Mac as full partner in the system is Oracle (prior to 1992, Macs were limited to acting only as clients connecting to Oracle databases). Other databases, such as those from Sybase and Ingres, can act as distributed databases on other, non-Mac, computers, but they limit Mac access to client functions only.

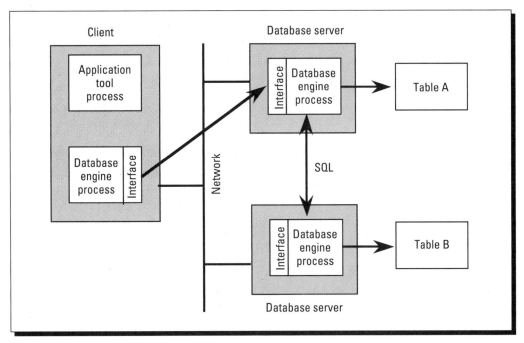

Figure 26-8: The distributed database.

Summary

In this chapter, we've described some of the ways that you can use applications running on other computing systems with your Mac. The methods described extend from terminal emulation over a network to client-server systems and distributed processing.

The following points were covered:

- ✔ Mac terminal emulators can be run over a network and connected to SNA, DECnet, and TCP/IP networks.

- ✔ Gateways are available for the three major networks, SNA, DECnet, and TCP/IP.

- ✔ Front-ending tools can be used to construct interfaces that are easier to use for almost any operating system.

- ✔ Macs can be either X Windows display servers or X Windows clients.

- ✔ The DAL query language can be used over a network to extract data from a variety of databases running on Unix, VMS, and IBM systems.

- ✔ Macs can control DOS-based applications on PCs over a network.

- ✔ The major distributed processing application available for Macs currently is the distributed database.

Appendixes

Appendix A
AppleTalk Packet Formats

This appendix contains drawings representing the formats of the various packet types used in AppleTalk. Figure A-1 is a layer-by-layer map of the AppleTalk packets described in this appendix. For further information on packet contents and program calls to the protocols, refer to *Inside AppleTalk*, 2nd Edition (Addison-Wesley, 1991).

List of figures in Appendix A:

A-13: Zone Information Protocol (ZIP).

A-14: ZIP GetNetInfoRequest, ZIP GetNetInfoReply.

A-15: ZIP Query, ZIP Reply, ZIP Notify.

A-16: AppleTalk Session Protocol (ASP).

A-17: Printer Access Protocol (PAP).

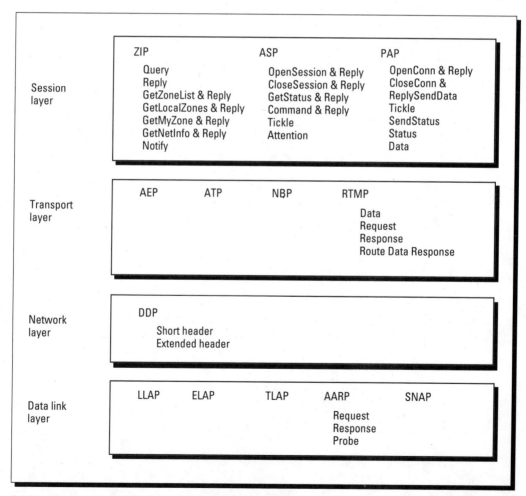

A-1: Layer-by-layer map of AppleTalk packets included in Appendix A.

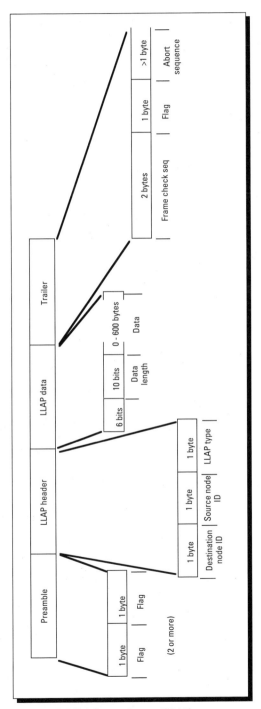

A-2: LocalTalk Link Access Protocol (LLAP).

A-3: Sub-Network Access Protocol (SNAP).

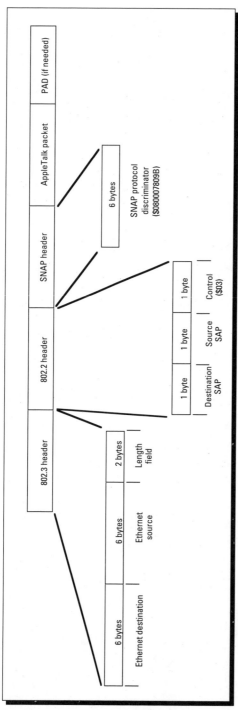

A-4: Ethernet Link Access Protocol (ELAP).

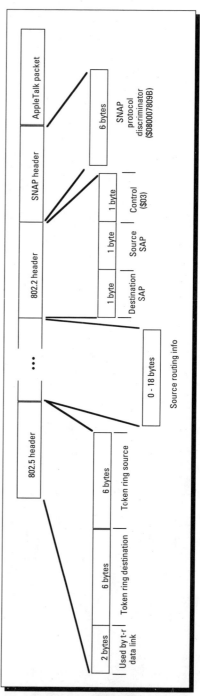

A-5: Token Ring Link Access Protocol (TLAP).

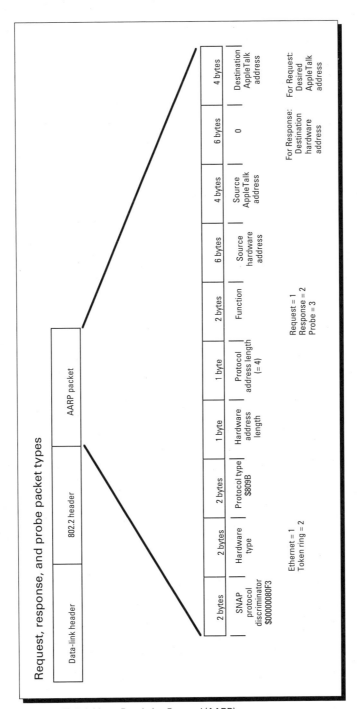

A-6: AppleTalk Address Resolution Protocol (AARP).

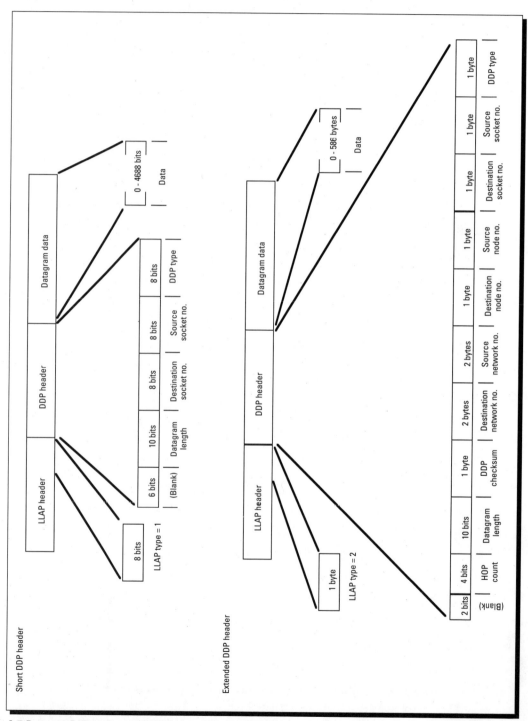

A-7: Datagram Delivery Protocol (DDP) (short and long headers).

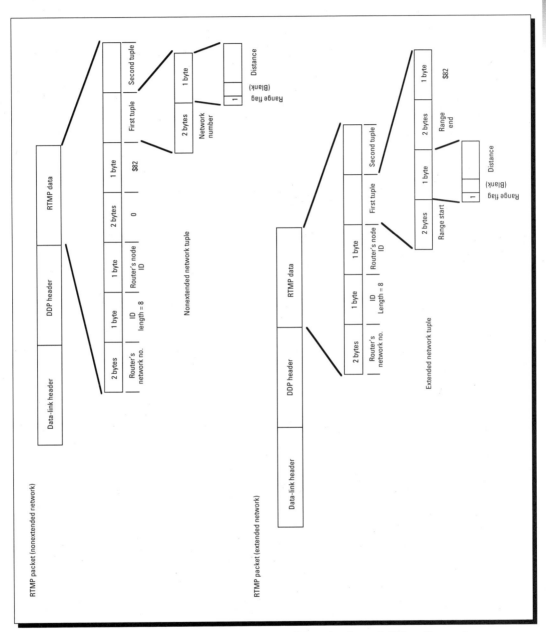

A-8: Routing Table Maintenance Protocol (RTMP) for nonextended (Phase 1) and extended (Phase 2) networks.

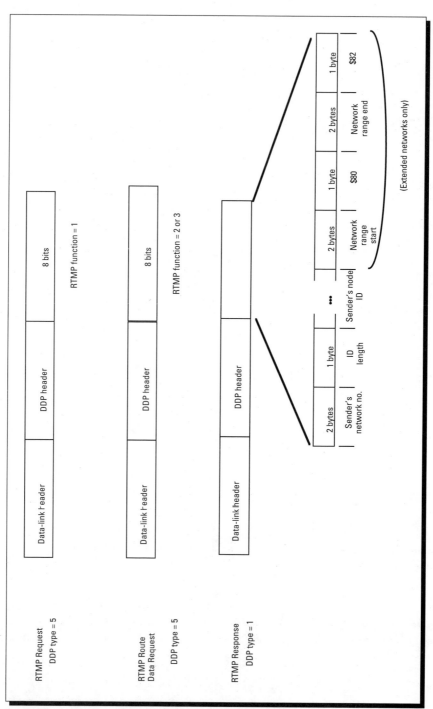

A-9: RTMP Request, RTMP Route Data Request, RTMP Response.

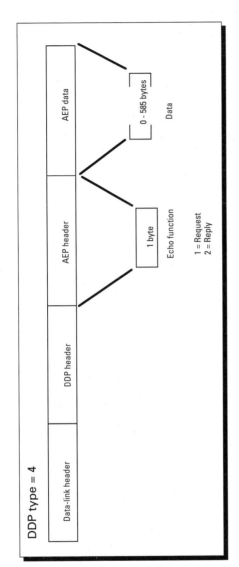

A-10: AppleTalk Echo Protocol (AEP).

DDP type = 4

| Data-link header | DDP header | AEP header | AEP data |

1 byte — Echo function
1 = Request
2 = Reply

0 - 585 bytes — Data

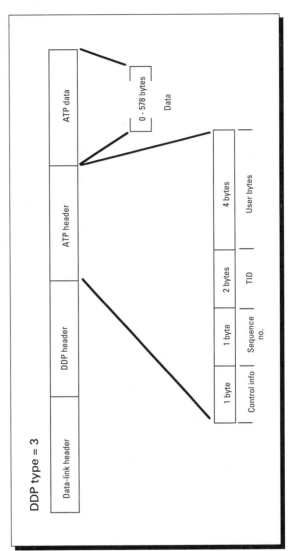

A-11: AppleTalk Transaction Protocol (ATP).

DDP type = 3

| Data-link header | DDP header | ATP header | ATP data |

1 byte — Control info
1 byte — Sequence no.
2 bytes — TID
4 bytes — User bytes

0 - 578 bytes — Data

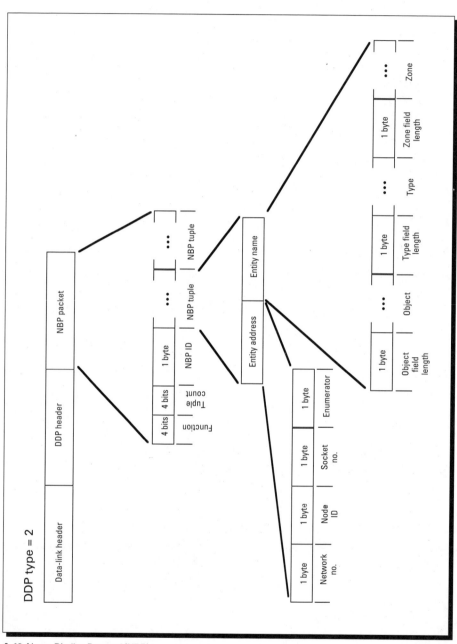

A-12: Name Binding Protocol (NBP).

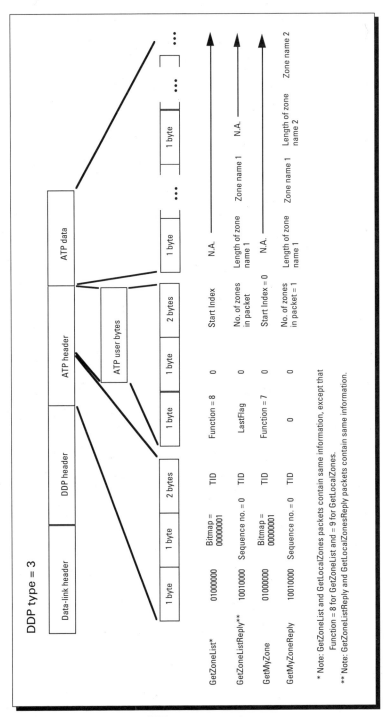

A-13: Zone Information Protocol (ZIP).

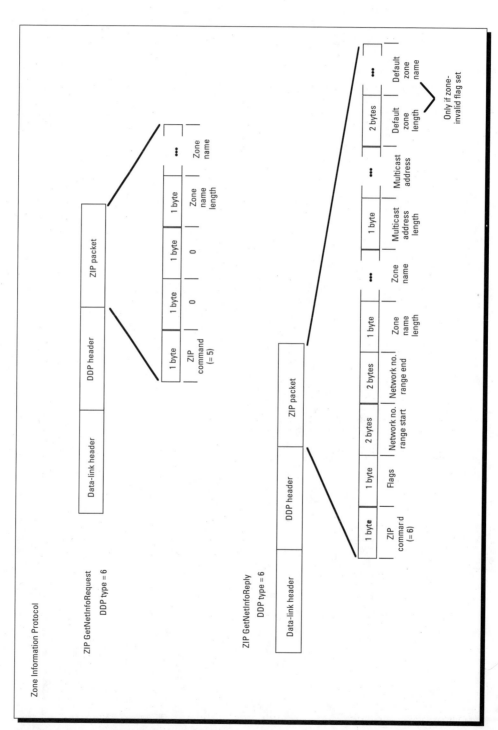

A-14: ZIP GetNetInfoRequest, ZIP GetNetInfoReply.

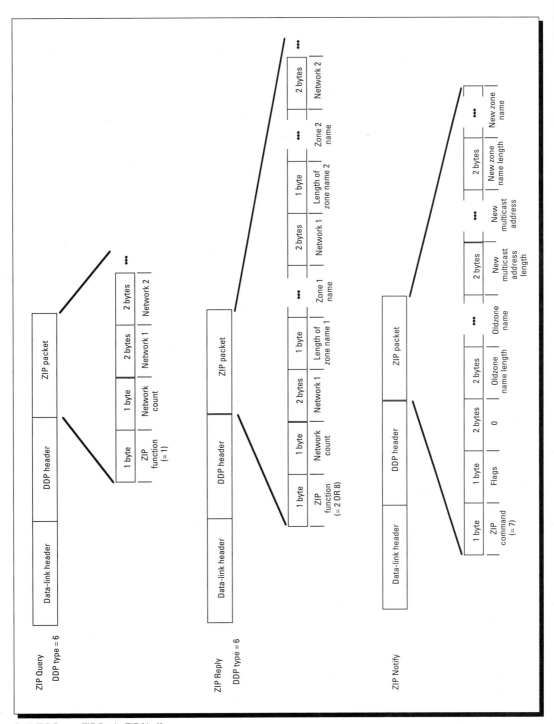

A-15: ZIP Query, ZIP Reply, ZIP Notify.

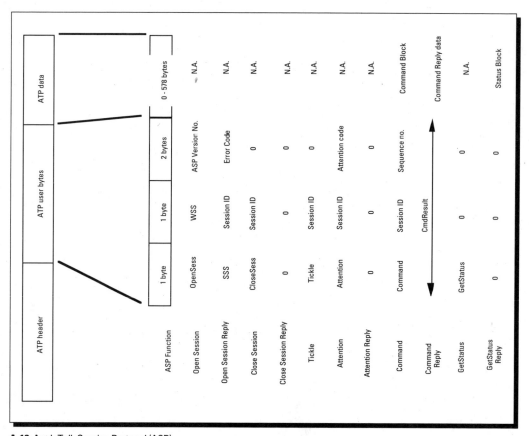

A-16: AppleTalk Session Protocol (ASP).

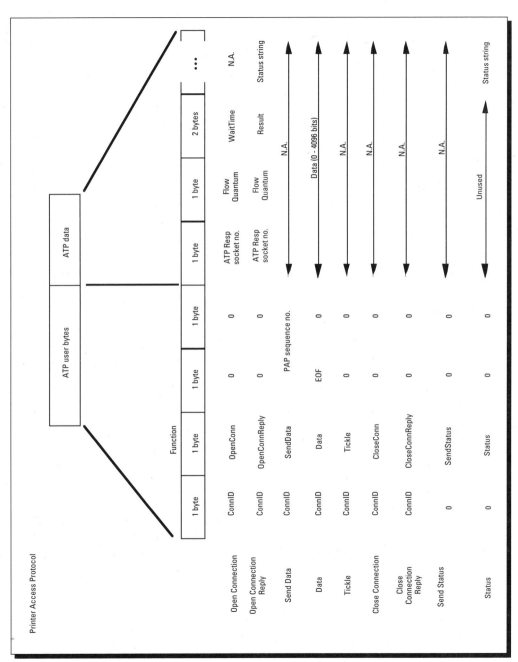

A-17: Printer Access Protocol (PAP).

Appendix B
List of Vendors

The following list is not intended as a comprehensive guide to the vendors listed in this book, but rather as a starting point of information.

Note that the descriptions are organized as follows:

Company name
A description of pertinent products offered by the company
The company address and phone number

3Com Corp.
Suppliers of 3+/3+Open network operating system and associated server hardware.
5400 Bayfront Plaza
Santa Clara, CA 95052-8145
(408) 764-5000

Acius, Inc.
Developers and suppliers of 4th Dimension relational database for the Macintosh.
10351 Bubb Road
Cupertino, CA 95014
(408) 252-4444

Actinet Systems, Inc.
Suppliers of ARCnet interface cards for the Mac.
360 Cowper, #11
Palo Alto, CA 94301
(415) 326-1321

AESP Inc.
Wiring and wire-accessory suppliers, especially for LocalTalk and PhoneNET.
1810 NE 144th St.
N. Miami, FL 33181
(305) 944-7710

The AG Group
Developers of LocalPeek and EtherPeek packet analysis software; NetWatchMan device monitoring software.
2540 Camino Diablo, Suite 202
Walnut Creek, CA 94596
(510) 937-7900

Alisa Systems Inc.
Developers and suppliers of AlisaTalk, AlisaShare VAX- and Unix-based file servers, AlisaPrint VAX- and Unix-based print servers, AlisaMail, VMS-based e-mail server, and MailMate/QM and MailMate/MM Mail, bridges for QuickMail and Microsoft Mail.
221 E. Walnut St., Suite 175
Pasadena, CA 91101
(818) 792-9474

ANDREW/KMW Systems Corp.
Source for IBM 5250 terminal emulation software and associated interface hardware for Macs and PCs.
4301 Westbank Dr., Suite A-100
Austin, TX 78746
(512) 314-3000

Andyne Computing Ltd.
Developers of GQL, query construction tool
for DAL and SQL.
> 552 Princess St., 2nd Floor
> Kingston, Ontario
> K7L 1C7
> Canada
> (613) 548-4355

Apple Computer, Inc.
Developer and supplier of the Macintosh and
LaserWriter II.
> 20525 Mariani Ave.
> Cupertino, CA 95014
> (408) 996-1010

Asante Technologies, Inc.
Source for Ethernet and token ring interface
cards for Macintosh computers.
> 404 Tasman Dr.
> Sunnyvale, CA 94089
> (408) 752-8388

ASD Software, Inc.
Developers of Planisoft group scheduling
software for Mac and Windows clients.
> 4650 Arrow Highway, Suite E-6
> Montclair, CA 91763
> (714) 624-2594

AT&T
Telecommunications service providers.
> Business Communications Services
> 295 N. Maple Ave.
> Basking Ridge, NJ 07920
> (908) 221-6153

Avatar Corp.
Source for IBM 3270 terminal emulation
software and associated interface hardware;
also supplier of LANWAY EtherTalk router and
SNA gateways.
> 65 South St.
> Hopkinton, MA 01748
> (508) 435-3000

Banyan Systems, Inc.
Developer and supplier of VINES network
operating system.
> 115 Flanders Road
> Westboro, MA 01581
> (508) 898-1000

Beagle Bros., Inc.
Developer of Flash file-transfer utility.
> 6215 Ferris Square, Suite 100
> San Diego, CA 92121
> (619) 452-5500

Belkin Components
General network wiring source.
> 1303 Walnut Pkwy.
> Compton, CA 90220
> (310) 515-7585, (800) 223-5546

Blyth Software
Developer of Omnis 5 and Omnis 7 rela-
tional databases, as well as DAL tool for
DOS, Windows, and OS/2.
> 1065 E. Hillsdale Blvd.
> Foster City, CA 94404
> (415) 571-0222

Brio Technology, Inc.
Developers of DataPrism SQL/DAL query
construction tool and DataPivot data-viewing
tool.
> 444 Castro St., Suite 700
> Mountain View, CA 94041
> (415) 961-4110

BT Tymnet
> Telecommunications service provider.
> P.O. Box 49019
> 560 N. First St.
> San Jose, CA 95161-9019
> (408) 922-7583

Cabletron Systems
Source for DNI Ethernet cards for Macintosh computers.
　35 Industrial Way
　Rochester, NH 03867
　(603) 332-9400

Caravelle Network Corp.
Developers of Mac-to-Mac file-transfer utility and Mac-to-Mac NetWORKS network monitoring software.
　301 Moodie Dr., Suite 306
　Nepean, Ontario
　K2H 9C4
　Canada
　(613) 596-2802

Cayman Systems, Inc.
Source of GatorBox EtherTalk routers and Ethernet interface cards for the Mac.
　26 Landsdowne St.
　Cambridge, MA 02139
　(617) 494-1999

cc:Mail, Div. of Lotus Corp.
Developer of cc:Mail e-mail products for DOS and Mac computers.
　2141 Landings Dr.
　Mountain View, CA 94043
　(415) 961-8800

CE Software, Inc.
Developer of QuickMail e-mail products for DOS and Macintosh computers.
　1801 Industrial Circle
　P.O. Box 65580
　W. Des Moines, IA 50265
　(515) 224-1995

Cisco Systems Inc.
Source for Ethernet routers and WAN-related products.
　1525 O'Brien Dr.
　Menlo Park, CA 94025
　(415) 326-1941

Compatible Systems Corp.
Developer of Ether•Route EtherTalk router, Ether•Write, an interface for LaserWriters, and various Ethernet interface cards for Macintosh computers.
　P.O. Drawer 17220
　Boulder, CO 80308-7220
　(303) 444-9352

Compumation Inc.
Developers of Print Central print server software.
　820 N. University Dr.
　State College, PA 16803
　(814) 238-2120

Connectivite Corp.
Developers of BOTH front-end software for IBM 3270 communication sessions.
　Talleyrand II, 220 White Plains Road
　Tarrytown, NY 10591
　(914) 631-5365

CSG Technologies
Developers of Network Supervisor resource-management software.
　530 William Penn Place, Suite 329
　Pittsburgh, PA 15219
　(412) 471-7170, (800) 366-4622

Cypress Research Corp.
Developers of FaxPro, networked fax server hardware and software for Macintosh and Windows clients.
　240 E. Caribbean Dr.
　Sunnyvale, CA 94089
　(408) 752-2700

Datability Software Systems, Inc.
Developer of RAF and MacRAF disk-server software that runs on the VMS operating system.
　One Palmer Terrace
　Carlstadt, NJ 07072
　(201) 438-2400

DataViz

Supplier of MacLink Plus file-translation software.

    55 Corporate Dr.
    Trumbull, CT 06611
    (203) 268-0030

Dayna Communications Inc.

Source for EtherPrint interface for LaserWriters, as well as Ethernet interface cards for Macs.

    50 S. Main St., Suite 530
    Salt Lake City, UT 84144
    (801) 531-0203

DayStar Digital Inc.

Source for LocalTalk interface card for 80286 and 80386 PCs and PS/2s.

    5556 Atlanta Hwy.
    Flowery Branch, GA 30542
    (404) 967-2077

Digital Communications Associates, Inc.

Developer and supplier of MacIRMA, IBM 3270 terminal software, and associated hardware, including AppleTalk-SNA gateway.

    1000 Alderman Dr.
    Alpharetta, GA 30202
    (404) 442-4000

Distributed Technologies Corp.

Suppliers of TalkManage network management software.

    275 Wyman St.
    Waltham, MA 02154
    (617) 684-0060

Dove Computer Corp.

Supplier of Ethernet interface cards for the Macintosh; also supplies DoveFax networkable fax modem.

    1200 N. 23rd St.
    Wilmington, NC 28405
    (919) 763-7918, (800) 788-DOVE

EDI Communications Corp.

Developer of MacToken token-ring diagnostic software for the Mac and IBM-PC.

    20440 Town Center Lane, Suite 4E1
    Cupertino, CA 95014
    (408) 996-1343

EMAC, Div. of Everex Systems Inc.

Supplier of Ethernet interface cards for Mac and Community-Mac DECnet software.

    48431 Milmont Dr.
    Fremont, CA 94538
    (800) 821-0806

Engage Communications

Developer of SyncRouter device for connecting AppleTalk WANs.

    756 Marlin Ave., Suite 4
    Foster City, CA 94404
    (415) 358-0264

Fairfield Software Inc.

Developer of ClearAccess, query construction tool for SQL and DAL.

    200 West Lowe St.
    Fairfield, IA 52556
    (515) 472-7077

Farallon Computing, Inc.

Source for PhoneNET wiring accessories, StarController LocalTalk and Ethernet active hubs, Timbuktu screen-sharing software, Liaison and PhoneNET Manager's Pack (includes CheckNet, TrafficWatch II and NetAtlas), and EtherMac series cards.

    2000 Powell St., Suite 600
    Emeryville, CA 94608
    (510) 596-9100

Fifth Generation Systems, Inc.

Supplier of SuperLaserSpool print-spooler software.

    10049 N. Raleigh Road
    Baton Rouge, LA 70809
    (504) 291-7221

Focus, Inc.
Supplier of TurboNet PhoneNET-clone connectors, TurboStar LocalTalk multiport repeater, and Ethernet interface cards for the Mac.
> 800 W. Cummings Park
> Woburn, MA 01801
> (800) 538-8866

Fox Software, Inc.
Developer of FoxBase relational database manager for PCs and Macs.
> 134 W. South Boundary
> Perrysburg, OH 43551
> (419) 874-0162

GAVA Corporation
Developers of VirusNET software that checks for viruses over a network of Macintoshes.
> 1001 4th Ave. Plaza, Suite 3200
> Seattle, WA 98154
> (206) 784-4736, (800) 767-0647

Gizmo Technologies
Developers of SendExpress file-transfer utility and ShadowWriter software for networked sharing of printers.
> P.O. Box 14177
> Fremont, CA 94539
> (510) 623-7899

Hayes Microcomputer Products, Inc.
Source for high-speed modems and Hayes InterBridge LocalTalk router.
> P.O. Box 105203
> Atlanta, GA 30348
> (404) 840-9200

Helios USA
Supplier of EtherShare Unix-based file and print-server software.
> 10601 S. De Anza Blvd., Suite 103
> Cupertino, CA 95014
> (408) 864-0690

Hewlett-Packard Co.
Source for LaserJet IIIsi laser printer (among others).
> 5301 Stevens Creek Blvd.
> Santa Clara, CA 95052
> (800) 752-0900

IDEAssociates, Inc.
Developer of IBM 5250 terminal emulation software and associated hardware for Mac and DOS computers.
> 29 Dunham Road
> Billerica, MA 01821
> (508) 663-6878

Information Presentation Technologies Inc.
Developer of uShare Unix-based file- and print-server and SunPartner file-exchange software.
> 555 Chorro St.
> San Luis Obispos, CA 93405
> (805) 541-3000

Insight Development Corp.
Developer of print drivers for Mac use of non-AppleTalk printers; also Mosaic products for printers on NetWare.
> 2200 Powell St., Suite 500
> Emeryville, CA 94068
> (510) 652-4115, (800) 825-4115

Insignia, Solutions
Developers of SoftPC DOS emulation software for the Mac.
> 526 Clyde Ave.
> Mountain View, CA 94043
> (800) 848-7677

Integrated Solutions Inc.
Developer of X-Windows tools for use with Apple Terminal Services and MacWorkStation.
> 1020 Eighth Ave.
> King of Prussia, PA 19406
> (215) 337-2282

InterCon Systems Corp.
Developer of TCP/Connect II TELNET
emulation software and NFS/Share NFS client
software for Macs.
    950 Herndon Pkwy., Suite 420
    Herndon, VA 22070
    (703) 709-9890

International Business Software
See **Novell**.

International Transware Inc.
Developers of InterTalk AppleTalk router
line.
    800 El Camino Real W., Suite 180
    Mountain View, CA 94040
    (415) 968-8888

Keyword Technologies
Developer of KeyPack document translation
for VMS server and Mac and PC clients.
    2816 Eleventh St., NE
    Calgary, Alberta
    T2E 7S7
    Canada
    (403) 250-1770

MacVONK
Source for inForum networked bulletin board
system and NetOctopus resource management
program.
    313 Iona Ave.
    Narbeth, PA 19072
    (215) 660-0606

Mainstay
Developer of Marco Polo document-retrieval
software and MarkUp group-editing software
for Macintosh computers.
    5311-B Derry Ave.
    Agoura Hills, CA 91301
    (818) 991-6540

MCI
Telecommunications service providers.
    1111 19th St., NW, Suite 500
    Washington, D.C. 20036
    (800) 444-6245

MDG Computer Services
Developers of NetUpdater updating software.
    634 S. Dunton
    Arlington Heights, IL 60005-2544
    (708) 818-9991, (708) 453-6330

Microcom
Source for high-speed modems and Carbon
Copy-Mac screen-sharing software.
    500 River Ridge Dr.
    Norwood, MA 02062-5028
    (617) 551-1000

Micro Dynamics, Ltd.
Developer of MARS document archive system.
    8555 16th St., Suite 802
    Silver Spring, MD 20910
    (301) 589-6300

Microsoft Corp.
Developer of Microsoft Mail for Macs and
PCs, MS Schedule+ group scheduler, and LAN
Manager network operating system.
    One Microsoft Way
    Redmond, WA 98052-6399
    (206) 882-8080

Miramar Systems
Developer of MacLAN Connect AFP-
compatible PC-based file-server software.
    201 N. Salsipuedes, Suite 204
    Santa Barbara, CA 93103
    (805) 965-5161

Mitem Corp.
Developer of MitemView front-ending
software for serial and network connections.
    2105 Hamilton Ave., Suite 350
    San Jose, CA 95125
    (408) 559-8801

Motorola, Inc.
Radio-Telephone Systems Group, developer
and supplier of Altair wireless Ethernet
system.
>3215 Wilke Road
>Arlington Heights, IL 60004
>(708) 632-2853

National Semiconductor Corp.
Developer of EtherNODE Ethernet interface
cards for Macs.
>2900 Semiconductor Dr.
>P.O. Box 58090
>Santa Clara, CA 95052-8090
>(408) 721-5000

Neon Software, Inc.
Developer of NetMinder LocalTalk and
Ethernet packet analysis software for Macs,
and RouterCheck router-monitoring software.
>1009 Oak Hill Road, Suite 203
>Lafayette, CA 94549
>(510) 283-9771

Network General Corp.
Developer and supplier of Sniffer hardware
for network packet analysis.
>4200 Bohannon Dr.
>Menlo Park, CA 94025
>(415) 688-2700

Network Resources Corp.
Developer and supplier of MultiGate Ethernet
routers, and MacFN and Mac2000 Ethernet
interface cards for the Mac.
>736 S. Hillview Dr.
>Milpitas, CA 95035
>(408) 263-8100

Nevada Western
General source for network wiring and wiring
accessories.
>615 N. Tasman Dr.
>Sunnyvale, CA 94089-1950
>(408) 734-8727

Novell Inc.
Source for NetWare network operating
system and DataClub distributed file-server
system.
>122 E. 1700 South
>Provo, UT 84606
>(801) 379-5900

Odesta Corp.
Developer of Double Helix relational database
and Odesta Document Management System
(ODMS).
>4084 Commercial Ave.
>Northbrook, IL 60062
>(708) 498-5615

ON Technology, Inc.
Source for Instant Update groupware, Meeting
Maker group scheduling software, and
Status*Mac (originally sold by Pharos Tech-
nologies).
>155 Second St.
>Cambridge, MA 02141
>(617) 876-0900

Oracle Corp.
Developer of Oracle multiplatform databases
and OracleCard front-end to databases.
>500 Oracle Pkwy.
>Redwood Shores, CA 94065
>(415) 506-7000

Pacer Software Inc.
Developer of PacerShare AFP-compatible
file-server software for VMS and Unix
systems, PacerTerm terminal emulator
software, PacerForum networked bulletin
board system, and PacerLink network
software for VMS and Unix systems.
>7911 Herschel Ave., Suite 402
>La Jolla, CA 92037
>(619) 454-0565

Personal Computer Peripherals Corp.
Supplier of NetStream multiuser backup
software for networks.
> 4902 Eisenhower Blvd., Suite 390
> Tampa, FL 33634
> (813) 884-3092

Pharos Technologies
See **ON Technology**.

Photonics Corp.
Developer of PhotoLink infrared-based
devices for connecting LocalTalk networks,
either in offices or between buildings.
> 200 E. Hacienda Ave.
> Campbell, CA 95008
> (408) 370-3033

Proteus Technology
Developers of Quota license server software
for networks.
> 9919 68th St.
> Edmonton, Alberta
> T6A 2S6
> Canada
> (403) 426-6794

Racal-Interlan, Inc.
Suppliers of Ethernet interface cards for Macs
and PCs.
> 155 Swanson Road
> Boxborough, MA 01719
> (508) 263-9929

Sassafras Software
Developers of KeyServer license management
software.
> Box 150
> Hanover, NH 03755
> (603) 643-3351

ShirtPocket Software
Developers of EasyShare background file-
server software for the Mac and 80286/80386-
based AFP-compatible file servers for
AppleTalk networks.
> P.O. Box 40666
> Mesa, AZ 85274-0666
> (602) 966-7667

Shiva Corporation
Source of FastPath 5 EtherTalk router,
NetBridge WAN device, NetModem 2400, and
V.32 shareable modems.
> One Cambridge Center
> Cambridge, MA 02142
> (617) 864-8500

Simware
Developer of SimMac IBM 3270 terminal
emulation software for Macs (also SimPC for
DOS computers).
> 20 Colonnade Road
> Ottawa, Ontario
> K2E 7M6
> Canada
> (613) 727-1779

Sitka Corporation
Source for TOPS distributed file-server system
and InBox e-mail program.
> 950 Marina Village Pkwy.
> Alameda, CA 94501
> (510) 769-9669

Soft-Switch Inc.
Source for various mainframe-based e-mail
gateways.
> 640 Lee Road
> Wayne, PA 19087-5698
> (215) 640-9600

SoftWriters, Inc.
Developers of VersionTerritory version-tracking software.
> P.O. Box 1308
> Round Rock, TX 78680
> (512) 244-3999

Solana Electronics
Developer of C-Server network interface for non-AppleTalk devices, I-Server AppleTalk half-router, and R-Server communications server.
> 7124 Convoy Court
> San Diego, CA 92111
> (619) 573-0800

Sonic Systems, Inc.
Suppliers of Radar resource management software and Ether TnT and TwP Ethernet interface cards for Macs.
> 333 W. El Camino, Suite 280
> Sunnyvale, CA 94087
> (408) 725-1400

Spider Island Software
Developers of TeleFinder graphical bulletin board and NetConnect option for use on networks.
> 4790 Irvine Blvd., Suite 105-347
> Irvine, CA 92720
> (714) 669-9260

Standard Microsystems Corp.
Source of ARCnet interface cards for Mac and DOS computers.
> 80 Arkay Dr.
> Hauppauge, NY 11788
> (516) 273-3100

StarNine Technologies, Inc.
Developers of numerous gateways between Mac-based e-mail programs and other e-mail systems.
> 2126 Sixth St.
> Berkeley, CA 94710
> (510) 548-0391

Symantec Corp.
Supplier of SAM virus checker.
> 10201 Torre Ave.
> Cupertino, CA 95014
> (408) 253-9600

Synergy Software
Developer and supplier of VersaTerm and VersaTerm-PRO terminal emulators.
> 2457 Perkiomen Ave.
> Mt. Penn, PA 19606
> (215) 779-0522

Talaris Systems Inc.
Supplier of various laser printers, including some with Ethernet interfaces.
> 6059 Cornerstone Court W.
> San Diego, CA 92121
> (619) 587-0787

TechGnosis Inc.
Developers of SequeLink SQL interface between Macs and SQL databases.
> 301 Yamato Road, Suite 2200
> Boca Raton, FL 33431
> (407) 997-6687

Technology Works
Source for Ethernet interface cards for Macs and GraceLAN resource management products.
> 4030 Braker Lane West, Suite 350
> Austin, TX 78759
> (512) 794-8533

Terranetics

Developers of SafeDeposit automatic backup software for AppleShare.

> 1538 North Martel Ave., Suite 413
> Los Angeles, CA 90046
> (818) 446-7692

Thomas-Conrad Corp.

Source of ARCnet interface cards for Mac and DOS computers.

> 1908-R Kramer Lane
> Austin, TX 78758
> (512) 836-1935

T.I.C., Inc.

Developers of hi-BBS networked bulletin-board system.

> 5253 Decarie Blvd., #550
> Montreal, Quebec
> H3W 3C3
> Canada
> (514) 483-1295

Touch Communications, Inc.

Developers of WorldTalk X.400 e-mail gateway for QuickMail and Microsoft Mail.

> 250 E. Hacienda Ave.
> Campbell, CA 95008
> (408) 374-2500

Traveling Software Inc.

Developers of LapLink Mac file-transfer software.

> 18702 N. Creek Pkwy.
> Bothell, WA 98011
> (206) 483-8088

Tri-Data Systems, Inc.

See **Avatar Corp**.

Trik, Inc.

Developers of NetDistributor software upgrade program and NokNok monitoring software for System 7 File Sharing.

> 400 W. Cummings Park, Suite 2350
> Woburn, MA 01801
> (617) 933-8810, (800) 766-0356

Ungermann-Bass, Inc.

Source of concentrators, routers, and WAN devices for many types of networks.

> 3900 Freedom Circle
> Santa Clara, CA 95052
> (408) 496-0111

United Data Corp.

Source for MacWorkStation software for Macs and other computers, including ALAC software for Microsoft Windows.

> 3755 Balboa St., Suite 203
> San Francisco, CA 94121
> (415) 221-8931

US Sprint Communications Co.

Telecommunications service providers.

> P.O. Box 8417
> 1200 Main St., 4th Floor
> Kansas City, MO 64105
> (800) 877-2000

Walker, Richer & Quinn, Inc.

Developer of Reflection series of VT1xx, VT2xx terminal emulation software.

> 2815 Eastlake Ave. East
> Seattle, WA 98102
> (206) 324-0350

Webster Computer Corp.

Source for MultiGate multiport EtherTalk routers.

> 2109 O'Toole Ave., Suite J
> San Jose, CA 95131-1303
> (408) 954-8054

White Pine Software

Source for Mac241 DEC terminal emulators for the Macintosh; also eXodus X-Windows server and VTXpress for the Macintosh.

    40 Simon St., Suite 201
    Nashua, NH 03060-3043
    (603) 886-9050

WilTel

Telecommunications service providers.

    P.O. Box 21348
    Tulsa, OK 74121
    (800) 642-2299

The Wollongong Group Inc.

Developers and suppliers of MacGateWay AT EtherTalk router and MacPathWay Access TELNET software for the Mac.

    1129 San Antonio Road
    Palo Alto, CA 94303
    (415) 962-7100

WordPerfect Corp.

Developer of WordPerfect Office for Mac and DOS computers.

    1555 N. Technology Way
    Orem, UT 84057
    (801) 225-5000 (800) 451-5151

Xinet Inc.

Source for Unix-based K-AShare file-server and K-Print print-server software for Macs.

    2560 Ninth St., Suite 312
    Berkeley, CA 94710
    (510) 845-0555

Appendix C
Glossary of Networking Terms

10Base2

An implementation of the Ethernet IEEE standard on thin coaxial cable, a baseband medium, at 10 megabits per second. The maximum segment length is just under 200 meters.

10Base5

The original Ethernet medium, an implementation of the Ethernet IEEE standard on twinaxial cable, a baseband medium, at 20 megabits per second. The maximum segment length is 500 meters.

10BaseT

An implementation of the Ethernet IEEE standard on 24 gauge unshielded, twisted-pair wiring, a baseband medium, at 10 megabits per second.

802.2

The third layer defined in the IEEE 802 LAN specifications, overlaying the 802.8, 802.4, 802.5, and FDDI protocols. 802.2, or Logical Link Control (LLC), is responsible for addressing and data link control, and is independent of the topology, transmission medium, and medium access control technique chosen.

802.3

Defined by the IEEE, these standards govern the use of the **CSMA/CD** (Carrier Sense Multiple Access/Collision Detection) network access method used by Ethernet networks.

802.4

Defined by the IEEE, these standards govern the use of the token bus network access method.

802.5

Defined by the IEEE, these standards govern the use of the token ring network access method.

AAUI (Apple Attachment Unit Interface)

The name used for Apple's new Ethernet physical interface, which uses a special connector and requires an external transceiver to complete a connection to the network.

active star

A network wired in a star topology with a concentrator or multiport *repeater* located at the center of the star. All wiring runs lead to the *concentrator*, which is responsible for retransmitting the network signal from one wiring run to the rest of the wiring runs attached to it.

address

A name, set of numbers, or sequence of bits used to identify devices on a network. Each computer, printer, server, or other device on the network must have a unique address. Addresses are necessary so that information transmitted on the network will get to the right destination. The network software keeps track of the addresses.

AFP (AppleTalk Filing Protocol)
The presentation-level protocol that governs remote file access in an AppleTalk network.

amplitude
The difference between the maximum and minimum voltage of an electrical signal.

analog
A form of transmission in which the waveform is continually varied over an infinite range of voltage.

ANSI (American National Standards Institute)
The principal organization in the United States dedicated to the development of voluntary standards for American industry.

API (Application Program Interface)
A series of specifications describing the types of data and commands that can be relayed from a program to other software or a software-controlled device, such as a network interface card.

APPC (Advanced Program-to-Program Communications)
Specifications for peer-to-peer communications in an IBM SNA network. See *LU6.2* and *SNA*.

AppleDouble
A file format specified by Apple for storing the data fork and resource fork of a Macintosh file in separate files on another computing system. Many file servers support the AppleDouble method for storing Mac files. The method allows you to share files with non-Mac users. With AppleDouble, other users simply access the data fork of a Mac file stored in the AppleDouble format.

AppleShare
Apple Computer's Mac-based file server software, using the AFP protocol.

AppleSingle
A file format specified by Apple for storing both the data fork and resource fork of a Macintosh file in a single file on another computing system.

AppleTalk
Apple Computer's networking software and protocols that provide the capabilities for communications and resource sharing among the computers, printers, and other peripherals attached to the network.

AppleTalk address
A number that uniquely identifies software processes in an AppleTalk network. For example, if the networking software includes a process that sends and receives a certain type of data, that process receives its own AppleTalk address. Processes of that type are called *socket clients*.

The address is composed of the socket number and the identification number of the node (the node ID) containing that socket number. This combination makes the address unique for each socket. See *socket*.

application layer
The layer of the OSI Reference Model that defines protocols for user or application programs. See *OSI Reference Model*.

ARCnet (Attached Resource Computer Network)
First developed by Datapoint Corporation, ARCnet is a local area network for IBM personal computers and compatibles. ARCnet uses the token-passing method.

ARP (Address Resolution Protocol)

A protocol in the TCP/IP protocol suite, ARP is responsible for translating an IP address into a physical address, such as an Ethernet address.

ARPAnet (Advanced Research Projects Agency)

See *TCP/IP*.

ASCII (American Standard Code for Information Interchange)

The ASCII code represents keyboard characters, control characters, and some graphics elements as an on/off pattern of 7 bits plus one more bit for an error-checking process known as *parity checking*. For example, the ASCII code for the letter "a" is 01100001 in binary, 61 in hexadecimal, and 97 in decimal.

Although initially developed as the code for representing text in a file on a single computer, the ASCII code is now also one of the most common codes used for transmitting data on networks of personal computers or between pieces of data processing equipment such as a computer and a printer. The ASCII code can represent 128 characters.

asynchronous communication

A method for transmitting data that sends one character at a time. Asynchronous also refers to commands, as in a windowing environment, that may be sent without waiting for a response from the previous command. See *synchronous communication*.

attenuation

The loss of signal strength that occurs as a signal is transmitted through a cable.

AWG (American Wire Gauge)

A standard for specifying the diameter of a wire. Larger AWG numbers represent wires with smaller diameters.

backbone network

A central network that connects a number of networks, usually of lower capacity. Those lower-capacity networks can pass data to each other over the backbone network. The backbone network normally is built with a high-capacity medium, such as an Ethernet or fiber-optic cable. The lower-capacity networks connect to the backbone using routers, half routers, or modems. Information sent from one device to another within a network stays in that network, but data sent from one network to another travels over the backbone. Individual devices can also connect directly to the backbone network; they do not have to be part of one of the lower-capacity networks.

balun

A device that connects a balanced line to an unbalanced line, for example, a twisted wire pair to coaxial cable. A balanced line is one in which both wires are electrically equal. In an unbalanced line, such as coaxial cable, one line (the central conductor) has different physical properties from the other (the surrounding concentric conductor).

bandwidth

The capacity of a network to carry information using a particular type of cable, as measured by the maximum number of bits per second (bps) the network can transmit. In a network, the higher the bandwidth, the greater the information-carrying capacity of the network, and the faster data can be transmitted from one device to another.

baseband

A type of network transmission that uses the entire bandwidth of a network to transmit a digital signal. The cables of a baseband network only carry one set of signals at a time. (See *broadband*, a type of transmission that can send multiple signals simultaneously.)

bridge

An electronic device that connects two networks so that devices on one network can communicate with devices on the other network. Bridges connect only networks that operate under the same communications protocols.

broadband

A method of transmitting data so that a single wire or cable can simultaneously carry many different channels of information. Cable television uses the broadband method to carry as many as 100 channels on a single coaxial cable. (Compare with *baseband*.)

broadcast transmission

A message sent over the network to all network devices. A network administrator planning to shut down the network for maintenance may send a broadcast transmission so that everyone on the network will know when the interruption will occur. Without the ability to send a broadcast transmission, the administrator would have to send messages to each user individually.

brouter

A device that can route specific protocols and bridge others, thus combining the capabilities of bridges and routers.

buffer

A temporary storage location in memory that provides uninterrupted data flow between devices, such as printers and keyboards, with fewer interruptions or pauses.

bus topology

A network topology in which a single cable is used to carry the network's signals. Computing devices are attached to the central cable (also known as a *backbone cable*) via taps.

carrier sense multiple access

See *CSMA*.

CCITT (Consultative Committee for International Telegraphy and Telephony)

An international standards-making body consisting of national telecommunications authorities.

cdev (Control Panel Device)

A utility program for the Macintosh. The cdev is found in the System Folder and appears as an option in the Macintosh Control Panel.

centralized server

A computer dedicated to providing network services to users or clients. Often called a *dedicated server*.

cheapernet

See *Thinnet*.

checksum

A simple method used for detecting errors in transmission of data. The bytes comprising the data are added together; this sum is appended to the end of the data packet. The receiver recomputes the sum of the bytes in the packet and compares it to the sum received from the sender to determine if any data has been garbled.

Chooser

A desk accessory included with the Macintosh system software. The desk accessory is used to select network services by service type (such as LaserWriter or AppleShare), device name, and zone name.

client

A relationship in which one device or computer program is dedicated to serving another device or program. For example, a workstation that requests services from a file server is a client of the server.

client-server

A networked computing system in which the two participating computers each use their own on-board processing capabilities to perform part of the task. In client-server systems, one of the two computers exerts more control over the transactions.

coaxial cable

An electrical cable that contains two separate wires. One wire is solid, and the other is a tube. The solid wire is inside the tube. Both wires have the same center point, or axis, which is why the cable is named *coaxial*. The solid wire carries data while the tube wire acts as a shield for the solid wire. The solid wire is surrounded by insulation to isolate it from the tube wire. The tube wire, which is made of a braided mesh, screen material, is in turn surrounded by insulation. Coaxial cables, also called *coax*, are the familiar wires used for cable television connections. Terminals used on IBM networks frequently have coaxial cables for their connections; many Ethernet networks also use coaxial cables.

collision

A situation that occurs when two devices on a network try to transmit at the same time and their transmissions "run into" each other. The signals are crossed, causing the data to become garbled. When a collision occurs, the data of each transmission is ruined and must be retransmitted. See *CSMA*.

crosstalk

The electrical interference between signals transmitted on wires.

CSMA (carrier sense multiple access)

A method used by network devices to gain access to a single channel on the network. Each device "listens" to the traffic on the network (or *senses the carrier*) and thus detects whether the network is clear, whether signals are already passing on the cables, or whether signals are about to pass. If the network is clear, a device signals its intent to begin transmitting.

Two refinements of CSMA are collision avoidance (CA) and collision detection (CD). Collision avoidance (CSMA/CA) is the process for resolving contention for the channel. *Contention* occurs when two devices both signal their intent to begin transmitting at the same time. When contention occurs, the transmitting workstations wait a random time interval, and then retransmit. The time interval is random so that when the devices begin retransmitting, chances are exceedingly small that they will start at the same time. An AppleTalk network system with LocalTalk cables uses the CSMA/CA technique.

The collision detection technique (CSMA/CD) senses when two transmissions occur on the same channel simultaneously. The main difference between the collision avoidance and collision detection methods is that transmitting devices using collision detection *listen* while transmitting. If the devices hear different signals than the ones transmitted, a *collision* is known to have occurred. Also, the receiving device doesn't send an acknowledgment character to the transmitting device. As with the collision avoidance method, the devices will wait a random amount of time before beginning to retransmit. Ethernet networks use the CSMA/CD technique.

CTERM (Communications Terminal Protocol)
Part of the virtual terminal service defined in layer 6 of the DECnet architecture.

daemon
A program running in the background on a Unix system. A daemon performs a single task the entire time that it is running.

data link layer
The layer of the OSI Reference Model that defines protocols governing data packets and transmissions. See *OSI Reference Model.*

datagram
In the Internet Protocols, a *datagram* is a packet containing destination address and data.

DDCMP (Digital Data Communications Message Protocol)
A data link protocol used in the DECnet architecture. DDCMP is used for point-to-point links between nodes in either asynchronous or synchronous modes. See *asynchronous communication* and *synchronous communication.*

DDP (Datagram Delivery Protocol)
The AppleTalk Datagram Delivery Protocol (DDP) is responsible for ensuring delivery of datagrams between AppleTalk sockets.

DECnet/DNA
The series of network protocols defined by Digital Computer, Inc. DNA, or Digital Network Architecture, contains the definitions of the protocols. DECnet is Digital's implementation of DNA.

disk server
Software that allows a user to treat a partition of another computer's hard disk as if it were a locally attached disk drive. The contents of that partition cannot be shared with other users, a characteristic that distinguishes a disk server from a file server, which does allow sharing.

distributed server
A server system in which computers can be both clients and servers at the same time. Distributed servers do not require the full resources of the computer and are often run in the background. Also commonly called a *peer-to-peer* system. See *peer-to-peer.*

DOS (Disk Operating System)
Single-user operating system developed by Microsoft. Primarily used on IBM and IBM-compatible computers but sometimes ported to other systems.

downtime
The time during which the network and/or its services are unavailable to users.

driver
Software for using a peripheral hardware device attached to a computer. For example, to control a printer from a Macintosh computer, the print driver program for that type of printer has to be added to the Macintosh's System Folder.

dynamically assigned socket
A socket that is allocated to the software whenever it is required. A *socket* is an addressable memory location in a node on the network. Transmissions are sent directly to a socket in a node rather than to the node in general. Nodes can have more than one socket. See *DDP.*

EBCDIC (Extended Binary Coded Decimal Interchange Code)
An 8-bit code for representing letters, numerals, punctuation marks, and other symbols. Primarily used in IBM equipment, EBCDIC defines 256 character codes. The other, more commonly used code for representing characters is *ASCII* (American Standard Code for Information Interchange).

electronic mail (e-mail)
The use of electronic data communications to exchange information with other users. Electronic mail uses personal addresses for each recipient to determine to whom mail should be sent.

emulation
See *terminal emulation.*

enterprise computing
The term currently used to describe corporate networks, which are composed of different types of computers running different operating systems and probably also using different network protocols. The goal of enterprise computing is interoperability.

Ethernet
A data link protocol jointly developed by Intel, Xerox, and DEC and subsequently adopted by the IEEE as a standard.

EtherTalk
The name given to AppleTalk protocols transmitted over Ethernet media.

FDDI (Fiber Distributed Data Interface)
A 100-megabit/sec LAN standard based on the token ring system. Currently designed to be used with fiber-optic cabling.

fiber-optic cable
See *Optical fiber.*

file-locking
A method of network data management in which a file is reserved for the first user who requests it. Other users are locked out of access to the file and thus prevented from altering the file at the same time another user is modifying the file.

file server
A computer specifically intended for storing files that people can share over the network. The computer being used as the file server might not be able to be used for other common workstation tasks. Workstations used for a single purpose like a file server are called *dedicated* devices because they are dedicated to a single function. Often a dedicated file server is kept away from work areas for security reasons and to prevent accidental or malicious use. However, not all file servers must be dedicated. Some networking software allows any workstation to handle file server tasks and still function as a workstation.

frame
A series of bytes of data encapsulated with a header. The data link layer sends frames back and forth. The term *frame* is often used interchangeably with the term *packet.* See *packet.*

frequency
The number of times per second an electrical signal cycles from maximum to minimum voltage and back again.

FTP (File Transfer Protocol)
An upper-layer protocol in the TCP/IP suite that provides services for copying files across the network.

full-duplex

A data communications term that indicates that both ends of a communications link can transmit data at the same time. See *half-duplex*.

gateway

An electronic device that connects two networks, each of which operate with a different set of protocols, such as AppleTalk and EtherTalk. The gateway translates all the protocols of one network into those of the other network so that workstations and other devices on the two networks can communicate with one another. Some gateways translate all the protocols from the physical layer up to the applications layer. Others translate only the protocols above the data link layer or the transport layer.

groupware

Also called *collaborative computing*. Groupware includes programs designed to handle group-related tasks such as scheduling meetings, sending messages and other information, and coauthoring documents. Other programs include networked bulletin board systems and group decision support systems.

half bridge

A device that connects a network to a communications link, such as the telephone lines. Often the half bridge connects to a modem which then connects to the communications link. Workstations on the network can then transmit through the half bridge, then to the modem, over telephone lines, and to another network. The other network may also be attached to telephone lines with a modem and a half bridge.

Because half bridges do not deal with any addressing information, messages sent through

half bridges are sent to the network, not to a particular workstation. The networking software then has to route the message to its proper destination. Half bridges can also connect a network to other dedicated circuits, such as a PBX.

Whereas a half bridge connects a network to an intermediate communications link, a *full bridge* connects one network to another. Conceptually, two half bridges, two modems, and the telephone lines create a full bridge between two networks.

half duplex

A data communications term that indicates that only one end of a communications link can transmit data at the same time; one end must wait for acknowledgment of its data transmission from the other end before it can continue with transmitting another data packet. See *full duplex*.

half router

A device that connects a network to a communications link, often using a modem. Unlike a half bridge, a half router maintains addressing information about the networks. Workstations on the network can send messages through the half router, then through the modem, over the telephone lines, through another modem and another half router, and then on to a workstation.

Because the router maintains the addressing information for both networks, messages can be properly routed to the correct workstations with a minimum of additional processing. See *router*.

HDLC (High-Level Data Link Control)

An ISO protocol for the data link layer. HDLC is used in both X.25 and OSI networks.

header

A listing of control information that is found at the front of a packet. A packet header usually includes an identification of packet type, source and destination addresses, sequence numbers, and other indicators of priority levels. See *frame* and *packet.*

hop

A pass of data through a router. Routers connect the networks physically and maintain addressing information for each network. By going through the router, data leaves one network and passes to another, or "hops" from one network to the other. See *router.*

ICMP (Internet Control Message Protocol)

The protocol used by the IP layer of TCP/IP stacks for exchanging messages that control routing.

IEEE (Institute of Electronic and Electrical Engineers)

A major standards-setting group in the United States. Part of the ISO.

IETF (Internet Engineering Task Force)

A group of network engineers and users responsible for controlling the implementation of protocols on the Internet. See *Internet.*

impedance

Measurement of a transmission medium's resistance to an alternating current. Impedance is measured in ohms. See *ohms.*

Internet

Called "The Internet." A collection of networks with a common routing backbone which encompasses such public networks as NSFnet (National Science Foundation Network) as well as private networks such as those at various universities. Not to be confused with the generic term *internet.*

internet

Two or more networks that are connected. Workstations in each network can share data and devices with other parts of the internet. Also called an *internetwork.*

The networks on an internet are connected through routers. A *router* is a device that physically connects the network cables and maintains network addresses. Data passing from one network to another passes through the router on its way to nodes on another network. See *router.*

interoperability

The capability to operate computers and exchange information in a heterogenous network.

IP (Internet Protocol)

A protocol located in layer 3 of the TCP/IP protocol suite, used to provide connection-less transmissions of data packets over a TCP/IP network.

IPX (Internetwork Packet Exchange)

A network layer protocol used by Novell NetWare to provide functions for addressing, routing, and switching packets.

ISDN (Integrated Services Digital Network)

An international communications standard that allows the integration of voice and data on a common transport mechanism.

ISO (International Standards Organization)

An international standards-making body responsible for the OSI network standards and the OSI Reference Model.

layer

One set of networking protocols that is part of a complete group or *suite* of protocols.

Processing at each layer performs one or more major functions necessary for transmitting data over a network.

One of the most common models of networking layers is the Open Systems Interconnection (OSI) Reference Model put forth by the International Standards Organization (ISO). In that model, seven layers of protocols dictate the processing of data before it can be transmitted to a receiving workstation. See *OSI Reference Model*.

LAN (local area network)

A network in one location. The size of the location can vary; for example, a network on one floor of an office building is a LAN. So is a network connecting all the buildings of a college campus. Networks connected by modems and telephone lines, however, are not LANs. Thus, a network connecting buildings in different cities is not a LAN (although the networks in each of the buildings probably are).

LANs provide the connections between workstations and peripherals such as printers and disk servers. Unlike telephone networks, in which all the lines and much of the equipment is owned by a telephone company, a LAN is typically owned by the company that uses it.

LAP (Link Access Protocol)

AppleTalk protocols for controlling the hardware interface to different network media, including ELAP for Ethernet and LLap for LocalTalk.

LAT (Local Area Transport)

A proprietary architecture developed by Digital Computer for terminal servers on Ethernet networks. LAT is designed to conserve network bandwidth and off-load processing from host computers.

link

See *data link*.

LLC (Logical Link Control)

Part of the IEEE LAN model (IEEE 802 standards). The logical link control layer presents a uniform interface to the user of the data link service, usually a network layer, and therefore reduces the need for the user to know what network medium is being used.

LocalTalk

The name for Apple Computer's low-cost connectivity products consisting of cables, connection boxes, cable extenders, and other cabling equipment for connecting computers and other devices. LocalTalk was formerly called the AppleTalk Personal Network Cabling System.

Sometimes the term *LocalTalk environment* is used to describe the capabilities of an AppleTalk network. A LocalTalk environment is merely an AppleTalk network connected with LocalTalk cabling and connectors. Calling the system a LocalTalk environment differentiates it from an AppleTalk network connected with some other type of media and having different capabilities, such as EtherTalk.

LU (Logical Unit)

An IBM term in SNA (Systems Network Architecture) networks to describe the software that uses the network.

LU 6.2

A logical unit (LU) used on networks that use the Systems Network Architecture (SNA) protocols. LU 6.2 is being implemented as part of APPC. APPC allows peer-to-peer communications so that computers with the same processing capabilities will be able to communicate with each other directly as peers. This, in turn, means that processing loads can be more evenly distributed on the network, and that computers need not resort to terminal emulation in order to talk to mainframes.

mail server

A network computer that acts as an electronic post office. People using the network transmit a message to the mail server, where the message is stored until the addressee checks the server and reads the message. Thus, a mail server has the electronic equivalent of post office boxes. With some mail servers, users can also store the messages after reading them.

MAN (Metropolitan Area Network)

A network capable of data communications over distances from a few miles to one hundred miles. Normally, a MAN is thought of as a network consisting of fewer than 1,000 nodes and using very high data rates (100 Mbps or higher).

Manchester encoding

A digital, self-clocking method of encoding that describes a bit value by the transition between two signals.

mapping

The redirection of local resources to network resources.

MIB (Management Information Base)

Information used by SNMP for maintaining the status and control of a network device. MIBs are specific to each type of device; information within the MIB is relayed by an SNMP agent to network management software either on request or when a problem occurs within the device.

modem

A device that takes digital data from a computer and encodes it in analog form

(modulation) for transmission over a phone line. It also performs the opposite process for incoming signals (demodulation). The term modem is derived from the terms *mo*dulator/*dem*odulator.

multicast address

A term used in network addressing. A multicast address is a group address that is meant for a certain subset of devices on the network. See *address*.

NBP (Name Binding Protocol)

An AppleTalk protocol used for translating device names to addresses.

network

A collection of individually controlled computers, printers, modems, and other electronic devices which are interconnected so that they can all communicate with each other. Networks also include all the software needed to run the network as well as the wires, cables, connection boxes, and other hardware that make the physical connections. Using a network, people can share data, programs, and send messages to each other. Networks also let people share resources, such as printers and disk storage units.

network interface controller (NIC)

A card (or set of chips) that fits inside a computer so that the computer can connect to a network. The card has a connector for attaching the network cable. Sometimes the network interface controller (or NIC) is called simply the *interface card*.

Different types of networks require different interface cards. The connectors are different sizes to accommodate the cables of different networks, and the chips on the card contain the hardware and software needed to implement the various protocols for a specific type of network.

network layer
The layer of the OSI Reference Model that defines protocols governing data routing.

NFS (Network File System)
A protocol defined by Sun Microsystems to extend TCP/IP network file services. NFS allows files on remote nodes of a network to appear as if they were stored on the local workstation.

node
An addressable device on a network, such as a LaserWriter or a Macintosh. Network processes running within a node are called *sockets* and are assigned *socket numbers*.

NVE (network-visible entity)
Any computing node or socket that can communicate with a network and be seen by other nodes or sockets. Your Mac, PC, LaserWriter, or file server are all network-visible entities.

ohm
An electrical unit of measurement used to measure the resistance of a transmission medium to the flow of electrons (that is, a current) through the medium. If the current is a direct current (DC), the term *resistance* is used. If the current is an alternating current (AC), the term *impedance* is used. Both resistance and impedance are measured in ohms.

ohmmeter
An electrical measuring device. Ohmmeters include a series of wiring posts with insulated wires for connecting to the circuit or electrical device to be measured, and also include either an analog display (a meter) or a digital display for showing the value of the measured quantity. Ohmmeters can also be used to measure voltages and/or electrical current.

optical fiber
A type of network cabling composed of thin glass fibers. In order for optical fibers to be used on a network, electrical signals are converted into pulses of light to be sent through the fibers. A receiving device then transforms the light pulses back into electrical signals and passes those signals on to the appropriate destination.

Fiber optics have an extremely high bandwidth for carrying information. Thus, they can transmit information at very high rates and can also carry many channels. Other benefits include maximum protection from eavesdropping, and virtually no susceptibility to electromagnetic interference or atmospheric disturbances, such as rain or lightning.

OSI Reference Model
A model for the modularization of network protocols and their functions. Each layer communicates only with the layer immediately above and below it. The OSI Reference Model has seven layers: physical layer, data link layer, network layer, transport layer, session layer, presentation layer, and application layer. OSI stands for *Open Systems Interconnection*.

packet
A group of bits, including address, data, and control elements, that are switched and transmitted together. See *frame*.

passive star
A network topology in which each wiring run is connected together at a common end. Each wiring run is called a *branch*, or *leg*, of the star. Unlike the active star, a passive star has no concentrator at the center. See *star topology*.

peer

A device treated as the equal of another device on the network. Networks that let workstations and other nodes communicate with each other as equals are called *peer-to-peer networks*.

port descriptor file

A file maintained by a router for network-related information for each of the router's ports. The port descriptor file includes the *port ID*, a number that designates the identity of the port for the internal processing use of the router; the *network number*, a number that labels the cable that is attached to the port with a unique number that identifies it as a separate network; and the *network address*, a number that designates the port's address on the network.

PPP (Point-to-Point Protocol)

A replacement protocol for SLIP, designed to provide router-to-router as well as host-to-network connections over asynchronous and synchronous links. See *asynchronous communication* and *synchronous communication*.

presentation layer

The layer of the OSI Reference Model that defines protocols governing data formats and conversions.

print server

A device (usually an additional workstation) that acts as a large buffer for files being sent to the printer. When users send data to the printer, the data is actually sent to the server and stored there until the printer is available. Then, the print server automatically sends the data to the printer to be printed.

A print server enables network users to send data to a printer even if the printer is busy with another job. Thus, users do not need to wait for an available printer on the network. If more than one print job is waiting on the server, the print-server software keeps track of the jobs and prints them in order. Some software allows for the reassignment of priorities to print jobs as well as job cancellation so that some people can get their work printed ahead of others.

print spooler

An application program or combination of hardware and software that allows users to print at the same time they are working on some other task.

The print spooler acts as a buffer for the files to be printed. The files are stored in the spooler until a printer is free for printing. The spooler then sends the file to the printer.

protocol

A procedural rule or convention for sending information over a network. Each network has its own way of transmitting data and divides the entire process into a series of specific functions. Each function requires a complete set of operating rules, or *protocols*.

The OSI Reference Model has become one of the primary models for network protocols. If companies developing communications protocols follow the OSI model, their networks can probably (with minor conversion routines) interconnect with most other networking protocols in use today.

The entire set of protocols used by a particular network is called its *family* or *suite* of protocols. A particular implementation of a protocol family in a computer is called that computer's *protocol stack*.

The protocols themselves are small programs that control a specific set of communications functions. However, none of the protocols can carry out full communications from start to finish. The protocols all have to work together in sequence.

protocol layers

The functional divisions of processing to send and receive data on a network. The layers refer to the main tasks the networking software has to accomplish to transmit and receive data.

protocol stack

The implementation of a specific protocol family in a computer or other node on the network. The protocol stack refers to the visual analogy of all of the layers of a set of protocols — a stack of protocols being implemented on a node.

punchdown block

A wiring device used by phone companies and network installers for connecting many wires together in one location. A typical punchdown block (type 66 block) has fifty rows of four contacts, or pins. Wires are pushed, or "punched down," onto a pin to make electrical contact using a special tool called a *punchdown tool*.

redundant path

A second path that a network packet may use to travel from its source to its destination. The redundant path is used when the primary path between two nodes is disrupted.

repeater

A hardware device that repeats the signals on a network. As signals pass over a line, they lose some of their power and pick up static. A repeater amplifies and conditions the signals on a network line.

Repeating a digital signal is sometimes called *regenerating the signal* because the repeater

device removes static (line noise) and boosts the signal strength so that it becomes louder as it passes over the line. By improving a signal, repeaters reduce the possibility of error when a workstation has to interpret the signal. Repeaters also enable the signals to be sent greater distances and therefore essentially extend the length of the network.

A repeater acts only at the physical layer of the network's protocols and therefore can only connect two networks with identical physical links.

ring topology

A network arrangement in which all the devices are connected in a circle, or ring. Data passes around the ring from node to node, always in the same direction. Each node essentially acts as a repeater and retransmits the messages to the next node.

IBM's token ring network uses the ring topology. In that system, a sequence of bits — the token — is passed around the network, and the node that has the token can have access to the network. When the node is through, it releases the token to be passed to the next node that wants access.

RIP (Routing Information Protocol)

A protocol for updating routing tables in TCP/IP networks.

router

A device that connects two networks together and maintains addressing information for each network. Workstations can pass information from one network to another by sending the information through the router.

Routers are often confused with bridges. A bridge physically connects two networks, but a bridge does not maintain the network addressing information. The router maintains a table of network addresses and is more effective in sending data to nodes on the different networks. See *bridge*.

SAA (Systems Application Architecture)
A set of network operating procedures developed by IBM that attempts to let nodes use different programming languages and applications on an IBM network. SAA is IBM's attempt to solve the problem of software incompatibility among its computers.

Prior to SAA, programs written for one type of IBM computer were not usable on other IBM computers. SAA's basic premise is that software for one IBM computer should work on any other IBM computer. The concept is called *device independence* for the software.

SDLC (Synchronous Data Link Control)
A data link protocol used in IBM's SNA networks. See *asynchronous communication* and *synchronous communication*.

segment
Any section of cable that is attached to a port of a repeater, bridge, or router.

server
A computer, workstation, or similar device that provides a service to network users or other devices on the network. The three most common types of servers on local area networks are the print server, file server, and mail server.

session
A term used to refer to the logical stream of data flowing between two programs that are communicating over the network. There are usually many different sessions originating from one particular node of a network. In AppleTalk, each session in a node has its own socket. See *socket*.

session layer
The layer of the OSI Reference Model that defines protocols that govern communications between applications. See *OSI Reference Model*.

shielded cable
A wire or circuit enclosed by a grounded metallic material. Shielding serves two purposes. First, it keeps outside electrical disturbances from reaching the wire and disrupting the signals passing over it. Second, shielding keeps the cable from emitting radiation that can disrupt radio and television reception, or that can be captured and interpreted by some unauthorized person.

SLIP (Serial Line Internet Protocol)
A TCP/IP-based protocol used to run IP over serial lines such as telephone circuits. See *TCP/IP* and *IP*.

SMDS (Switched Multimegabit Data Service)
A high-speed networking technology offered by telephone companies.

SMTP (Simple Mail Transfer Protocol)
The electronic mail protocol defined for TCP/IP networks.

SNA (Systems Network Architecture)
A set of communications protocols developed by IBM for synchronous transmission of data.

SNA is popular on networks that include an IBM mainframe computer. SNA includes protocol layers for the data structures, formats, control of the data links, and maintaining data transmission.

A key purpose of SNA is to allow different types of computers to communicate over the network. Users of the SNA network are unaffected by the way the network provides its services, or by the equipment necessary to maintain the network. See *asynchronous communication* and *synchronous communication*.

SNADS (SNA Distribution Services)

Part of the SNA networking architecture, designed for transferring messages within SNA.

SNMP (Simple Network Management Protocol)

A protocol in the TCP/IP suite for managing objects on the network. SNMP uses agents on managed devices to maintain a MIB (Management Information Base) and transmit MIB data to the management software upon request.

socket

Any addressable entity in a node on an AppleTalk network. Sockets are "owned" by the software processes that create them. For example, if a communications program obtains a socket for receiving messages, that socket can only be used to receive messages for that program. Messages that arrive for some other program arrive through their own sockets. The software processes that own the sockets are called the *socket clients*.

socket number

The number that identifies a particular socket. Each node may have the capability to allocate many sockets. The socket number identifies which one is being used by a particular software process.

split-horizon routing

A technique for maintaining routing tables of individual routers. If a router A is attached (via a network) to one port of another router (B), then router B only

informs router A of networks that are reachable through the other ports of router B. Router A is thus not informed of networks that are attached to the same port of Router B as the one router A is attached to.

SPX (Sequenced Packet Exchange)

The transport Layer protocol used by Novell NetWare. Provides a connection-oriented, guaranteed delivery link between workstations.

SQL (Structured Query Language)

A data manipulation language standardized by ANSI and used in most relational database systems.

star topology

A centralized network with the main computer in the center and all the nodes connected to it. For LANs, a device known as an *active hub, concentrator,* or *star controller* replaces the main computer at the center of the network.

The central device controls each workstation. For one workstation to communicate with another, the message passes through the central device, also called the *hub.* The hub controls access and transmission along all of the connecting lines. For example, the part of a telephone network that includes a local telephone exchange is a star network because communications between any two telephones must first pass through the local exchange. The exchange is, essentially, the hub of that star network.

Star networks are simple to control because all control takes place at one point. Also, problems are easy to isolate because the workstations are not directly connected to one another. However, the two disadvantages of the star network are the cost of the central computer and the vulnerability of the overall network if the hub fails. Unlike bus networks that can still operate if a device fails, star networks fail completely if the hub fails. See *hub* and *ring topology*.

store-and-forward

A message-passing technique in which messages are temporarily stored at intermediate points before being retransmitted to the next destination.

synchronous communication

A data transmission method in which a packet of data is sent, and the sender and receiver stations resynchronize their clocks. See *asynchronous communication*.

TCP (Transmission Control Protocol)

The transport layer protocol of the TCP/IP protocol suite. TCP provides connection-oriented, end-to-end transport of packets between workstations.

TCP/IP (Transmission Control Protocol/ Internet Protocol)

A set of protocols designed to let many networks interconnect.

TCP/IP is the standard for internetwork communication established in the U.S. Department of Defense network known as ARPAnet. ARPA, also called DARPA, stands for the Advanced Research Projects Agency. ARPAnet is the research and development arm of the Department of Defense.

TCP/IP is rapidly becoming a de facto standard for network interconnections for universities and research organizations. It has been associated with Unix networks because various companies selling Unix devices have built the TCP/IP protocols into the devices.

TELNET

An upper-layer TCP/IP protocol that provides virtual terminal services and allows users to log onto remote nodes.

terminal emulation

The process of making a personal computer imitate a terminal, often a "dumb" terminal.

Terminal emulation is necessary in certain systems because mainframes expect all the terminals on a network to have similar input/output requirements. Specifically, the terminals need to use and understand the same control characters that indicate different processing procedures. Programs called *emulators* allow a personal computer to emulate a terminal. The programs store the meaning of the control characters and the various procedures in the personal computer's memory. When the computer receives the control character over the network from the mainframe, the computer responds with the proper procedure. Similarly, the personal computer translates its input characters and control keys into the form the mainframe expects and understands. To the mainframe, it appears as if the personal computer is the proper type of terminal.

terminator

A device attached to the end of a cable to prevent unwanted signals from being transmitted on the line or link. A terminator resistance matches the characteristic impedance of the line so that signals arriving at the end of the cable do not find an impedance discontinuity and are thus not reflected.

Thicknet

Cabling scheme using 50-ohm coaxial cable with N-type connectors. Thicknet uses a 50-ohm coaxial cable as the backbone for the network. The cable has an outer diameter of

0.37 to 0.41 inches, depending on the type of insulation; also note that Thicknet cable has two layers of shielding.

Thinnet
Cabling scheme using 50-ohm coaxial cable with BNC-type connectors — thinnet coax is 0.20 inches in outer diameter and has a single layer of shielding. Sometimes called *cheapernet.*

timeout
The process by which a computing task determines if a connection is still active or valid. The task maintains a clock counter to determine if a packet is delivered properly within a predetermined period of time. If the receiver does not acknowledge receipt of the packet within that time period, the sender either tries again or closes the connection.

token ring
A network that connects workstations in a closed ring and that uses token passing to enable nodes to use the network. A token is a set of bits that the networking software uses to grant access to the network. Token passing refers to the process of passing the token from node to node on the network until one node wants to use the network. That node then keeps the token while it is using the network. See *ring topology.*

topology
The physical layout of a network, including the cables and devices. The topology of a network is its roadmap and can show which devices can communicate directly and which cannot because they don't share a connection path. Typical topologies used on local area networks are the bus, star, and ring.

Topology can also mean the possible logical connections along the network. Logical connections are those that permit nodes to communicate through some additional software processing instead of directly through physical connections.

transceiver
A device used as an interface between a workstation and the network to which it is attached. The transceiver performs the task of transmitting frames onto the cable and receiving them from it. It also monitors signal levels on the medium and detects collisions and other error conditions.

transport layer
The layer of the OSI Reference Model that defines protocols that govern message structure. Provides some error checking. See *OSI Reference Model.*

tuple
A type of data in which two values are paired with each other because the two items are related; for example, in the routing table, the two items are a network number and the distance the network is away, measured in hops.

twisted-pair cable
Ordinary telephone wire consisting of two insulated copper strands twisted about each other to reduce outside interference of their signals. Twisted-pair wiring is relatively inexpensive, easy to install, easy to modify, and may already exist in many installations as part of the telephone network. See *shielded cable.*

UDP (User Datagram Protocol)
Part of the TCP/IP protocol suite. The protocol is used as an alternative to TCP for unacknowledged datagrams.

VAX (Virtual Address Extension)
A series of computers manufactured by Digital Computer.

Vines (Virtual Network Software)
Banyan's network operating system based on Unix and its protocols.

virtual terminal
A definition of a standardized terminal for a network that can accommodate different type of terminals. Protocols are used to prevent incompatibilities among the different types of terminals. Signals to and from the nonstandard terminals are converted into signals that would come from the standard terminal. Therefore, all the terminals appear to be the same to the host computer.

VMS (Virtual Memory System)
A proprietary operating system used by Digital Computer for its VAX computers.

WAN (Wide Area Network)
A network that spans many geographically separated locations. The WAN links between each local network are provided by a telecommunications service, such as leased line, SMDS, or other long-distance carriers. See *SMDS*.

workstation
A computer on a network, usually reserved for end users.

ZIP (Zone Information Protocol)
The AppleTalk protocol used to exchange information on zone names and locations between routers.

ZIT (Zone Information Table)
Table maintained within an AppleTalk router, relating zone names to the router's ports.

zone
A collection of networks on an AppleTalk internet. A zone can consist of a single network or a number of networks.

One of the main reasons for breaking a network into a zone is to reduce the amount of searching a user has to do to find a resource on the network. For example, to use a particular printer on the network, the user can search various zones instead of searching the entire network.

Although grouping an internet into zones is usually done on some logical basis such as work loads or business departments, the zones do not have to be physically contiguous. A network in one building might be part of the same zone as a network in another building.

Appendix D
Networking Acronyms

This appendix lists common networking acronyms and their meanings.

AARP	AppleTalk Address Resolution Protocol
AAUI	Apple Attachment Unit Interface
ADSP	AppleTalk Data Stram Protocol
AEP	AppleTalk Echo Protocol
AFP	AppleTalk Filing Protocol
ANSI	American National Standards Institute
API	Application Program Interface
APPC	Advanced Program-to-Program Communication
ARAP	AppleTalk Remote Access Protocol
ARP	Address Resolution Protocol
ASCII	American Standard Code for Information Interchange
ASP	AppleTalk Session Protocol
ATP	AppleTalk Transaction Protocol
AURP	AppleTalk Update-Based Routing Protocol
AWG	American Wire Gauge
CCITT	Consultative Committee for International Telegraphy and Telephony
CRC	Cyclic Redundancy Check
CSMA/CA	carrier sense multiple access/collision avoidance
CSMA/CD	carrier sense multiple access/collision detection
CTS	Clear to Send
DDP	Datagram Delivery Protocol
DNA	Digital Networking Architecture
DOS	Disk Operating System
ELAP	Ethernet Link Access Protocol
FCS	Frame Check Sequence
FDDI	Fiber Distributed Data Interface
FTP	File Transfer Protocol

IDG	Interdialog Gap
IEEE	Institute of Electronic and Electrical Engineers
IETF	Internet Engineering Task Force
IFG	Interframe Gap
IPX	Internet Package Exchange
ISDN	Integrated Services Digital Network
ISO	International Standards Organization
LAN	Local Area Network
LLAP	LocalTalk Link Access Protocol
MAN	Metropolitan Area Network
MHS	Message Handling Service
MIB	Management Information Base
NPB	Name Binding Protocol
NFS	Network File System
NIC	network interface controller
NVE	network-visible entity
OSI	Open Systems Interconnection
PAP	Printer Access Protocol
PPP	Point-to-Point Protocol
RAM	Random Access Memory
ROM	Read-Only Memory
RTMP	Routing Table Maintenance Protocol
RTS	Ready to Send
SAA	Systems Application Architecture
SLIP	Serial Line Internet Protocol
SMTP	Simple Mail Transfer Protocol
SNA	Systems Network Architecture
SNMP	Simple Network Management Protocol
SPX	Sequenced Packet Exchange
SQL	Structured Query Language
TCP/IP	Transmission Control Protocol/Internet Protocol
TID	Transaction ID
TLAP	Token-Ring Link Access Protocol

UTP   Unshielded Twisted Pair

VAX   Virtual Address Extension

WAN   Wide Area Network

ZIP   Zone Information Protocol
ZIT   Zone Information Table

Index

Macworld Authorized Editions

Macworld Guide to Microsoft Word 5
by Jim Heid
Macworld magazine's
"Getting Started" columnist

New from the bestselling author of *Macworld Complete Mac Handbook*

Learn the new Word the easy way with this *Macworld* Authorized Edition.

Highlights:
- Up-to-date for Word 5 — covers all new features
- With step-by-step instructions for mastering everyday word processing tasks

- FREE Illustrated Quick Reference Card includes keyboard shortcuts and type tips

$22.95 [$29.95 Canada]
ISBN: 1-878058-39-8
448 pages. Available now.

Macworld Authorized Editions

Macworld Guide to System 7
by Lon Poole
Macworld magazine's "Quick Tips" Columnist

"You'll find everything you need to know about System 7 in this book."
— Bob Levitus, author of *Dr. Macintosh*

This *Macworld* Authorized Edition is the most recommended guide to System 7.

Highlights:

- Optimize the new features of System 7
- Valuable hardware and software compatibility lists

- Scores of undocumented insider tips and secrets
- NEW! System 7.1 Update covers system enhancements and bug fixes

$24.95 [$33.95 Canada]
ISBN: 1-878058-16-9
384 pages. Available now.

Macworld Authorized Editions

Macworld Music & Sound Bible
by Christopher Yavelow

"Invaluable for anyone interested in music and sound on the Mac."
— Alan Kay, Mac Guru

Finally, the definitive guide to music, sound, and multimedia on the Mac.

Highlights:

- Covers the latest hardware, software, and techniques in music and sound
- With dozens of interview and forewords written by industry notables including Herbie Hancock, Craig Anderton, Alan Kay, Patrick Moraz, Jaron Lanier, and more
- Over 1000 pages crammed with everything you need to know about using music, MIDI, and digital audio in composition, performance, film, video, multimedia, and programming
- Over 500 illustrations and figures

$37.95 [$47.95 Canada]
ISBN: 1-878058-18-5
1300 pages. Available June.

Macworld Authorized Editions

Macworld Complete Mac Handbook
by Jim Heid, *Macworld* magazine's "Getting Started" Columnist

The most complete guide to getting started, mastering, and expanding your Mac.

Highlights:

- Loaded with tips and techniques for using the Mac and Mac software better
- For beginners or seasoned veterans
- FREE *Macworld* System 7 Reference Card!

$26.95 [$35.95 Canada]
ISBN: 1-878058-17-7
576 pages. Available now.

Macworld Read Me First Book
Edited by Jerry Borrell, *Macworld* magazine's Editor-in-Chief

Macworld's experts recommend the best hardware and software configurations and offer start-up advice.

Highlights:

- A friendly and authoritative guide for first-time users
- With sections from *Macworld* magazine's most popular experts
- Optimize hardware and software to meet your individual needs

$22.95 [$30.95 Canada]
ISBN: 1-878058-19-3
336 pages. Available now.

Future *Macworld* Titles

Macworld Guide to Microsoft Excel
by David Maguiness

Build spreadsheets quickly with this Macworld Authorized Edition to Excel 4.

Highlights:
- Crunch numbers easily with this quick start guide to Excel — task-by-task instructions make it simple
- Use the straightforward tutorials and start working right away
- FREE Illustrated Quick Reference Card
- Tabbed for easy look-ups

$22.95 [$29.95 Canada]
ISBN: 1-878058-40-1
448 pages. Available July.

Macworld Guide to Microsoft Works 3
by Barrie A. Sosinsky

Get inside the new Works so you can work more productively.

Highlights:
- Up-to-date for the newest release
- Learn to use all the applications in Works — for instant results
- FREE Illustrated Quick Reference Card

$22.95 [$29.95 Canada]
ISBN: 1-878058-42-8
448 pages. Available July, subject to software availability.

Order Form

Order Center: **(800) 762-2974** (7 a.m.–5 p.m., PST, weekdays)

or **(415) 312-0650**

Order Center FAX: **(415) 358-1260**

Quantity	Title & ISBN	Price	Total

Subtotal	
CA residents add applicable sales tax	
IN residents add 5% sales tax	
Canadian residents add 7% GST tax	
Shipping	
TOTAL	

Shipping & Handling Charges

Subtotal	U.S.	Canada & Int'l.	Int'l. Air Mail
Up to $20.00	Add $3.00	Add $4.00	Add $10.00
$20.01–40.00	$4.00	$5.00	$20.00
$40.01–60.00	$5.00	$6.00	$25.00
$60.01–80.00	$6.00	$8.00	$35.00
Over $80.00	$7.00	$10.00	$50.00

In U.S. and Canada, shipping is UPS ground or equivalent. For Rush shipping call (800) 762-2974.

Ship to:

Name _____

Company _____

Address _____

City/State/Zip _____

Daytime phone _____

Payment: ☐ Check to IDG Books   ☐ Visa   ☐ MasterCard   ☐ American Express

Card # _____   Expires _____

Please send this order form to: IDG Books, 155 Bovet Road, Ste. 610, San Mateo, CA 94402. Allow up to 3 weeks for delivery. Thank you!

BK=BOBNTWK

Fold Here

Place
stamp
here

IDG Books Worldwide, Inc.
155 Bovet Road
Suite 610
San Mateo, CA 94402

Attn: Order Center / Macworld Networking Handbook

IDG Books Worldwide Registration Card
Macworld Networking Handbook

Fill this out — and hear about updates to this book and other IDG Books Worldwide products!

Name _____

Company/Title _____

Address _____

City/State/Zip _____

What is the single most important reason you bought this book? _____

_____

Where did you buy this book?
- ❏ Bookstore (Name _____)
- ❏ Electronics/Software store (Name_____)
- ❏ Advertisement (If magazine, which? _____)
- ❏ Mail order (Name of catalog/mail order house _____)
- ❏ Other: _____

How many computer books do you purchase a year?
❏ 1 ❏ 6-10
❏ 2-5 ❏ More than 10

How did you hear about this book?
- ❏ Book review in: _____
- ❏ Advertisement in: _____
- ❏ Catalog
- ❏ Found in store
- ❏ Other: _____

What are your primary software applications?
_____
_____
_____

How would you rate the overall content of this book?
- ❏ Very good   ❏ Satisfactory
- ❏ Good   ❏ Poor
- Why? _____

What chapters did you find most valuable? _____

What chapters did you find least valuable? _____

What kind of chapter or topic would you add to future editions of this book? _____

_____

Please give us any additional comments. _____

_____

Thank you for your help!

❏ I liked this book! By checking this box, I give you permission to use my name and quote me in future IDG Books Worldwide promotional materials. Daytime phone number_____ .

❏ FREE! Send me a copy of your computer book and book/disk catalog.

Fold Here

Place
stamp
here

IDG Books Worldwide, Inc.
155 Bovet Road
Suite 610
San Mateo, CA 94402

Attn: Reader Response / Macworld Networking Handbook